Family Law in Scotland

Family Law in Scotland

J M Thomson, LLB, FRSE
Regius Professor of Law
University of Glasgow

Third edition

Edinburgh
Butterworths/Law Society of Scotland
1996

United Kingdom	Butterworths, a Division of Reed Elsevier (UK) Ltd, 4 Hill Street, EDINBURGH EH2 3JZ and Halsbury House, 35 Chancery Lane, LONDON WC2A 1EL
Australia	Butterworths Pty Ltd, SYDNEY, MELBOURNE, BRISBANE, ADELAIDE, PERTH, CANBERRA and HOBART
Canada	Butterworth Canada Ltd, TORONTO and VANCOUVER
Ireland	Butterworth (Ireland) Ltd, DUBLIN
Malaysia	Malayan Law Journal Sdn Bhd, KUALA LUMPUR
New Zealand	Butterworths of New Zealand Ltd, WELLINGTON and AUCKLAND
Puerto Rico	Butterworth of Puerto Rico, Inc, SAN JUAN
Singapore	Malayan Law Journal Pte Ltd, SINGAPORE
South Africa	Butterworth Publishers (Pty) Ltd, DURBAN
USA	Michie, CHARLOTTESVILLE, Virginia

Law Society of Scotland
26 Drumsheugh Gardens, EDINBURGH EH3 7YR

ISBN 0 406 07013 X

Typeset by Phoenix Photosetting, Chatham, Kent
Printed and bound in Great Britain by
Mackays of Chatham PLC, Chatham, Kent

Preface

Although it is almost 10 years since the first edition of this book, its purpose remains the same, *viz* to provide a clear and concise account of the rules of Scots law which govern family relationships. Since the last edition, the law in relation to children has been transformed as a result of legislation culminating in the Children (Scotland) Act 1995. I have written this edition as though the 1995 Act was fully in force: however, apart from a few minor provisions, it is anticipated that Part I will be commenced in November 1996 and Parts II, III and IV in April 1997. As a consequence, the chapters on the law of parent and child have been largely rewritten and the treatment of the law relating to children in need has been extended. While the law on husband and wife has not been the subject of such dramatic changes, I have endeavoured to take into account all the important developments since the last edition, especially in the area of financial provision on divorce.

I am grateful to my colleague, Tom Mullen, for writing the section on the Child Support Act 1991, which has largely overtaken the law of aliment in respect of maintenance for children. I would also like to thank Joan Rose for reading chapters 13 and 14 on children in need and giving me the benefit of her rich experience of the children's hearing system. I owe a special debt to Professor Kenneth Norrie who gave generously of his time to answer my questions on the construction of the 1995 Act and was prepared to engage in stimulating debate when I had the temerity to disagree with his views. Finally, I would like to thank Elaine McLelland, my research assistant, who organised much of the new material for this edition with unassuming expertise. I, of course, remain responsible for any errors in the text. The 1995 Act apart, I have attempted to take account of legal developments up to 1 March 1996.

Joe Thomson
The Law School
University of Glasgow
4 March 1996

Abbreviations

Bell, *Principles:* Professor G J Bell, *Principles of The Law of Scotland* (10th edn, 1899)

Clive: Dr Eric Clive, *The Law of Husband and Wife in Scotland* (3rd edn, 1992)

Erskine, *Institute:* Professor John Erskine, *The Institute of the Law of Scotland* (8th edn, 1870)

Stair: Sir James Dalrymple, Viscount Stair, *Institutions of the Law of Scotland* (Tercentenary edn, 1981)

Wilkinson and Norrie: A B Wilkinson and K McK Norrie *The Law Relating to Parent and Child in Scotland* (1993)

Contents

Table of statutes

Table of cases

Introduction

In this short introduction, it is proposed to explain the selection of subjects chosen for extended treatment and to discuss the policies underlying some of the most important features of contemporary family law.

Since the end of the eighteenth century, the nuclear family has become the essential family unit in Scotland.[1] This comprises a man and a woman who have a sexual relationship and their children. Before their relationship can give rise to mutual legal rights and obligations, as a general rule, the couple have to marry. More importantly, it is only when a couple have been married that the law regulates their income and capital when their relationship breaks down, in the form of financial provision on divorce. Similarly, a spouse, but not a cohabitee, has important legal rights in respect of succession to a proportion of the deceased spouse's estate.[2]

In spite of evidence that a considerable number of couples are now living in stable sexual relationships outside marriage,[3] the vast majority of couples eventually marry. Accordingly, the law of husband and wife remains of fundamental importance. Scots law, however, has begun to recognise that non-married couples (cohabitees) face similar problems to married couples, especially when their relationships break down. While there has been no attempt to create a legal status of cohabitee, the legislature has provided cohabitees with certain rights in relation to particular matters, for example, the occupation of the home in which the cohabitees are, or have been, living.[4]

While marriage retains its fundamental importance in Scots family law, it should be noted that it is of very little legal significance for the spouses *during* the marriage. Until the later years of the nineteenth

---

1 Before that time the extended family in the form of clans was important, at least in the Highlands of Scotland.
2 On the spouses' rights to succession, see *infra* Ch 3.
3 Statistical information on this subject is notoriously inexact, but approximately 14% of couples who live together are unmarried. For statistical data, see *The Effects of Cohabitation in Private Law* SLC Discussion Paper No 86, para 1.3.
4 See *infra* Ch 5. For futher proposals for reform of the law in relation to cohabitees, see generally *The Effects of Cohabitation in Private Law* SLC Discussion Paper No 86.

century, a woman lost many important rights on marriage, for example, in relation to her property. Since then, the law has endeavoured to achieve legal equality between the spouses by enacting that for various purposes, for example, contract, delict and property, the spouses should be treated as though they were unmarried.[1] But while legal equality may have been achieved, the application of rules which ignore the fact that the persons concerned are married, leads, particularly in relation to property matters, to results which are both artificial and unjust. Consequently, legislation has introduced special rules for spouses which take into account the fact that they are married.[2]

Of course, marriage does continue to give rise to rights and obligations for the spouses. Spouses, but not cohabitees, owe a duty to aliment (ie maintain) each other during the marriage.[3] Moreover, when parents are married at the date of a child's conception or subsequently, the father will automatically have parental responsibilities and rights in relation to the child;[4] if the couple never marry, only the child's mother will have parental responsibilities and rights unless and until the father obtains them as a consequence of a court order or agreement with the mother. But the most important legal consequence of marriage is that a court can award financial provision for the spouses if the marriage ends in divorce.[5]

Judicial divorce has been possible in Scots law since the Reformation in 1560, but divorce was not a prevalent feature of Scottish society until this century. The reasons for this are complex. While the grounds for divorce were restricted to the defender's adultery or desertion until the Divorce (Scotland) Act 1938, religious disapproval of divorce must also have acted as a considerable restraint. As a result of the increasing secularisation of Scottish society in the twentieth century, the social upheavals of two world wars and the emphasis on personal fulfilment in sexual relationships, divorce has become an accepted part of contemporary Scottish society. The law has responded to the demand for easier divorce with the introduction of a system based, theoretically at least, on the non-fault principle of irretrievable breakdown of marriage.[6] It is estimated that in Scotland at least one in three marriages now ends in divorce. As a divorced

---

1 On contract and delict, see *infra* Ch 3: on property, see *infra* Chs 4 and 5.
2 See, for example, s 25 of the Family Law (Scotland) Act 1985: discussed *infra* Ch 4.
3 On aliment, see *infra* Ch 3.
4 Section 3(1)(b) of the Children (Scotland) Act 1995: discussed *infra* Ch 9.
5 On financial division on divorce, see *infra* Ch 7.
6 Divorce is discussed *infra* Ch 6.

person will often enter a second marriage, it is not too cynical to suggest that we now live in a society where serial polygamy is common.

Given this high incidence of divorce, it is crucial that the law provides a system of financial provision which will enable the income and capital of the spouses to be redistributed in a fair manner after divorce. Until 1964, divorce was treated as judicial death: financial provision took the form of treating the defender as though dead and awarding the pursuer the legal rights to which a spouse would have been entitled from the defender's estate. That system was replaced[1] by one which gave the judge who was hearing the claim discretion to make financial provision which appeared just in the circumstances. Any advantages of flexibility which this system may have had were outweighed by the uncertainty that ensued. A much more sophisticated system has been introduced which provides a set of principles to be used in determining the financial provision which should be awarded in the circumstances of a particular marriage.[2] This gives greater certainty on the outcome of possible litigation and so enables spouses and their legal advisers to negotiate a settlement without recourse to the courts.

The current divorce law can be criticised on the ground of its complexity which inhibits the parties from being able to end their marriage with the minimum of legal intervention. On the other hand, the reform of the law on financial provision has, because of the increase in certainty as to the outcome of litigation, enabled the parties or their legal advisers to reach a settlement more frequently than in the past. It is generally accepted that modern family law should encourage spouses to settle the property and other issues which arise when their marriage breaks down without recourse to litigation, thereby saving scarce legal aid resources. Scots law, at present, only does this to a limited extent and it is the present writer's view that the grounds of divorce should be further simplified and that more support should be given to conciliation services to help spouses reach agreement on such issues as property, financial provision and looking after their children.[3]

While marriage continues to remain a condition for the legal regulation of the relationship between a man and a woman who are living

---

1 Part V of the Succession (Scotland) Act 1964; later replaced by s 5 of the Divorce (Scotland) Act 1976.
2 Sections 8–17 of the Family Law (Scotland) Act 1985, discussed *infra* Ch 7.
3 The Scottish Law Commission has recommended further simplification of the grounds of divorce: see *Report on the Reform of the Ground of Divorce* (SLC No 116). At the time of writing, these reforms have not been enacted. For discussion of the proposals, see *infra* p 119.

together, Scots law has always recognised that parents owe duties towards their children, albeit that the parents have never married. However, the extent of a child's rights which were exigible from his or her parents – and remoter relatives – depended for centuries upon whether or not the child was legitimate. A child is legitimate if he or she was conceived or born during the parents' marriage. During this century, piecemeal reforms have alleviated the legal position of the illegitimate child but as a result of the Law Reform (Parent and Child) (Scotland) Act 1986,[1] the legal position of an illegitimate child has, for all but a few minor purposes, been equated with that of a legitimate child. But since an illegitimate child is more likely to be a member of a one-parent family than a legitimate child, he or she will more often suffer social disadvantages stemming from impoverished economic circumstances.

While parents owe responsibilities and obligations towards their children, for example, the duty of aliment, they enjoy important rights in respect of the care and upbringing of their child. The nature and extent of these parental responsibilities and rights has been one of the most controversial aspects of modern family law – in particular, the question of when these rights cease and children can assert their liberty to make their own decisions on such important matters as contraception or medical treatment. Scots law has recently been reformed so that the views of the child at the centre of the decision-making process are adequately represented.

Given the prevalence of divorce, an important issue for modern family law is to attempt to ensure that the children of the family are well looked after when the parents separate. Scots law has adopted the welfare principle as the criterion for the determination of such issues.[2] In practice, however, the courts are reluctant to disturb the arrangements which have *de facto* been operative prior to the divorce, thus preserving the *status quo ante*: this is generally thought to be in the best interests of the child. Thus the law merely underpins the self-regulation by the parents themselves of the care of their children. Since in the vast majority of cases the mother will *de facto* be looking after any children when the marriage breaks down, the preservation of the *status quo* which is currently endorsed by the courts when applying the welfare principle, reinforces the traditional view that the care of a child is primarily the responsibility of the mother. However, the law has recently been reformed to stress that

---

1 The 1986 Act is discussed in detail, *infra* Chs 8 and 9.
2 See *infra* Ch 11.

children need both parents and that parental responsibilities continue even where the child no longer lives with the parent concerned.

In a modern society, the state has a crucial role in supporting children who are at risk when their families have become dysfunctional. State agencies have certain powers and duties to help in this situation.[1] Scots law also has a system of children's hearings which can provide compulsory measures of supervision for children in need.[2] The danger of any welfare-based system is, of course, that a parent's prima facie right to bring up a child and the child's prima facie right to be brought up in his or her family environment may be given insufficient weight when it is thought that the removal of the child from the family is desirable for the child's welfare. A delicate balance has therefore to be found and procedural safeguards must exist so that the rights of parents and children to each other are given proper consideration. After disturbing cases which suggested that this balance did not sufficiently favour family autonomy,[3] the law has recently been reformed in order to give greater weight to the rights of the children and parents concerned.[4]

One of the most remarkable features of contemporary Scottish family law is that much of the law is of very recent origin. The last ten years have, for example, seen the full scale reform of financial provision on divorce,[5] illegitimacy[6] and parental responsibilities and rights.[7] These reforms are the result of the work of the Scottish Law Commission which is largely responsible for having provided Scotland with a system of family law which is capable of meeting the needs of contemporary Scottish society and our obligations under the United Nations Convention on the Rights of the Child[8].

1 See *infra* Ch 13.
2 See *infra* Ch 14.
3 For example, the removal of children from their parents in Orkney which led to a public inquiry under Lord Clyde and his subsequent Report: HC Papers 1992–93, No 195.
4 Parts II and III of the Children (Scotland) Act 1995 which enact the major recommendations of the White Paper *Scotland's Children* (1993) Cm 2286.
5 By the Family Law (Scotland) Act 1985: discussed *infra* Ch 7.
6 By the Law Reform (Parent and Child) (Scotland) Act 1986: discussed *infra* Ch 8.
7 By Pt I of the Children (Scotland) Act 1995: discussed *infra* Ch 10.
8 International Legal Materials 1448.

1 Getting married

ENGAGEMENTS

It is customary for a couple to become engaged for a period before they marry. At common law, an engagement was a contract and wrongful failure to implement the promise to marry gave rise to an action in damages. These damages included not only compensation for pecuniary loss arising from the breach, for example, the cost of preparations for the wedding, but also for *solatium* to compensate the innocent party's injured feelings and wounded pride.[1] The Scottish Law Commission took the view that actions for breach of promise had become anachronistic in the late twentieth century and recommended abolition.[2]

By s1(1) of the Law Reform (Husband and Wife) (Scotland) Act 1984, it is declared that:

> 'No promise of marriage or agreement between two persons to marry one another shall have effect under the law of Scotland to create any rights or obligations; and no action for breach of any such promise or agreement may be brought in any court in Scotland, whatever the law applicable to the promise or agreement.'[3]

The extent of this provision is wide. First, an engagement is no longer a legally enforceable contract. Therefore any contractual remedies for breach of promise are no longer competent in Scottish courts.[4] Second, by stipulating that a promise or agreement to marry does not create any rights or obligations in Scots law, it would appear that the section excludes any delictual liability which might arise from a breach of promise. For example, if a man deliberately lied when he promised to marry a woman, she would appear to have no right to sue

---

1 *Hogg v Gow* May 27, 1812 F C.
2 Report of the Scottish Law Commission on *Outdated Rules in the law of Husband and Wife* (1983) SLC No 76.
3 By s 1(2) the provision is expressly made retrospective.
4 This is so, whatever the proper law of the promise or agreement.

6

him in delict on the ground of his fraudulent misrepresentation.[1]
Thus, unlike the parallel English legislation,[2] which only prevents
agreements to marry operating as contracts, the Law Reform
(Husband and Wife) (Scotland) Act 1984 prohibits delictual as well
as contractual remedies.

The 1984 Act does not address itself to any of the property issues
which can arise between engaged couples. Where the marriage does
not take place, any property dispute, for example, over the ownership
of a house which was bought with a view to marriage, will be governed by the general principles of the law of property.[3] Where the
couple do marry, however, any property acquired during the engagement for use as a family home, or to be used in the home, will be
regarded as matrimonial property for the purpose of financial provision on divorce.[4]

There are no special property rules in relation to gifts between
engaged couples. If the gift is intended to be outright, for example, a
birthday present, it need not be returned if the engagement is broken
off. Where a gift is made expressly or impliedly[5] conditional on the
marriage taking place, it must be returned if the condition fails: and
the donor may use the *condictio causa data causa non secuta*[6] to
recover the property.

Unlike the position in England,[7] there are no specific provisions in
respect of gifts of engagement rings. In one sheriff court case it was

1 Similarly there would be no right to sue in negligence, if the promise was made
   carelessly, for example, if without taking reasonable care to discover whether he
   had the capacity to marry the promisee, a man gives a promise to marry which he
   cannot fulfil.
2 Section 1(1) of the Law Reform (Miscellaneous Provisions) Act 1970.
3 In *Grieve v Morrison* 1993 SLT 852, an engaged couple bought a house, title to
   which was taken in joint names. Part of the price was the free proceeds from the
   sale of the woman's previous house. When the marriage did not take place, the
   woman failed to recover the proceeds because she had not established that the
   transfer of the proceeds to purchase the new house was made in consideration that
   the marriage would take place. Instead, the court ordered a division and sale under
   which both parties obtained half the free proceeds from the sale of the new house.
   On actions for division and sale, see *infra* Ch 5.
4 Section 10(4) of the Family Law (Scotland) Act 1985, discussed *infra* Ch 7.
   Similarly, moveable property obtained in prospect of the marriage is subject to the
   presumption of equal shares in household goods: s 25 of the Family Law (Scotland)
   Act 1985, discussed *infra* Ch 4.
5 For example, the gift of family jewellery.
6 Stair I 7.7. Before the *condictio* is applicable, it must be clear that the transfer of the
   property was subject to a mutually agreed understanding that it was made in consideration that the marriage would take place: *Grieve v Morrison* 1993 SLT 852.
7 Section 3(2) of the Law Reform (Miscellaneous Provisions) Act 1970, where there
   is a rebuttable presumption that the gift of the ring is made unconditionally.

held that the gift of an engagement ring is made unconditionally[1] but in another,[2] it was thought that the ring was returnable if the marriage did not take place – unless the donor had unjustifiably broken off the engagement. A third possibility is that the ring is given on the implied condition that it should be returned if the marriage does not take place for any reason. Given that engagements now give rise to no legal rights or obligations between the parties, it is thought that it would be consistent with the policy of the 1984 Act if engagement rings were presumed to be outright gifts; but that this presumption should be able to be rebutted on proof that the gift was intended to be subject to the condition that it should be returned if the marriage did not take place.

Where a couple receive engagement presents from third parties, it is thought that these are returnable if the marriage does not take place.[3]

THE FORMALITIES OF MARRIAGE

A marriage will not be valid unless the parties have capacity to marry and the marriage conforms to the formalities required by the law of the place where the marriage is celebrated. In this section, the formal requirements of a valid marriage celebrated in Scotland are discussed. Scots law recognises two possible methods of marrying *viz* regular or formal marriages and irregular or informal marriages.

REGULAR MARRIAGES – FORMAL MARRIAGES

The law on the formalities of regular marriages was the subject of the Kilbrandon Committee's Report in 1969[4] and in the light of the Committee's recommendations, the law was radically altered and simplified by the Marriage (Scotland) Act 1977.[5]

There are two types of regular marriage in Scotland, a civil ceremony and a religious ceremony. But before either can take place, the parties must follow certain civil preliminaries.[6]

1 *Gold v Hume* (1950) 66 Sh Ct Rep 85.
2 *Savage v M'Allister* (1952) 68 Sh Ct Rep 11.
3 Stair I 7.7.
4 *The Marriage Law of Scotland* Cmnd 4011.
5 As amended by the Law Reform (Miscellaneous Provisions) (Scotland) Act 1980, s 22. See generally *Clive* Ch 4. References in this section are to the 1977 Act unless otherwise stated.
6 Accordingly, the proclamation of banns has no legal significance in Scots law.

Civil preliminaries

(i) Marriage notices

Each of the parties to a marriage which is intended to be solemnised in Scotland, whether it is to be a religious or civil ceremony, must submit a notice of intention to marry – a marriage notice – to the district registrar for the registration district in which the marriage is to be solemnised.[1] There is no need for either party to be resident in that registration district nor, indeed, in Scotland: but as one of the parties must appear to finalise arrangements for a civil ceremony or, alternatively, collect the marriage schedule for a religious ceremony, in practice, one of the parties must be present in Scotland before the date of the ceremony.

The marriage notice is accompanied by the prescribed fee and the birth certificate of the party submitting it. If either party has been married before and the marriage has been dissolved, a copy of the decree of divorce or declarator of nullity must be included: similarly, if either party is a widow or widower, the death certificate of the former spouse must be submitted.[2] If one of the parties is domiciled abroad,[3] he or she must 'if practicable' submit a certificate issued by a competent authority in the state in which the party is domiciled that he or she 'is not known to be subject to any legal incapacity (in terms of the law of that state) which would prevent his marrying':[4] this is known as a certificate of capacity.[5]

On receipt of the marriage notice, the registrar enters the following prescribed particulars in a marriage notice book *viz* the party's name, address, marital status, date of birth and the proposed date of the marriage.[6] The names – but not the addresses – of the parties and the proposed date of the marriage are then displayed in a 'conspicuous' place at the registration office.

Any person claiming to have reason to submit an objection to an intended marriage, can inspect any entry relating to the marriage in

1 Section 3(1).
2 Section 3(1) (a) and (b). An extract of an entry in the Register of Divorces is sufficient evidence of the decree of divorce or declarator of nullity: s 28A(5) of the Registration of Births, Deaths and Marriages (Scotland) Act 1965.
3 And has not been resident in the UK for more than 2 years.
4 Section 3(5).
5 Where the *lex domicilii* does not recognise the party's divorce, but the divorce would be recognised in Scotland, a marriage can go ahead without a certificate of capacity: s 3(5)(b) as added by para 21 of Sch 1 to the Family Law Act 1986. See also ibid, s 50.
6 Section 4: the particulars are prescribed in the Marriage (Prescription of Forms) (Scotland) Regulations 1977 (SI 1977/1671) para 4.

the marriage notice book. The objection to the marriage must be submitted in writing to the district registrar.[1] Where the objection is concerned with a trivial matter, for example, an inaccuracy as to the age of the parties, the district registrar can, after notifying the parties, make the correction.[2] However, if the objection goes to the capacity of either party to marry,[3] for example, if it is alleged that one of them is already a party to a subsisting marriage, then the district registrar must notify the Registrar General, and the completion or issue of the marriage schedule is suspended until the matter has been investigated by the Registrar General.[4] If after investigation the Registrar General is satisfied that there is no legal impediment, he will inform the district registrar and the marriage can go ahead: but if there is a legal impediment, the Registrar General must direct the district registrar to take all reasonable steps to ensure that the marriage does not take place.[5]

It will be obvious that there must be sufficient time for objections to be made and any subsequent investigations to be carried out. As a general rule, there is a minimum waiting period of fourteen days from the receipt of the marriage notice and a civil ceremony[6] or the issue of a marriage schedule for a religious ceremony.[7] However, the Registrar General has a dispensing power to allow a marriage to be celebrated within a shorter period if the circumstances justify doing so. This power is used sparingly.[8]

(ii)   Marriage schedule

After the usual waiting period has expired and the district registrar is satisfied that the parties have capacity to marry, he makes up the marriage schedule. The schedule contains the details of the parties and serves as an initial record of the marriage for registration purposes. Where there is to be a religious ceremony, in addition, the marriage schedule acts as a licence authorising the celebrant to proceed. If more than three months have elapsed since the receipt of a marriage

---

1 Section 5(1).
2 Section 5(2)(a).
3 Section 5(4).
4 Section 5(2)(b).
5 Section 5(3).
6 Section 6(4)(a).
7 Section 19(1).
8 Nevertheless there was a case known to the author where a marriage had been arranged for two years but the parties failed to submit their marriage notices: after some frantic telephone calls, the Registrar General was prepared to issue the marriage schedule on the morning of the wedding!

notice, the Registrar General has discretion to direct the district registrar not to complete the marriage schedule unless a new marriage notice is submitted.[1] A marriage schedule for a religious ceremony will not be issued to the parties earlier than seven days before the ceremony.[2]

Civil marriage

If there is to be a civil ceremony, the district registrar retains the marriage schedule till the date of the marriage. The ceremony is usually conducted by the registrar and takes place in his office. Where, however, one of the parties is unable to attend the registrar's office because of serious illness or serious bodily injury, then, provided delay of the wedding is undesirable, the registrar can, on application by either party, solemnise the marriage anywhere in his registration district, for example, a hospital.[3] There is no restriction on the time when the ceremony must take place but in practice it will be during the registrar's normal office hours.

Both parties must be present with two witnesses professing to be over sixteen.[4] The marriage schedule is completed and the district registrar explains to the parties the nature of marriage in Scots law. The parties declare there are no legal impediments and are then asked if they take each other as husband and wife. The registrar declares them to be married and the marriage schedule is signed by both parties, the witnesses and the registrar. The marriage is then registered.

Religious marriage

If there is to be a religious ceremony, the district registrar issues the marriage schedule *to the parties*. This is because the schedule acts as a licence to the celebrant to solemnise the marriage. A religious ceremony can be carried out at any time, for example, in the evening if the couple come from a farming community, and any place, for example, in a hotel. But the date and place chosen must be specified in the marriage schedule.[5]

The authorised celebrant is a person who is[6]
a) a minister of the Church of Scotland; or
b) a minister, clergyman, pastor, priest or other marriage celebrant of

1 Section 6(3).
2 Section 6(4)(b).
3 Sections 18(3) and (4). A civil ceremony cannot otherwise be performed in any other place except a registrar's office.
4 Section 19(2).
5 Section 6(5).
6 Section 8(1).

a religious body prescribed in regulations made by the Secretary of State: the religious bodies prescribed are the major Christian churches and denominations;[1] or

c) celebrants nominated by other religious bodies as a marriage celebrant and registered as such by the Registrar General under s 9 of the 1977 Act. Only religious bodies can nominate celebrants, who need not be priests but must be over 21. The nominee is authorised for three years in the first instance. A religious body is defined as 'an organised group of people meeting regularly for common religious worship'. Non-Christian religions, such as Islam or Hinduism are clearly included, but as they must engage in religious worship, groups such as Humanists would appear to be excluded; or

d) temporarily authorised by the Registrar General under s 12 of the 1977 Act. There is no restriction on these persons except that they must be over 21. In practice, they are celebrants who are registered under s 9 but whose area of operation does not extend to the place where the marriage is to be celebrated, ministers from outside Scotland who have been asked to solemnise a marriage in Scotland, or ministers who are in Scotland on pulpit exchange with a recognised religious body. The authorisation must be in writing and is limited either to the marriage specified in the authorisation or for a specified period.

In the case of a) and b), the celebrant must follow the form of ceremony approved by the church: in the case of c) and d), the ceremony must be in an appropriate form which includes and is not inconsistent with (i) a declaration of the parties, in the presence of each other, the celebrant and two witnesses, that they accept each other as husband and wife and (ii) a declaration thereafter by the celebrant that they are husband and wife.

In all religious marriages, the approved celebrant must not proceed unless (i) the parties produce a marriage schedule issued in accordance with the Act, (ii) *both* parties are present, and (iii) there are two witnesses professing to be over sixteen.[2] After the ceremony, the marriage schedule is signed by both parties, the witnesses and the celebrant. The schedule must be returned to the district registration office for registration within three days of the ceremony.[3] This is traditionally the task of the best man who pays the registration fee as part of his wedding gift!

1 See the Marriage (Prescription of Religious Bodies) (Scotland) Regulations 1977 (SI 1977/1670).
2 Section 13(1).
3 Section 15(2).

Effect of irregularities

A marriage solemnised under the Marriage (Scotland) Act 1977 will not be invalidated by non-compliance with these formalities provided both parties were present at the ceremony and the marriage was duly registered.[1] There must be some form of ceremony, but otherwise the marriage will not be invalidated by formal defects. The scope of s 23A was considered by Lord Clyde in *Saleh v Saleh*.[2] The pursuer sought a declarator of nullity. The parties had originally intended to be married by a Church of Scotland minister in Grangemouth. Marriage notices were lodged but the registrar was unable to issue a marriage schedule as there was doubt as to the defender's freedom to marry. Faced with this difficulty, the couple decided to be married in a mosque in Edinburgh. No marriage notices were lodged with the appropriate district registrar nor was any marriage schedule made up, far less issued. Nevertheless the ceremony took place and the matour issued a certificate recording the ceremony. But because of the absence of a completed marriage schedule, the marriage could not be, and was not, registered. In granting the declarator, Lord Clyde held that this was not a case where s 23A was applicable because, while the parties were present at the ceremony, there was no registration. Lord Clyde thought that s 23A could save a marriage when, for example, the schedule had been issued prior to the time limits or if the person who conducted the ceremony was not an approved celebrant or a marriage schedule was not produced at the ceremony, always provided that the parties were present and the schedule had been issued, signed and registered.

However, even if the marriage can be saved by s 23A, the parties and the celebrant may be liable to criminal sanctions for breach of the Act, for example, if a person falsifies or forges a marriage schedule.[3] However, the validity of a marriage is still challengeable on such grounds as lack of legal capacity of the parties or absence of true consent.

Conclusion

The purpose of legal preliminaries to the solemnisation of marriage is to ensure that the parties to a marriage have legal capacity to marry. As a result of the Marriage (Scotland) Act 1977, all persons who wish

---

1 Section 23A, inserted by s 22 of the Law Reform (Miscellaneous Provisions) (Scotland) Act 1980.
2 1987 SLT 633.
3 See s 24 for a full list of offences.

to enter into a regular marriage in Scotland must follow the same preliminary procedure whether or not they intend to have a civil or a religious ceremony. This makes for simplicity and uniformity.

Moreover, it is submitted that the current rules give sufficient time
for objections to be made and appropriate investigations to take
place. The procedure itself is admirably simple, without the com-
plexities of residence requirements for the parties.

In relation to the ceremony itself, there are for religious marriages
no limitations on the time or place of the wedding. It is thought, however, that the restriction of civil ceremonies to the district registrar's
office, unless one of the parties is seriously ill or injured, is unneces-
sarily restrictive and that steps should be taken to enable a couple to
have a civil ceremony when and wherever they wish.

IRREGULAR MARRIAGES[1]

(i)   Introduction

Before the Reformation in 1560, Scots law recognised the validity of
irregular marriages. These involved no ecclesiastical formalities
whatsoever. There were three kinds.
a) A declaration by the parties that they took each other as husband
   and wife: marriage *per verba de praesenti*. The consent of the parties was sufficient to constitute the marriage and there was no
   need for the presence of an episcopally ordained priest or witnesses.
b) A promise to marry at some future date followed by sexual intercourse on the faith of that promise: marriage *per verba de futuro
   subsequente copula*. The sexual intercourse on the faith of the
   promise was deemed to be agreement to marry. Not surprisingly,
   perhaps, there was no need for the presence of an episcopally
   ordained priest or witnesses.
c) Marriage constituted by the tacit agreement of the parties to marry
   presumed from a period of cohabitation with habit and repute that
   they were husband and wife: marriage by cohabitation with habit
   and repute.

After the Reformation these forms of irregular marriage continued to
be recognised as constituting valid marriages in Scots law. The first
two forms of irregular marriage were abolished by s 5 of the
Marriage (Scotland) Act 1939 which came into force on 1 July 1940.[2]

1 For full discussion see *Clive* Ch 5.
2 The section was not retrospective.

However, the third form, marriage by cohabitation with habit and repute, remains a valid method of constituting marriage in Scotland.

Because many of the older cases involved irregular marriages, it is proposed to outline the salient features of *de praesenti* and *de futuro* marriages and then to consider marriage by cohabitation with habit and repute in some detail.

(ii) Marriage by declaration de praesenti

The essence of this form of marriage was that the parties seriously and genuinely exchanged present consent to marriage. The couple were married as soon as consents were exchanged. Consummation was not required: *consensus non concubitus facit matrimonium.* Because there was no need for witnesses, there could be formidable problems of proof, particularly where one of the alleged spouses had died and the issue arose in a claim by the other for rights of succession.[1]

The exchange of consents had to take place in Scotland.[2] This explains the popularity of elopements from England to marry at Gretna Green. Eventually, a residence requirement of at least 21 days was introduced by the Marriage (Scotland) Act 1856. The *de praesenti* marriage has not been a competent form of contracting a marriage since 1 July 1940.[3]

(iii) Marriage by promise subsequente copula

In this form of irregular marriage, if a promise was made of marriage at some date in the future and sexual intercourse took place on the faith of the promise, the couple were taken to be married at the date of the intercourse. The theory was that while mutual consent was essential to marriage, where a woman permitted sexual intercourse in reliance on a man's promise to marry her, it was to be presumed that there and then the parties had exchanged consents to present marriage and, if this presumption was not rebutted, a marriage was constituted by promise *subsequente copula.*[4] Both the promise and the sexual intercourse had to take place in Scotland.

In time, this form of marriage was treated with scepticism. As Lord Sands explained in *N v C:*[5]

---

1 See, for example, *Dunn v Dunn's Trustees* 1930 SC 131.
2 *Macdonald v Macdonald* (1863) 1 M 854.
3 Section 5 of the Marriage (Scotland) Act 1939.
4 See *N v C* 1933 SC 492.
5 Ibid at 501.

'According to the theory of the law, when two persons who are
engaged to be married indulge in sexual intercourse, presumably they there and then exchange matrimonial consent and
become married persons. But, according to the view which pre-
vails in those sections of the community in which antenuptial
fornication is most apt to occur, they do nothing of the kind.
They yield to desire and indulge in immoral intercourse, robbed
doubtless of some of its danger by the prospect of future marriage . . . Parents, employers and clergymen in rural Scotland
have often had occasion to deal sorrowfully with a girl whose
betrothed had got her in the family way. I much doubt if it has
ever happened that the girl advanced the plea in excuse that she
was a married woman . . . Marriage by promise *cum subsequente copula* is a plant nourished by the law which has never
taken root in the understanding or the conscience of the common people'.

It is therefore not surprising that this has not been a competent form
of contracting a marriage since 1 July 1940.[1]

(iv)   Marriage by cohabitation with habit and repute

The Marriage (Scotland) Act 1939 did not abolish the third form of
irregular marriage, marriage by cohabitation with habit and repute.
The theoretical basis of the doctrine has been the subject of controversy.[2] It is not simply a matter of evidence. While there is a presumption from long cohabitation as husband and wife, that a couple
have been married,[3] this is rebuttable by evidence that the alleged
ceremony did not take place. However, marriage by cohabitation
with habit and repute is not merely a rule of evidence that the parties
are prima facie to be presumed to have married by declaration *de
praesenti* or promise *cum subsequente copula*, for if that were so,
marriage by cohabitation with habit and repute would have been
impliedly abolished by the Marriage (Scotland) Act 1939. Instead,
the basis of the doctrine is that the parties' *tacit* consent to marry,
inferred from, and combined with, cohabitation with habit and repute
constitutes marriage: a legitimate enunciation by the parties to themselves and others of their matrimonial consent which has never

1 Section 5 of the Marriage (Scotland) Act 1939.
2 See, for example, Ashton-Cross 'Cohabitation with Habit and Repute' (1961) JR
   21.
3 Or before 1 July 1940, that the couple had married by *de praesenti* consents or
   promise *cum subsequente copula*.

expressly been put into words.[1] Because of their cohabitation with habit and repute that they are married, the law presumes that the parties have *tacitly* agreed to be married, with the result that they *are* married unless evidence is led that they never intended to take each other as husband and wife.

The requirements

(i) There must be cohabitation, ie the couple must live together: merely to have sexual intercourse is not enough.[2]

(ii) The cohabitation must be as husband and wife: not as man and mistress or man and housekeeper. However, cohabitation which began on an indeterminate footing can ripen into a marriage if the couple later cohabit as husband and wife.[3] However, where a couple live together with the intention that they will marry at a future date, since they are not cohabiting as husband and wife, they cannot become married as a result of the doctrine of marriage by cohabitation with habit and repute.[4] A *fortiori* the doctrine does not apply when a couple live together without any intention of ever marrying.[5]

(iii) The cohabitation must take place in Scotland.

(iv) The cohabitation must be sufficiently long for the court to infer that the parties tacitly agreed to marry. At one time it was thought that this must be at least a year,[6] but in *Shaw v Henderson*[7] Lord Stott emphasised that there was no hard and fast rule: all that is required is that the evidence of cohabitation is sufficient for an inference of tacit agreement to be drawn. Eleven months cohabitation was enough in that case. It is ultimately a question of fact.[8]

1 *Campbell v Campbell* (1866) 4 M 867 at 924–925.
2 *Quaere* whether a couple can cohabit for this purpose if they do not have sexual intercourse.
3 See, for example, *Nicol v Bell* 1954 SLT 314 (woman began as man's housekeeper, became his mistress but on the birth of his child was treated as his wife: they were married as a result of 20 years' cohabitation as his wife).
4 See, for example, *Low v Gorman* 1970 SLT 356; *Mackenzie v Scott* 1980 SLT (Notes) 9.
5 See, for example, *Gow v Lord Advocate* 1993 SLT 275. 'The case must be viewed against the background of modern social conditions where it is not at all uncommon for a man and woman to live together openly in an intimate relationship while retaining a distinct disinclination to enter the marriage state': at 276 per Lord Caplan.
6 See, for example, *Campbell v Campbell* (1866) 4 M 867; *Wallace v Fife Coal Co Ltd* 1909 SC 682.
7 1982 SLT 211.
8 *Petrie v Petrie* 1911 SC 360 per Lord Dundas.

(v)   The parties must be reputed to be husband and wife and this reputation must be 'uniform and undivided'.[1] But it is not fatal if some persons know that the couple are not married, provided they are generally thought by friends and society in general to be husband and wife.[2] But if a substantial number of relatives and friends do know that the couple are not married[3] or are merely contemplating marriage, the doctrine will not apply.[4]

(vi) The parties must have legal capacity to marry.[5] If, for example, one of the parties is already married to a third party, the doctrine cannot apply: but, once the impediment is removed by the death or divorce of the existing spouse then, as the party will now have capacity to marry, the doctrine is applicable. But the parties can only rely upon the cohabitation with habit and repute which occurs after the impediment has been removed.[6] Thus if A who is married to B begins to cohabit with C in 1975 and B dies in 1995, the period of relevant cohabitation only begins with B's death in 1995: the period of cohabitation – albeit with habit and repute – between 1975 and 1995 is irrelevant, except as background material.[7] Where a relationship begins illicitly, it may, of course, be difficult to establish the necessary repute that the couple are living as husband and wife. But the doctrine will still be applicable once the parties are aware that the impediment has been removed.[8] No weight is now given to the old idea that a relationship which begins illicitly should prima facie be presumed to continue illicitly.

---

1   *Kamperman v MacIver* 1994 SLT 763 (a period of six and a half months not necessarily insufficient).

2   *Shaw v Henderson* 1982 SLT 211. Nor is it fatal that the woman continued to use her maiden name: *Donnelly v Donnelly's Executor* 1992 SLT 13.

3   *Low v Gorman* 1970 SLT 356.

4   *Mackenzie v Scott* 1980 SLT (Notes) 9.

5   A couple who were parties to a regular marriage and then divorced, have capacity to marry again as a result of the doctrine of cohabitation with habit and repute: *Mullen v Mullen* 1991 SLT 205.

6   *Low v Gorman* 1970 SLT 356; in *Kamperman v MacIver* 1994 SLT 763, the Second Division held that such cohabitation is not wholly irrelevant as it is part of the background material which could colour the nature of the cohabitation after the impediment is removed.

7   *Kamperman v MacIver* 1994 SLT 763.

8   *Campbell v Campbell* (1866) 4 M 867. The case proceeded on the assumption that the parties knew of the death of the first husband. Thus it would appear that the presumption of tacit consent would be rebutted if the parties continued to believe that the impediment existed.

As Lord Caplan observed in *Gow v Lord Advocate*[1]

'. . . if the parties clearly showed an inclination to adopt the married state before they became free to marry, this could reflect on their attitude to the relationship if cohabitation continues when freedom to marry arises'. Whether a man and a woman have cohabited as husband and wife with the necessary repute to draw the inference of tacit consent is essentially a question of fact.[2]

Procedure

A party to the alleged marriage by cohabitation with habit and repute will raise an action in the Court of Session for declarator of marriage. It should be emphasised, however, that the couple are married by virtue of the doctrine: there is no need for a declarator to establish the marriage. A declarator has been granted where the couple were married by cohabitation with habit and repute albeit that they had separated before the husband's death.[3] By the nature of the doctrine it will be difficult to establish exactly when the couple were married. While the matter is not free from difficulty, there is force in Clive's view that the date should be when there was sufficient relevant cohabitation with habit and repute, for the inference of tacit consent to be drawn.[4] When a declarator has been granted, the Principal Clerk of Session will intimate the relevant details to the Registrar General to enable the marriage to be registered.[5]

Conclusion

Marriage by cohabitation with habit and repute is a distinctive feature of Scots family law but it is not a common occurrence. There are only about two declarators a year. The question arises whether the doctrine is worth retaining. While Scots law continues to consider a valid marriage – as opposed to cohabitation per se – as a condition *sine qua non* of the legal regulation of the property of the parties to a sexual relationship when it comes to an end, it is probably of value. Its illogicalities cannot be denied. For example, it requires the parties to *pretend* that they are married. Accordingly, it cannot provide a solution to the legal problems of a couple who openly cohabit as unmarried persons.

1 1993 SLT 275 at 276.
2 *Kamperman v MacIver supra*.
3 *Morris v Morris* 1987 GWD 39–1437.
4 See *Clive* p 57 ff.
5 Section 21 of the Marriage (Scotland) Act 1977.

Where the doctrine is valuable is in the situation where a couple purport to enter a regular marriage but, unknown to the parties, they do not have legal capacity to marry at the time of the ceremony. As we shall see in the next chapter, in these circumstances the marriage is void. If, however, the impediment is subsequently removed and the couple continue to cohabit as husband and wife, they will *become* married as a result of the doctrine.[1] Thus marriage by cohabitation with habit and repute can be useful in creating the status of husband and wife when the couple's original marriage was void as a result of a legal impediment at the time of the original ceremony.

Nevertheless, it has been recommended that the doctrine be abolished.[2]

---

1 This certainly follows if the parties know that the impediment has been removed: *quaere* if they thought (wrongly) that the impediment continued.
2 *Family Law: Pre-consolidation Reforms*, SLC Discussion Paper No 85, paras 2.1–2.19.

2 Legal impediments to marriage – void and voidable marriages

INTRODUCTION

As we saw in the last chapter,[1] as a result of s 23A of the Marriage (Scotland) Act 1977, non-compliance with the formalities for regular marriages laid down in the Act will not affect the validity of the marriage provided both parties were present at the ceremony and the particulars of their marriage were duly registered. However, a marriage may be defective if the parties lack legal capacity to enter into the contract or if there is not true consent or the marriage cannot be consummated as a result of the incurable impotency of one or both of the parties. In this chapter we shall examine the impediments to marriage which are recognised by Scots law.

VOID AND VOIDABLE MARRIAGES

As a general rule, where such an impediment exists the marriage will be void in Scots law. There is one exception to this principle, namely, where the marriage has not been consummated as a result of the incurable impotency of one or both of the parties. In this case, the marriage is voidable.

Where a marriage is void, it prima facie has no legal effect whatsoever. There is no need for the parties to obtain a declarator of nullity of marriage in the Court of Session. However, any person who has a legitimate interest may seek a declarator of nullity from the Court of Session on the ground that the marriage was void. In certain circumstances, a void marriage may have legal consequences. For example, a child conceived during a void marriage is presumed to be the child of the mother's 'husband'[2] and he will have parental responsibilities and rights over the child if he and the mother entered into

---

1 *Supra* p 13.
2 Sections 5(1) and (2) of the Law Reform (Parent and Child) (Scotland) Act 1986, discussed *infra* Ch 8.

the 'marriage' believing in good faith at that time that the marriage was valid.[1] Moreover, if a declarator of nullity is obtained by one of the parties, the court has the same powers to award financial provision for the parties as it does in actions of divorce.[2]

In the case of a voidable marriage, the marriage subsists unless and until a declarator of nullity of marriage is obtained from the Court of Session. Only a party to the marriage can seek declarator and, unlike the case of a void marriage, declarator cannot be obtained if one of the parties is dead. However, the effect of the decree is to declare that the marriage has never existed, ie it has retroactive effect. Nevertheless, the court can award the parties financial provision in the same way as in an action of divorce.[3] Nor does the retroactive effect of the decree affect the status of any children of the marriage.[4] Given that the sole ground of a voidable marriage is the incurable impotency of one or both of the parties, the number of children affected will be small, but, as we shall see, with modern reproductive techniques, the existence of children of a voidable marriage is not impossible.[5]

CAPACITY TO MARRY

We shall now consider the grounds on which a marriage is void in Scots law as a result of the parties' lack of legal capacity to enter into the marriage.

Non-age

By s 1(1) of the Marriage (Scotland) Act 1977, no person domiciled[6] in Scotland may marry before he or she attains the age of sixteen. Thus, for example, a fifteen year old girl who is domiciled in Scotland has no legal capacity to contract a marriage in Scotland or any other country in the world, even if the law of the foreign country allows its domiciliaries to marry below the age of sixteen. However, where a Scottish domiciliary is over the age of sixteen, he

---

1 Section 3(1) and (2) of the Children (Scotland) Act 1995 discussed *infra* Ch 10.
2 Section 17(1) of the Family Law (Scotland) Act 1985. Financial provision on divorce is discussed in detail *infra* Ch 7.
3 Ibid.
4 Section 4 of the Law Reform (Miscellaneous Provisions) Act 1949.
5 See *infra* p 152ff.
6 Domicile is a complex legal concept: its essence is a person having his or her permanent home in Scotland or who has a Scottish domicile of dependence as a result of his or her parent being domiciled in Scotland.

or she has legal capacity to marry a foreign domiciliary who is under the age of sixteen, provided the ceremony takes place abroad and the foreign party has capacity under his or her *lex domicilii* and the law of the country where the ceremony takes place (the *lex loci celebrationis*).[1]

By s 1(2) of the Marriage (Scotland) Act 1977, a marriage solemnised between persons either of whom is under the age of sixteen is void. Consequently, even if one or both of the parties have capacity to marry under the age of sixteen under their *lex domicilii*, the marriage is void if the ceremony takes place in Scotland. However the 1977 Act specifically refers to a marriage 'solemnised' in Scotland. It is open to argument, therefore, that provided the parties have capacity to marry below the age of sixteen under their *lex domicilii*, they can become married by cohabitation with habit and repute and a period of cohabitation prior to attaining the age of sixteen would be relevant for the purpose of the doctrine. However, in the case of a Scottish domiciliary who purports to marry under the age of sixteen, only periods of cohabitation after the impediment has been removed, ie after he or she has reached the age of sixteen, will be relevant in establishing a new marriage by cohabitation with habit and repute.[2]

Forbidden degrees of relationship

By s 2(1) of the Marriage (Scotland) Act 1977, a marriage between a man and any woman related to him in a degree specified in column 1 of Schedule 1 to the Act, or between a woman and any man related to her in a degree specified in column 2 of that Schedule, shall be void if (a) either the marriage is solemnised in Scotland or (b) either party is domiciled in Scotland at the time of the ceremony. The list is exclusive in the sense that where the relationship is not mentioned in the Schedule, the parties may validly marry[3] unless it would be contrary to their *lex domicilii* or the *lex loci celebrationis* for them to do so. The lists are as follows:

---

1 Contrast the position in English law: see s 2 of the Marriage Act 1949; *Pugh v Pugh* [1951] 2 All ER 680, [1951] P 482.
2 *AB v CD* 1957 SC 415: see generally *Clive* pp 77–79.
3 Section 2(3) of the Marriage (Scotland) Act 1977. Similar principles apply to marriages by cohabitation with habit and repute: see *Clive* p 79.

Man &

Woman &

1 – Relationships by consanguinity

Column 1	*Column 2*
Mother	Father
Daughter	Son
Father's mother	Father's father
Mother's mother	Mother's father
Son's daughter	Son's son
Daughter's daughter	Daughter's son
Sister	Brother
Father's sister	Father's brother
Mother's sister	Mother's brother
Brother's daughter	Brother's son
Sister's daughter	Sister's son
Father's father's mother	Father's father's father
Father's mother's mother	Father's mother's father
Mother's father's mother	Mother's father's father
Mother's mother's mother	Mother's mother's father
Son's son's daughter	Son's son's son
Son's daughter's daughter	Son's daughter's son
Daughter's son's daughter	Daughter's son's son
Daughter's daughter's daughter	Daughter's daughter's son

2 – Relationships by affinity

Daughter of former wife	Son of former husband
Former wife of father	Former husband of mother
Former wife of father's father	Former husband of father's mother
Former wife of mother's father	Former husband of mother's mother
Daughter of son of former wife	Son of son of former husband
Daughter of daughter of former wife	Son of daughter of former husband

2A – Relationships by affinity

Mother of former wife	Father of former husband
Former wife of son	Former husband of daughter

3 – Relationships by adoption

Adoptive mother or former adoptive mother	Adoptive father or former adoptive father
Adopted daughter or former adopted daughter	Adopted son or former adopted son

The prohibited relationships arise from (a) blood ties (consanguinity), (b) marriage (affinity), and (c) adoption.

(a) Consanguinity

Prima facie we are concerned with persons who are genetically related. However, where a woman gives birth to a child as a result of a fertilised ovum donated by another woman, she is to be treated as the child's mother, and not the woman who donated the egg.[1] Therefore, the child cannot marry the woman who gave birth to him even though she is not genetically related to him; but he could marry the donor who is genetically related to him, as she is not his mother for any legal purpose. Similarly, where a husband agrees to the artificial insemination of his wife using a donor's sperm (AID), the husband is treated as the father of the child for all legal purposes and not the donor.[2] Accordingly, the AID child cannot marry her mother's husband even though she is not genetically related to him; but she could marry the donor, who is genetically related to her, as he is not her father for any legal purpose.[3] Such children will also be deemed to be genetically related to the other members of the family, for example, grandparents or siblings.

For the purpose of consanguinity, half-blood is treated as full blood[4] and illegitimacy is irrelevant.[5] For example, a man cannot marry his half-sister, ie his mother's daughter by a man who was not his father or his father's daughter by a woman who was not his mother. Similarly, a woman cannot marry her illegitimate son or her legitimate son's illegitimate son. It should be noted that first cousins are free to marry.

(b) Affinity

A degree of affinity is only created by marriage and not merely by the fact that sexual intercourse has taken place between the persons concerned. Thus a man cannot prima facie marry his mother in law ie the mother of his former wife, but he can marry the mother of his former or, indeed, current mistress. Similarly, he cannot prima facie marry his father's former wife, but he can marry his father's mistress even if she has cohabited with his father for many years and borne him children. Step-brothers and step-sisters are free to marry.

---

1 Sections 27(1) and 29 of the Human Fertilisation and Embryology Act 1990.
2 Ibid, ss 28(2), (4) and 29.
3 For further discussion of these provisions see *infra*, p 152ff.
4 Section 2(2)(a) of the Marriage (Scotland) Act 1977.
5 Para 17 of Sch 1 to the Law Reform (Parent and Child) (Scotland) Act 1986.

However, in certain circumstances, a marriage between persons related by affinity is not prohibited. First, persons who are related within the degrees of affinity in paragraph 2, may marry provided that both parties have attained the age of 21 at the time of the marriage and the younger party has not at any time before attaining the age of eighteen lived in the same household as the other party and been treated by the other party as a child of the family.[1] For example, a man may now marry his father's former wife provided both are over the age of 21 and, if he is the younger party, he has not lived in the same household as his stepmother and been treated by her as a child of the family before he had reached the age of eighteen. If he has been so treated, the parties cannot marry.[2] In other words, provided the parties related within the degrees of affinity specified in paragraph 2 have never assumed, in effect, the roles of parent and child, they are free to marry if both are over the age of 21. Secondly, persons who are related within the degrees of affinity in paragraph 2A, may marry provided both parties have attained the age of 21 and the marriage is solemnised (a) in the case of a man marrying his mother-in-law or his daughter-in-law, after the deaths of his former wife and her father or the deaths of his son and his son's mother and (b) in the case of a woman marrying her father-in-law or her son-in-law, after the deaths of her former husband and his mother or the deaths of her daughter and her daughter's father.[3] Thus, it is still only in very exceptional circumstances that parents-in-law and children-in-law will be able to marry.

(c)   Adoption

The Act only prohibits marriage between adoptive parents and their adopted children.[4] Thus, if H and W adopt C (male), C cannot marry

---

1 Section 2(1A) of the Marriage (Scotland) Act 1977, as inserted by para 2(b) of Sch 2 to the Marriage (Prohibited Degrees of Relationship) Act 1986. Either party can petition the Court of Session for declarator that the conditions are satisfied which enable them to marry: see s 2(5) of the Marriage (Scotland) Act 1977, as inserted by para 2(c) of Sch 2 to the Marriage (Prohibited Degrees of Relationship) Act 1986: on the 1986 Act, see Nichols 1986 SLT (News) 229.
2 Sexual intercourse between the couple would also be a criminal offence: Criminal Law (Consolidation) (Scotland) Act 1995, s 2.
3 Section 2(1B) of the Marriage (Scotland) Act 1977, as inserted by para 2(b) of Sch 2 to the Marriage (Prohibited Degrees of Relationship) Act 1986.
4 Where a couple, who have commissioned a surrogate child, obtain parental rights under s 30 of the Human Fertilisation and Embryology Act 1990, they are treated as being related to the child for the purpose of the law on prohibited degrees of marriage: s 41 of the Adoption (Scotland) Act 1978 as applied by the Parental Orders (Human Fertilisation and Embryology) (Scotland) Regulations 1994, SI 1994/2804.

W, his adoptive mother: but if H and W then adopt C_2 (female), C can marry C_2, unless they are genetically brother and sister.[1]

There are two major policy reasons for having prohibited degrees. The first, in relation to consanguinity, is biological. Marriage to a close relative greatly increases the risk of conceiving a physically or mentally handicapped child. However, marriage between first cousins is permitted even though there is an enhanced risk of conceiving a physically or mentally handicapped child, particularly if the woman is in her mid-thirties or older. Secondly, it is argued that to allow marriage between persons who are closely related will give rise both to feelings of disgust in society generally and possible disruption within the family concerned. This can be the only justification for prohibitions in respect of affinity and adoption. However, if this were thought to be an important policy objective, why does the law, for example, permit adopted brothers and sisters to marry, even if for many years they believed they were siblings by blood? Moreover, it is thought that a total prohibition of marriage between persons who are only related by affinity is difficult to defend in modern society. The amendments to the Marriage (Scotland) Act 1977 made by the Marriage (Prohibited Degrees of Relationship) Act 1986 are therefore to be welcomed but they do not, in the present writer's view, go far enough. It is, for example, difficult to believe that there would be objections in allowing a step-daughter to marry her mother's former husband when her mother had died, even if he had treated her, before the age of 18, as a child of the family. The prohibition on the grounds of affinity survives only for historical reasons and it is submitted that it is an intrusion on personal liberty which serves little, if any, purpose.[2]

Parties of the same sex

Marriage in Scots law has always been regarded as a union between a man and a woman.[3] A marriage will therefore be void if the parties purporting to marry are of the same sex.

In *Corbett v Corbett*,[4] the High Court in England had to consider the criteria for determining a person's sex for the purpose of the law of marriage. The couple went through a ceremony of marriage which

---

1 Adoption and parental rights orders (*supra*) do not affect the prohibitions on the grounds of consanguinity; so an adopted child cannot marry his genetic mother or father etc: s 41 of the Adoption (Scotland) Act 1978.
2 It has been recommended that the remaining limitations on marriage between a person and the parent of his or her former spouse should be abolished: *Family Law: Pre-consolidation Reforms* SLC Discussion Paper No 85, paras 3.6–3.13.
3 Stair I 4.1–I 4.6.
4 [1970] 2 All ER 33, [1971] P 83.

was never consummated. Their relationship deteriorated and the 'husband' sought a declaration that the marriage was void on the ground that the respondent was also male. Evidence was brought that the respondent had been born with male external genitalia and gonads but was a transsexual, ie psychologically he regarded himself as a woman imprisoned in a man's body. Prior to the ceremony he had undergone sex realignment surgery and as a result of this and hormone treatment, his physical appearance approximated to that of the gender which he had always psychologically considered himself to be, ie a woman. Ormrod J held that, in spite of the sex realignment surgery, the respondent was nevertheless male. In the cells of biological males, there is present Y, as well as X, chromosomes: no Y chromosomes are present in the cells of a biological female. The sex realignment surgery had not altered the respondent's cell structure and, as there was a Y chromosome present, he remained biologically male.

Having been satisfied that the respondent was biologically male, Ormrod J went on to hold that for the purpose of the law of marriage, the parties biologically had to be of different sexes. He maintained that the concept of marriage as hitherto understood required that one party had to be biologically male and the other biologically female.[1] Accordingly, as both parties in this case were biologically male, he granted decree of nullity.

It is thought that Scottish courts would follow the approach taken by Ormrod J in this case. Marriage in Scots law has traditionally been considered to be exclusively a heterosexual relationship. More controversially, perhaps, it is submitted that Scots law would also regard biological criteria, including chromosomal or cellular make up, as determinative of sex for this purpose.[2]

However this criterion has been criticised as giving insufficient weight to psychological factors as a determinant of a person's sex.[3] But, unless and until there is a fundamental re-assessment of the nature and purpose of marriage in contemporary Scottish society, there is force in the contention that marriage in Scots law presupposes that only parties of different biological sexes can fulfil the traditional obligations arising from the status. The criterion laid down in *Corbett v Corbett*[4] at least has a measure of certainty even if it has

1 Ibid at 106, per Ormrod J.
2 See, for example, *X-Petitioner* 1957 SLT (Sh Ct) 61.
3 See, for example, Kennedy (1973) Anglo American Law Review 112; Thomson (1980) 6 Journal of Medical Ethics 92.
4 [1970] 2 All ER 33, [1971] P 83.

the unfortunate result of denying post-operative transsexuals the right to marry persons whom they regard as being of the opposite sex.[1]

Underlying the decision in *Corbett* was the fear that if post-operative transsexuals were held to have capacity to marry, the question would arise whether a pre-operative transsexual could marry a person of the same biological sex, and if so, the way would then be open for homosexuals to argue that they were free to marry persons of the same sex. While the psychology of the transsexual is, of course, fundamentally different from that of the homosexual, there is no doubt that a considerable body of public opinion would not countenance the possibility of homosexual 'marriages'. By restricting marriage to biologically heterosexual couples, the decision in *Corbett* prevents this development. But for as long as Scots law regards marriage as a condition *sine qua non* for the legal regulation of cohabitation, parties to a homosexual relationship remain deprived of the right to have the economic and other consequences of their cohabitation governed by appropriate legal rules.

Prior subsisting marriage

A person who is already a party to a valid marriage lacks legal capacity to enter into a subsequent marriage while the first marriage continues to subsist.[2] There is no legal impediment if the first marriage is void: if, however, it is only voidable, it will operate as a bar to a second marriage unless and until a declarator of nullity of marriage has been obtained.[3]

Even although the parties entered into marriage with the belief held in good faith that any prior marriage had ended as a result of the death of the spouse or divorce, the marriage will still be void if, in fact, the prior marriage was subsisting at the time of the ceremony. However, if a decree of declarator of nullity were obtained, financial provision for the spouses is available.[4] Moreover, once the prior marriage is dissolved and the impediment to marriage is thereby removed, the parties may become married as a result of subsequent cohabitation with habit and repute.[5]

1 This has been held not to constitute a breach of article 12 of the European Convention on Human Rights (the right to marry and found a family): see *Rees v UK* 1987 9 EHRR 56; *Cossey v UK* (Ser A No 184, Judgment 17 Sept 1990) (1991) 13 EHRR 622, [1991] 2 FLR 92.
2 See generally *Clive* pp 76–77.
3 Even although a declarator of nullity of marriage renders the marriage retrospectively null, it will probably not operate to validate a second marriage which was entered into before declarator was obtained.
4 *Supra* p 22.
5 *Supra* p 19.

Where one of the parties is aware of this impediment, the innocent party may obtain damages for fraud. This can be illustrated by the case of *Burke v Burke*.[1] In this case H was living with W1. He went through a ceremony of marriage with the pursuer, W2. He told her that he was divorced from W1. He also informed W2 that he was working night shifts but he spent his evenings with W1. When W2 discovered that no divorce had taken place, she sought declarator of nullity and aliment for her child which had been conceived during the 'marriage'. The court held that W2 did not have to prove the validity of the first marriage: she could rely on the presumption *omnia rite et solemniter acta esse*. The onus lay on the defender to establish, which in the circumstances he was unable to do, that the first marriage was void. Accordingly, she obtained declarator and aliment for the child. In addition, the court held that the pursuer was entitled to damages in delict as a result of the defender's fraud, and the court awarded her £2,500.

As we have seen, a marriage will be void even although the parties believed, in good faith, that a prior marriage had been dissolved as a result of the death of the spouse. This can raise difficulties for a person whose spouse has disappeared and who wishes to enter a second marriage. At common law, there was a very strong presumption of life and a person who had disappeared was presumed to live to a ripe old age.[2] This presumption could be rebutted by evidence establishing beyond reasonable doubt that a spouse was dead but even so, a subsequent marriage was void if the spouse was in fact still alive.

This unsatisfactory position was resolved as a result of the Presumption of Death (Scotland) Act 1977.[3] Under this statute, any person with sufficient interest may petition the Court of Session[4] or the sheriff court[5] for a declarator of death. The court may grant decree if satisfied on a balance of probabilities that either—

a) the missing person is dead – including the date and time of death; or

1 1983 SLT 331.
2 Stair IV 45.17. See, for example, *Muhammad v Robertson or Kettle or Muhammad* 1972 SLT (Notes) 69.
3 See generally *Clive* Ch 29.
4 The Court of Session has jurisdiction if a) the missing person was domiciled in Scotland, or habitually resident in Scotland for one year, at the date when last known to be alive, or b) if the pursuer is the spouse of the missing person and is domiciled in Scotland or habitually resident in Scotland for one year, at the date when the action is raised: s 1(3) of the 1977 Act.
5 The sheriff court has jurisdiction on the same grounds but in addition where jurisdiction is based on a) *supra* the last known place of residence of the missing person must have been in the sheriffdom and where it is based on b) *supra* the pursuer must have been resident in the sheriffdom for at least 40 days before the date of the action.

b) the missing person has not been known to be alive for a period of at least seven years: in this case, the court will declare the missing person to have died at the end of the day occurring seven years after the date on which he was last known to be alive.[1]

The 1977 Act therefore covers two situations. In the first, a person has disappeared in circumstances which point to his death at a particular time, for example, if a person was travelling in an aeroplane which disappeared. Here, there is no need to wait seven years before bringing the action. In the second, a person has simply gone missing and there are no circumstances to suggest that he is dead. Here no action can be raised until seven years have elapsed during which there is no evidence that the missing person is alive.

A declarator of death is effective 'for all purposes including dissolution of a marriage to which the missing person is a party'.[2] Once a marriage has been dissolved as a result of a decree, 'the dissolution of the marriage shall not be invalidated by the circumstance that the missing person was in fact alive at the date specified in the decree'.[3] Thus if a person has obtained a declarator of death of a missing spouse, that person will have capacity to enter a subsequent marriage and this later marriage is not affected even if the missing spouse was in fact alive at the date of the later ceremony.

Although there are provisions for the variation or recall of the declarator if the missing person is found to be alive within five years of the date of the decree, no variation or recall 'shall operate so as to revive a marriage of the missing person dissolved by virtue of a decree in an action of declarator'.[4]

It should be noted that any person, for example, a beneficiary under the missing person's will, may apply for declarator. If it is granted, it will have the effect of dissolving the missing person's marriage, even although the missing person's spouse continues to entertain the belief that the missing person is still alive and does not wish the marriage to be dissolved.

Finally, by s 13 of the 1977 Act it is a defence to a charge of bigamy for the accused to prove that at no time within a period of seven years immediately preceding the date of a subsequent 'marriage' had he or she any reason to believe that a prior spouse was alive.[5]

1 Presumption of Death (Scotland) Act 1977.
2 Ibid, s 3(1).
3 Ibid, s 3(3).
4 Ibid, s 4(5).
5 It is possible to call the Lord Advocate as a defender in an action of declarator of death, but as a general rule the missing person should be called as defender: *Horak v Lord Advocate* 1984 SLT 201.

DEFECTIVE CONSENT

Marriage is a contract and like any other contract requires consent. Accordingly, it will be null if the parties did not truly consent to take each other as husband and wife. Defective consent can arise for several reasons.

Mental illness or defect

As a result of mental illness or defect, one or both parties to a marriage may not be capable of understanding the nature of marriage and giving true consent thereto. However, the fact that a person is suffering from a mental illness, for example, depression, does not necessarily prevent the giving of a valid consent provided the necessary capacity is present at the time. Marriage has been said to be a simple contract. Accordingly persons of limited intelligence can validly consent to marriage.

It has been held[1] that there is a very heavy burden on any person denying the validity of a marriage to establish that one or both parties were incapable of understanding the nature of marriage as a result of feeble mindedness or mental illness at the time of the ceremony. However, if this burden can be discharged, the marriage will be void. A person may be of sound mind but physically or mentally weak ie facile: as a result, such persons may easily be persuaded to act against their interests. For example, an unscrupulous nurse might persuade a rich old lady who is ill in hospital to marry him. In the absence of force and fear,[2] such a marriage is valid! Scots law has firmly rejected the contention that a marriage can be voidable on the grounds of facility and circumvention or undue influence.[3]

Intoxication

A party may lack capacity to consent as a result of drunkenness or abuse of drugs at the time of the ceremony. The effect of alcohol or drugs must be extreme before capacity is lost. However, in *Johnston v Brown*,[4] the pursuer, Mary Brown, obtained declarator of nullity of marriage on the ground that at the time of the ceremony and for three days thereafter she was so inebriated that she lacked capacity to consent to the marriage. Accordingly, the marriage was void.

1 *Long v Long* 1950 SLT (Notes) 32.
2 See *infra* p 34ff.
3 *Scott v Kelly* 1992 SLT 915.
4 (1823) 2 S 495.

Error

The parties' apparent consent may be vitiated by error with the result
that the marriage is void. However, the scope of operative error in
relation to marriage is strictly limited.

It is accepted that where a party is in error as to the nature of the
ceremony, the marriage is void. For example, if A goes through a ceremony of marriage with B, believing it to be merely a betrothal, the
marriage is void.[1] Similarly, if there is an error as to the identity of the
other party, the marriage is void.[2] The error is only operative in cases
of impersonation. Thus when Jacob married Leah, believing he was
marrying Rachel, the marriage would have been void in Scots law as
a result of error.[3]

However, an error as to identity was held not to have arisen in the
case of *M' Leod v Adams*.[4] The defender had deserted from the army.
Using a false name to avoid detection by the authorities, he told a
young and gullible widow that he was a sergeant in the Black Watch.
The couple married by exchanging *de praesenti* consents whereupon
the defender promptly deserted his wife, taking her savings with him.
Lord Sands held that there was no operative error as the widow
clearly intended to marry the man before her and accordingly there
was no error as to the identity of the parties to the marriage.[5]

It is settled that an error as to the qualities of a party to the marriage
does not operate to vitiate consent. 'Errors in qualities or circumstances vitiate not: as if one supposing he had married a maid, or
chaste woman, had married a whore.'[6] In the contract of marriage
parties take each other 'for better or worse' and the Scottish courts
have refused to imply resolutive conditions into the contract which
would be inconsistent with this fundamental principle.[7] Moreover, in
Lang v Lang,[8] the Inner House of the Court of Session held that it was
irrelevant that an error as to qualities was induced by the fraudulent
misrepresentation or concealment of facts by the spouse concerned.

The pursuer in this case sought a declarator of nullity on the

1 See, for example, *Ford v Stier* [1896] P 1; *Valier v Valier* (1925) 133 LT 830.
2 Stair I 9.9.
3 *Gen* Ch 29 v 21–30.
4 1920 1 SLT 229.
5 Declarator of nullity was however granted on the grounds that the marriage was a
   sham: see *infra* p 37.
6 Stair I 9.9.
7 There is one exception: the marriage is voidable if one or both of the parties are
   unable to consummate the marriage as a result of incurable impotency. See *infra*
   p 38ff.
8 1921 SC 44: overruling *Stein v Stein* 1914 SC 903.

ground that he had been induced to marry the defender as a result of her representation that she was pregnant by him when, in fact, she was carrying another man's child. The Court maintained that neither concealment of pregnancy *per alium* nor a fraudulent misrepresentation of the true source of a disclosed pregnancy was a ground of nullity in Scots law as these merely gave rise to errors as to qualities of the spouse and were therefore not sufficiently essential to vitiate consent. The contract of marriage therefore constitutes an exception to the general law of contracts where a contract is voidable if it was induced as a result of a fraudulent misrepresentation.[1]

The limited scope of operative error in relation to marriage can be the cause of considerable injustice. While a person in the position of the pursuer in *Lang v Lang*[2] could seek divorce, he may well have to wait five years before he has a relevant ground.[3] The fraudulent misrepresentation cannot constitute grounds for divorce as behaviour for this purpose is restricted to the defender's conduct '*since the date of the marriage*'.[4]

Force or fear: duress

As a matter of principle, a marriage will be void if a party's consent was obtained as a result of force or fear.[5]

First, the will of the party must have been overcome as a result of force or fear. The test is a subjective one[6], ie was this particular person overcome by force or fear, not whether a person of reasonable fortitude would have been terrified. As Clive has pointed out:[7]

'There is a built-in protection against abuse of a subjective standard. The more trivial the force or fear, the more difficult it will be to convince the court that it did in fact overcome the will of the person subject to it'.

The Scottish cases are concerned with arranged marriages. It is accepted that where a child marries out of deference to the parents' wishes, the marriage is not void. But unremitting pressure, intention-

1 As it also does in respect of a plea of facility and circumvention or undue influence: *Scott v Kelly* 1992 SLT 915 discussed *supra* p 32.
2 1921 SC 44.
3 Ie five years' non-cohabitation: s 1(2)(e) of the Divorce (Scotland) Act 1976. See *infra* Ch 6.
4 Section 1(2)(b) of the Divorce (Scotland) Act 1976: see *infra* Ch 6.
5 Stair I 4.1; I 4.6.
6 *Mahmood v Mahmood* 1993 SLT 589; *Mahmud v Mahmud* 1994 SLT 599.
7 *Clive* p 89.

ally sustained by the parents[1] or the threat of being cut off from financial support and being sent to a foreign country,[2] go beyond the limits of proper parental influence and can constitute duress.[3]

The force or fear may emanate from a third party, for example, state authorities. It has been held that fear of incarceration for political reasons can be sufficient.[4] In the leading English case of *Buckland v Buckland*[5] Buckland was accused of corrupting a young girl in Malta. These charges were false but in order to avoid imprisonment, Buckland went through a ceremony of marriage with the girl. His petition for a decree of nullity was granted but the Court of Appeal emphasised that it would not have succeeded if he had actually been guilty of defiling the girl. In other words, the fear must have been unjustifiably imposed. Accordingly, if a man is forced to marry a girl whom he has made pregnant because of the threat that paternity proceedings would be brought against him unless he did so, he could not rely on the fear as it was justly imposed.

Clive has argued[6] that this distinction is hard to justify as the consent is no more free where the fear is justly imposed. However, this may well be a case where reasoning from legal principle must give way to considerations of public policy.[7]

Sham marriages

Parties may enter into marriage, not because they intend to live together as husband and wife, but for some ulterior purpose, for example, to avoid deportation. In England, in the absence of force or fear, such marriages are valid.[8] However, in Scotland, such marriages may be treated as void on the grounds that the parties did not have real consent to marry.

In the leading case of *Orlandi v Castelli*[9] the pursuer, a Scots woman of Italian origin, met the defender who was an Italian. In order to enable him to remain in Scotland when his residence permit

---

1 *Mahmud v Mahmud supra*. It was irrelevant that the pursuer in this case was a young man rather than a girl.
2 *Mahmood v Mahmood* 1993 SLT 589. The disapproval of the parents or the child's community is not per se enough.
3 While it may be easier to infer duress when, as in *Mahmud*, the 'marriage' was never consummated and the parties never lived together, in *Mahmood* declarator was granted even though the marriage was consummated.
4 *H v H* [1953] 2 All ER 1229, [1954] P 258. Cf *Silver v Silver* [1955] 2 All ER 614.
5 [1967] 2 All ER 300, [1968] P 296.
6 *Clive* p 90.
7 See generally Davies (1972) 88 LQR 549.
8 See, for example, *Silver v Silver* [1955] 2 All ER 614.
9 1961 SC 113.

expired, the couple went through a civil marriage ceremony. Both were Roman Catholics and held the view that a civil ceremony did not constitute a valid marriage and a religious ceremony was necessary. The marriage was never consummated. Lord Cameron held that if the pursuer could establish her averments, declarator of nullity would be granted. In his Lordship's opinion:

> '. . . *where it can be established* that there is no true matrimonial consent and that the ceremony was only designed as a sham or as an antecedent to true marriage, it is competent to found upon the absence of that consent for the purpose of setting aside a marriage regularly celebrated'.[1]

This decision was followed in *Mahmud v Mahmud*[2] where Lord Kincraig held that a civil marriage was void where it was satisfactorily proved that a Moslem couple did not regard themselves as married until a religious ceremony had taken place. In *Akram v Akram*[3] Lord Dunpark expressed the principle as follows:[4]

> '. . . there is no doubt that Scots civil law has always applied the consensual principle to the contract of marriage so that *if it be proved* that, notwithstanding the trappings of a formal marriage ceremony, the parties thereto did not exchange their consent *for the purpose of obtaining married status*, the ceremony must be denied the legal effect it was designed to produce.'

It is accepted that given a regular marriage ceremony, prima facie the parties' consent is presumed. There is therefore a heavy onus on the pursuer to establish that the parties did not consent to be married. While the parties' religious beliefs will be important evidence of the absence of true consent, it is thought that the principle will apply even if there is no religious element, though the difficulty of rebutting the presumption of consent will be formidable. However, if it can be shown that the parties' predominant purpose when going through the ceremony was some ulterior motive, for example, to evade immigration rules, and not to enter upon the status of husband and wife, the marriage is void for absence of true consent.

Clive has argued[5] that a marriage will only be void as a sham, if it can be shown that at the time of the ceremony, the parties had a positive intention not to be married. Proof that they had a predominant

---

1 Ibid at 120; italics added.
2 1977 SLT (Notes) 17.
3 1979 SLT (Notes) 87.
4 Ibid at 88; italics added.
5 *Clive* p 93.

ulterior motive for entering upon the marriage is not sufficient. But as he himself admits,[1] it is doubtful whether the parties would draw the distinction between having an intention not to marry and marrying for a predominant ulterior motive. It is submitted that Clive's distinction is too subtle. Instead it is thought that a marriage is void as a sham if it is established that at the time of the ceremony the parties purported to consent to marriage, not for the purpose of living together as husband and wife, but for some other ulterior motive.[2]

In *Akram v Akram*[3] Lord Dunpark granted decree with reluctance. He was concerned that it might well be contrary to public policy to annul a marriage on proof of a predominant ulterior motive when, as a result of the ceremony, the parties had achieved their aims, for example, to avoid deportation. Indeed he suggested that the principle of personal bar 'might well be extended to cover cases in which the proved ulterior purpose was to circumvent any law of the land'.[4] It is thought, however, that the solution to the problem is to reduce even further the importance of marriage in, for example, the immigration rules, so that there is no advantage in being parties to a sham marriage.

There is authority for the view that a marriage is void as a sham where only one party withheld true consent. In *M'Leod v Adams*,[5] for example, although the marriage was not void as a result of the young widow's error,[6] declarator of nullity was granted on the ground that the soldier did not intend to marry her when they purported to exchange *de praesenti* consent. Lord Sands held that the defender did not intend to marry her and only wished to discover the whereabouts of the widow's money, steal it and leave:

> 'The marriage ceremony was a detail in the execution of this crime. . . . His statement that he took her as his wife was a falsehood, and the marriage was simulate on his part.'[7]

However, a person is personally barred from pleading his or her own unilateral and uncommunicated reservation of true consent in an action of declarator of nullity.[8]

---

1 Ibid.
2 This is certainly the thrust of Lord Dunpark's reasoning in *Akram v Akram* 1979 SLT (Notes) 87, cited *supra* p 36.
3 1979 SLT (Notes) 87.
4 Ibid at 89.
5 1920 1 SLT 229.
6 *Supra* p 33.
7 1920 1 SLT 229 at 231.
8 *Akram v Akram* 1979 SLT (Notes) 87 at 88, per Lord Dunpark; *Clive* p 95.

It has, however, been recommended that sham marriages should no longer be treated as void.[1]

Validation of marriages void for absence of consent

There is some authority for the principle that a marriage which is void as a result of absence of consent will be validated if the parties choose to overlook the impediment and continue to live as husband and wife.[2] However, it is thought that the better view is that a couple will become married as a result of the doctrine of marriage by cohabitation with habit and repute, in the same way as if their original marriage was void because of a temporary impediment to their marriage.

VOIDABLE MARRIAGES – INCURABLE IMPOTENCY

The parties' consent is the essential element of marriage in Scots law: *consensus non concubitus facit matrimonium*. However, a marriage is voidable if, and only if, one or both of the parties is at the time of the ceremony permanently and incurably impotent. As Lord President (Clyde) explained in *L v L*,[3] *potentia copulandi* is a resolutive condition of the contract of marriage: if it is not fulfilled the marriage is a nullity. But before the marriage will be treated as null, a party to the marriage must obtain a declarator of nullity of marriage from the Court of Session whereupon the marriage is retrospectively void from the date of decree.[4] It has been recommended that incurable impotency should cease to be a ground on which a marriage is voidable.[5]

The meaning of incurable impotency

Impotency means incapacity to have sexual intercourse. The Scottish courts have taken the view that sexual intercourse involves full and

---

1 *Family Law: Pre-consolidation Reforms* SLC Discussion Paper No 85, paras 3.16 ff.
2 *Clive* p 97 ff.
3 1931 SC 477 at 481.
4 *Supra* p 22.
5 *Family Law: Pre-consolidation Reforms* SLC Discussion Paper No 85, paras 3.20–3.29. There are only about 8 declarators of nullity a year and it is doubtful whether they are all concerned with incurable impotency. The numbers concerned are therefore very small. It is true that specific matrimonial relief on the ground of incurable impotency is anomalous: there is no specific relief, for example, if a spouse marries when suffering from sterility or an incurable or infectious disease, for example, AIDS. It is argued by the Commission that divorce on the ground of irretrievable breakdown should be a sufficient remedy in cases of incurable impotency.

complete sexual intercourse: *vera copula perfecta* accomplished *modo naturalis*. Partial penetration by the husband of the wife is not enough.[1] However, once full penetration has been achieved, the marriage has been consummated. It is irrelevant that the husband has used a contraceptive sheath.[2] Moreover, impotency is incapacity for sexual intercourse not capacity to procreate. Consequently, sterility does not amount to impotency. If a spouse is capable of sexual intercourse but refuses to consummate the marriage, that is not a ground of nullity in Scots law though it could give rise to grounds for divorce.[3]

The impotency may be the result of physical or psychological causes. It may exist only in relation to the other spouse: *quoad hanc* (vis à vis the wife) or *quoad hunc* (vis à vis the husband). Indeed, both spouses may be impotent in relation to each other: *quoad hanc et quoad hunc*!

The impotency must exist at the date of the marriage and must be permanent and incurable at the date of the action for declarator of nullity. The courts have taken a realistic approach on the question of incurability and have held that the issue is whether the impotency is incurable in the context of the particular marriage. Thus, for example, in *M v W or M*,[4] the husband suffered from a nervous or psychological inability to consummate the marriage. He was advised by his doctor that the impotency was curable if he had hormone treatment and had the full support and help of his wife. After the hormone treatment was administered, his wife refused to have sexual intercourse with him. The Inner House held that the husband's impotency was incurable *quoad hanc* as the cure involved both the hormone treatment and the wife's help which had not been forthcoming.[5]

While this decision illustrates the court's sympathy towards the pursuer, it must be restricted to its own special facts: a potent spouse cannot argue that he is impotent *quoad hanc* merely because his wife refuses to have sexual intercourse with him since this would, in effect, be recognising wilful refusal to consummate as a ground of nullity.

If the impotency is curable, where the action is brought by the potent spouse, decree is not granted until the impotent spouse has had

---

1 *J v J* 1978 SLT 128.
2 *Baxter v Baxter* [1947] 2 All ER 886, [1948] AC 274, HL, an English case which it is thought would be followed in Scotland.
3 On the behaviour ground: s 1(2)(b) of the Divorce (Scotland) Act 1976, see *infra* Ch 6.
4 1966 SLT 152.
5 But the Lord President (Clyde) thought that the question was whether the husband was impotent throughout the marriage rather than whether it was curable at the date of the action.

an opportunity to undergo the necessary treatment: if the defender refuses treatment, decree will then be granted.[1] If the impotent spouse is the pursuer, the action will fail if reasonable steps could be taken to effect a cure. Where the treatment carries a risk to life or intolerable pain, the impotent spouse is not expected to undergo such an ordeal, and the impotency will be regarded as incurable.[2]

The potent spouse can obviously bring an action. But in *F v F*,[3] the Inner House held that because impotency was an involuntary condition, the impotent spouse can also seek a declarator of nullity on the ground of his or her own incurable impotency.

Personal bar

A spouse may be personally barred from obtaining declarator of nullity on the ground of incurable impotency. Personal bar will arise if with knowledge of the impotency and the availability of a legal remedy, the pursuer has either approbated the marriage or taken advantage of, or derived benefits from, the matrimonial relationship with the result that it would be unfair or inequitable to permit the pursuer to treat the marriage as null.[4]

Two points should be noticed. First, personal bar will only arise if the pursuer knows of the facts and the availability of a legal remedy. But knowledge of the law will prima facie be assumed and the onus should therefore be on the pursuer to show that he or she did not have knowledge of a legal remedy. Secondly, it is the pursuer's *conduct* which constitutes approbation or the taking of advantages etc which renders it unfair or inequitable to grant decree. The following are illustrations of the principle.

Delay

Delay per se is not enough,[5] but if it would result in serious prejudice to the defender, it could be so.[6]

Knowledge of impotency

Where the pursuer entered into the marriage with knowledge of the defender's impotency this will result in personal bar. By marrying in

---

1 *WY v AY* 1946 SC 27.
2 Such risks are unlikely to arise in the context of modern medicine.
3 1945 SC 202.
4 *CB v AB* (1885) 12 R (HL) 36 at 38, per Lord Selborne.
5 See, for example, *Allardyce v Allardyce* 1954 SC 419.
6 *AB v CB* 1961 SC 347.

these circumstances, the pursuer has adopted or homologated the defender's failure to perform a condition whose failure would otherwise have entitled the pursuer to have the marriage resolved.[1] Conversely, an impotent spouse who has allowed the potent spouse to enter the marriage with knowledge of the impotency is personally barred from seeking declarator on the ground of his or her own impotency.[2]

Children

Personal bar will arise where the pursuer has homologated or adopted the voidable marriage by agreeing to adopt a child or have a child by artificial insemination.[3]

---

1 *L v L* 1931 SC 477 at 481, per Lord President (Clyde).
2 It is submitted that this is an example of *rei interventus*.
3 *AB v CB* 1961 SC 347. *Quaere* if the child was conceived by *fecundatio ab extra* during an unsuccessful attempt to consummate the marriage.

3 The legal consequences of marriage I

INTRODUCTION

In this and the following two chapters it is proposed to discuss the major legal consequences of marriage for the spouses. This chapter is concerned with a miscellaneous range of subjects but the treatment is not intended to be exhaustive and certain important matters, for example, evidence, bankruptcy and taxation, are thought to be out-with the scope of a student text on family law. In Chapters 4 and 5, the implications of marriage on the law of property are discussed in some detail.[1]

The twentieth century has seen a drastic decline in the legal conse-quences of marriage.[2] In the interests of equality between the spouses, many changes in the law have taken the form of treating the spouses as though they were unmarried. But, particularly in relation to property, as long as our society continues to perceive that the pri-mary responsibility for child rearing should be the mother's, formal legal equality will often result in a wife's economic dependence on her husband, as in fact she does not have the same opportunities to acquire property during the marriage. However, as we shall see,[3] under our system of financial provision on divorce the courts can compensate a wife for economic disadvantages suffered by her as a result of the marriage. Moreover, when a marriage is terminated by death, Scots law protects the surviving spouse by providing the sur-vivor with legal rights to a proportion of the deceased's estate which cannot be defeated by the deceased. It is perhaps not too cynical to observe that during the marriage the legal consequences of being married are, with some important exceptions such as aliment[4] and the right to occupy the matrimonial home,[5] relatively insignificant com-pared with being married when the marriage is terminated by divorce or death.

1 *Infra* p 61 and p 73.
2 See generally, *Clive* Part II.
3 *Infra* Ch 7.
4 Discussed *infra* p 49.
5 *Infra* Ch 5.

PERSONAL EFFECTS[1]

Nationality

Marriage has no effect on nationality. If a wife is a citizen of the United Kingdom and Colonies before marriage she remains so: if not, she retains her existing nationality. A foreign spouse of a British citizen can acquire British citizenship by naturalisation.[2] Marriage does, however, remain important in the context of immigration.[3]

Adherence

It is the duty of the spouses to live together, ie adhere. But, it is a duty which could never be specifically implemented and actions of adherence are no longer competent.[4] Where a spouse refuses to adhere without reasonable cause, that spouse is, however, regarded as being in desertion.[5]

At one time, the husband had the right to choose where the matrimonial home should be, and provided his choice was genuine and reasonable, a wife was in desertion if she refused to live there with him.[6] This right has now been abolished.[7]

Domicile

Arising from the wife's duty to live with her husband, the rule developed that a wife's domicile depended on that of her husband. Accordingly, while the marriage subsisted, a wife could not have a domicile which was different from her husband's. The wife's domicile of dependency was abolished by s 1 of the Domicile and Matrimonial Proceedings Act 1973 and a wife can now acquire an independent domicile.[8]

---

1 See *Clive* Ch 11.
2 The previous system whereby a foreign spouse could, on marriage to a British citizen, acquire British citizenship by registration has been phased out: see, generally, the British Nationality Act 1981, s 8; *Clive* pp 151–152.
3 *Clive* pp 152–153.
4 Section 2 of the Law Reform (Husband and Wife) (Scotland) Act 1984.
5 Discussed in the context of divorce, *infra* Ch 6.
6 See, for example, *Stewart v Stewart* 1959 SLT (Notes) 70.
7 Section 4 of the Law Reform (Husband and Wife) (Scotland) Act 1984.
8 By s 1(2) of the 1973 Act, a wife who had a domicile by dependence retains that domicile unless and until it is changed by acquisition or revival of another domicile, on or after the Act came into force.

Sexual relations

If a spouse is unable to consummate the marriage as a result of incurable impotency, the marriage is voidable. Similarly, if a spouse wilfully refuses to have sexual intercourse, this could give rise to an action of divorce.[1] If a spouse voluntarily has sexual intercourse with a third party during the subsistence of the marriage, this can give rise to an action of divorce on the ground of adultery.[2]

At one time, it was thought that a husband could not be guilty of raping his wife if he had sexual intercourse with her without her consent: this was based on the view that, on marriage, a wife is prima facie deemed to have surrendered her person to her husband. Where there was evidence, for example, if the couple were *de facto* separated, from which it could be inferred that the wife was no longer prepared to surrender her body to her husband, then he could be prosecuted for rape and not merely indecent assault.[3] The High Court of Justiciary has now held that these rules are anachronistic and that a husband can be guilty of raping his wife even although the couple are living together.[4] In the course of his judgment the Lord Justice-General (Emslie) said:[5]

> 'Nowadays it cannot seriously be maintained that by marriage a wife submits herself irrevocably to sexual intercourse in all circumstances. It cannot be affirmed nowadays, whatever the position may have been in earlier centuries, that it is an incident of modern marriage that a wife consents to intercourse obtained only by force. There is no doubt that a wife does not consent to assault upon her person and there is no plausible justification for saying today that she nevertheless is to be taken to consent to intercourse by assault.'

Of course, even although a husband can now be charged with the rape of his wife, there remain formidable problems of proof.[6]

On marriage, a spouse lacks capacity to enter into another marriage, unless the existing marriage is terminated by divorce or death.

1 Based on s 1(2)(b) of the Divorce (Scotland) Act 1976, discussed *infra* Ch 6.
2 Section 1(2)(a) of the Divorce (Scotland) Act 1976, discussed *infra* Ch 6.
3 *HM Advocate v Duffy* 1983 SLT 7; *HM Advocate v Paxton* 1985 SLT 96.
4 *S v HM Advocate* 1989 SLT 469.
5 Ibid at 473.
6 In *S v HM Advocate*, for example, the jury found the charge of rape not proven.

Name

There is no legal requirement for a wife to take her husband's surname on marriage. It is, however, still common for a wife to use her husband's surname but this is mere usage. In formal legal documents a married woman will sign using her maiden name and her husband's surname, for example, Mrs Elizabeth Smith (maiden name) or Brown (husband's name).[1]

OBLIGATIONS

Contract

At common law a wife had no contractual capacity. However, in time the courts recognised exceptions to the general rule and in a series of statutes culminating in the Married Women's Property (Scotland) Act 1920, a married woman was deemed to 'be capable of entering into contracts and incurring obligations . . . as if she were not married'.[2] Now s 24(1) of the Family Law (Scotland) Act 1985 provides that subject to the provisions of any enactment, marriage shall not of itself affect 'the legal capacity of the parties to the marriage'. Thus marriage per se has no effect on the contractual capacity of the spouses.

At common law, a wife was presumed to have been placed by her husband in charge of his domestic affairs and consequently she could pledge his credit for household expenses, for example, food, clothing etc. This was known as the wife's *praepositura*. The *praepositura* was thought to have become anachronistic and has been abolished.[3] However, it is, of course, possible that one spouse may expressly appoint the other to act as his or her agent in a particular transaction. Moreover, one spouse may impliedly authorise the other to act as his or her agent by acquiescing in a series of transactions. For example, if a husband has paid the accounts incurred by his wife at a dress shop, he will remain liable to pay future accounts unless he has informed the shopkeeper that he will no longer be prepared to pay her accounts in the future: merely to tell his wife no longer to pledge his credit is not sufficient to avoid liability.[4]

---

1 For the form of names used in court proceedings, see *Clive* p 156 ff.
2 Section 1: for a full account of these developments, see *Clive* p 222 ff.
3 Section 7 of the Law Reform (Husband and Wife) (Scotland) Act 1984.
4 The husband's liability to pay his wife's debts incurred before marriage has been abolished: s 6 of the Law Reform (Husband and Wife) (Scotland) Act 1984.

When a wife enters into an obligation with a third party which benefits her husband, for example, the grant of a standard security to guarantee her husband's debts, there is no presumption in Scots law that she acted under the undue influence of her husband.[1]

Thus, as a result of recent reforms, spouses enjoy the same contractual capacity as they would have had if they were unmarried.

Delict

At common law, spouses could not sue each other in delict. The anachronistic nature of this rule can be illustrated by the case where, as a result of a husband's negligent driving, the wife was injured: it was indefensible that she could not sue her husband, particularly as the loss would ultimately fall on her husband's insurance company. This position was modified by s 2 of the Law Reform (Husband and Wife) Act 1962 which provides that each of the spouses has 'the like rights' to bring proceedings against the other in respect of a delict 'as if they were not married': however, where the action is brought during the subsistence of the marriage, the court has a discretion to dismiss the proceedings if it appears that no substantial benefit would accrue to either party if the action continued.[2] The court's discretion is unlikely to be invoked as the action must proceed if a benefit accrues to the *pursuer*, even although the couple, as a family unit, will not benefit.[3]

Under the Damages (Scotland) Act 1976, where a spouse has died as a result of a delict by a third party, the surviving spouse has a right to damages for loss of support, including a reasonable sum for loss of the deceased's personal services[4], funeral expenses and compensation for grief, distress and the loss of the deceased's society.[5] However, claims under the Damages (Scotland) Act 1976 can also be brought by members of the deceased's 'immediate family', for example, children. In an important step towards the recognition of

1 *Mumford v Bank of Scotland; Smith v Bank of Scotland* 1995 SCLR 839 (IH) 1994 SLT 1288 (OH). Cf the position in English law: *Barclay's Bank v O'Brien* [1994] 1 AC 180.
2 Law Reform (Husband and Wife) Act 1962, s 2(2).
3 It has been proposed that since the discretion in s 2(2) is anomalous and unnecessary, it should be repealed: *Family Law: Pre-consolidation Reforms* SLC Discussion Paper No 85, paras 5.1–5.7.
4 Section 9 of the Administration of Justice Act 1982, discussed *infra*, p 48. See, for example, *Ingham v John G Russell Transport Ltd* 1991 SCLR 596.
5 Section 1(3) and (4) of the Damages (Scotland) Act 1976 as amended by s 1(1) of the Damages (Scotland) Act 1993. Compensation is not reduced where a wife married her husband knowing that he was suffering a fatal disease allegedly caused by the negligence of the defender: *Phillips v Grampian Health Board* 1989 SLT 538.

cohabitation, the deceased's 'immediate family' includes, 'any person, not being the spouse of the deceased, who was immediately before the deceased's death, living with the deceased as husband and wife.'[1] As a member of the deceased person's immediate family, the cohabitee is entitled to the same damages as a surviving spouse. This demonstrates the recognition by Parliament that 'a significant minority of caring and stable relationships exist outside marriage.' A surviving *divorced* spouse can only obtain damages for loss of support and funeral expenses.[2]

While it is not necessary that the deceased was under a legal obligation to aliment the claimant, the relative must show that loss of support has been or is likely to arise as a result of the delict. Thus, where both spouses work and pool their wages and enjoy an enhanced standard of living, but each is *in fact* supporting himself or herself, there may be little, if any, damages for loss of support: 'the loss of jam on the family bread and butter does not give rise to what can currently be termed a claim for loss of support.'[3] Where a housewife was killed, her husband and child obtained damages for the loss of her services as a housekeeper.[4]

The Damages (Scotland) Act 1976 is concerned with the situation where the delict results in death. Where a person is injured, it was held at common law that the defender did not owe a duty of care to the victim's spouse or relatives if they suffered loss as a result of the delict. Accordingly, the family could not sue for damages.[5] Moreover, the victim could not sue for losses sustained by a relative, for example, a spouse, who had given up his or her job to nurse him.[6] As a result of s 8 of the Administration of Justice Act 1982,[7] where a person has sustained personal injuries, the injured person can now recover damages which amount to reasonable remuneration for necessary services rendered to him or her by a relative.[8] For these

1 Section 14 of the Administration of Justice Act 1982, amending para 1 of Sch 1 to the 1976 Act.
2 Sections 1(4) and 10(2) of the Damages (Scotland) Act 1976.
3 *Mitchell v Gartshore* 1976 SLT (Notes) 41 per Lord Grieve at 42. The case was concerned with the analogous action at common law but it is submitted it still applies to a claim under the Damages (Scotland) Act 1976.
4 *Brown v Ferguson* 1990 SLT 274.
5 *Robertson v Turnbull* 1982 SLT 96.
6 *Edgar v Lord Advocate* 1965 SC 67.
7 As amended by s 69 of the Law Reform (Miscellaneous Provisions) (Scotland) Act 1990.
8 Damages can also be awarded as reasonable remuneration for necessary services to be rendered by a relative after the date of the action: s 8(3). This reverses the decision in *Forsyth's Curator Bonis v Govan Shipbuilders* 1988 SLT 321.

purposes, a relative includes a cohabitee. The pursuer ie the injured person, will then account to the relative for any damages recovered under this provision.[1]

When the victim is not earning, at common law, he or she had no right to sue for loss of earnings. This was particularly unfair to wives who had given up their job to look after the home or children. Section 9 of the Administration of Justice Act 1982 now provides that an injured person who has been providing *unpaid* personal services to a relative, can sue for damages if as a result of the injuries, he or she is unable to continue to do so. For these purposes, a relative includes a cohabitee. The personal services must be services which a) were or might have been expected to have been rendered by the injured person before the injury; b) were of a kind which when rendered by a person other than a relative would ordinarily be obtainable on payment; and c) the injured person but for the injuries in question might have been expected to render gratuitously to a relative. These would include a wife's or cohabitee's unpaid housekeeping services to her husband or cohabitee, a mother's unpaid child rearing services to her children or a husband's unpaid DIY maintenance for the benefit of his wife and family.[2] Because the personal services must have been rendered gratuitously before s 9 applies, the Act recognises the fact that work at home is still prima facie unpaid, but that its economic value to the community is such that justice demands that the injured person receive compensation even though he or she has not suffered patrimonial loss.[3]

INCOME SUPPORT

For the purpose of obtaining income support it is necessary to aggregate the needs and resources of certain persons who are living together. The requirements and resources of a married couple who are members of the same household are aggregated but so also are those of an unmarried couple who are living together as husband and wife.[4]

---

1 Section 8(2). Damages will not be paid if the relative has expressly agreed that no payment should be made for these services: s 8(1) and (3). For an example of the operation of the provisions, see *Denheen v British Railways Board* 1986 SLT 249. There is, however, no equivalent to s 8(2) in respect of recovery of damages for future services under s 8(3).
2 See, for example, *Ingham v John G Russell Transport Ltd* 1991 SCLR 596.
3 Of course, if the victim was being paid for his or her services, they could recover damages for loss of wages in the usual way.
4 Sections 136(1) and 137(2) of the Social Security Contributions and Benefits Act 1992.

The relationship between the system of state support and the private law obligation of aliment is discussed in the next section.

ALIMENT

The nature and extent of the obligation

A husband has a duty to aliment, ie *maintain* his wife, and a wife has a duty to aliment her husband.[1] There is no obligation on cohabitees to aliment each other.

A spouse's duty to aliment is 'to provide such support as is reasonable in the circumstances', having regard to the matters which a court is required or entitled to consider in determining the amount of aliment awarded.[2] The effect of this provision is that a spouse will always have a prima facie right to aliment from the other, but the extent of the defender's duty to aliment will depend on the same factors as govern quantification of an award.

The factors which must be considered are set out in s 4(1). They are:

'a) the needs and resources of the parties;[3]
 b) the earning capacities of the parties;[4]
 c) generally, all the circumstances of the case.'

Section 4(3)(a)

In relation to s 4(1)(c), s 4(3)(a) provides that the court '*may*, if it thinks fit, take account of any support, financial or otherwise, given by the defender to any person whom he maintains as a dependant in his household, whether or not the defender owes an obligation of aliment to that person'. The effect of this provision can be illustrated by the following example: H leaves W, who is unemployed, and sets up home with his mistress, M. H supports M financially. In an action for aliment brought by W against H, the court *may* take into account the fact that H is supporting M. If it does, there will be less resources available for W and consequently a smaller amount of aliment will be awarded. Section 4(3)(a) reverses the previous rule under which financial or other support *in fact* made by a defender to a third party

---

1 Section 1(1)(a) and (b) of the Family Law (Scotland) Act 1985. References in this section are to the 1985 Act unless otherwise stated. Obligations of aliment exist between parents and children: these are discussed *infra* Ch 9.
2 Section 1(2).
3 'Needs' means present and foreseeable needs; 'resources' means present and foreseeable resources: s 27.
4 The court is concerned with earning *capacity*, not merely a party's likely future earnings: consequently a claimant cannot elect to be unemployed.

was *not* taken into account, unless he was under a legal obligation to aliment that person, for example, his child.[1] It is submitted that the courts should be prepared to exercise their discretion under s 4(3)(a), particularly where the defender is a low wage earner. If H, in the example, was earning very little, then if the fact that he was supporting M was taken into account, W would probably receive no aliment at all. This is a sensible result in the circumstances for it allows W to have full recourse to income support and other benefits. If it were not taken into account, the amount of aliment awarded would be small: even if H paid it regularly, W would be no better off financially, since the aliment would merely reduce the amount payable in income support.

Where either spouse is being financially or otherwise supported by a third party, this will be a relevant factor under s 4(1)(c) as it is clearly one of the circumstances of the case. For example, in an action for aliment by a wife against her husband, the court was entitled to take into account the fact that the husband's cohabitee was contributing to their joint outlays: but the joint incomes of the husband and cohabitee could not simply be aggregated as that would subject the cohabitee to an obligation of aliment to the wife, which the cohabitee did not owe.[2]

Section 4(3)(b)

In relation to s 4(1)(c), s 4(3)(b) provides that the court 'shall not take account of any conduct of a party unless it would be manifestly inequitable to leave it out of account'. The effect of this provision is that a spouse has a prima facie right to aliment from the other, even although the pursuer has committed adultery,[3] has behaved in an intolerable way, or refuses to adhere. Moreover, in assessing the amount of aliment such conduct is to be ignored by the court, unless it would be 'manifestly inequitable to leave it out of account'.[4] It is submitted that it should only be in very extreme circumstances that the pursuer's conduct should be taken into account to reduce the

---

1 *Henry v Henry* 1972 SLT (Notes) 26. Moreover, a pursuer's entitlement to income support was ignored, with the result that defenders could be ordered to pay awards of aliment which they could not afford while continuing to support the third party: *McAuley v McAuley* 1968 SLT (Sh Ct) 81; *McCarrol v McCarrol* 1966 SLT (Sh Ct) 45.
2 *Munro v Munro* 1986 SLT 72; *Firth v Firth* 1990 GWD 5–266. Cf *Pryde v Pryde* 1991 SLT (Sh Ct) 26.
3 Discussed in the context of divorce, *infra* Ch 6.
4 Section 4(3)(b).

amount of aliment which would otherwise be awarded.[1] When a marriage is breaking down, there is usually fault on both sides: certainly, it is most unjust to penalise a spouse financially for conduct, for example, adultery, which is a symptom not a cause of matrimonial breakdown. Nor does this raise injustice to the defender. The purpose of aliment is to oblige the spouses to maintain each other *during the marriage*: the obligation to aliment ends on divorce. Consequently, if the defender feels aggrieved at being obliged to aliment a pursuer who has committed adultery or other matrimonial misconduct, the remedy is to sue for divorce.[2] On divorce, the obligation to aliment ceases and, instead, financial provision can be ordered which will hopefully result in a financial clean break between the spouses.[3] And it is thought this approach is consonant with current public policy which is to encourage marriages which have irretrievably broken down, as evidenced inter alia by matrimonial misconduct, to be decently buried.

Defences

Section 2(8) gives a general defence to a claim for aliment[4] if the defender makes an offer to receive the pursuer into the defender's household and to fulfil the obligation of aliment, *provided* it is reasonable to expect the pursuer to accept the offer. In considering whether it is reasonable for the pursuer to accept the defender's offer, s 2(9) enjoins the court to look at all the relevant circumstances including conduct and any decree, for example, an interdict against violence,[5] which has been obtained. So, for example, if W has been the victim of H's domestic violence, she will obtain aliment even though she is unwilling to adhere and despite the fact that H makes her an offer to return to his household: as a result of H's conduct, the offer is not one which it would be reasonable to expect W, the victim of his violence, to accept. Even if she had committed adultery, it is thought that H would not have a defence if he had been violent

1 One example might be where the pursuer's conduct had reduced the defender's resources: for example, by injuring the defender so that his earning capacity was impaired. Another is illustrated by the facts of *Kyte v Kyte* [1987] 3 WLR 1114 where the wife had actively encouraged her husband's attempts at suicide! In *Walker v Walker* 1991 SLT 649 Lord Clyde stated that where the defender had lied as to his income and assets this *was* conduct which it would be manifestly inequitable to leave out of account.
2 See *infra* Ch 6.
3 See *infra* Ch 7.
4 Except where the claim is brought by or on behalf of a child under the age of 16: see *infra* Ch 9.
5 Discussed *infra* Ch 5.

towards her; because of the violence, it is still not reasonable to expect W to return. Moreover, her adultery will not lead to any reduction in the amount of aliment awarded as it is thought that adultery per se is not conduct which it would be manifestly inequitable to leave out of account.[1]

Where a couple have agreed to separate, s 2(9) provides that the mere fact that they have agreed to live apart does not of itself establish that it is unreasonable to expect the pursuer to accept the defender's offer. Thus, if a couple agree to part and W later seeks aliment, if H makes her an offer to return to his household, this may constitute a s 2(8) defence because it is not unreasonable to expect the pursuer to accept such an offer merely because they have earlier agreed to part. Of course, other circumstances, for example, H's drinking or adultery or violence while they lived together, may make it unreasonable to expect W to accept H's offer.

Aliment where the parties are living together

At common law, a spouse who was being inadequately maintained had to leave the matrimonial home before an action for aliment could be brought.[2] Section 2(6) provides that an action for aliment is competent notwithstanding that the pursuer is living in the same household as the defender. Thus, for example, a wife can sue her husband for an adequate housekeeping allowance. But it is a defence to an action in these circumstances if the defender can show that he is fulfilling his obligation to aliment the pursuer and intends to continue doing so.[3]

The nature of an award

On granting a decree of aliment s 3(1) provides that the court may, if it thinks fit,
a) order the making of a periodical payment, whether for a definite or an indefinite period or until the happening of a specified event: but the court cannot substitute a lump sum for a periodical payment;[4]
b) order the making of alimentary payments of an occasional or special nature, for example, hospital expenses: these will usually be small amounts;

---

1 Section 4(3)(b), discussed *supra* pp 50, 51.
2 *M'Donald v M'Donald* (1875) 2 R 705.
3 Section 2(7).
4 Section 3(2). A defender cannot be ordered to provide security for an alimentary payment: *MacDonald v MacDonald* 1995 SLT 72.

c) backdate awards to the date of bringing the action or, on special cause shown, even earlier;
d) award less than the amount claimed even if the claim is undisputed.[1]

The prohibition of lump sum payments and the continued insistence that the award take the form of a periodical payment reflects the fact that aliment is an obligation which arises from, and continues throughout, marriage. As we shall see,[2] on divorce it is envisaged that financial provision will generally take the form of capital ie lump sum payments, to encourage a financial clean break between the parties.

A decree of aliment can, on an application by either party, be varied or recalled if there has been a material change of circumstances since the date of decree.[3] Thus, for example, if the value of the original award has been undermined by inflation, the decree may be varied upwards; conversely, if the defender has been made redundant since the date of the original award the decree can be varied downwards, or indeed, recalled. The mere fact that at the time of the original award the court proceeded upon a particular hypothesis which turned out to be incorrect is not a material change of circumstances.[4] In an action for variation, the court has the same powers, for example, to backdate awards as in an original application for aliment.[5] The Act is retrospective and its powers in relation to variation apply to awards made before its date of commencement.[6]

Procedural matters

A spouse may bring a claim for aliment *simpliciter* in the Court of Session or the sheriff court.[7] In practice a claim for aliment is often brought along with other proceedings, for example, separation. In

1 This overrules *Terry v Murray* 1947 SC 10, where it was held that the court was bound to grant decree for the amount claimed in an undefended action for aliment.
2 *Infra* Ch 7.
3 Section 5(1); *Walker v Walker* 1991 SLT 649. There is, however, no need for a change of circumstances before a decree of interim aliment can be varied: *Bisset v Bisset* 1993 SCLR 284.
4 *Walker v Walker* 1995 SLT 375.
5 Section 5(2) impliedly incorporating s 3: see *Hannah v Hannah* 1988 SLT 82. However, there is authority that in a variation, the court cannot backdate beyond the date of the decree sought to be varied: *Walker v Walker* 1991 SLT 649, *sed quaere*.
6 1 September 1986; see *Matheson v Matheson* 1988 SLT 238; *Nixon v Nixon* 1987 SLT 602.
7 Section 2(1).

addition, in an action for aliment or in an action for divorce, separation, declarator of marriage or declarator of nullity of marriage, the
court can order interim aliment until the final disposal of the action.[1]
When decree of divorce has been granted, but a claim for financial
provision is still pending, an award of interim aliment remains competent.[2] Because an action for interim aliment is not technically an
action of aliment within the meaning of the 1985 Act,[3] it has been
held that the court does not have the power to vary or recall a decree
of aliment with *retrospective* effect.[4] The factors in s 4 have also been
held to be relevant to a claim for interim aliment.[5]

As interim aliment is awarded to a party to the proceedings, it does
not matter that the proceedings finally establish that, for example,
because the marriage was void, the parties did not owe an obligation
to aliment each other because they were never spouses. A pursuer in
an action of declarator of nullity can apply for interim aliment
although denying the existence of the marriage.[6]

The relationship between aliment and income support

It will be clear that the guidelines in s 4 are sufficiently wide to allow
a court considerable discretion in assessing the amount of aliment.
However, apart from the prima facie exclusion of matrimonial conduct and the fact that the defender's financial or other support to a
third party may be taken into account, there are few guidelines on
how the court should exercise its discretion. Wealthy couples should
be able to negotiate an appropriate figure with the advice of their
lawyers. But where the couple is in the lower income bracket, there
may not be enough money to aliment the family adequately when the
marriage breaks down, particularly if the wage earner has become
involved with another family. Consider the following example.

---

1 Section 6(1).
2 *Neill v Neill* 1987 SLT (Sh Ct) 143.
3 Section 2(2) and (3) as amended by para 36 of Sch 4 to the Children (Scotland) Act
   1995.
4 *McColl v McColl* 1993 SLT 617. This can cause difficulties if the award of aliment
   is backdated to cover the period when the defender was obliged to pay an award of
   interim aliment. Because the decree of interim aliment cannot be recalled with retrospective effect, the defender would have to pay both the backdated award of aliment *plus* any arrears of interim aliment.
5 *McGeachie v McGeachie* 1989 SCLR 99: for the s 4 factors, see *supra* p 49 ff. An
   appeal from an award of interim aliment is possible with leave of the sheriff:
   MacInnes v MacInnes 1990 GWD 13–690; *Richardson v Richardson* 1991 SLT (Sh
   Ct) 7.
6 Section 17(2).

EXAMPLE

H, who is a small wage earner, deserts W who is unemployed in order to live with his mistress, M. H supports M financially and does not provide aliment for W. What can W do?

(i) At common law, W could pledge her husband's credit for necessaries – if she could obtain food and clothing on credit. This right was distinct from her *praepositura* and has not been abolished.[1] The third party who supplied W with the necessary support can recover from H, provided H was liable to aliment W. H's liability to the third party is based on principles of recompense.[2]

(ii) W could bring an action for aliment against H. However, if the court exercised its discretion and took into account the fact that he was supporting M, W would receive little, if any, aliment.[3] If this factor were ignored, it could cause hardship to M, who is unable to obtain income support because of the cohabitation rule.[4]

(iii) In practice W would apply for income support. There is no longer an obligation on a spouse to seek a decree of aliment before applying for income support. As we have seen, in financial terms, W is no worse off: indeed, she could be better off, than if an award of aliment had been obtained from H.[5] At the very least, she receives regular income and there is no problem of enforcement of a decree of aliment against H.[6]

By s 78(6) of the Social Security Administration Act 1992 a man is liable to maintain his wife and children up to the age of 16[7] and a woman is liable to maintain her husband and children up to that age (ie the spouses are liable relatives). Where income support is paid to or on behalf of a person who is not being alimented by a liable

---

1 On the *praepositura*, see *supra* p 45. It is thought that the right has not been affected by the repeal of s 3(2) of the Married Women's Property (Scotland) Act 1920.
2 See *Clive* pp 224–225.
3 Section 4(3)(a) discussed *supra* p 49. However, if W's entitlement to income support was ignored as a resource, W would obtain *some* aliment: but this would simply reduce her income support and leave her no better off financially.
4 *Supra* p 48.
5 *Supra* p 50.
6 On enforcement of decrees, see *Clive* p 175 ff.
7 Children between the ages of 16 and 18 are included if either parent is receiving income support: s 78(6)(d) of the 1992 Act.

relative, the Secretary of State can take proceedings against the liable relative to make a contribution towards the amount of support paid.[1] The sheriff, having regard to all the circumstances, including the defender's resources, can order the defender to pay such sum, weekly or otherwise, as may be appropriate.[2] Thus in the above example, the Secretary of State could take proceedings against H (the liable relative) who has failed to aliment W (the dependant) for a contribution towards the amount of income support W has received.[3] If W has a decree of aliment against H, the Secretary of State can enforce the decree.[4]

But, in practice, the Secretary of State will only take proceedings against a liable relative, if the relative's resources are in excess of the following: the income support, including any premiums and housing costs, which the relative could claim, plus a quarter of the relative's net earnings.[5] If H is on a low wage, it is unlikely that he would have income in excess of the formula and the Secretary of State would therefore not approach him for a contribution. Approximately, only eleven per cent of the money paid out in income support is recovered from liable relatives.

It should be noticed that for the purposes of the Social Security Administration Act 1992, neither a man nor a woman is a liable relative in respect of a former spouse. However, parents are liable relatives in respect of their children.[6]

SUCCESSION

Introduction

As submitted at the outset, in modern family law it is important for a person to have been married. This is particularly true in relation to

1 Section 106 of the 1992 Act.
2 The sheriff's discretion is very wide: the sheriff can, for example, order the liable relative to pay only a small fraction of the income support paid out: *Secretary of State for Social Services v McMillan* 1987 SLT 52.
3 The court can order payments to be made to W rather than the Secretary of State: in other words, the Secretary of State, in effect, raises an action of aliment on behalf of W: s 106(4)(b) and (c) of the 1992 Act.
4 Section 108 of the 1992 Act.
5 The formula was first published in the *Report of the Committee on One-Parent Families* (the Finer Report) (Cmnd 5629) (1974) para 4.188. It has subsequently been modified: it is not clear whether the formula will continue to be applied.
6 The aliment of children is discussed *infra* Ch 9. If A and B have a child C, A is a liable relative in respect of B if B is looking after C: it does not matter if A and B are divorced or were never married: s 107 of the 1992 Act.

succession where Scots law gives the surviving spouse certain rights to succeed to a proportion of the deceased spouse's estate which cannot be defeated by testamentary deed. In this section it is proposed to give an outline of these rights:[1] as they are closely integrated to similar rights enjoyed by the deceased's children it is convenient to discuss these at this stage.

Legal rights

Since the Succession (Scotland) Act 1964,[2] a surviving husband is entitled to his *jus relicti* out of his deceased wife's estate; a surviving wife is entitled to her *jus relictae* out of her deceased husband's estate; and children[3] are entitled to *legitim* out of their deceased parent's estate. Since they are identical it is proposed to call the *jus relicti* and the *jus relictae* by the composite term 'relict's right'.[4]

The relict's right is to a third of the deceased's free moveable estate, if the deceased is survived by children or to a half of the deceased's free moveable estate, if there are no surviving children. *Legitim* is the right to a third of the deceased parent's free moveable estate if survived by a spouse or to a half of the deceased's free moveable estate if there is no surviving spouse. Moveable estate consists of money, shares, pictures, cars etc, but excludes heritable property (heritage), of which the most important property is likely to be the matrimonial or family home. Thus, for example, if H dies survived by W and children, W is entitled to a third of his free moveable estate as her *jus relictae*, the children are entitled to a third of his free moveable estate as *legitim* and the deceased can only effectively test on the remaining third. But if the estate includes heritable property, for example, the matrimonial home, H is free to dispose of the property as he wishes by testamentary deed, as legal rights are not exigible out of heritage. So H could, by will, leave his house to his mistress, M.

Legal rights may be discharged in the lifetime of the spouses or parents. Similarly, legal rights may be renounced after a spouse's or parent's death, expressly, or impliedly by acceptance of testamentary provisions which were intended by the deceased to be in satisfaction

---

1 For a full treatment, see *Clive* Ch 30.
2 References in this section are to the 1964 Act unless otherwise stated.
3 Scots law makes no distinction between legitimate and illegitimate children in this context: para 7(2) of Sch 1 to the Law Reform (Parent and Child) (Scotland) Act 1986, discussed *infra* Ch 8.
4 This is the term used by *Clive*.

of legal rights.[1] If, however, the surviving spouse or children elect to take legal rights, they will forfeit any testamentary provisions in testamentary deeds executed after 1964, unless forfeiture is expressly excluded.[2]

Prior rights

Where a spouse dies intestate,[3] ie without a will, the surviving *spouse* enjoys substantial prior rights out of the intestate estate.

By s 8, the surviving spouse is entitled to the dwelling house in which he or she was ordinarily resident at the date of the death of the intestate.[4] If the house is worth more than £110,000, the surviving spouse is entitled to a sum of £110,000 instead.[5] In addition, the surviving spouse is entitled to the furniture and plenishings of a dwelling house[6] in which he or she was ordinarily resident at the date of the death of the intestate. However, if the value of the furniture or plenishings exceeds £20,000, the surviving spouse is entitled to such parts of them as he or she may choose, to a value not exceeding £20,000.

By s 9, the surviving spouse is entitled to financial provision out of the intestate's estate. If the intestate is survived by issue,[7] however remote, the surviving spouse is entitled to £30,000: in other cases, the surviving spouse is entitled to £50,000.[8] Where the net intestate estate is less than £30,000 or £50,000, as the case may be, the surviving spouse is entitled to the whole of the intestate estate. Where it is more, the surviving spouse's financial provision is borne by the heritable and moveable parts of the estate in proportion to the respective amounts of those parts.[9]

---

1 By s 13 (as amended by the Law Reform (Miscellaneous Provisions) (Scotland) Act 1968 Sch 1), acceptance of a provision in a post-1964 testamentary disposition is, in the absence of express provision to the contary, deemed to be an implied renunciation of legal rights in so far as they would conflict with the settlement.
2 Section 13: for deeds executed pre-1964, see *Ballantyne's Trs v Ballantyne* 1993 SLT 1237.
3 For these purposes intestacy includes partial intestacy.
4 If more than one house qualifies, the surviving spouse has 6 months to elect which house is to be subject to prior rights.
5 Section 8(1) as amended. The current amounts were set by the Prior Rights of Surviving Spouses (Scotland) Order 1993 (SI 1993/2690).
6 It does not matter if the dwelling house did not form part of the deceased's intestate estate.
7 There is now no distinction between legitimate and illegitimate issue: Sch 2 to the Law Reform (Parent and Child) (Scotland) Act 1986 amending s 36(1) of the 1964 Act.
8 The current sums were set by SI 1993/2690.
9 Section 9(3).

After satisfaction of these prior rights, the spouse is entitled to claim legal rights from the remaining free moveable estate.[1] Only then is the remaining intestate estate distributed to the deceased's heirs.[2]

It will be obvious that a surviving spouse's prior rights will exhaust the value of most estates. Consequently, the surviving spouse may well be better off if the deceased dies intestate rather than leave a testamentary deed bequeathing all the estate to the surviving spouse. For in this latter case, any surviving children will be entitled to claim *legitim*: but on an intestacy, children can only succeed to the intestate estate after satisfaction of the surviving spouse's prior rights.

Conclusion

As a result of the system of prior rights, a surviving spouse is generously treated on an intestacy. Where the deceased has left a will, the system of legal rights affords some degree of protection for the deceased's surviving spouse and family. However, there is nothing to stop the deceased from defeating claims to legal rights by converting all the property into heritage and disposing of it by testamentary deed to whomsoever he or she chooses.[3] Moreover, the same result can be achieved if the deceased has transferred his or her moveable property to a third party during his or her lifetime. The inter vivos transfer must be genuine: a simulate or sham transaction will not suffice.[4]

It should be noted that marriage does not have the effect of revoking prior testamentary writings. It is a question of construction whether a legacy to the deceased's 'wife' or 'husband' means the deceased's spouse at the time the will was executed or the person who was the deceased's spouse at the date of death.[5]

In the present writer's view, there is force in the argument that at present the deceased's family may be over protected. While protection for a spouse is perhaps justified, it is difficult to see why *adult* children should be entitled to *legitim*, when they may have had no

---

1 Discussed *supra* p 57.
2 These will in the first place be the deceased's children and their issue. No distinction is now made between legitimate and illegitimate issue: Sch 2 to the Law Reform (Parent and Child) (Scotland) Act 1986 amending s 36(1) of the 1964 Act. For a full list of heirs see s 2: on representation see s 5.
3 In these circumstances, the surviving spouse has an equitable claim for continuing aliment from the deceased spouse's estate: see *Clive* p 658 ff.
4 See *Clive* p 682 ff.
5 See *Clive* p 686 ff.

interest in their parent's welfare before his or her death. Nevertheless, the Scottish Law Commission has recommended further strengthening of the protection of the deceased's family by *inter alia* allowing legal rights to be exigible out of both moveable and heritable property.[1]

1 *Report on Succession* SLC No 124, paras 3.15–3.16. For the proportions of the legal shares, see paras 3.18–3.29.

4 The legal consequences of marriage II: moveable property

INTRODUCTION

Until the Married Women's Property (Scotland) Act 1881[1], as a general rule all moveable property – money, shares, furniture etc – owned by a wife or subsequently acquired by her during marriage, for example, by legacy, passed to her husband as a result of his *jus mariti*. The husband could do anything he wished with the property. There were limited exceptions to this rule such as alimentary provisions in favour of the wife under a marriage contract and the wife's *paraphernalia*, ie her dresses and jewellery, including their receptacles. The 1881 Act abolished the *jus mariti*.[2] Where a wife owned heritable property, for example, land or a house, it remained hers, but the property was administered by her husband as a result of his *jus administrationis*.[3] The *jus administrationis* was abolished by the Married Women's Property (Scotland) Act 1920.[4]

As a result of the Acts of 1881 and 1920, Scots law accepted that marriage should have no effect on the property rights of spouses during marriage and that for this purpose they should be treated as strangers. In relation to the property of spouses, Scots law is a separate property system. This is enshrined in s 24 of the Family Law (Scotland) Act 1985 which provides that:

'. . . marriage shall not of itself affect –
(a) the respective rights of the parties to the marriage in relation to their property'.

Scots law therefore proceeds on the basis that prima facie the ordinary rules of property apply to spouses, as though they were unmarried. The separate property system thus achieves legal equality

---

1 For the history of the law, see *Clive* p 231 ff.
2 Section 1(1).
3 Until 1881, income arising from her lands, for example, rents, belonged to the husband by virtue of his *jus mariti* as the rents were, of course, moveable property.
4 Section 1.

between the spouses in respect of their property. But, in practice, this can lead to injustice, as it is still expected in our society that women should bear the major burden of child rearing and consequently, wives often do not have the same opportunity as their husbands to acquire property during the marriage.[1] Moreover, the separate property system ignores the fact that when spouses acquire property, they do not regard themselves as strangers. Often they will pool their resources to purchase a matrimonial home and other domestic property. Further, property, for example, a car, is often bought not for the use and enjoyment of the purchasing spouse but for the use and enjoyment of the family. In relation to such property, the application of the ordinary rules of the law of property is difficult and likely to lead to unrealistic results.

It has now been recognised in Scotland that the property rules relating to spouses – and to a lesser extent cohabitees – cannot ignore the 'family' element in their property transactions. Consequently, special property rules have been introduced which are specifically applicable to spouses and do not treat them as strangers.

Thus while the basic property regime for spouses in Scots law is still that of a separate property system, there are now some special property rules which recognise that the parties are married and these are designed to take into account the 'family' element in the spouses' property dealings. These rules have, to some extent, alleviated the injustices which in practice arise from the strict application of the separate property system.

The law as it relates to moveable property is examined in this chapter: the law in relation to the matrimonial home is considered in Chapter 5.

WEDDING PRESENTS

The ownership of a wedding present depends on the intention of the donor. Did the donor intend the gift to be owned in common by the spouses or only by one of the spouses? There is no difficulty if there is direct evidence of the donor's intention. But problems can arise if such evidence is not available.

In *McDonald v McDonald*[2] the sheriff took the view that 'the practical rule which is normally applied is to regard as the owner of the present the spouse from whose friends or relatives the gift was

---

1 A wife can now obtain compensation for economic disadvantages suffered by her as a result of marriage in the form of financial provision on divorce: see *infra* Ch 7.
2 1953 SLT (Sh Ct) 36.

received'.[1] Moreover, because a gift was intended to be *used* by the spouses, for example, an electric toaster or bathroom scales, it does not follow that the donor intended that the present should be *owned* in common by them.[2] Sometimes, however, the donor's intention can be inferred from the nature of the gift: thus, for example, a necklace can be presumed to be a gift to the wife and a set of guns can be presumed to be a gift to the husband. Although Clive has suggested[3] that in the absence of evidence of the donor's intention, common ownership of a wedding present should be presumed, it is doubtful whether this is in fact the current law of Scotland.

GIFTS BETWEEN SPOUSES

The ordinary law of donation applies in relation to the transfer of corporeal moveable property between spouses. Accordingly, the presumption *against* donation is prima facie applicable.[4] But as gifts between spouses are not uncommon, the presumption is not difficult to rebut.[5] Thus, for example, if H transfers a dress to W, while the onus is on W to show that H intended to make a gift of the dress to her, the presumption can easily be rebutted if W brings evidence that the transfer took place on her birthday or on their wedding anniversary or at Christmas. In addition to rebutting the presumption against donation, the transferee must establish that the property has been delivered to him or her, before the ownership of the property passes to the donee. This can give rise to difficulties where the property is already in the matrimonial home before the gift is made.[6]

The common law rule that gifts between spouses were revocable during the donor's lifetime has been abolished.[7]

1 1953 SLT (Sh Ct) 36.
2 *Traill v Traill* 1925 SLT (Sh Ct) 54.
3 *Clive* p 241.
4 *Jamieson v M'Leod* (1880) 7 R 1131; *Smith v Smith's Trustees* (1884) 12 R 186; *Beveridge v Beveridge* 1925 SLT 234 at 236.
5 There is no presumption against donation in transfers of property between parent and child: Stair I 8.2.
6 See generally *Clive* p 241 ff.
7 Section 5 of the Married Women's Property (Scotland) Act 1920. The gift may, however, be struck down as a gratuitous alienation under s 34 of the Bankruptcy (Scotland) Act 1985, if the donor becomes bankrupt.

CORPOREAL MOVEABLES BOUGHT BY THE SPOUSES

It is a cardinal principle of a system of separate property that the spouse who buys or otherwise acquires corporeal moveable property, for example, a motor car, prima facie owns it: so if H buys a motor car, he is the owner. Where both spouses contribute to the purchase price, they own the property in common in proportion to their contributions to the price. But in the absence of evidence of joint contribution to the price, the common law did not assume common ownership merely because the property was used by both spouses and the family.[1]

Apart from the problems of proving which of the spouses paid for the property, perhaps many years after the date of its purchase, the separate property system could give rise to injustices in the following situations:

a) Where W gives up her job for several years to look after the children of the family she will lose the opportunity to earn and acquire property. The common law gave her no proprietary interest in the property acquired by H during that period.

b) Where both spouses are working and they agree that, for example, H's earnings should be used to run the household while W used her earnings to purchase antiques or lay down vintage claret, the common law gave H no proprietary interest in the property purchased by W.

The injustices of the application of the system of separate property in practice are obvious, and Parliament has intervened to alleviate the position to some extent.

Household goods

Section 25(1) of the Family Law (Scotland) Act 1985[2] provides that 'if any question arises (whether during or after a marriage) as to the respective rights of ownership of the parties to a marriage in any household goods obtained in prospect of or during the marriage other than by gift or succession from a third party, it shall be presumed, unless the contrary is proved, that each has a right to an equal share in the goods in question'. In other words, there is a presumption that the household goods are *owned* in common by the spouses.[3]

Household goods are defined[4] as 'any goods (including decorative or ornamental goods) kept or used at any time during the marriage in

1 *Harper v Adair* 1945 JC 21 at 28 per Lord Justice General (Normand); *Preston v Preston* 1950 SC 253 at 261 per Lord Keith.
2 References in this section are to the 1985 Act unless otherwise stated.
3 *Kinloch v Barclay's Bank* 1995 GWD 24–1316.
4 Section 25(3).

any matrimonial home[1] for the joint domestic purposes of the parties
to the marriage'. However, (a) money or securities, (b) any motor car,
caravan or other road vehicle[2] and (c) any domestic animal, are
expressly excluded.[3]

Consider the following examples:

1. If H buys antique paintings *before* the marriage, the presumption
    of common ownership does not apply as the property was
    acquired before marriage. But if before marriage, H buys a
    Chinese carpet with the intention that it is to be used in the matri-
    monial home after marriage, the presumption of equal shares will
    apply as the goods were bought in prospect of marriage.
2. If W inherits a grandfather clock during the marriage the pre-
    sumption of common ownership will not apply as property
    acquired by gift or succession from a third party is excluded.
3. If H wins £10,000 on the lottery during the marriage and invests
    £5,000 in a building society and uses the remainder to buy
    antiques which are kept in the matrimonial home, the presumption
    of equal shares does not apply to the money deposited with the
    building society, as money and securities are expressly excluded,
    but it will apply to the antiques as these are household goods.
4. If W buys a motor car during the marriage which is used by H for
    work and leisure purposes, the presumption of common owner-
    ship does not apply, as road vehicles are expressly excluded.

It must be stressed that s 25 only gives rise to a *presumption* of
equal shares in household goods: it is therefore open to the purchasing spouse if he or she alleges that the goods were not intended to be
owned in common, to bring evidence to rebut the presumption and
establish that they were to be owned outright by the purchasing
spouse. However, s 25(2) provides that the presumption of equal
shares will not be rebutted merely by the fact that 'while the parties
were married *and living together* the goods in question were purchased from a third party by either party alone or by both in unequal
shares'. Consider the following examples:

1. During the marriage and while the spouses were living together, H
    buys a silver tea pot from a dealer. Prima facie the tea pot is house-
    hold goods and the presumption of equal shares applies. The mere
    fact that H bought the tea pot from a third party using his own
    money, is not in itself sufficient to rebut the presumption.
    Consequently the tea pot is owned in common by H and W.

1 This has the same meaning as 'matrimonial home' in s 22 of the Matrimonial
  Homes (Family Protection) (Scotland) Act 1981: see *infra* Ch 5.
2 For example, a bicycle!
3 Section 25(3)(a), (b) and (c).

2. During the marriage and while the spouses were living together, H buys a silver tea pot from a dealer. Prima facie the tea pot is household goods and the presumption of equal shares applies. But if H could show that *before* the marriage he had collected silver, not with the prospect of marriage, this fact combined with the fact that he bought the tea pot from a third party using his own money, could be sufficient to rebut the presumption and establish that the tea pot was intended for his collection, to be owned along with the rest of the silver, outright by H.[1]

3. During the marriage but when the spouses were not living together, H buys a silver tea pot from a dealer. Prima facie the tea pot is household goods and the presumption of equal shares applies. But as the tea pot was bought when the couple were not living together, s 25(2) does not apply and the fact that H bought the tea pot from a third party using his own money may in itself be sufficient to rebut the presumption of common ownership and consequently establish that the tea pot is owned outright by H.

There may be difficulties in the interrelationship between s 25 and the law of gifts between spouses.[2] If H purchases a painting during the marriage, prima facie s 25 applies as the painting comes under household goods and therefore there is a presumption of common ownership. If H transfers the painting to W on her birthday, W may be able to rebut the presumption *against* donation and establish that H intended the painting to be an outright gift to her. It is submitted that, if W can do so, she would thereby rebut the presumption of equal shares in household goods in s 25.

The examples given are perhaps esoteric and the theoretical difficulties in s 25 must not be thought to undermine its evident utility. In the vast majority of cases the presumption will not be capable of being rebutted and consequently spouses will be taken to have equal shares in the normal contents of the matrimonial home, *viz* consumer durables, for example, furniture, carpets, televisions, fridges, cookers and kitchen utensils. Moreover, the definition of household goods[3] demands that not only must the goods be kept or used in the matrimonial home but also that they must be kept or used 'for joint domestic purposes'. Thus corporeal moveables used exclusively for a spouse's business, for example, a word processor, or hobby, for example, golf clubs, will be excluded. But difficulties arise where property is bought both as a collector's item and for use by the spouses, as in the exam-

---

1 If the tea pot was kept in a display cabinet and never used, arguably it is not household goods as it has not been kept or used for *joint domestic purposes.*

2 *Supra* p 63.

3 Section 25(3).

ple of the silver tea pot: such property could be defined as household goods so giving rise to the problems outlined above.[1]

More difficult to justify, perhaps, is the exclusion of motor cars, caravans or other vehicles, as these are often bought as a result of a couple pooling their resources: the application of the separate property system may give a result which is entirely fortuitous. The exclusion of family pets is, on the other hand, quite understandable.

It should also be noted that as common owners, either spouse can apply for an action of division and sale of the property.[2]

Furniture and plenishings in the matrimonial home

The Matrimonial Homes (Family Protection) (Scotland) Act 1981 contains provisions which enable a spouse – and in certain circumstances a cohabitee – to continue living in a matrimonial home although the marriage or relationship is breaking down.[3] It was appreciated by Parliament that these rights would be of limited value if the spouse who owned the furniture and plenishings of the home could sell them, leaving the house empty. Accordingly, a spouse or cohabitee who has a right to occupy the matrimonial home[4] can apply under s 3(2) of the Act for an order granting the applicant the possession or use in the matrimonial home of any of its furniture and plenishings owned by the other.[5] 'Furniture and plenishings' means any article situated in the matrimonial home which is owned or hired by either spouse[6] and 'is reasonably necessary to enable the home to be used as a family residence'.[7] In the present writer's view a s 3(2) order is not available when the spouses own the property in common. But here a spouse can apply for an interdict to stop the other spouse preventing the applicant from using or possessing the property.[8]

---

1 *Supra* p 66.
2 Actions for division and sale are discussed in the context of heritage; see *infra* p 89.
3 The 1981 Act is discussed *infra* Ch 5. References in this section are to the 1981 Act unless otherwise stated.
4 See *infra* Ch 5. For definition of matrimonial home, see *ibid*, s 22.
5 Section 3(2).
6 Or is being acquired by either spouse under a hire-purchase agreement or conditional sale agreement.
7 Section 22: vehicles, caravans or houseboats are expressly excluded. For the definition of matrimonial home, see *infra* Ch 5.
8 Section 3(2) was, of course, enacted before s 25 of the Family Law (Scotland) Act 1985, discussed *supra* p 64 ff. Since the presumption of common ownership will usually apply, the scope of s 3(2) is greatly reduced. Ironically, it can be argued that the remedy of a non-owning spouse under s 3(2) is more sophisticated than that of a common owner at common law. However, it is possible that s 3(2) may be capable of being interpreted as including household goods owned in common by the defender and the applicant: *sed quaere*.

The court[1] must first make an order declaring that the applicant has occupancy rights in respect of the matrimonial home.[2]

Under s 3(2), the court can then make such an order as appears just and reasonable having regard to all the circumstances of the case including inter alia:

a) the conduct of the spouses;
b) the needs and financial resources of the spouses;
c) the needs of any children of the family;
d) the extent, if any, to which the matrimonial home, or any item of furniture and plenishings is used in connection with a trade, business or profession of either spouse.[3]

An interim order can be made, provided the non-applicant has been afforded an opportunity of being heard or represented before the court.[4] But the court cannot make an order if the effect of the order would be to exclude the non-applicant spouse from the matrimonial home: for example, an order for the sole and exclusive possession or use of the fitted carpets throughout the home.

Where the furniture or plenishings are being paid up under a hire purchase or a conditional sale agreement, an order does not prejudice the rights of the hirer or creditor to recover the property for non-performance of any obligations under the agreements.[5] But the spouse in whose favour the order is made is entitled to make any payments under the agreements in lieu of the debtor.[6] Similarly, he or she can carry out any essential repairs to the furniture and plenishings.[7] On the application of either spouse, the court can apportion any such expenditure between the spouses.[8]

The effect of a s 3(2) order is therefore to override the property rights of a spouse in relation to the furniture and plenishings of the matrimonial home, to the extent that the applicant is entitled to the use and possession of the relevant property for the duration of the order. It must be stressed that s 3(2) only regulates the possession and use of the property. Its ownership will, of course, be determined by reference to s 25 of the Family Law (Scotland) Act 1985[9] and the common law rules. Moreover, the definition of furni-

1 The Court of Session or the sheriff court: s 22.
2 Section 3(1): *Welsh v Welsh* 1987 SLT (Sh Ct) 30.
3 Section 3(3).
4 Section 3(4); *Welsh v Welsh* 1987 SLT (Sh Ct) 30.
5 Section 3(2).
6 Sections 2(5)(a) and 3(2).
7 Ibid.
8 Section 2(5)(b).
9 Discussed *supra* p 64.

ture and plenishings in the 1981 Act is narrower than that of household goods for the purposes of s 25, since it is only furniture and plenishings which are *reasonably necessary* to enable the home to be used as a family residence which can be the subject of a s 3(2) order.[1] The following examples illustrate the interrelationship between the two provisions.

1. H buys a bed during the marriage. The presumption of equal shares applies and is not rebutted. H and W therefore own the bed in common. Although a bed is an article reasonably necessary to enable the home to be used as a family residence, W cannot apply for a s 3(2) order for the use and possession of the bed because s 3(2) only applies where the furniture and plenishings are owned solely by one of the spouses. However, at common law, W as common owner would be entitled to an interdict preventing H from disposing of the bed.[2]

2. During the marriage, H inherits a dining room suite from his grandmother. The presumption of equal shares does not apply[3] and the suite is owned outright by H. But if they are the only table and chairs in the house, W can apply for a s 3(2) order for their use and possession as they are articles reasonably necessary to enable the home to be used as a family residence.

3. H inherits an oil painting during the marriage. The presumption of equal shares does not apply. H therefore owns the painting outright. But as the painting is not reasonably necessary to enable the home to be used as a family residence, W will be unable to obtain a s 3(2) order for the use and possession of the painting.

Again it should be emphasised that these theoretical difficulties should not be allowed to detract from the evident utility of s 3(2). It is further recognition that the incidents of ownership of property may have to be overridden in the interests of the family for whose benefit the property was acquired. In particular, it should be noticed that the needs of the children of the family will be an important factor in determining whether or not a s 3(2) order should be made.[4]

---

1 Section 22.
2 Since the bed is common property and H and W each own a one half *pro indiviso* share of its value, an action for division and sale is competent to enable H to realise his share. This is discussed in the context of heritage, *infra* Ch 5. Theoretically, H could attempt to sell his pro indiviso share of the bed, if anyone would like to buy half a bed!
3 Household goods inherited from third parties are expressly excluded by s 25(1) of the 1985 Act.
4 Section 3(3).

MONEY AND SECURITIES

As we have seen[1] money and securities are expressly excluded from
the presumption of equal shares in household goods.[2] The ownership
of money or securities will therefore be determined by the ordinary
property rules, ie in accordance with the separate property system.
Thus, for example, if H deposits £5,000 in a building society account
in his name, the money in the account prima facie belongs to him. It
is, however, open to W to claim, for example, that the money was
transferred by her to H to invest and consequently belongs to her. She
will have the benefit of the presumption against donation[3] and she is
not restricted in the type of evidence she can bring to substantiate her
claim.[4]

Problems have arisen in relation to joint bank accounts. When an
account is opened in the joint names of the spouses, this may, depending on the terms of the agreement with the bank, oblige the bank to
honour cheques drawn by either spouse or, in the case of a deposit
account, to pay money over to either of the spouses when called upon
to do so. The fact that the account is in joint names does not determine
the ownership of the money in it. Where one spouse has been the sole
contributor of the funds in the account, it will be presumed, in the
absence of evidence of donation, that the account was opened for
administrative convenience only and the money in the account belongs
to the contributing spouse. Where *both* spouses contributed to the fund,
it will be readily inferred that they intended the account to be used as a
common purse and that the money in the account is owned in common.[5]

Where a spouse draws on a joint account to buy property, prima
facie the property belongs to that spouse outright – even although the
account was opened for administrative purposes only.[6] However,
where the spouse purchases household goods, the presumption of
equal shares will apply by virtue of s 25 of the Family Law (Scotland)
Act 1985.[7]

Similar principles will apply to money invested in a building
society.

---

1 *Supra* p 65.
2 Section 25(3)(a) of the Family Law (Scotland) Act 1985.
3 Discussed *supra* p 63.
4 *Smith v Smith* 1933 SC 701.
5 Ie the court will infer donation to the extent necessary to give each spouse a half
   share of the money in the account.
6 Unless there is evidence that the property was bought as a joint investment.
7 Discussed *supra* p 64 ff.

SAVINGS FROM HOUSEKEEPING

One of the harshest consequences of the system of separate property was where, for example, a husband provided a wife with a house-keeping allowance and the wife, being thrifty, was able to save some of the money. Because the husband had intended the money to be used to run the home, donation could not be inferred. Consequently, the husband was the owner of the savings made by the wife.[1] The Married Woman's Property Act 1964 attempted to alleviate the position. It provided that savings made by a wife from a housekeeping allowance made to her by her husband, should be presumed to be owned jointly by the spouses in the absence of an agreement to the contrary. The 1964 Act was defective in that it was not applicable to savings made by a husband from a housekeeping allowance paid to him by his wife: in these circumstances, any savings would still be owned by the wife. This discriminatory element has been removed. Section 26 of the Family Law (Scotland) Act 1985 provides:

'If any question arises (whether during or after a marriage) as to the right of either party to a marriage to money derived from any allowance made by either party for their joint household expenses or for similar purposes, or to any property acquired out of such money, the money or property shall, in the absence of any agreement between them to the contrary, be treated as belonging to each party in equal shares'.

It will be clear that s 26 applies both to allowances made by a husband to his wife and a wife to her husband. The allowances must be for 'their joint household expenses or for similar purposes'. It is not thought that money given to a spouse for payment of mortgage instalments would be included within the definition.[2] Money or property 'derived from the allowance' has been given a wide meaning. In *Pyatt v Pyatt*[3] Lord Fraser held that the prize money won by a wife on Littlewoods Football Pools was 'derived from' the allowance when the wife had taken the stake money from her housekeeping. The winnings had resulted both from the allowance which had provided the stake money and the wife's luck. As the stake money had been essential, the prize money had been derived from the allowance and consequently the husband was entitled to half the winnings.

---

1 *Smith v Smith* 1933 SC 701; *Preston v Preston* 1950 SC 253. This did not apply to savings from aliment paid by a husband when the couple were separated.
2 *Tymoszczuk v Tymoszczuk* (1964) 108 Sol Jo 676 (interpreting the similar phrase in the 1964 Act); but cf *Re John's Assignment Trusts, Niven v Niven* [1970] 2 All ER 210, n, [1970] 1 WLR 955.
3 1966 SLT (Notes) 73.

The application of s 26 can lead to some odd results. Consider the following example. W gives H a housekeeping allowance. H uses some of the allowance to bet on a horse. H wins £1,000. He puts £500 in a building society account and buys a second hand caravan with the rest of the money. Following *Pyatt v Pyatt*[1] W is entitled to half the £500 in the building society account ie £250 and is an owner in common of the caravan.[2] W is not entitled to choose the full £500 in the account in lieu of her half share of the caravan.[3]

MARRIED WOMEN'S POLICIES OF ASSURANCE (SCOTLAND) ACT 1880

Where A takes out an insurance policy for the benefit of B, B has no rights in the policy until it is delivered to B or the rights under the policy have been intimated to B. There is an exception to this principle where a husband or wife takes out a life policy on his or her life for the benefit of the other spouse (or children): in these circumstances, the policy is deemed to be held by the insured in trust for the beneficiaries who take an immediate right without the necessity of delivery or intimation of the policy to them.[4]

1 Ibid.
2 Section 25 of the Family Law (Scotland) Act 1985 is inapplicable, as caravans are expressly excluded from the definition of household goods: s 25(3)(b), see *supra*.
3 Moreover, if H used the £1,000 together with £1,000 of his own savings in order to buy a pony, W would own a quarter of the pony! Domestic animals are also excluded from s 25: s 25(3)(c).
4 Married Women's Policies of Assurance (Scotland) Act 1880, s 2 as amended by the Married Women's Policies of Assurance (Scotland) (Amendment) Act 1980: see *Clive* p 263 ff.

5 The legal consequences of marriage III: the matrimonial home

INTRODUCTION

The most important heritable property which spouses are likely to possess is their matrimonial home. Increasingly, a married couple is likely to live in accommodation which is owned by one or both of the spouses.[1] In Scots law, title to heritable property is held on feudal tenure. When property is sold, the deeds must be recorded in the Register of Sasines or the interest registered in the Land Register of Scotland. Until recording or registration, the buyer does not have a real right in the property, ie he is not the owner with a proprietary interest which is good against the world: as against the seller, however, the buyer will have a personal right to sue for breach of contract, if the seller disposes of the property to a third party before recording or registration. Many couples will be unable to purchase a matrimonial home outright and will have to borrow the necessary sum from a bank or building society (the heritable creditor). Until the loan is repaid, the bank or building society will have a heritable security (a mortgage) over the house: this enables the heritable creditor to sell the house if the loan (and interest thereon) is not repaid. This form of heritable security is known as a standard security, which is itself recorded in the Register of Sasines or registered in the Land Register of Scotland.

Many couples, of course, cannot afford to buy their home. Instead, they will simply rent accommodation. Since 1974, a lease of residential property cannot be granted for more than 20 years.[2] Accordingly,

---

1 In their survey, *Family Property in Scotland* (HMSO 1981), Manners and Rauta found that 37% of all matrimonial homes in Scotland were owner-occupied: ibid Table 2.1. In 57% of these, title was taken in the joint names of the spouses: ibid Table 2.4. Among homes purchased after 1977, the proportion where the title was taken in joint names rose to 78%. It is thought that the proportion of matrimonial homes where title is taken in joint names will continue to rise. See Scottish Law Commission, *Report on Matrimonial Property* (SLC No 86).
2 Land Tenure Reform (Scotland) Act 1974, s 8.

most leases are not for long periods but are terminable by notice, stipulated in the lease. However, tenants enjoy a considerable measure of security of tenure, in both the public and private housing sector, as a result of legislation.[1] The person who has security of tenure is the tenant. Joint tenancies are possible, but it is more usual for the tenancy to be in the name of one of the spouses, usually the husband.

It will be obvious that where, for example, property is owned by a husband or a tenancy has been taken in his name, his wife may experience difficulties in relation to her continued occupation of the matrimonial home if their marriage begins to break down. As a result of the Matrimonial Homes (Family Protection) (Scotland) Act 1981[2] (the 1981 Act), the rights of a spouse to occupy the matrimonial home have been greatly improved: these rights will be discussed, at some length, in this chapter. However, before doing so, consideration must be given to the operation of the system of separate property on the question of the ownership of the matrimonial home.

THE OWNERSHIP OF THE MATRIMONIAL HOME

Title in the name of one of the spouses

When a person purchases heritable property, title to which is taken in that person's name, it is a cardinal principle of the Scots law of property that that person is the owner of the property. Thus, for example, if H buys a house, title to which is taken in H's name, he is the owner of the house. This is an inevitable consequence of a system of separate property. The fact that the house is to be used as the matrimonial home is irrelevant to the question of its ownership.

When a house is purchased solely from the funds of one of the spouses, then the application of the separate property principle is justified. But, in practice, it is more likely that a house will be purchased through the means of a mortgage. A couple will often agree to pool their resources in order to acquire their matrimonial home. For example, a wife may make a direct financial contribution to the downpayment or the mortgage instalments. Alternatively, the spouses may agree that while the husband's earnings are used to pay the instalments, the wife's earnings will be used for household expenses: in

---

1 See in particular the Rent (Scotland) Act 1984, the Housing (Scotland) Act 1987, and the Housing (Scotland) Act 1988. Discussion of these statutes is outwith the scope of the present book.
2 Throughout this chapter, references are to the 1981 Act unless otherwise stated.

these circumstances, the wife will have made an indirect contribution to the acquisition of the matrimonial home. Yet, if the title has been taken in the husband's name, he will be the sole owner of the house, even although it could not have been purchased without the wife's direct or indirect financial assistance. The injustice of the application of the separate property principle in these circumstances is readily apparent.

In England, a wife who has made a direct or indirect financial contribution towards the acquisition of the matrimonial home may obtain an interest in the property because a court can in these circumstances infer that the couple intended that the husband was holding the property on a constructive trust for the benefit of the wife. The extent of the wife's interest in the house is proportional to the size of her contribution.[1] The question arises whether such a solution is possible in Scots law. At one time it was thought that the scope of a constructive trust was limited because, as a result of the Blank Bonds and Trusts Act 1696, proof of the existence of the trust was restricted to the writ or oath of the alleged trustee.[2] For example, if W transferred funds to H which H used to purchase a house, title to which was taken in H's name, W could not argue that H held the property on trust for W unless she could prove by H's writ or oath that he held the house on trust for her. However, the 1696 Act has been repealed.[3] Consequently, in the example, W may be able to argue that since there is a fiduciary relationship between her and H, H was holding the property on a constructive trust for her benefit.[4] This would enable her to obtain an accounting from H if he had sold the house to a bona fide third party.[5] It remains to be seen whether the Scottish courts will be prepared to develop the law upon such lines.

Where, for example, H obtained the funds from W by telling her that he would put the title in joint names, W could sue H in delict if he did not do so.[6] If W transferred the money in the erroneous belief that title would be taken in joint names, then even in the absence of

---

1 On these developments see Pearce and Stevens *The Law of Trusts and Equitable Obligations* (1995) p 636 ff.
2 See, for example, *Clive* p 254 ff.
3 Section 11(1) and Sch 5 of the Requirements of Writing (Scotland) Act 1995.
4 See Norrie 1995 JR 209.
5 If the third party was not in good faith, ie knew of W's interest or did not give value for the property, for example if H gave the house to the third party as a gift, W could claim the property from the third party.
6 *Marshall v Lyall and Marshall* (1859) 21 D 514.

fraud on his part, W would have a claim for recompense under principles of unjust enrichment.[1]

Where a spouse has made a direct or indirect contribution to the acquisition of a house, title to which has been taken in the name of the other spouse, it is possible to regulate the beneficial ownership of the property by agreement. While this agreement need not be in writing,[2] it is thought that such an agreement will not be readily inferred. Even if such an agreement existed it would only be binding between the spouses, and would not prevent the spouse with legal title selling the property to a third party, who is entitled to rely on the title as it appears in the Register of Sasines or the Land Register of Scotland.

As we shall see,[3] on divorce a spouse will prima facie receive half the value of, inter alia, the matrimonial home. But as Clive has observed, 'property questions between spouses do not arise only on divorce'.[4]

Title in the name of both of the spouses

As we have seen, spouses are increasingly taking title to the matrimonial home in joint names.[5] While this will alleviate many of the problems discussed in the previous section, to take title in both names raises its own difficulties.

Where title to a house is taken in joint names, the property is regarded as common property. This means that while the property is possessed undivided, each of the spouses has his or her own separate title to half of the property, ie each spouse owns a one half *pro indiviso* share of the value of the property.[6] Accordingly, each is entitled during his or her lifetime to dispose of their share, by selling or donating it to a third party, against the wishes of the co-owning spouse.[7] Similarly, each is free to dispose of his or her share by will.

Complications have arisen from the conveyancing practice of taking the title in the names of husband and wife *and the survivor*. This

---

1 Similarly an action for recompense would lie if W made improvements to the property in the belief that the house was hers: *Newton v Newton* 1925 SC 715.
2 Section 1(1) and (2) of the Requirements of Writing (Scotland) Act 1995; *Denvir v Denvir* 1969 SLT 301.
3 *Supra* Ch 7.
4 *Clive* p 319.
5 *Supra* p 73.
6 If the title is in joint names, it is presumed that prima facie each owner has a one half *pro indiviso* share. If the proportions are not to be so then the parties should have an agreement stipulating what the actual proportions are: see *supra*.
7 But see *McLeod v Cedar Holdings Ltd* 1989 SLT 620 where H took out a further heritable security over property owned by H and W. H had forged W's signature. The Inner House granted W reduction in respect of her *pro indiviso* share.

is known as a special destination. On the death of, for example, the husband, his share of the property will automatically pass to his wife, the survivor. This has the advantage that the wife will receive the deceased husband's *pro indiviso* share free from all her husband's debts.[1] But there are difficulties. While the spouses remain free to dispose of their share during their lifetime,[2] a special destination may prevent a spouse disposing of his or her share by will. Where both spouses have contributed to the purchase of the property, the courts will readily infer from a special destination to the survivor that there is a contractual relationship between the parties, and neither can revoke the arrangement by testamentary deed.[3] Where only one of the parties has purchased a house, this principle does not apply to the spouse who bought the property and he or she remains free to dispose of his or her *pro indiviso* share by will – but not, of course, the other spouse's share. Moreover, since the latter has in effect received his or her share as a gift, the court will readily imply that the donee took the gift under the condition that the donor should obtain that share if the donor is the survivor, and consequently the donee cannot dispose of his or her share by will. But, even in these circumstances, the donee is free to dispose of his or her share during his or her lifetime.[4] In spite of its advantages, because of these difficulties the use of special destinations to husband and wife and survivor should be discouraged.

THE OCCUPATION OF THE MATRIMONIAL HOME

In the last section, we discussed the question of the ownership of the matrimonial home. In this section we shall consider the different but related question of the occupation of the matrimonial home. There are two situations: a) where one spouse has the legal title to the property or is the tenant and the other spouse has no proprietary interest in the property and b) where both spouses have an interest in the property.

1 Unless, of course, the creditors have a heritable security over the husband's share: see *Barclay's Bank v McGreish* 1983 SLT 344, criticised by Morton, 1984 SLT (News) 133.
2 *Steele v Caldwell* 1979 SLT 228.
3 *Perrett's Trustees v Perrett* 1909 SC 522.
4 *Hay's Trustee v Hay's Trustees* 1951 SC 329. Where title is taken in joint names of H and W and survivor, if H wishes to transfer his one half *pro indiviso* share to W during H's lifetime, *both* H and W should convey their respective shares to W thus evacuating the survivorship clause.

Where one spouse has legal title or is the tenant

At common law, the legal owner or the tenant had the right of exclusive possession of his or her property. Thus, if, for example, H owned the matrimonial home, he could tell W to leave: if W refused, H could obtain an interdict preventing her access to the house. While H remained under a duty to aliment W, this did not oblige him to continue to allow W to occupy the matrimonial home.[1] The common law rule that a spouse who owned or was the tenant of a matrimonial home was entitled to order the non-owning spouse to leave has been radically altered as a result of the Matrimonial Homes (Family Protection) (Scotland) Act 1981.[2]

The nature of the statutory rights

By s 1(1) where one spouse, 'the entitled spouse', is the owner or tenant of the matrimonial home[3] and the other spouse, 'the non-entitled spouse' is not the owner or tenant,[4] then the non-entitled spouse has the following statutory rights –
a) if in occupation to continue to occupy the matrimonial home;
b) if not in occupation to enter into and occupy the matrimonial home.[5]
These statutory rights of a non-entitled spouse to occupy the matrimonial home expressly include the right to do so 'together with any child of the family'.[6]

The effect of this provision is to give the non-entitled spouse a positive right to occupy the matrimonial home together with any child of the family. 'Matrimonial home' has a wide meaning. It includes any house, caravan, houseboat or other structure which has been provided as or become a *family* residence.[7] Although the term 'family residence' is used, it is clear that it is not limited to a family where there are children. It is enough that a house has been acquired with the intention that it should be used as a family home; the couple do not need to have lived there.[8] Conversely, if the house was

1 *MacLure v MacLure* 1911 SC 200; *Millar v Millar* 1940 SC 56.
2 See generally, *Clive* Ch 15.
3 Or is permitted by a third party to occupy the home: s 1(1). This only arises if the third party has waived his or her right to occupy the home in favour of the entitled spouse: s 1(2); *Murphy v Murphy* 1992 SCLR 62.
4 Or is not permitted by a third party to occupy the home: s 1(1).
5 Section 1(1) as amended by s 13(2) of the Law Reform (Miscellaneous Provisions) (Scotland) Act 1985.
6 Section 1(1A), added by s 13(3) of the Law Reform (Miscellaneous Provisions) (Scotland) Act 1985.
7 Section 22: any garden or outbuildings, for example a garage, are included.
8 *O'Neil v O'Neil* 1987 SLT (Sh Ct) 26.

acquired without the intention that it should be used as a family residence, it can, nevertheless, become a matrimonial home for the purposes of the 1981 Act. For example, if H bought a flat before he met and married W, it will become a matrimonial home if W lives there after their marriage.[1] If there are two or more family residences, for example, a town house and a country cottage, the non-entitled spouse will have a statutory right to occupy both (or more) houses. On the other hand, if one spouse has acquired a house in which he or she lives separately from the other spouse this will not constitute a matrimonial home, even if children of the family also reside there.[2] A child of the family includes any child or grandchild of either spouse or any person brought up or treated by either spouse as if he or she was a child of that spouse: the age of the child is irrelevant.[3] Thus, for example, a severely handicapped adult son or daughter of either spouse will be a child of the family for the purposes of the 1981 Act.

The statutory rights arise as soon as the spouses marry and the entitled spouse acquires a matrimonial home. The rights continue throughout the marriage even if the couple separate. However, they cease when the marriage ends in death or divorce.[4] Most importantly, the rights of the non-entitled spouse are not defeated if during the marriage, the matrimonial home is sold or otherwise disposed of to a third party.[5]

Upkeep and maintenance of the matrimonial home

For the purpose of securing the statutory rights of occupation, a non-entitled spouse has the right, without the consent of the entitled spouse, inter alia to pay any rent, mortgage instalments etc instead of the entitled spouse; to carry out essential repairs; to carry out non-

---

1 But it will not be matrimonial property for the purpose of fair division under s 9(1)(a) of the Family (Scotland) Act 1985: discussed *infra* Ch 7.

2 Section 22, as amended by s 13(10) of the Law Reform (Miscellaneous Provisions) (Scotland) Act 1985. Similarly, where one spouse provides the other with a house where the other spouse lives separately it has been held that this is not a matrimonial home within the meaning of the 1985 Act: *McRobbie v McRobbie* 1983 (unreported) OH.

3 Section 22, as amended by para 30 of Sch 4 to the Children (Scotland) Act 1995.

4 Where on divorce, the court makes an incidental order entitling the applicant spouse to continue to occupy the matrimonial home after the divorce, certain of the rights in s 2 to take steps in relation to the upkeep of the home and its contents, will continue: s 14(5) of the Family Law (Scotland) Act 1985. On financial provision, see *infra* Ch 7. Nevertheless it is common and accepted practice to incorporate craves for relief under the 1981 Act in divorce proceedings: *Nelson v Nelson* 1988 SLT (Sh Ct) 26.

5 Discussed in detail *infra* p 85 ff.

essential repairs approved by a court as appropriate for the reasonable enjoyment of the occupancy rights; and to take any other steps necessary to ensure the occupancy of the matrimonial home.[1] The court has the power to apportion such expenditure between the spouses.[2]

Regulatory orders

By s 3 the court has the power to regulate the spouses' occupancy of the matrimonial home. An order may be sought by either the entitled or non-entitled spouse. The court can make orders declaring or enforcing the applicant's rights of occupation, restricting the non-applicant's occupancy rights and regulating the occupancy rights of both spouses. While the court is obliged to declare that the applicant has occupancy rights when it is satisfied that the property constitutes a matrimonial home,[3] the exercise of its other powers under s 3 is discretionary. By s 3(3) the court is obliged to make such an order as appears –

> 'just and reasonable having regard to all the circumstances of the case including –
> (a) the conduct of the spouses in relation to each other and otherwise;
> (b) the respective needs and financial resources of the spouses;
> (c) the needs of any child of the family;
> (d) the extent (if any) to which –
>   (i) the matrimonial home . . . is used in connection with a trade, business or profession of either spouse; and
> (e) whether the entitled spouse offers or has offered to make available to the non-entitled spouse any suitable alternative accommodation.'

Interim orders are possible if considered necessary or expedient[4] and compensation is available for loss or impairment of occupancy rights.[5] However, a court cannot make an order under s 3(3) if its effect would be to exclude the entitled spouse from the matrimonial home. While the power to grant declarator of a non-entitled spouse's statutory rights is important, in practice little use has been made of the court's powers to make regulatory orders under s 3(3).

1 Section 2(1). The court is the Court of Session or the sheriff court.
2 Section 2(2).
3 Section 3(3). Indeed, it would appear that declarator is essential before other relief can be given under s 3: *Welsh v Welsh* 1987 SLT (Sh Ct) 30.
4 Section 3(4): the non-applicant spouse must have been afforded an opportunity of being heard or represented in court.
5 Section 3(7).

Exclusion orders

By s 4 of the Act, the court has, however, the power to exclude either of the spouses from the matrimonial home. The order may be sought by either the entitled or non-entitled spouse.[1] By s 4(2) the court:

> '*shall* make an exclusion order if it appears to the court that the making of an order is *necessary* for the protection of the applicant or any child of the family from any *conduct* or threatened or reasonably apprehended conduct of the non-applicant spouse which is or would be injurious to the physical or mental health of the applicant or child'.[2]

In spite of the mandatory wording of s 4(2), by s 4(3)(a) the court shall not make an exclusion order if it would be unjustified or unreasonable having regard to all the circumstances of the case including the factors specified in s 3(3).[3] Interim exclusion orders are available[4] but the necessity criterion must still be satisfied.[5]

The construction of s 4 initially caused the Scottish courts much difficulty. At first there was a reluctance to grant an interim order when the court was proceeding on affidavit evidence. In *Bell v Bell*,[6] and *Smith v Smith*,[7] the Inner House of the Court of Session held that the necessity criterion in s 4(2) was a 'high and severe' test. The judges indicated that it would be unlikely to be satisfied unless the applicant was living in the matrimonial home at the time of the application. This caused considerable apprehension until the Lord Justice Clerk (Wheatley) attempted to remove such fears in *Colagiacomo v Colagiacomo*:[8]

---

1 See, for example, *Brown v Brown* 1985 SLT 376; *Millar v Millar* 1991 SCLR 649 where the applicant was the entitled spouse. A local authority has title to sue for an exclusion order under s 76 of the Children (Scotland) Act 1995, discussed *infra* p 263.

2 Italics added.

3 *Supra* p 80. Exclusion orders are also not available if the matrimonial home is part of an agricultural tenancy or has been let as an incident of employment: s 4(3)(b).

4 Section 4(6): the non-applicant spouse must be afforded an opportunity of being heard or represented before the court. It has been held that affidavit evidence is of little value to the defender and a proof should take place at an early stage, unless the circumstances are exceptional: *Armitage v Armitage* 1993 SCLR 173.

5 *Bell v Bell* 1983 SLT 224; *Smith v Smith* 1983 SLT 275; *Ward v Ward* 1983 SLT 472.

6 1983 SLT 224.

7 1983 SLT 275.

8 1983 SLT 559.

'If there is any misconception that following *Bell v Bell* an interim exclusion order will only be granted if the parties are both occupying the matrimonial home, the sooner that misconception is removed the better. The fact that only one of the parties is occupying the matrimonial home is a factor to be taken into account but is not per se to be regarded as a conclusive one'.[1]

While exclusion orders were granted in later cases where the applicant had left the matrimonial home,[2] s 4(1) was amended expressly to provide that an application for an exclusion order can be made, 'whether or not that spouse [the applicant] is in occupation at the time of the application'.[3]

In *Bell v Bell*[4] and *Smith v Smith*[5] the judges also indicated that an exclusion order should not be made if a matrimonial interdict, prohibiting the molestation of the applicant, would be sufficient protection.[6] This could lead to a 'Catch 22' situation: a wife, for example, could not be granted an interim exclusion order unless she had applied for a non-molestation interdict, but if she obtained such an interdict, an exclusion order would not be granted without evidence that the husband had been in breach of the interdict.[7] However, in *Brown v Brown*,[8] Lord Dunpark held that a matrimonial interdict was not a prerequisite for an exclusion order although in considering whether it would be unjustified or unreasonable to make the order,[9] the sheriff or Lord Ordinary must consider inter alia whether a matrimonial interdict would suffice. Moreover, when granting a s 4 order, the judge should state the reasons why an interdict did not afford sufficient protection.[10] On the facts of *Brown*, for example, an interdict was not enough as the husband was only violent when he was drunk and this conduct would not be affected by the existence of an interdict.[11]

---

1 Ibid at 562.
2 See, for example, *Ward v Ward* 1983 SLT 472; *Brown v Brown* 1985 SLT 376.
3 Section 13(5) of the Law Reform (Miscellaneous Provisions) (Scotland) Act 1985. In *Millar v Millar* 1991 SCLR 649 a spouse obtained an exclusion order although she had left the home ten months before: the delay was not the fault of the pursuer.
4 1983 SLT 224.
5 1983 SLT 275.
6 Matrimonial interdicts are granted under s 14 of the Act: discussed *infra* p 92 ff.
7 As happened in *Smith v Smith* 1983 SLT 275.
8 1985 SLT 376.
9 Section 4(3).
10 *McCafferty v McCafferty* 1986 SLT 650.
11 See also, for example, *Oliver v Oliver* 1988 GWD 26–1110.

Lastly, there are dicta in *Bell v Bell*[1] to support the contention that an interim exclusion order should only be made if the court was satisfied that the applicant would be in danger of 'serious injury or irreparable damage' if the order was not granted. However, in *McCafferty v McCafferty*[2] the Inner House of the Court of Session held that these dicta were an unnecessary gloss on the necessity test which stipulates that it is sufficient that the non-applicant's conduct or threatened or reasonably apprehended conduct 'is or would be injurious to the physical or mental health of the applicant or child'.

In spite of these developments, it has never been doubted that the criterion for an exclusion order is not easy to satisfy. The applicant must satisfy the court that the order is *necessary* for the protection of the applicant or any child of the family because the non-applicant's *conduct* (or threatened or reasonably apprehended conduct) is or would be injurious to the physical or mental health of the applicant or child.[3] The fact that on a balance of convenience test, it is desirable that the applicant and the child of the family should have exclusive occupation of the matrimonial home will not suffice.[4] While s 4(2) expressly includes harm to the applicant's or child's mental as well as physical health,[5] this must be occasioned by the non-applicant's *conduct* and not merely be the result of the breakdown of the marriage.[6]

Finally, it should always be remembered that even if the necessity test is satisfied, the court can refuse an exclusion order if in all the circumstances of the case, including the factors listed in s 3(3), it would be unjustified or unreasonable to do so.[7] But as Lord Dunpark observed in *Brown v Brown*,[8] the Inner House of the Court of Session

'had difficulty in envisaging circumstances in which an order which is necessary for the protection of the spouse may be "unjustified or unreasonable" . . . .'.

1 1983 SLT 224 per Lord Robertson at 231 and Lord Grieve at 232.
2 1986 SLT 650 per Lord Justice Clerk (Ross) at 652, Lord Robertson at 654 and Lord Dunpark at 655.
3 In *Barbour v Barbour* 1990 GWD 3–135, for example, it did not appear that an exclusion order was necessary to protect anyone. Cf *Raeburn v Raeburn* 1990 GWD 8–424.
4 *Smith v Smith* 1983 SLT 275. In *Hampsey v Hampsey* 1988 GWD 24–1035, the Sheriff Principal (Caplan) held that a sheriff has 'no power to grant an exclusion order simply because the best interests of the child required it'. See also *Millar v Millar* 1991 SCLR 649.
5 *McCafferty v McCafferty* 1986 SLT 650.
6 *Matheson v Matheson* 1986 SLT (Sh Ct) 2.
7 It is ironic that the needs of the children is one of the s 3(3) factors and is, therefore, only relevant when considering whether it would be unjustified or unreasonable to make an exclusion order!
8 1985 SLT 376 at 378. See also *Millar v Millar* 1991 SCLR 649 at 651 per Sheriff Principal Maguire.

Nevertheless the court has suspended the operation of an exclusion order for three months in order to enable the defender to find alternative accommodation: this is difficult to accept given that the exclusion order was *ex hypothesi* 'necessary'.[1] In *McCafferty v McCafferty*,[2] Lord Dunpark said that in an application for an exclusion order the court should ask four questions:

'(1) What is the nature and quality of the alleged conduct?
 (2) Is the court satisfied that the conduct is likely to be repeated if cohabitation continues?
 (3) Has the conduct been or, if repeated, would it be injurious to the physical or mental health of the applicant or to any child of the family?
 (4) If so, is the order sought necessary for the future protection of the physical or mental health of the applicant or child?'[3]

The necessity for an exclusion order will only be established if the court is satisfied that a matrimonial interdict will not afford sufficient protection, but as we have seen,[4] a matrimonial interdict is not a prerequisite for an exclusion order.

It will be clear that the success of an application for an exclusion order will greatly depend on the readiness of the judge at first instance, the Lord Ordinary or the sheriff, to find the necessity test satisfied. This is important, for an appellate court will not interfere with a judge's discretion unless 'no reasonable Lord Ordinary [or sheriff] could have reached the decision, and that he was completely wrong.'[5]

Whatever the difficulties inherent in the legislation and experienced in practice, it cannot be doubted that the protection afforded by s 4 is an important step forward in the protection of wives and children who are the victims of domestic violence. The necessity criterion can be criticised as too narrow, but it will clearly cover at least the most blatant forms of domestic violence. Moreover, there is much in the contention that where a marriage is breaking down, the

---

1 *Mather v Mather* 1987 SLT 565.
2 1986 SLT 650.
3 Ibid at 656.
4 *Supra* p 82.
5 *McCafferty v McCafferty* 1986 SLT 650 per Lord Robertson at 655. In *Brown v Brown* 1985 SLT 376, Lord Dunpark held that an appellate court could only interfere if the judge at first instance did not apply the proper test or the decision was wholly unwarranted on the facts. In *Coster v Coster* 1992 SCLR 210, an appeal from a sheriff refusing an exclusion order was allowed on the basis that the sheriff had given too much weight to whether the pursuer had alternative accomodation available rather than the averments of serious assault by the defender.

needs of any children of the family should be paramount and that the courts should have the power to exclude a spouse from the matrimonial home when, giving paramount consideration to the welfare of the children of the failing marriage, on the balance of convenience it is desirable that the spouse looking after the children should have exclusive occupation of the matrimonial home. To some extent, however, this has been remedied by the introduction of exclusion orders under s 76 of the Children (Scotland) Act 1995.[1]

Statutory rights and third parties

A non-entitled spouse's statutory right of occupation is not prejudiced as the result of the entitled spouse's dealings with the property.[2] Dealings include the sale or lease of the matrimonial home or grant of a heritable security over it.[3] Thus, for example, while the entitled spouse may still sell the matrimonial home, the purchaser will take the property subject to the non-entitled spouse's statutory rights of occupation. Moreover, by s 6(1)(b) the purchaser is not entitled to occupy the matrimonial home or any part of it while the non-entitled spouse continues to enjoy statutory rights of occupation in relation to that property. While this provision is laudable in so far as it protects the non-entitled spouse's statutory rights vis à vis third parties, it clearly causes conveyancing difficulties as the statutory rights are not

---

1 Discussed *infra* p 263.
2 Section 6(1)(a). This protection does not apply where the entitled spouse occupies the home by permission of a third party or shares the occupation of the home with a third party: s 6(2)(a) and (b).
3 Dealing does not include the compulsory acquisition of the property or the transfer of property by operation of law, for example, bankruptcy. By s 41 of the Bankruptcy (Scotland) Act 1985, the sequestration can be recalled if the petition for sequestration was wholly or mainly to defeat the occupancy rights of the non-entitled spouse. Moreover, by s 40 of the Bankruptcy (Scotland) Act 1985, a debtor's spouse or ex-spouse are protected in their occupation of the family home, in that the consent of the debtor's spouse is required before the sale of the debtor's interest in the property. Further, an application by the permanent trustee to obtain the relevant consent can be refused by the court or an order postponed for a period of up to twelve months in the interests of inter alia the debtor's spouse or children of the family. If the debtor lives in the family home with a child of the family, but separated from the other spouse, it is the debtor's consent which is relevant: thus the interests of the children of the family will be safeguarded. On the application of s 40, see *Salmon's Trustee v Salmon* 1989 SLT (Sh Ct) 49. A child of the family has the same meaning as in the 1981 Act except that where the child is not the child or grandchild of the debtor, the child must have been *accepted* by the debtor as a child of the family: cf the 1981 Act where the child must have been treated as a child of the family.

recorded in the Register of Sasines or registered in the Land Register of Scotland. Thus, a third party could buy a house in good faith and in reliance upon the Registers, only to find that he cannot occupy the property because it is a matrimonial home in which the non-entitled spouse of the seller has statutory rights of occupation.

The 1981 Act provides various solutions to this problem. A non-entitled spouse can renounce in writing the statutory rights in relation to a particular matrimonial home, provided that, at the time it was made, the non-entitled spouse swore or affirmed before a notary public that the renunciation was made freely and without coercion of any kind.[1] Where such a renunciation is made, the property is no longer subject to statutory rights of occupancy.[2]

Similarly, occupancy rights are not effective against a third party if the non-entitled spouse has consented to the dealing.[3] When a non-entitled spouse refuses to consent to the dealing, the court has power to dispense with the consent on the ground, inter alia, that it is being unreasonably withheld.[4] A non-entitled spouse will be taken to have withheld consent unreasonably if (i) the entitled spouse had been led to believe that the consent would be forthcoming and there has been no change of circumstances which would prejudice the non-entitled spouse or (ii) the entitled spouse having taken all reasonable steps, has been unable to obtain an answer to a request for consent.[5] In all other cases, the onus rests on the entitled spouse to show that the non-entitled spouse has unreasonably withheld consent to the dealing. Before the court can consider this issue, the proposed dealing must have reached a stage of negotiations where price and other conditions have been discussed: it is not enough that the entitled spouse proposes to put the property up for sale.[6] In determining whether the consent is being unreasonably withheld the court will consider all the circumstances of the case, including the factors listed in s 3(3).[7] In

---

1 Sections 1(5) and (6). It is not necessary that the non-entitled spouse comes to Scotland to swear or affirm provided it is done before a person authorised to administer oaths or receive affirmations under the law of the country where the non-entitled spouse swears or affirms.
2 Section 6(3)(a)(ii).
3 Section 6(3)(a)(i).
4 Section 7(1). The other grounds for dispensation are that the non-entitled spouse is unable to consent because of physical or mental disability; or cannot be found after reasonable steps have been taken to trace the spouse; or is under the age of 16! This could only arise in the case of a marriage celebrated abroad.
5 Section 7(2).
6 *Fyfe v Fyfe* 1987 SLT (Sh Ct) 38. This effectively prevents the entitled spouse from selling the property on the open market without the non-entitled spouse's consent.
7 Section 7(3). For the s 3(3) factors, see *supra* p 80.

O'Neil v O'Neil[1] where the non-entitled spouse had no intention of living in the house but was merely withholding consent as a bargaining lever in relation to a financial settlement on divorce, the court indicated that her consent was being withheld unreasonably. If the court dispenses with the non-entitled spouse's consent to the dealing,[2] the third party is not affected by the statutory rights.

There are also exceptions when the entitled spouse entered into a binding obligation in respect of the dealing before the marriage[3] or commencement of the Act.[4] If the entitled spouse has permanently ceased to be entitled to occupy the matrimonial home, for example by selling it to a third party, the non-entitled spouse's statutory rights cease to be exercisable against a third party if the non-entitled spouse has, at any time thereafter, not occupied the property for a continuous period of five years.[5] For example, H is the entitled spouse who sells the matrimonial home to X in 1988 and W leaves the matrimonial home in January 1990: then provided W does not occupy the matrimonial home for any period during the next five years, her statutory rights of occupation will not be enforceable against X after January 1995.

However, in practice the most important exception is to be found in s 6(3)(e).[6] This provides that the non-entitled spouse's rights are not enforceable against a third party where –

> 'the dealing comprises a sale to a third party who has acted in good faith, if there is produced to the third party by the seller –
> (i) an affidavit sworn or affirmed by the seller declaring that the subjects of sale are not or were not at the time of the dealing a matrimonial home in relation to which a spouse of the seller has or had occupancy rights; or
> (ii) a renunciation of occupancy rights or consent to the dealing which bears to have been properly made or given by the non-entitled spouse.'[7]

1 1987 SLT (Sh Ct) 26. The house was only a matrimonial home because the husband had hoped that his wife would live there: see *supra* p 78.
2 The court will proceed as expeditiously as possible, but there must be evidence to justify dispensing with consent: see *Longmuir v Longmuir* 1985 SLT (Sh Ct) 33.
3 Section 6(3)(c).
4 Section 6(3)(d).
5 Section 6(3)(f), added by s 13(6)(c) of the Law Reform (Miscellaneous Provisions) (Scotland) Act 1985.
6 As amended by s 13(6)(b) of the Law Reform (Miscellaneous Provisions) (Scotland) Act 1985; and para 31(1) of Sch 8 to, and Sch 9 to, the Law Reform (Miscellaneous Provisions) (Scotland) Act 1990.
7 The time of the dealing in the case of a sale of the property is the date of delivery of the deed transferring title to the property: s 6(3)(c) as amended by s 13(6)(b)(iv) of the Law Reform (Miscellaneous Provisions) (Scotland) Act 1985.

Provided the third party is in good faith, then if such an affidavit is sworn or affirmed, the buyer will take the property free from the occupancy rights of the seller's non-entitled spouse. If the affidavit is false, the non-entitled spouse will have recourse against the entitled spouse for compensation for loss of occupancy rights as a result of the entitled spouse's fraud.[1] The provision is so worded that it enables a seller who is not married to swear or affirm that the property is not a matrimonial home but also enables a seller who is married and whose spouse does have statutory rights in relation to the matrimonial home to swear or affirm when the property which is subject to the dealing is not *in fact* a matrimonial home. A similar affidavit is used to protect the rights of a heritable creditor[2] in respect of a matrimonial home which is subject to a mortgage, being prejudiced by a non-entitled spouse's statutory rights of occupation.[3]

Where a dealing has occurred and the third party has taken the property subject to the non-entitled spouse's statutory rights, the third party can apply to a court for an order dispensing with the consent of the non-entitled spouse to the dealing, if, inter alia, the consent was unreasonably withheld.[4] If successful, the third party will then take the property free from the non-entitled spouse's statutory rights.

Since the 1981 Act came into effect, in spite of initial conveyancing difficulties, these provisions have been the cause of little, if any, litigation. In particular, where a third party has relied on a s 6(3)(e) affidavit, there has been no reported case in which a non-entitled spouse has claimed that occupation rights are nevertheless enforceable against the third party because of an absence of good faith. Nevertheless, these provisions remain controversial among conveyancers and the Scottish Law Commission is considering further proposals for reform.[5]

Where both spouses have legal title or are joint tenants

The statutory rights of occupation of the matrimonial home are only available to a non-entitled spouse, ie a spouse who has no proprietary interest in the property. Where a spouse has a proprietary interest in

---

1 Section 3(7).
2 For example, a bank or building society.
3 Section 8(1) and (2), as amended by s 13(7) and (8) of the Law Reform (Miscellaneous Provisions) (Scotland) Act 1985; and para 31(2) of Sch 8 to, and Sch 9 to, the Law Reform (Miscellaneous Provisions) (Scotland) Act 1990.
4 Section 7.
5 These are discussed in *Family Law: Pre-consolidation Reforms* SLC Discussion Paper No 85, paras 6.1–6.29. In the present writer's view only the minor modifications suggested in paras 6.19–6.25 are either necessary or desirable.

the matrimonial home, at common law, he or she is entitled to occupy it. However, the 1981 Act contains important provisions which strengthen the position of a spouse who has a joint legal title and it is these provisions which will be discussed in this section.

Although it was contrary to principle that a co-owner or co-tenant could be ejected by the other from the common property, there was a suggestion in *Price v Watson*[1] that this was possible. Section 4(7) of the 1981 Act has clarified the position: it provides that where both spouses are entitled, or permitted by a third party, to occupy a matrimonial home, it shall be incompetent for one spouse to bring an action of ejection from the matrimonial home against the other spouse. Moreover, while at common law either co-owner could carry out necessary repairs and pay essential outgoings, there was no power to carry out non-essential repairs. The 1981 Act gives co-owners the power to do so and allows a court to apportion the expenditure between them.[2]

As we have seen,[3] where the spouses are common owners of the matrimonial home, each spouse is free to sell his or her own half *pro indiviso* share of the property without the agreement of the other. This could lead to problems where the purchaser insisted on occupying the property. Section 9(1) of the 1981 Act provides that the right to occupy the matrimonial home enjoyed by a co-owning spouse is not to be prejudiced by reason only of any dealing of the other spouse in respect of the property and that a third party shall not by reason only of such a dealing be entitled to occupy the matrimonial home or any part of it. The effect of this provision is that while a co-owning spouse is still entitled to sell his or her half *pro indiviso* share, the purchaser of the interest is unable to occupy the matrimonial home while the other co-owning spouse continues to reside there.[4]

It was an axiomatic principle of the common law that where property was held in common, either of the co-owners was entitled to obtain a decree of division and sale to realise his or her share of the value of the property. The court had no discretion to refuse the decree. Thus, for example, in *Dickson v Dickson*,[5] the Lord Ordinary (Kincraig) held that a husband was entitled to a decree of division and sale in respect of property he owned in common with his wife: it was irrelevant that she would not agree to the sale as she wished to

---

1 1951 SC 359.
2 Sections 2(4)(a) and (b) and (6).
3 *Supra* p 76.
4 When a co-owning spouse becomes bankrupt, the provisions of s 40 of the Bankruptcy (Scotland) Act 1985, are applicable to protect the occupancy rights of the other co-owning spouse and children of the family: see *supra* p 85 note 3.
5 1982 SLT 128.

use the house as a home for herself and the children of the family. Thus by applying for a decree of division and sale, a spouse could frustrate the underlying purpose of owning a matrimonial home, ie to provide a home for the co-owning spouse and their family. Section 19 provides a partial solution to this problem. Where a matrimonial home is owned in common by a married couple, if one of the spouses brings an action for the division and sale of the property, the court has a discretion, after having regard to all the circumstances of the case, to refuse or postpone the granting of the decree or only to grant the decree subject to conditions. The court is expressly directed to consider the factors listed in s 3(3)[1] and whether the spouse bringing the action has offered to make suitable alternative accommodation available to the other spouse.[2] It is not clear where the onus lies in s 19 applications. In *Hall v Hall*[3] the Sheriff Principal (Caplan), arguing by analogy with dispensation of consent under s 7,[4] held that the onus lay on the spouse seeking the sale to show that the sale is reasonable. On the other hand, in *Berry v Berry*,[5] Lord Sutherland held that as a co-owner has a *prima facie* right to an action of division and sale, the onus lay on the defender to show why it was unreasonable for the sale to go ahead. In practice, however, the court will not allow a sale to go ahead when the continued occupation of the matrimonial home is clearly in the interests of the defender and the family. The needs of children are important.[6] In *Crow v Crow*,[7] Lord Wylie held that s 19 had made very material inroads into the rights of *pro indiviso* proprietors who were married. In particular, he stressed that the needs of the family were

1 *Supra* p 80.
2 Section 19(a) and (b). The offer must be of specific alternative accomodation; a general offer to help a co-owning spouse find somewhere to live is not enough. See *Hall v Hall* 1987 SLT (Sh Ct) 15.
3 Ibid. See also *Milne v Milne* 1994 SLT (Sh Ct) 57, where the approach in *Hall* was followed.
4 Discussed *supra* p 86.
5 1988 SCLR 296. The sale was ordered in this case. The most appropriate method of sale is by private treaty in open market: *Berry v Berry (No 2)* 1989 SLT 292. Where a spouse refused to pay a capital sum payment as financial provision on divorce, he was forced to sell his *pro indiviso* share of the former matrimonial home to his co-owning former spouse: *Scrimgeour v Scrimgeour* 1988 SLT 590. This was an exceptional case.
6 See, for example, *Milne v Milne* 1994 SLT (Sh Ct) 57 (W and children lived in home for 18 years: not fair and reasonable that they should have to move). Significantly, in *Berry v Berry* the couple had no children: but a home was not required for the children in *Hall v Hall*, yet the sale was refused. In *Rae v Rae* 1991 SLT 454, *Berry* was distinguished on the ground that in *Rae* the home was required for the wife and child of the marriage.
7 1986 SLT 270.

crucial. Accordingly, he had no hesitation in postponing the grant of a decree of division and sale beyond a date when the marriage would be terminated by divorce.[1] So, for example, if H applied for an action of division and sale, the court can now delay granting decree until any children of the marriage reach the age of 18, even although the couple may divorce before the youngest child has reached that age.

It is important to note that s 19 is only applicable when the co-owners are spouses. If, after divorce, an ex-spouse applies for an action of division and sale, he or she must be granted decree. Moreover, if during the marriage, a spouse sells his or her half *pro indiviso* share to a third party, the third party is entitled to a decree of division and sale as s 19 only applies when both spouses are common owners of the property.[2]

Where both spouses are joint owners of the matrimonial home, ie entitled spouses, the court has the same powers under s 3 to make regulatory orders in respect of its occupation as it has when there is an entitled and non-entitled spouse.[3] Similarly, the court may make an exclusion order under s 4 where both spouses are entitled, in exactly the same way as in the case of an entitled and non-entitled spouse.[4] The availability of exclusion orders as an important step towards the protection of wives and children from domestic violence cannot be over-estimated.

TENANCIES

By s 13(1) of the 1981 Act, a non-entitled spouse can apply to a court for an order transferring the tenancy of the matrimonial home from the entitled to the non-entitled spouse subject to the non-entitled

---

1 Indeed a divorce action was pending in this case.
2 However, this 'dodge' may be caught by s 9(1)(a) which provides that the co-owning spouse's rights 'in that home' are not to be prejudiced by any dealing of the other spouse. Curiously, s 9(2) appears to apply ss 6(3) and 7 to the situation where both spouses are entitled. But these provisions would appear to be concerned with the statutory rights of occupation of non-entitled spouses: it could hardly have been Parliament's intention that, for example, a spouse could be compelled to sell his or her *pro indiviso* share on the grounds of withholding consent unreasonably. *Sed quaere.*
3 *Supra* p 80.
4 *Supra* p 81 ff.

spouse paying just and reasonable compensation to the entitled spouse. Notice must be given to the landlord who has to be given an opportunity to be heard in the proceedings. In considering whether the tenancy should be transferred the court is directed to consider the factors in s 3(3)[1] and whether the non-entitled spouse is suitable to become a tenant and to perform the obligations in the lease. There are exceptions where the matrimonial home is, for example, part of an agricultural holding or a croft.[2] An order granting an application under s 13(1) can be made on granting a decree of divorce or declarator of nullity of marriage.[3]

Where both spouses are joint or common tenants there is a similar right to apply to a court for an order vesting the tenancy in the applicant's name solely, provided that the applicant pays just and reasonable compensation to the other spouse.[4]

Where an entitled spouse is the tenant of a matrimonial home, the non-entitled spouse retains possession of the tenancy, and therefore the protection of the Rent (Scotland) Act 1984, if the entitled spouse leaves the home.[5]

MATRIMONIAL INTERDICTS

A spouse's right to occupy the matrimonial home can, of course, be undermined as a result of the other spouse's violent behaviour. Since this is so, it is thought to be convenient to discuss the law relating to matrimonial interdicts in this section.

In the leading case of *Tattersall v Tattersall*, the Lord President (Emslie) opined[6] that 'interdict in the law of Scotland is designed only to prevent the apprehended commission of a wrong'. Interdict is granted at common law to protect proprietary rights. Thus in *MacLure v MacLure*,[7] for example, a husband who owned a hotel

---

1 *Supra* p 80. Thus in *McGowan v McGowan* 1986 SLT 112, Lord Kincraig ordered the transfer of a tenancy in H's name to his W. H had been violent during the marriage and had had an adulterous affair. W was living with the son of the marriage in overcrowded conditions with her married daughter. Lord Kincraig thought it would be a 'travesty of justice' if H was allowed to retain occupation of the matrimonial home.
2 For a full list, see s 13(7) and (8).
3 Section 13(2) as amended by para 11 of Sch 1 to the Family Law (Scotland) Act 1985.
4 Section 13(9).
5 Section 2(8), reversing the decision in *Temple v Mitchell* 1956 SC 267.
6 1983 SLT 506 at 509.
7 1911 SC 200.

which was also used as the matrimonial home obtained an interdict against his wife who had no interest in the property from entering the hotel. However, interdict is also granted to protect the integrity of the person and therefore one spouse can obtain interdict against molestation by the other.[1] However, it is a fundmental principle of Scots law that an interdict must be granted in sufficiently precise terms to leave the defender in no doubt as to what he or she can or cannot do and that the conduct prohibited should be no wider than is necessary to curb the defender's illegal actions. Thus in *Murdoch v Murdoch*[2] an interim interdict preventing a husband from telephoning his wife or calling at her house was incompetent by reason of being too wide.

The major drawback of an interdict at common law was the question of enforcement. Where there was an alleged breach of interdict, a petition and complaint had to be brought with the concurrence of the Lord Advocate or procurator fiscal, to establish to the courts that breach of interdict had taken place.[3] The action was a civil one and the police had no power to arrest a person merely because he or she was in breach of interdict, though they could, of course, intervene if a crime or offence, for example, an assault, had occurred.

The 1981 Act introduces a system of matrimonial interdicts to which the court must, in certain circumstances, attach a power of arrest. Where a power of arrest is attached to an interdict, a police constable may arrest the defender without warrant if he has reasonable cause to suspect that he or she is in breach of an interdict.

Section 14(1) of the 1981 Act provides that it shall not be incompetent for a court to entertain an application by a spouse for a matrimonial interdict by reason only that the spouses are living together as man and wife. This clarifies the doubt which had existed at common law about the competency of an application for interdict when the spouses are living together.[4]

By section 14(2) a matrimonial interdict means an interdict, including an interim interdict, which—

'(a) restrains or prohibits any conduct of one spouse towards the other spouse or a child of the family, or
(b) prohibits a spouse from entering or remaining in a matrimonial home or in a specified area in the vicinity of the matrimonial home.'

1 This was certainly the case if the spouses were living apart: it was uncertain whether interdict was available when they were cohabiting: but see now s 14, discussed *infra*.
2 1973 SLT (Notes) 13.
3 *Gribben v Gribben* 1976 SLT 266.
4 See *supra* note 1.

There is little difficulty in relation to s 14(2)(a) interdicts, ie non-molestation interdicts. It appears that the criteria in *Murdoch v Murdoch*[1] are still followed and that the interdict must specify the conduct prohibited which should be no wider than necessary to prevent the illegal act, ie the molestation of the other spouse or a child of the family.

More difficulties have been experienced in relation to s 14(2)(b) interdicts, which have the effect of banning the defender from the matrimonial home. Where an entitled spouse seeks a s 14(2)(b) interdict to exclude a non-entitled spouse from the home, the interdict is being used to protect the applicant's proprietary rights. In *Tattersall v Tattersall*[2] the Inner House of the Court of Session held that it was not competent for a non-entitled spouse who has no proprietary rights to seek a s 14(2)(b) interdict to exclude the entitled spouse from enjoying the incidents of ownership of his or her property. Instead, the non-entitled spouse must seek enforcement of his or her *statutory* rights to occupy the matrimonial home, and resort must be made to a s 4 exclusion order, when interdicts preventing the entitled spouse from entering or remaining in the matrimonial home can also be granted.[3] Where both spouses are entitled, since an action of ejection is no longer competent,[4] it is thought that neither spouse can obtain an interdict under s 14(2)(b) excluding the other from the matrimonial home in which he or she has a one half *pro indiviso* share: once again resort must be made to a s 4 exclusion order.

Thus the effect of *Tattersall v Tattersall*[5] is that a s 14(2)(b) interdict can only be granted to an entitled spouse against a non-entitled spouse. Otherwise an exclusion order must be sought under s 4. The important distinction between the two remedies is that a s 14(2)(b) interdict can be granted when, on the balance of convenience, it is just to do so while a s 4 exclusion order cannot be made unless the court is satisfied it is *necessary* to do so.[6]

Where a s 14(2)(b) interdict has been granted to an entitled spouse and consequently the non-entitled spouse has been excluded from the matrimonial home, it will, of course, be open to the non-entitled spouse to obtain declarator of his or her statutory rights of occupation

1 1973 SLT (Notes) 13.
2 1983 SLT 506.
3 Sections 4(4)(a) and (5)(a).
4 Section 4(7), *supra* p 89.
5 1983 SLT 506.
6 See *supra* p 83.

and seek a s 3 regulatory order to re-enter the home and, if necessary, a s 4 exclusion order.

Where a matrimonial interdict is made which is ancillary to an exclusion order under s 4,[1] s 15(1)(a) provides that the court *must* attach a power of arrest to such an interdict, if this is requested by the applicant. In relation to any other matrimonial interdict, for example, a non-molestation interdict under s 14(2)(a),[2] the court has a discretion by s 15(1)(b) to refuse a request to attach a power of arrest where 'it appears to the court that in all the circumstances of the case the power is unnecessary'. It will be noticed, therefore, that a court has no discretion to refuse to attach a power of arrest when the interdict is ancillary to an exclusion order and a power of arrest is requested by the applicant.

When a power of arrest is attached to a matrimonial interdict, a police constable may arrest the non-applicant spouse without a warrant, if the policeman has reasonable cause for suspecting that the defender is in breach of the interdict.[3]

In spite of the theoretical difficulties surrounding s 14(2)(b), nevertheless it is thought that the introduction of matrimonial interdicts, with powers of arrest, marks an important advance in Scots law for the protection of a spouse or child of the family from domestic violence. It should be stressed that before making an exclusion order under s 4, the court must have determined that a non-molestation interdict under s 14(2)(a) would not be sufficient to protect the applicant spouse or the children of the family, and that an exclusion order is therefore necessary for their protection.

COHABITEES

Couples who are unmarried may also experience difficulties in relation to the occupation of their 'family' accommodation when their relationships begin to break down. The 1981 Act takes the important step of providing some relief to an unmarried cohabiting couple in these circumstances. There are two situations. Where a couple are cohabiting and one partner is entitled to occupy the house and the

---

1 Including an interim order. Interdicts prohibiting the non-applicant spouse from entering or remaining in the matrimonial home, can be granted as ancillary to an exclusion order, ss 4(4) and (5). These are matrimonial interdicts for the purpose of s 15.
2 Or an 'exclusion' interdict under s 14(2)(b).
3 Section 15(3). For full discussion of the procedure, see *Clive* p 311 ff. Minor amendments to s 15(2) and (4) were made by s 64 of the Law Reform (Miscellaneous Provisions) (Scotland) Act 1990.

other partner is not entitled, the non-entitled partner may apply to a court for the grant of occupancy rights in relation to the house in which they are cohabiting.[1] Occupancy rights can be granted for a period not exceeding six months,[2] although the initial period can be extended for further periods of up to six months with no overall limit. A non-entitled partner's rights of occupation are the same as those of a non-entitled spouse.[3] A cohabiting couple is defined as a man and a woman who are living with each other as if they were man and wife.[4] In determining whether a couple are cohabiting for the purpose of an application for occupation rights under s 18(1), the court must consider all the circumstances of the case including the length of their relationship and whether they have any children.[5] The couple must be cohabiting as man and wife at the time of the conduct giving rise to the application for occupancy rights[6] but the applicant need not be residing in the house at the time of the application.[7] When an order granting occupancy rights is in force, certain provisions of the 1981 Act apply to the couple:[8] in particular, regulatory and exclusion orders are available under ss 3 and 4 as are the provisions relating to matrimonial interdicts.[9] However the non-entitled partner's occupancy rights are not protected from dealings by the entitled partner with third parties.

The second situation is where both partners are entitled to occupy the house. Here there is no need for an application under s 18(1): but the same provisions of the 1981 Act apply to the couple as though a s 18(1) order was in force.[10] The entitled partners do not have to be

1 Section 18(1), as amended by s 13(9)(a) of the Law Reform (Miscellaneous Provisions) (Scotland) Act 1985. A person has been held not to be homeless for the purposes of the Housing (Scotland) Act 1987, where she had a right to apply for occupancy rights under s 18(1): *McAlinder v Bearsden & Milngavie DC* 1986 SLT 191.
2 Ibid.
3 Section 18(6) as amended by s 13(9)(a) of the Law Reform (Miscellaneous Provisions) (Scotland) Act 1985.
4 Section 18(1). Homosexual couples are therefore excluded.
5 Section 18(2). In *Armour v Anderson* 1994 SLT 1127, the Lord President (Hope) emphasised that s 18(2) only applies to determine whether or not a couple are cohabiting for the purpose of a s 18(1) application.
6 *Armour v Anderson supra.*
7 However, the longer they have been apart the less likely the court will exercise its discretion under s 18(1) and grant occupancy rights: *Verity v Fenner* 1993 SCLR 223 (apart for 11 months: applicant had a home in Northern Ireland: occupancy rights not granted).
8 Section 18(3).
9 A tenancy transfer order under s 13 is also available.
10 Section 18(3). Unlike the position of entitled spouses, there is no restriction on the grant of a decree in an action of division and sale where the house is owned in common by the entitled partners.

residing together at the time of the proceedings: it is enough that they were living together at the time of the conduct which gave rise to the action. Thus, for example, where entitled joint tenants were living together as husband and wife at the time of the man's misconduct, his partner obtained a tenancy transfer order in an action brought ten months after she had left the house.[1]

It must be stressed that when one cohabiting partner is non-entitled, the protection afforded by these provisions of the 1981 Act does not apply unless and until there has been a successful application by the non-entitled partner for occupancy rights. Thus, for example, in *Clarke v Hatten*,[2] an entitled partner was unable to use the 1981 Act to obtain *inter alia* a matrimonial interdict, as the non-entitled partner, whose violence she had fled, had not applied for occupancy rights.[3] A non-entitled spouse, on the other hand, has statutory rights of occupation of the matrimonial home as a result of simply being married. Although the protection afforded a spouse is also more extensive, nevertheless the 1981 Act is at least a first step towards the recognition by Scots law that the needs of an unmarried couple when their relationship is deteriorating are similar to those of spouses whose marriage is breaking down, and that legal remedies should be available to persons in this situation regardless of their marital status.[4]

1 *Armour v Anderson* 1994 SLT 1127. The same principle would apply if an entitled partner sought an exclusion order under s 4 against the other entitled partner.
2 1987 SCLR 527.
3 It would have been different if both partners were entitled as s 18(3) would operate. The entitled partner could seek an interdict at common law: see *supra* p 92.
4 For proposals for further extension of cohabitees' rights, see *The Effects of Cohabitation in Private Law* SLC Discussion Paper No 86, paras 7.2–7.10

6 Divorce

INTRODUCTION

Divorce on the ground of adultery has been recognised at common law since the Reformation and divorce for desertion was introduced by statute in 1573.[1] Until the Divorce (Scotland) Act 1938, these remained the only two grounds of divorce. The 1938 Act introduced further grounds: cruelty, incurable insanity, sodomy and bestiality.[2] With the exception of incurable insanity, the grounds of divorce were fault-based and divorce was perceived as a punishment for the defender's matrimonial offence. Divorce for incurable insanity was manifestly a non-fault ground and to this can be traced the idea that divorce should be regarded as a remedy to enable a spouse to escape from a dead marriage. This view of divorce gradually became more prevalent. For example, as the result of judicial and statutory developments,[3] any requirement of moral fault on the part of a defender was whittled away from the concept of cruelty, so that the pursuer could obtain a divorce whenever the defender's conduct was detrimental to the pursuer's health.

By the 1960s the movement for the reform of divorce law on the basis of a 'non-fault' ground of irretrievable breakdown of marriage had built up considerable momentum.[4] The Law Commission took the view that a system based on the matrimonial offence did not achieve the objectives of a good divorce law which were –

  '(i) to buttress, rather than to undermine, the stability of marriage; and
  (ii) where, regrettably, a marriage has irretrievably broken down, to enable the empty legal shell to be destroyed with the maximum fairness, and the minimum bitterness, distress and humiliation.'[5]

---

1 Act 1573, c 55.
2 The Act also enabled a marriage to be dissolved on the ground of the presumed death of one of the spouses.
3 Most importantly s 5 of the Divorce (Scotland) Act 1964.
4 See, for example, *Putting Assunder: A Divorce Law for Contemporary Society*, Society for Propagation of Christian Knowledge, 1966.
5 *Reform of the Grounds of Divorce: The Field of Choice*, Cmnd 3123 para 15.

However, the Law Commission considered that it was impracticable to make irretrievable breakdown of marriage the sole ground of divorce. How was breakdown to be established without some form of inquisitorial procedure alien to an adversarial system of adjudication? Would not this involve a new system of courts or tribunals manned by social workers rather than lawyers? Was not the equation of matrimony with a commercial partnership too revolutionary a concept for contemporary British society? The Scottish Law Commission recommended merely the addition of new separation grounds to the existing grounds of divorce but considered that the legal effect of the grounds was that they established that a marriage had in fact broken down.[1]

In England, a compromise was reached between the concept of non-fault divorce based on irretrievable breakdown and the existing matrimonial offences in the Divorce Reform Act 1969, later consolidated in the Matrimonial Causes Act 1973. While irretrievable breakdown was to be the sole ground of divorce it could only be established by proof of at least one of five guideline facts, which included modified versions of the previous matrimonial offences and two new facts based on separation.[2] The Divorce (Scotland) Act 1976 follows a similar compromise.[3]

IRRETRIEVABLE BREAKDOWN OF MARRIAGE

If a system of divorce is based on the sole ground of irretrievable breakdown of marriage as opposed to the concept of matrimonial offence, two consequences should follow. First, a pursuer should be entitled to a divorce whenever the marriage has in fact broken down irretrievably. It is irrelevant that the defender's conduct was morally blameless. Moreover, and more importantly, it is irrelevant that the pursuer's conduct could be perceived to have contributed to the failure of the marriage. If, for example, a pursuer has committed adultery, this should not be held against him or her: the adultery is merely a symptom of the breakdown.

Second, even though the defender's conduct amounted to what had formerly been a matrimonial offence, for example, adultery, the pursuer should not be entitled to a divorce unless the marriage has in fact broken down. There should therefore be built into the system

1 *Divorce: The Grounds Considered* (1967) (Cmnd 3256).
2 Section 1 of the Matrimonial Causes Act 1973.
3 See, generally, *Clive*, Chs 20–23.

provisions for establishing whether or not reconciliation is possible
and to encourage reconciliation where this possibility exists.

As a result of the fact that the current Scottish divorce law is a
compromise between the concept of irretrievable breakdown and
matrimonial offences, the full implications of a non-fault theory of
divorce have been ignored. Section 1(1) of the Divorce (Scotland)
Act 1976[1] provides that irretrievable breakdown of marriage is the
sole ground of divorce in Scots law 'if, but only if, it is established in
accordance with the following provisions of the Act'. Section 1(2)
provides that irretrievable breakdown will be established on proof of
a) the defender's adultery, b) the defender's behaviour, c) the
defender's desertion for two years, d) the non-cohabitation of the parties for two years and their consents, or e) the non-cohabitation of the
parties for five years. Thus, a pursuer will be unable to obtain a
divorce unless he or she can prove one of the facts or guidelines in s
1(2), even though the marriage has in fact irretrievably broken down.
Conversely, a pursuer will be entitled to a divorce if one of the facts
or guidelines is established, even although the marriage has not in
fact irretrievably broken down. In other words, proof of a s 1(2) fact
or guideline is both a necessary and sufficient condition of establishing irretrievable breakdown within the meaning of the Act.
Irretrievable breakdown in the context of Scottish divorce law is simply an artificial legal construct enabling a party who can prove one or
more of the facts and guidelines in s 1(2) to obtain a divorce.[2] The
concept of matrimonial fault has therefore not been eroded from the
Scots law of divorce. Moreover, because the Act is not concerned
with whether a marriage has *in fact* broken down irretrievably, it is
significant that it contains no provisions for compulsory attempts at
reconciliation nor is there any obligation on solicitors to discuss with
clients the possibility of reconciliation.[3] If, however, it appears to the
court that there is a reasonable prospect of reconciliation, the court
can continue the action for an attempt to be made,[4] but in practice it
is unlikely that reconciliation is possible once the action has begun.

The result of the reforms introduced by the 1976 Act has been

1 References in this chapter are to the 1976 Act unless otherwise stated.
2 The phrase could as well be 'abracadabra', see WA Wilson, 1976 SLT (News) 27.
3 Cf s 6 of the Matrimonial Causes Act 1973. However a Court of Session Practice
   Note of 11 March 1977 enjoins practitioners to encourage clients to seek marriage
   counselling if the clients might benefit. There are also provisions in the Court of
   Session and sheriff court rules under which parties can be advised to attempt conciliation in respect of the residence of any children of the marriage. Rules 170B(15)
   and 260D(10) (Court of Session): Rule 132F (Sheriff Court). See infra p 216 ff.
4 Section 2(1).

simply to widen the grounds of divorce. In these circumstances, it is hypocritical to regard irretrievable breakdown as the sole ground of divorce: the provisions of s 1(2) constitute grounds for divorce in Scots law, not simply facts or guidelines to determine whether a marriage has in fact irretrievably broken down.

THE GROUNDS OF DIVORCE

Adultery

By s 1(2)(a) irretrievable breakdown of marriage is established if 'since the date of the marriage the defender has committed adultery'.

Adultery has been defined as voluntary sexual intercourse between a married person and a person of the opposite sex, not being the married partner. The sexual intercourse must be voluntary; thus a woman who is the victim of rape is not guilty of adultery.[1]

The physical requirements of adultery were discussed by Lord Wheatley in *MacLennan v MacLennan*.[2] The pursuer sought a divorce on the ground of his wife's adultery. She had gone to the United States and returned with a child which the pursuer could not have fathered. Her defence was that she had conceived the child as a result of artificial insemination from a donor (AID). While Lord Wheatley regarded the wife's conception of a child by AID without her husband's consent as 'a grave and heinous breach of the contract of marriage', it did not amount to adultery. Adultery involved a mutual surrender of the sexual and reproductive organs and some degree of penetration of the woman's vagina was necessary: in Lord Wheatley's words adultery necessitated 'physical contact with an alien and unlawful sexual organ, and without that element there cannot be what the law regards as adultery'.[3] He therefore dismissed the argument that adultery could be committed by a woman 'when alone in the privacy of her bedroom, she injects into her ovum by means of a syringe the seed of a man she does not know and has never seen'.[4]

A defender's adultery is only relevant if it has occurred 'since the date of the marriage'. Thus, if a young man commits adultery with a

---

1 The fact that a person believes in good faith that he or she is not married, does not prevent them from being guilty of adultery: *Sands v Sands* 1964 SLT 80.
2 1958 SC 105.
3 Ibid at 114.
4 Ibid at 114. AID without the husband's consent could give rise to a divorce based on s 1(2)(b), as would other forms of sexual gratification not involving sexual intercourse.

married woman and subsequently marries, his spouse cannot rely upon his pre-marital adultery to found an action of divorce. A single isolated act of adultery will suffice.

The standard of proof is on the balance of probabilities.[1] Corroboration is not required[2] but the defender's adultery must be established by evidence emanating from a source other than a party to the marriage.[3] Where the defender has been found guilty of rape or incest by a United Kingdom court evidence of his conviction can be used to establish adultery, provided a third party identifies the defender as the person convicted.[4] Moreover a finding of adultery in earlier matrimonial proceedings is admissible in divorce proceedings to establish adultery, but, once again, a third party must identify the defender as the party in the earlier proceedings.[5]

In an action of divorce on the ground of adultery, the pursuer may be met by certain defences.

(i)   Lenocinium

The common law defence of *lenocinium* was preserved by s 1(3) of the 1976 Act. The defence of *lenocinium* is difficult to define.[6] The essence of the defence is that the pursuer actively promoted the defender's adultery or was art and part in the offence. This would cover, for example, a husband who encouraged his wife to take up prostitution or a wife who suggested to her husband that they should join a 'spouse swapping' party. The defence can be illustrated by the leading case of *Gallacher v Gallacher*,[7] where a husband sent a letter to his wife entreating her to do something to enable him to divorce her. A few months later, the wife fell passionately in love with another man. In divorce proceedings based on adultery, the action failed on account of *lenocinium*. The court refused to accept the husband's contention that the adultery arose as a result of the wife's passion for her lover rather than his letter. As Lord Anderson said,[8]

'No woman invited by her husband to commit adultery would go into the street and offer herself to the first man she met.

1 Section 1(6).
2 Civil Evidence (Scotland) Act 1988, s 1(1). This is also the case for establishing the other grounds.
3 Ibid, s 8(1) and (3).
4 Section 10 of the Law Reform (Miscellaneous Provisions) (Scotland) Act 1968; *Andrews v Andrews* 1971 SLT (Notes) 44.
5 Section 11 of the Law Reform (Miscellaneous Provisions) (Scotland) Act 1968.
6 *Gallacher v Gallacher* 1928 SC 586 per Lord Justice Clerk (Alness) at 591.
7 1928 SC 586.
8 1928 SC 586 at 599.

Affection for her lover must always be a cause, and it may be the main cause of her lapse from virtue'.

However, the husband's letter had been the reason why she had even contemplated adultery. Lord Ormidale took the view[1] that –

'Passion no doubt was a factor before she finally fell, but I have no doubt that but for the letter and invitation of her husband, she would have resisted and not responded to the advances [of her lover]'.

Thus the pursuer's conduct does not have to be *the* cause *(causa causans)* of the adultery: it is sufficient if it is a cause *(conditio sine qua non)*.

Six years later, Gallacher again attempted to obtain a divorce.[2] This time he was successful. The wife had continued to live with her lover but the court held that her continuing adulterous relationship was no longer caused by the pursuer's letter. Lord Hunter[3] maintained that the husband's act of connivance six years before could not be regarded as a perpetual licence to the wife to commit adultery for the rest of her lifetime: on the facts, the defender no longer required his encouragement. Consequently, the defence of *lenocinium* failed as the wife could no longer show that her husband's letter was a cause of her continuing her adulterous affair.

It is important to stress that before *lenocinium* can be established, the pursuer must actively encourage the defender's adultery. In *Thomson v Thomson*,[4] the pursuer thought that his wife was having an affair. When she asked him for money to visit friends, he suspected she was going to meet her lover. Nevertheless he gave her the money she requested but had her followed by inquiry agents. They discovered her committing adultery in Gateshead! The wife's defence of *lenocinium* failed on the ground that since she believed she had succeeded in keeping the knowledge of her affair from her husband, he could not have been actively encouraging her to commit adultery when he gave her the money she requested – albeit that he suspected how she would in fact use it. Similarly, it is not *lenocinium* to hire inquiry agents to watch a spouse suspected of adultery.[5]

---

1 Ibid at 595.
2 1934 SC 339.
3 Ibid at 346.
4 1908 SC 179.
5 For proposals that *lenocinium* should be replaced by a defence of actively promoting or encouraging adultery, see *Family Law: Pre-consolidation Reforms* SLC Discussion Paper No 85, paras 8.2–8.4.

(ii)   *Condonation*

By s 1(3) of the 1976 Act, the defender's adultery will not be a
ground of divorce if it has been 'condoned by the pursuer's cohabitation with the defender in the knowledge or belief that the defender
has committed the adultery'. Section 13(2) provides that for the purposes of the Act 'the parties to a marriage shall be held to cohabit
with one another only when they are in fact living together as man
and wife'. Thus the parties must in fact live together as husband and
wife before the defence is operative:verbal forgiveness[1] or an isolated
act of sexual intercourse will not suffice. But s 1(3) must be read with
s 2(2) of the Act. Section 2(2) provides that adultery will not be condoned unless the pursuer has continued or resumed cohabitation with
the defender at any time after the end of a period of three months
from the date on which cohabitation was continued or resumed.
Some examples will illustrate how this section operates: in all cases
it is assumed that the pursuer knows or believes the defender has
committed adultery.

1. If the pursuer continues to cohabit with the defender for less than
   three months, adultery is not condoned.
2. If the pursuer continues to cohabit with the defender for more than
   three months, adultery is condoned.
3. If the pursuer continues to cohabit with the defender for less
   than three months but then resumes cohabitation, the adultery
   will be condoned if cohabitation takes place at any time after a
   three month period beginning from the date when he knew or
   believed the defender was committing adultery and continued to
   cohabit.

   For example:
   a) P learns of D's adultery on 31 January. P continues to cohabit
       with D for a week. If P resumes cohabitation, for however short
       a period after 30 April, the adultery will be condoned, as the
       resumption of cohabitation took place outside the three month
       period beginning on 31 January.
   b) P learns of D's adultery on 31 January. P continues to cohabit
       with D for a week. If P resumes cohabitation on 1 April, the
       adultery will not be condoned if P leaves before 1 May. But if
       the cohabitation continues beyond or is resumed after 30
       April, the adultery will be condoned, as cohabitation has
       taken place outside the three month period beginning on 31
       January.

---

1 This was the position at common law: *Annan v Annan* 1948 SC 532.

4. If P ceases cohabitation with D but resumes cohabitation for less than three months, the adultery will not be condoned.
5. If P ceases cohabitation with D but resumes cohabitation for more than three months the adultery will be condoned.
6. If P ceases cohabitation with D but resumes cohabitation for less than three months, the adultery will be condoned if cohabitation takes place at any time after a three month period from the date of the initial resumption. For example:
   a) P learns of D's adultery. He ceases to cohabit for a year. P resumes cohabitation on 31 January. P continues to cohabit with D for a week. If P resumes cohabitation, for however short a period after 30 April, the adultery will be condoned, as cohabitation has taken place outwith the three month period beginning on 31 January when cohabitation was first resumed.
   b) P learns of D's adultery. He ceases to cohabit for a year. P resumes cohabitation on 31 January. P continues to cohabit with D for a week. If P resumes cohabitation on 1 April, the adultery will not be condoned if he leaves before 1 May. But if cohabitation continues beyond or is resumed after 30 April, the adultery will be condoned, as cohabitation has taken place outwith the three month period beginning on 31 January.

It is thought that s 1(3) only operates as a defence in relation to the adultery on which the action is founded. Thus if the pursuer cohabited in the knowledge or belief that the defender committed adultery with A, it would not operate as a bar to an action based on the defender's adultery with B. Similarly, if the pursuer knew or believed that the defender has committed specific acts of adultery, s 1(3) would not operate in relation to other acts of adultery which subsequently came to the pursuer's knowledge.

(iii) *Collusion*

If the parties *agree* to put up a false case or keep back a relevant defence, this will operate as an absolute bar to a divorce if discovered before decree is granted: if discovered after decree has been granted, the decree can be reduced.[1] Collusion will be a bar to a divorce based on any of the five grounds.[2]

---

1 *Walker v Walker* 1911 SC 163.
2 See generally *Clive* pp 439–440. For proposals that collusion should cease to be a bar, see *Family Law: Pre-consolidation Reforms* SLC Discussion Paper No 85, paras 8.5–8.8.

Behaviour

By s 1(2)(b) irretrievable breakdown of marriage is established if –

> 'since the date of the marriage the defender has at any time
> behaved (whether or not as a result of mental abnormality and
> whether such behaviour has been active or passive) in such a
> way that the pursuer cannot reasonably be expected to cohabit
> with the defender'.

The defender's conduct must have occurred after the date of the marriage: a spouse's behaviour before the marriage is irrelevant. Thus, for example, a husband cannot use s 1(2)(b) to obtain a divorce on the ground that he was induced to marry the defender as a result of her fraudulent misrepresentation that she was pregnant by him: the wife's behaviour, ie the lie, took place *before* the date of the marriage.[1] Similarly, a wife who discovers that her husband had committed a heinous offence before the marriage, cannot rely on this offence to obtain a divorce.[2]

Before s 1(2)(b) is applicable, the defender must have behaved. What does behaviour mean in this context? A mere physical condition does not per se constitute behaviour. For example, if a defender is incontinent, that in itself does not amount to behaviour. But if an incontinent spouse refused to wear protective underwear, the refusal to do so would constitute behaviour. However, it is settled that symptoms of an illness can in certain circumstances amount to behaviour. If, for example, a spouse became violent as a result of an illness, the violence would clearly constitute behaviour. But it can be difficult to determine when the symptom of an illness is merely a physical condition and when it amounts to behaviour. Thus, a husband's sleepiness and general lack of interest in his family caused by schizophrenia has been held to amount to behaviour[3] and bad personal hygiene as a result of disseminated sclerosis has not.[4]

A solution to this problem may be that the 1976 Act includes behaviour 'whether such behaviour has been active or passive'. In *Thurlow v Thurlow*[5] it has been accepted in England that where as a result of a debilitating illness a spouse is unable to fulfil the obligations of marriage, this failure can constitute behaviour for the

---

1 On fraudulent misrepresentation, see *supra* p 33 ff.
2 Cf *Hastings v Hastings* 1941 SLT 323.
3 *Fullarton v Fullarton* 1976 SLT 8. However, the effect of the behaviour on the pursuer was not serious enough for the divorce to be granted.
4 *Grant v Grant* 1974 SLT (Notes) 54.
5 [1975] 2 All ER 979, [1976] Fam 32.

purposes of divorce. As the 1976 Act has expressly enacted that
behaviour may be passive,[1] it is thought that the principle in *Thurlow*
has been transplanted into Scots law. Thus if an illness prevents a
spouse from fulfilling the obligations of married life, this passive
negative behaviour – as opposed to the illness – can amount to
grounds for divorce.[2]

The fact that a defender's behaviour is caused by mental illness is
irrelevant: s 1(2)(b) expressly states that conduct will constitute
behaviour 'whether or not as a result of mental illness'.[3]

The pursuer must establish that the defender behaved 'in such a
way that the pursuer cannot reasonably be expected to cohabit with
the defender'. The test is a compromise between a subjective and
objective test. The criterion is whether the particular pursuer can, at
the time of the action,[4] reasonably be expected to cohabit with the
defender. Thus a highly sensitive spouse may not reasonably be
expected to put up with conduct which a spouse of ordinary fortitude
could withstand.[5] But because of the phrase 'reasonably be
expected', utterly trivial conduct (for example, snoring)[6] or socially
useful conduct (membership of a lifeboat or mountain rescue team)
will not constitute grounds for divorce, however sensitive the pursuer
may be.

1 There is no express reference to passive behaviour in s 1(2)(b) of the Matrimonial
  Causes Act 1973.
2 If this thesis be accepted doubt must be cast on such pre-1976 cases as *H v H* 1968
  SLT 40, where a wife's frigidity which was caused by neurotic depression was held
  not to constitute cruelty. However, the frigidity would now amount to passive
  behaviour and the fact that it was a symptom of an illness is irrelevant.
3 In so doing the 1976 Act follows the policy of s s 5 of the Divorce (Scotland) Act
  1964; *Williams v Williams* [1963] 2 All ER 994, [1964] AC 698, HL.
4 In *Findlay v Findlay* 1991 SLT 457, H drank and stayed out late. W suspected H
  was seeing another woman. The couple separated. At the time of the proof, W was
  living with another man. Her association was not per se enough to conclude that she
  could no longer reasonably be expected to cohabit with H. Lord Prosser stressed
  that there had to be a causal link between H's behaviour and the conclusion that W
  could not reasonably be expected to live with H. On the facts, H's behaviour led to
  W's separation and new relationship: there was therefore a causal link.
  Accordingly, because she was now living with another man, she could not reasonably be expected to cohabit with H at the time of the divorce action. See also *Knox
  v Knox* 1993 SCLR 381.
5 See, for example, *Livingstone-Stallard v Livingstone-Stallard* [1974] 3 All ER 766,
  [1974] Fam 47; *O'Neill v O'Neill* [1975] 3 All ER 289, [1975] 1 WLR 1118, CA.
  In *Meikle v Meikle* 1987 GWD 26–1005, a wife who came from a town background
  and went to live on her husband's hill farm obtained a divorce on the grounds that
  her husband spent too much time at work and she was disillusioned with life in the
  country.
6 Assuming, of course, that snoring constitutes behaviour.

The range of behaviour which could satisfy s 1(2)(b) is as wide as human conduct. It includes both physical[1] and verbal assaults. Moreover, as Lord Davidson explained in *Hastie v Hastie*,[2]

'. . . conduct on the part of a defender, by word or act, may be of such a nature that even if there is no risk of a repetition it is so destructive of a marriage relationship as to make it unreasonable to expect the pursuer to cohabit with the defender'.

In relation to sexual behaviour, this would include, for example, excessive demands for sexual intercourse, wilful and unjustified refusal of sexual intercourse,[3] non-adulterous sexual relations with a third party and homosexual activities.[4] Excessive drunkenness[5] or other abuse of drugs would also suffice.

The mere fact that the pursuer has continued to cohabit with the defender after the alleged behaviour took place does not per se prevent the pursuer relying upon it for the purpose of s 1(2)(b). A woman who has been the victim of violence may continue to live with her husband after the assaults through fear or because she has simply nowhere else to go.[6] But where the alleged behaviour is objectively trivial, the longer the pursuer remains with the defender, the more difficult it will be to establish that the pursuer cannot reasonably be expected to cohabit with the defender as a result of that conduct. The pursuer's conduct after separation, for example forming a new relationship, may be used as evidence to establish that the pursuer cannot reasonably be expected to live with the defender.[7]

The standard of proof is on the balance of probabilities.[8] Corroboration is not required. By s 3(1) of the 1976 Act, if a decree

1 The assault need not be directed at the pursuer: *AB v CB* 1959 SC 27.
2 1985 SLT 146 at 148: wife's false accusation that husband was engaging in an incestuous association. See also *MacLeod v MacLeod* 1990 GWD 14–767: husband's unfounded suspicions of wife's adultery. A husband's boast that he was having an affair has been held to constitute unreasonable behaviour even although the wife could not establish adultery: *Stewart v Stewart* 1987 SLT (Sh Ct) 48.
3 In *Mason v Mason, Times* 5 December 1980, CA, a wife's limitation of sexual intercourse to once a week was held in England not to be such that her husband could no longer reasonably be expected to cohabit.
4 *White v White* 1966 SC 187.
5 *Campbell v Campbell* 1973 SLT (Notes) 82.
6 See, for example, *Britton v Britton* 1973 SLT (Notes) 12; *Bradley v Bradley* [1973] 3 All ER 750, [1973] 1 WLR 1291, CA.
7 *Findlay v Findlay* 1991 SLT 457; *Knox v Knox* 1993 SCLR 381. However, there must be a causal link between the defender's behaviour and the conclusion that the pursuer cannot reasonably be expected to cohabit with the defender. See *supra* p 107, n 4.
8 Section 1(6).

of separation[1] has previously been granted in respect of the same or substantially the same facts, an extract of the decree may be regarded as sufficient proof of these facts in an action for divorce on the ground, inter alia, of behaviour, but the court must still receive further evidence from the pursuer of what has occurred between the parties since the date of the decree.[2] Finally, where the behaviour relied upon led to a criminal conviction of the defender by a United Kingdom court, s 10 of the Law Reform (Miscellaneous Provisions) (Scotland) Act 1968 is applicable.[3]

There are no specific defences in relation to s 1(2)(b) but collusion will constitute an absolute bar.[4]

Desertion

By s 1(2)(c) irretrievable breakdown of marriage is established if –

> 'the defender has wilfully and without reasonable cause deserted the pursuer; and during a continuous period of two years immediately succeeding the defender's desertion –
> (i) there has been no cohabitation between the parties, and
> (ii) the pursuer has not refused a genuine and reasonable offer by the defender to adhere'.

This ground falls into two parts. First, the defender must have deserted the pursuer. Second, this initial desertion must be followed by two years' non-cohabitation during which the pursuer has not refused a genuine and reasonable offer to adhere.

The initial desertion

First, the defender must have *wilfully* deserted the pursuer ie the defender must intend to leave the pursuer and end their married life. As it must be wilful, there is no desertion if the defender is mentally ill and incapable of forming the necessary intention. Nor is there desertion if the defender is separated from the pursuer against his will, for example, as a result of imprisonment.

Second, in order to amount to desertion, the pursuer must be willing to adhere at the date on which the defender leaves. Thus if a couple agree to separate, this is not desertion, as neither was willing to

---

1 See *infra* p 116.
2 This will usually simply be that the parties have neither lived together or had sexual relations since the date of the decree of separation.
3 Discussed in the context of adultery, *supra* p 102.
4 Collusion is discussed in the context of adultery, *supra* p 105.

adhere when they parted.[1] It must be stressed that the pursuer's willingness to adhere is only required to establish initial desertion: there is no need for the pursuer to continue to be willing to adhere beyond the initial period of the separation.

Third, there must be withdrawal of cohabitation. The fact that sexual relations have ceased between the couples is not sufficient.[2] But it is possible that if the couple live in separate households, ie no longer cohabit, the factual element of desertion will be satisfied even although they are living under the same roof.[3]

Fourth, the defender's desertion must be without reasonable cause. This could include, for example, the pursuer's adultery or behaviour which would justify a divorce under s 1(2)(b).[4] The reasonable cause must be known[5] to the defender at the date when he or she left.

Two years' non-cohabitation

Once the initial period of desertion is established, the pursuer is entitled to a divorce if 'during a continuous period of two years immediately succeeding the defender's desertion' the parties have not cohabited and the pursuer has not refused a genuine and reasonable offer by the defender to adhere.

The parties will be held to cohabit only when 'they are in fact living together as man and wife'.[6] The fact that the couple have had sexual intercourse during the two year period does not constitute

---

1 If, for example, the wife later wished to resume cohabitation, then, if, when she calls him to adhere, he unreasonably refuses, desertion by the husband begins at that date. It is thus necessary for the wife to communicate to her husband her change of mind. But where, for example, a couple are temporarily living apart, both being willing to adhere, then if the wife decides that she is never going to return to her husband, desertion begins at that date and there is no need for the wife to communicate this fact to her husband.

2 *Lennie v Lennie* 1950 SC (HL) 1.

3 Ibid at 5 and 16.

4 Behaviour before the marriage could perhaps constitute just cause for separation, although it would not constitute grounds for divorce or separation under s 1(2)(b): *Hastings v Hastings* 1941 SLT 323. See *supra* p 106.

5 Cf *Wilkinson v Wilkinson* 1943 SC (HL) 61 (pursuer's adultery unknown to defender is reasonable cause). But at that time the pursuer had to be willing to adhere throughout the desertion period and could not call on the defender to adhere if the pursuer had been guilty of a matrimonial offence, albeit unknown to the defender at the date when he left. The *Wilkinson* principle was reversed in relation to adultery by s 5(1) of the Divorce (Scotland) Act 1964. It is thought that it does not apply to other grounds of reasonable cause in the context of the 1976 Act: for full discussion, see *Clive* p 420 ff.

6 Section 13(2).

cohabitation.[1] The parties must resume life together as husband and wife.[2]

Resumption of cohabitation before two years have elapsed from the date of the initial desertion may not operate to prevent the pursuer obtaining a divorce. By s 2(4) of the 1976 Act it is provided that in considering whether the two year period has been continuous, no account shall be taken of any period or periods of cohabitation not exceeding six months in all: but no such period or periods count as part of the period of non-cohabitation. In other words, period(s) of cohabitation which amount to less than six months do not break the continuity of the period of non-cohabitation but they do not count towards it.

EXAMPLE 1

D deserts P on 1 January 1993. The couple resume cohabitation on 1 January 1994. They separate on 1 April 1994. The action for divorce can be brought after 1 April 1995. The three months period of cohabitation between 1 January 1994 and 1 April 1994 does not break the continuity of the two years non-cohabitation but does not count towards it.

EXAMPLE 2

D deserts P on 1 January 1993. The couple resume cohabitation on 1 November 1994. They separate on 30 June 1995. A divorce action cannot be brought on the ground of D's desertion on 1 January 1993. The period of cohabitation between 1 November 1994 and 30 June 1995 is greater than six months. The continuity of the non-cohabitation after the desertion has been broken and it is therefore impossible to establish that they have not cohabited for a *continuous* period of two years immediately succeeding the initial desertion on 1 January 1993. If P was deserted by D on 30 June 1995, a divorce action could be brought after 30 June 1997.

During the two year period of non-cohabitation after the initial desertion, the couple's intentions are irrelevant. Thus, provided that the pursuer was willing to adhere when the defender left, it does not matter that a week later the pursuer was unwilling to have the defender back. The only factor which would prevent a divorce in these

1 *Edmond v Edmond* 1971 SLT (Notes) 8.
2 The absence of sexual intercourse probably does not prevent a couple from being regarded as living together as man and wife.

circumstances would be if the pursuer during the two years non-cohabitation refused a genuine and reasonable offer by the defender to return.[1] If such an offer was made *after* the two year period had expired, the pursuer can refuse to accept it and still sue for divorce on the ground of desertion.

The standard of proof is on the balance of probabilities.[2] Corroboration is not required. The pursuer may be able to use s 3 of the 1976 Act if a decree of separation has previously been granted on the ground of desertion.[3]

It should be emphasised that provided there is initial desertion and the couple have not cohabited for the immediately succeeding two years, the pursuer may seek a divorce at any time after the two year period has elapsed. This illustrates how desertion is still conceived as a matrimonial offence. However, there is a defence if after the expiry of the two year period of non-cohabitation the pursuer resumes cohabitation and cohabits with the defender at any time after the end of three months from the date when cohabitation was first resumed.[4] This defence operates in a similar way to condonation of adultery.[5] Collusion will operate as an absolute bar.[6]

Non-cohabitation for two years

By s 1(2)(d) irretrievable breakdown of marriage is established if –

'there has been no cohabitation between the parties at any time during a continuous period of two years after the date of the marriage and immediately preceding the bringing of the action and the defender consents to the granting of the decree'.

First, there must be no cohabitation between the parties for the requisite period. Section 13(2) provides that 'the parties to a marriage shall be held to cohabit with one another only when they are in fact living together as husband and wife'. Interpreted literally, a couple who are not *in fact* living together as husband and wife are not cohabiting for the purpose of s 1(2)(d). The reason why they are not in fact living together is irrelevant. Thus, for example, if a couple are not living together because the husband is in prison or in hospital or working abroad, they are not cohabiting within the meaning of the 1976 Act.

1 Whether the offer is genuine and reasonable is a question of fact in the particular case.
2 Section 1(6).
3 Discussed in relation to behaviour, *supra* pp 108, 109.
4 Section 2(3).
5 Discussed *supra* p 104.
6 Discussed in the context of adultery, *supra* p 105.

It is hoped that Scottish courts will not follow the interpretation of the parallel English provisions[1] laid down by the Court of Appeal in *Santos v Santos*.[2] There it was held that a couple are not to be treated as living apart for the purpose of divorce merely because they are physically separated: in addition, it is necessary that one of them had formed the intention that the marriage had broken down and no longer wished to continue with their married life. This requirement of a mental element is an unwarranted gloss on the wording of the English legislation. *A fortiori* it should not be followed in Scotland. There is no ambiguity in the wording of s 13(2) and, construed literally, there is no need for a mental element: physical separation will suffice.

Conversely, a couple may not be cohabiting within the meaning of s 13(2) even although they live in close physical proximity. They will only be treated as cohabiting if they are in fact living together *as husband and wife*. The absence of sexual relations will be an important factor in determining whether they are living in that capacity – but absence of sexual relations per se will probably not be enough. But if sexual relations have ceased, or the spouses provide no services for each other or if they have no joint social life, then it is possible to argue that they are not living together as husband and wife even although they occupy the same house. In these circumstances, it is hoped that Scottish courts would take the approach of the Court of Appeal in *Fuller v Fuller*.[3] After their marriage had deteriorated H left the matrimonial home. W and their former lodger became lovers. When H fell ill W took pity on H and allowed him to return. While W looked after his domestic needs, she and her lover continued to live together in the matrimonial home. The Court held that the spouses had been living apart: for while they lived in the same house – indeed in the same household – they were not living together *in the capacity* of husband and wife. If similar circumstances arose in Scotland, it is submitted that the spouses should be treated as not cohabiting as they were not in fact living together as husband and wife, but rather as patient and nurse.

The non-cohabitation must be for a continuous period of at least two years after the date of the marriage and immediately preceding the bringing of the action. As in the case of desertion, by s 2(4) resumption of cohabitation for a period or periods not exceeding six

1 Section 1(6) of the Matrimonial Causes Act 1973.
2 [1972] 2 All ER 246, [1972] Fam 247, CA.
3 [1973] 2 All ER 650, [1973] 1 WLR 730, CA.

months in all does not break the continuity of the period of non-cohabitation but does not count towards it.[1]

Finally, the defender must positively consent to the granting of the decree. Consent can be withdrawn at any time before decree. Moreover in *Boyle v Boyle*[2] Lord Maxwell held[3] that 'it is perfectly open to a defender to withhold consent for any reason he thinks fit or for no reason'. Thus the defender's consent can be used as a bargaining counter between the parties in reaching agreement over ancillary matters like financial provision on divorce.

The standard of proof is on the balance of probabilities.[4] Corroboration is not required, and the divorce can proceed as a simplified divorce application.[5] The pursuer may be able to rely on s 3 of the 1976 Act if a decree of separation has previously been granted on the ground of non-cohabitation.[6]

Non-cohabitation for five years

By s 1(2)(e) irretrievable breakdown of marriage is established if 'there has been no cohabitation between the parties at any time during a continuous period of five years after the date of the marriage and immediately preceding the bringing of the action'.

In relation to the meaning of non-cohabitation and continuity of a non-cohabitation, including the application of s 2(4), this ground raises precisely the same legal issues as those in s 1(2)(d).[7] The difference is, of course, that the period of non-cohabitation is five years and the consent of the defender is not necessary. Accordingly, a defender who has not been guilty of a matrimonial offence can be divorced against his or her will. The rationale of this ground, however, is that since the parties have not cohabited for five years, the marriage has in fact broken down irretrievably and consequently should be legally brought to an end.

The defender is able to apply for financial provision on divorce.[8] But, in addition, in order to avoid excessive financial hardship to a defender, s 1(5) provides that a court is not bound to grant decree by

---

1 Section 2(4) is discussed in the context of desertion *supra* p 111.
2 1977 SLT (Notes) 69. See also *Donnelly v Donnelly* 1991 SLT (Sh Ct) 9.
3 Ibid at 69.
4 Section 1(6).
5 Section 2 of the Divorce Jurisdiction, Court Fees and Legal Aid (Scotland) Act 1983; Evidence in Undefended Divorce Actions (Scotland) Act Order 1983 (SI 1983/949). Simplified divorce procedure is discussed *infra* p 117.
6 Discussed in relation to behaviour, *supra* p 108 ff.
7 Discussed *supra* p 112.
8 Discussed *infra* Ch 7.

reason of s 1(2)(e), 'if in the opinion of the court *the grant of decree* would result in grave financial hardship to the defender'.[1] Several points should be noticed:

1. The defence is only available where the grave financial hardship arises from the grant of the divorce, not the breakdown of the marriage. Most marriage breakdowns will result in some financial hardship for the spouses but s 1(5) only applies if the *divorce* will cause grave financial hardship to the defender. This immediately limits the scope of the defence.

2. The divorce must result in *grave* financial hardship. Obviously, s 1(5) will not be available to wealthy spouses who will be able to afford to make generous financial provision on divorce. But very poor couples will also be excluded. For example, in *Boyd v Boyd*[2] H left W in 1959 after twenty years of marriage. During the next twenty years H paid W aliment of only £4.50 a week. On divorce, H could only offer W a periodical allowance of £5.00 a week. A s 1(5) defence failed on the ground that as a result of the breakdown of the marriage, W had suffered financial hardship but this would not be increased if she were divorced: indeed she would be 50p a week better off!

It is to be hoped that for the purpose of s 1(5), the Scottish courts will follow the decision of the Court of Appeal in *Reiterbund v Reiterbund*[3] where it was held that in considering whether or not a spouse would suffer grave financial hardship on divorce, the defender's entitlement to income support if the divorce was granted, should be taken into account. Where the spouses are poor, the defender may be no worse off when aliment ceases on divorce because he or she may be entitled to as much or more in the form of income support and other benefits.

In practice, therefore, s 1(5) will only be available to middle class, middle-aged women, particularly, where their husbands are in pensionable employment and the pension is payable to their *widow* on death. The Act recognises this by specifically providing that hardship includes 'the loss of the chance of acquiring any benefit'.[4] In *Nolan v Nolan*[5] the s 1(5) defence succeeded because the defender would lose the chance of obtaining the benefit of two-fifths of the husband's index-linked pension payable to his

---

1 Italics added. Section 1(5) is not an absolute bar to obtaining a divorce. The court has discretion to grant the decree of divorce even if satisfied that it would result in grave financial hardship to the defender: *Norris v Norris* 1992 SLT (Sh Ct) 51.
2 1978 SLT (Notes) 55.
3 [1975] 1 All ER 280, [1975] Fam 99, CA.
4 Section 1(5).
5 1979 SLT 293.

widow if the husband predeceased her. Lord Cowie was not satisfied that the husband's offer to take out an insurance policy for his
wife's benefit compensated sufficiently for the loss of her contin-
gent right to his index-linked pension.[1] If, however, the husband
had had sufficient resources to compensate the defender adequately, the defence would not have succeeded.

3. Unlike the parallel provision in England,[2] s 1(5) only operates if
the divorce will result in grave *financial* hardship. Accordingly,
there is no defence if other hardship will arise, for example, if
divorce is contrary to the defender's religious beliefs[3] or the
defender will be ostracised by his or her community, if the divorce
is granted.[4]

It is submitted that since the marriage has irretrievably broken down
as a result of at least five years of non-cohabitation, the s 1(5) defence
should be construed narrowly and only be applicable in exceptional
cases of grave financial hardship arising from the divorce.[5]

The same rules as to standard of proof and collusion apply as in
s 1(2)(d).[6] The divorce can proceed as a simplified divorce action.[7]

JUDICIAL SEPARATION

The grounds for judicial separation are exactly the same as the
grounds for divorce and the same defences apply.[8] When a decree of
separation is granted, the parties' obligation to adhere comes to an
end. The marriage still subsists, however, and the spouses remain
under their obligation to aliment each other[9] and their obligations of
fidelity and tolerable behaviour continue. Thus, for example, a
divorce can be sought on the ground of adultery committed after the

1 Since the portion of any rights in an occupational pension scheme acquired during
the marriage must now be shared fairly between the spouses on divorce, the scope
of s 1(5) in this respect is even further reduced: s 10(5) of the Family Law
(Scotland) Act 1985, discussed *infra* Ch 7.
2 Section 5 of the Matrimonial Causes Act 1973.
3 *Waugh* v *Waugh* 1992 SLT (Sh Ct) 17.
4 This aspect of the s 5 defence has rarely, if ever, succeeded in England: see, for
example, *Rukat v Rukat* [1975] 1 All ER 343, [1975] Fam 63, CA.
5 Indeed the Scottish Law Commission has recommended that the s 1(5) defence be
abolished: *Family Law: Pre-consolidation Reforms* SLC Discussion Paper No 85,
paras 8.9–8.11.
6 Discussed *supra* p 114.
7 Simplified divorce procedure is discussed *infra* p 117.
8 Section 4.
9 Discussed *supra* p 49 ff. A pursuer can seek a decree of separation without craving
for aliment: *Gray v Gray* 1991 SCLR 422.

decree of separation. If a decree of separation is obtained the same facts can be used as a ground for a subsequent divorce.[1] The Scottish Law Commission has recommended that judicial separation should be abolished.[2]

PROCEDURAL MATTERS

Jurisdiction

The Court of Session has jurisdiction to entertain an action of divorce if either of the parties to the marriage a) is domiciled in Scotland on the date when the action is begun or b) was habitually resident in Scotland throughout the period of one year ending with that date.[3] A sheriff court has jurisdiction if a) or b) is satisfied and either party to the marriage –

(i) was resident in the sheriffdom for a period of 40 days ending with that date, or

(ii) was resident in the sheriffdom for a period of not less than 40 days ending not more than 40 days before the said date, and has no known residence in Scotland at that date.[4]

There is no minimum period of marriage which must elapse before an action of divorce can be brought.

Proof

As a general principle, a divorce cannot be granted unless the ground of action has been proved, whether or not the action has been defended.[5] But where an action is undefended, proof is, unless the court otherwise directs, by way of affidavits instead of parole evidence. A simplified procedure – in effect a do-it-yourself divorce – is possible in relation to divorces based on s 1(2)(d) and (e). However

---

1 Section 3.
2 *Family Law: Pre-consolidation Reforms* SLC Discussion Paper No 85, paras 8.9–8.11.
3 Section 7 of the Domicile and Matrimonial Proceedings Act 1973.
4 Section 8(2) of the Domicile and Matrimonial Proceedings Act 1973 as amended by the Divorce Jurisdiction, Court Fees and Legal Aid (Scotland) Act 1983, Sch 1, para 18. The parties are not free to agree that a sheriff has jurisdiction where neither is resident in the sheriffdom, however convenient the forum: *Singh v Singh* 1988 SCLR 541.
5 There is no need for corroboration but there must be evidence emanating from a source other than a party to the marriage: Civil Evidence (Scotland) Act 1988, ss 1(1), 8(1), (3).

its scope is severely restricted. An application can proceed if, and only if –
  (i) in relation to a divorce based on s 1(2)(d) the other spouse consents;
 (ii) there are no proceedings pending in any court which could have the effect of bringing the marriage to an end;
(iii) there are no children of the marriage under the age of sixteen;
(iv) neither party is seeking financial provision on divorce; and
 (v) neither party is suffering from a mental disorder.
The simplified procedure is an exception to the rule that in divorce actions the evidence from a source other than one or both of the spouses is required.

Conclusion

This chapter has primarily been an attempt to outline the substantive Scots law of divorce. In theory, the right to a divorce is restrictive but, in practice, little difficulty is experienced in obtaining the necessary grounds. The vast majority of divorces are undefended[1] and there have been few reported decisions on the legal difficulties which the grounds in the 1976 Act raise. In short, it would appear that in relation to establishing a ground of divorce, as opposed to ancillary matters such as financial provision and the residence of children, the role of the court is largely administrative. But there must still be cases where a marriage has in fact irretrievably broken down, yet divorce is not possible because a s 1(2) ground cannot be established.

It is submitted that further reform of the Scots law of divorce is desirable. We should accept that in late twentieth century society, there is and will continue to be a high rate of matrimonial breakdown.[2] The primary concerns of a modern divorce law should be to attempt to protect the children of the marriage as much as possible and to provide a fair system for the re-allocation of the family's income and capital. Accordingly there is force in the view that if the spouses are agreed on these matters, they should be able to divorce by consent provided the court approves of the settlement. If the couple are not agreed, then the court, on an application by one of the spouses, should allow the couple a period of say six months in which, with the assistance of their legal advisers, a settlement could be reached. If this is not achieved during that period, the court on the

1 Approx 90%.
2 At present, approximately one in three marriages end in divorce.

application of one of the parties should then make orders relating to parental responsibilities[1] and financial provision and grant decree, without the necessity of any grounds for divorce.[2]

In its discussion paper, *The Ground for Divorce*,[3] the Scottish Law Commission put forward a radical proposal that divorce should be obtained by the lapse of a period after notice had been given, on the lines suggested in the preceding paragraph; delayed divorce on demand. However, in its final Report[4] this proposal was abandoned. Instead, the Commission recommended that desertion be abolished as a ground of divorce and the periods of non-cohabitation for the purposes of s 1(2)(d) and (e) be reduced to one year and two years respectively.[5] It remains to be seen whether these reforms will be enacted.[6] However, it is hoped that the momentum for more radical change in the system of divorce has not been dissipated and that the merits of delayed divorce on demand come to be more generally recognised.[7]

1 On parental responsibilities, see *infra* Ch 11.
2 On steps towards a more rational system of divorce, see *Clive* p 396 ff.
3 SLC Discussion Paper No 76.
4 *Report on Reform of the Ground for Divorce* (SLC No 116).
5 Paras 1.1–1.2 respectively.
6 These reforms were dropped from the Law Reform (Miscellaneous Provisions) (Scotland) Bill 1990 for political reasons.
7 In England, reform of the law of divorce along these lines has met with considerable support – and opposition.

7 Financial provision on divorce

INTRODUCTION

A major function of contemporary family law is to provide a system of rules whereby a couple's capital and income can be redistributed in a just way when their marriage ends in divorce. Before the enactment of the Family Law (Scotland) Act 1985, Scots law left this important matter largely to the discretion of the judges.[1] The Scottish Law Commission considered the options for reform in a very full and detailed report[2] which led to the system of financial provision on divorce in the Family Law (Scotland) Act 1985.[3] Before considering this system in detail, several important issues must be discussed.

For many couples who divorce, there is little property or income to be redistributed.[4] In 1980, a capital sum was awarded in only 6% of divorces granted and a periodical allowance was awarded to an ex-wife in only 22% of divorces granted: the average capital sum was £4,500 and the average periodical allowance to an ex-wife was £18 per week. As Clive has observed,[5]

'it seems only realistic to recognize that in a large proportion of cases the law of financial provision on divorce is irrelevant to the actual financial provision of divorced people. Any hope of improving the general condition of one-parent families cannot to any material extent depend on improvements in the law of financial provision on divorce'.

---

1 The Divorce (Scotland) Act 1976, s 5(2). For a short discussion of the pre-1985 law, see the second edition of this book p 120 ff.
2 *Report on Aliment and Financial Provision* (SLC No 67).
3 References in this chapter are to the 1985 Act unless otherwise stated. For a useful commentary see Nichols *The Family Law (Scotland) Act 1985* (2nd ed 1991) and *Clive* Ch 24. The 1985 Act came into force on 1 September 1986. On the effect of the Act on the practice of solicitors, see *The Impact of the Family Law (Scotland) Act 1985 on Solicitors' Divorce Practice* Scottish Office Central Research Unit Papers (November 1990).
4 See Doig *The Nature and Scale of Aliment and Financial Provision on Divorce* (Scottish Office Central Research Unit, 1982); Manners and Rauta *Family Law in Scotland* (OPCS Social Survey Division, 1981).
5 'The financial consequences of divorce: reform from the Scottish perspective' in *State, Law and the Family* (1984, ed Freeman) p 197.

Nevertheless, where couples do have considerable assets, they are surely entitled to a rational system of redistribution of their property and income when their marriage ends in divorce.

A major difficulty in determining the criteria for financial provision on divorce is that any system must endeavour to accommodate the different kinds of marriages which end in divorce. These would include short childless marriages where both spouses work, medium range marriages where there are dependent children or long marriages where the wife has given up paid employment and has no prospect of such in the future. The Scottish Law Commission concluded that given the variety of marriages, there was no one principle which, if followed, would produce a satisfactory financial settlement in every case. For example, in a short childless marriage it is simply not fair – even if it were practicable – that a spouse should, as a result of financial provision, be placed in the same financial position he or she would have enjoyed if the marriage had not broken down. On the other hand, if a wife has given up her career in order to look after the children of the marriage and has, in effect, been an unpaid housekeeper for many years, why should she lose the expectation that her husband would maintain her in her old age, merely because the marriage has ended in divorce? Again, even after a short marriage the financial needs of a wife who is unable to earn because she is looking after dependent children may not be met merely by the equal division of the spouses' capital assets.

Accordingly, the Scottish Law Commission took the view that it was necessary to provide a set of principles or objectives which were to be achieved by a system of financial provision on divorce but which, at the same time, would allow the courts to retain a considerable degree of discretion so that orders could be made which took account of the particular circumstances of the marriage in question.

Finally, it must be stressed at the outset that the provisions of the 1985 Act are only concerned with financial provision for *spouses*. As we shall see,[1] in Scots law children have an independent right to aliment from their parents or those who have accepted them as children of their family.[2] When a marriage breaks down, the children will often live with one of their parents and not with the other. In these circumstances, the absent parent *ie* the parent with whom the child does not live, is obliged to pay maintenance assessment for the child until the child is 16.[3] In addition, there is the possibility that that

---

1 *Infra* p 174 ff.
2 Section 1(1)(c) and (d).
3 On maintenance assessment, see *infra* p 183 ff.

parent will have to pay aliment to the child. The child's claims for
maintenance assessment and/or aliment are determined *before* a court
considers financial provision for the spouses. In this way, Scots law
gives primacy to the financial needs of the children of a family when
a marriage ends in divorce.

THE NATURE OF THE ORDERS

By s 8(1) of the Family Law (Scotland) Act 1985, in a divorce
action,[1] the court[2] has the power to make one or more of the following orders by way of financial provision for the applicant.

(i)   An order for the payment of a capital sum or the transfer of property

The court has the power to make orders for the payment of a capital
sum and/or a transfer of property.[3] Such an order can be made either
at the date of divorce or within a period specified by the court.[4]
Moreover, the court can stipulate that the order is to come into effect
at a specified future date.[5] So where, for example, a couple's only
substantial asset is the matrimonial home, if this would have to be
sold to raise the finance necessary for the payment of a capital sum,
the court may delay the operation of such an order until a specified
date, for instance, when the youngest child of the family has reached
the age of 18 and the property is no longer required as a matrimonial
home.

The court can order that a capital sum be paid by instalments.[6] This
is important where a couple's assets are not in an easily realisable
form. If, for example, a wife was granted a capital sum of £20,000 but
the husband's assets were tied up in a small business, the court could
order that the £20,000 be paid in five annual instalments of £4,000. It

1 The regime on financial provision also applies in an action of declarator of nullity:
   s 17.
2 Ie the Court of Session or the sheriff court: s 27.
3 Section 8(1)(a) and (aa) as amended by para 34 of Sch 8 to, and Sch 9 to the Law
   Reform (Miscellaneous Provisions)(Scotland) Act 1990. The court can also order a
   capital sum payment in respect of lump sums due under pension schemes:
   s 8(1)(ba) as inserted by s 167(1) of the Pensions Act 1995, discussed *infra* p 131.
4 Section 12(1)(a) and (b).
5 Section 12(2). See, for example, *Little v Little* 1990 SLT 230 approved by the Inner
   House 1990 SLT 785: in this case, the major assets – the defender's interest in a
   pension fund – was not in an easily realisable form, thus justifying the court in
   delaying payment of one half the capital sum for six years.
6 Section 12(3).

will also be useful where a spouse has few capital assets but a high income. The advantages of a capital sum, payable by instalments, over periodical allowances is that the total capital sum awarded cannot be varied[1] and it will not therefore be perceived by the payer as an indefinite financial burden.

A property transfer order obliges one of the parties to transfer the ownership of his/her property to the other.[2] For example, if H and W are common owners of the matrimonial home, the court could order H to transfer his one half *pro indiviso* share of the house to W.[3] This is useful where the children of the parties are to reside with W after the divorce. A property transfer order and a capital sum payment can be made in the same action.[4]

(ii) Periodical allowances

It is an axiomatic principle of the 1985 Act that before ordering a periodical allowance, the court must be satisfied that the payment of a capital sum or a transfer of property order is inappropriate or insufficient in the circumstances.[5] Moreover, a periodical allowance can only be made if it is justified by one of the principles in s 9(1)(c),(d) or (e).[6] Thus, the whole thrust of the Act is that the 'normal' orders for financial provision should take the form of capital sum payments or transfer of property orders rather than periodical allowances. This is to encourage 'a clean break' with the consequence that the spouses

1 The date or method of payment of an order can be varied on a material change of circumstances: s 12(4).
2 By section 13 of the Matrimonial Homes (Family Protection)(Scotland) Act 1981, the court can order the transfer of a tenancy of a matrimonial home: discussed *supra* pp 91, 92.
3 H and W would both convey their one half *pro indiviso* shares to W.
4 Section 8(1)(a) and (aa) as amended by para 34 of Sch 8 to, and Sch 9 to, the Law Reform (Miscellaneous Provisions)(Scotland) Act 1990. Before the 1990 Act, doubts had been raised whether an order for both a capital sum payment and a property transfer was competent: *Walker v Walker* 1990 SLT 229; cf *Little v Little* 1990 SLT 230. The Inner House indicated that such an order was competent: *Walker v Walker* 1991 SLT 157.
5 Section 13(2). 'If a pursuer seeks an award of periodical allowance she must aver and prove that the conditions in section 13(2) are satisfied. If she does not do so, the principle of the "clean break" embodied in the 1985 Act prevents the court from considering the question of periodical allowance at all': *Mackin v Mackin* 1991 SLT (Sh Ct) 22 at 24 per the Sheriff Principal (Ireland). Where the pursuer has obtained a substantial capital sum payment and/or property transfer order, it is most unlikely that the criteria in s 13(2) will be satisfied and no periodical allowance should be made: *McConnell v McConnell* (30 November 1994, unreported) IH.
6 Ibid. The principles are discussed in detail, *infra* p 140 ff. See *Thirde v Thirde* 1987 SCLR 335. The pursuer's pleadings must refer to the principle(s) in s 9(1)(c)–(e) being relied upon.

cease to be economically dependent on each other after the divorce. It is clear therefore why the court's power to order a capital sum to be paid by instalments is so important.

Accordingly, it should only be in exceptional circumstances that orders for periodical allowances should be made. The order can be for a definite or indefinite period or until the happening of a specified event.[1] If there has been a material change of circumstances, a periodical allowance can be varied or recalled and an order for a periodical allowance can be converted into the payment of a capital sum or property transfer order.[2]

A periodical allowance ends with the death or remarriage of the payee,[3] but it continues if the payer dies, though the executor can apply to the court to recall the order.[4]

(iii)   Incidental orders

In addition to making orders for capital sums, transfers of property and periodical allowances, the court has the power to make incidental orders. These are listed in s 14. They include an order for the sale of the couple's property,[5] the valuation of their property[6] and a declarator as to the ownership of any disputed property.[7] The court can also make an order regulating the occupation of the matrimonial home and the use of its furniture and plenishings,[8] including an order regulating liability as between the parties for outgoings in respect of the home and its contents.[9] Under these provisions, the court can exclude one of the parties from the matrimonial home. While an order subsists as to the occupation of the matrimonial home and its

1 Section 13(3). See, for example, *Mitchell v Mitchell* 1993 SLT 419.
2 Section 13(4). The making of a maintenance assessment in respect of a child living with the payee is a material change of circumstances: s 13(4A) as added by s 2(4) of the Child Support (Amendments to Primary Legislation) (Scotland) Order 1993, SI 1993/660. Any variation or recall can be backdated to the date of the application or, on cause shown, to an earlier date: s 13(4)(b). On variation, the periodical allowance can be made for a definite or indefinite period or until the happening of a specified event: s 13(5) impliedly incorporating *inter alia* s 13(2). See, for example, *Kerray v Kerray* 1991 SLT 613.
3 Section 13(7)(b).
4 Section 13(7)(a) and (4).
5 Section 14(2)(a). See, for example, *Porter v Porter* 1990 SCLR 752; *Reynolds v Reynolds* 1991 SCLR 175.
6 Section 14(2)(b).
7 Section 14(2)(c).
8 Section 14(2)(d); see *Little v Little* 1989 SCLR 613, approved by the Inner House, 1990 SLT 785.
9 Section 14(2)(e).

contents, the occupant spouse retains[1] the powers of management conferred by the Matrimonial Homes (Family Protection) (Scotland) Act 1981.[2] However, the provisions of the 1981 Act protecting a spouse's occupancy rights against dealings with third parties[3] do not apply, but it has been suggested[4] that the power[5] of the court to make any expedient ancillary order coupled with its common law powers, for example, interdict, may be sufficient to stop adverse dealings.

Other incidental orders include an order that security should be given for any financial provision[6] and an order as to the date from which any interest on any amount awarded should run.[7] In *Geddes v Geddes*,[8] the Inner House of the Court of Session held that a court could order interest to run from a date *prior* to the date of decree, provided it was justified by the principles in s 9 and reasonable to do so.[9] For example, H and W separate and W lives in the matrimonial home until the divorce five years later. H is prima facie entitled to a capital payment of half the net value of the house at the date of separation, the relevant date.[10] The court can order interest on the capital sum payment to run from the relevant date rather than the date of divorce *ie* H will get the capital sum payment *plus* five years' interest on that sum. The interest represents consideration for W's exclusive use of the matrimonial home for five years. The provision is also useful where payment of a capital sum is postponed until a future date because the payer's assets are not easily realisable at the date of divorce; for example, H's pension interests or rights under a life insurance policy.[11] Here, although the capital sum payment does not have to be paid for several years, the court can order interest to be paid to W during this period thus compensating her for the deferment of the payment.[12]

Powers also exist for the payment or transfer of property to a trustee on behalf of a party to the marriage[13] and for setting aside or varying any term in an antenuptial or postnuptial marriage settlement.[14] Finally, the court can make any ancillary order which is

---

1 Section 14(5)(a).
2 Ie s 2(1), (2), (5)(a) and (9) of the 1981 Act, discussed *supra* Ch 5.
3 Discussed *supra* p 85.
4 Nichols *The Family Law (Scotland) Act 1985*, (2nd ed) para 4.28.
5 Section 14(2)(k).
6 Section 14(2)(f).
7 Section 14(2)(j).
8 1993 SLT 494.
9 On the s 9 principles, see *infra* p 126ff.
10 Discussed *infra* p 127.
11 Discussed *infra* p 130 ff.
12 *Bannon v Bannon* 1993 SLT 999.
13 Section 14(2)(g).
14 Section 14(2)(h).

expedient to give effect to the principles set out in s 9[1] or any order
made under s 8(2).[2]

Armed with this plethora of powers, the court can make orders for
financial provision which can be tailormade for the particular couple
concerned.

THE PRINCIPLES

In an application for financial provision, s 8(2) provides that the court
shall make such order, if any, as is justified by the principles set out
in s 9 and is reasonable having regard to the resources of the parties.[3]
Resources include the couple's present and foreseeable resources.[4]
Thus, the court's discretion is limited in that the order must be justified by the s 9 principles, but the discretion is still wide as, even if
justified by the principles, the order must still be reasonable in the
light of the couple's resources. This discretion can be used to reduce
an award of financial provision which is otherwise due, in the light of
both the payer's[5] and payee's[6] resources at the date of the divorce. For
example, if W is prima facie entitled to a capital sum payment of
£50,000 but H's resources have substantially declined since the couple separated, the court can reduce the capital sum to be paid because
it is not reasonable for H to pay such a large amount in the light of his
resources at the date of divorce.[7] However, this discretion cannot be
used to increase an award beyond that justified by the s 9 principles.[8]
The s 9(1) principles will now be discussed.

1 Discussed *infra*.
2 Section 14(2)(k). See *McDonald v McDonald* 1993 SCLR 132; *Murley v Murley*
   1995 SCLR 1138.
3 Section 8(2)(a) and (b).
4 So, for example, a spouse's interest in a pension fund is a resource for these purposes: *Gribb v Gribb* 1995 SCLR 1007.
5 *Buczynska v Buczynski* 1989 SLT 558 (capital sum reduced because payee (wife)
   had resources which did not constitute matrimonial property).
6 *Welsh v Welsh* 1994 SLT 828.
7 In *Wallis v Wallis* 1993 SLT 1348, there are dicta in the speeches of Lord Keith at 1351
   and Lord Jauncey at 1352 to the effect that amending legislation might be necessary
   to achieve this result: however, it is thought that s 8(2)(a) and (b) does not inhibit a
   court reducing an award in the way described above. While (a) and (b) are cumulative in the sense that an award must be justified by s 9 principles and reasonable in the
   light of the parties' resources, it does not follow that the court can make no order at
   all if the order which is prima facie justified by the s 9 principles is unreasonable in
   the light of the payer's resources: instead the court can *reduce* the award to a reasonable level. In these circumstances, it is still justified by s 9 principles. *Sed quaere*.
8 *Latter v Latter* 1990 SLT 805. Section 8(2)(a) and (b) are cumulative in this sense;
   see discussion in preceding note. If otherwise, the s 9 principles would be otiose
   and the financial provision would simply be whatever the court in its discretion
   regarded as reasonable.

Principle 9(1)(a):   The net value of the matrimonial property should be shared fairly between the parties to the marriage

The first principle is s 9(1)(a). This provides that the net value of the matrimonial property should be shared fairly between the parties to the marriage. The net value of the matrimonial property is the value of the property at the relevant date, after deduction of any outstanding debts incurred by the parties either during the marriage or before the marriage, so far as they relate to matrimonial property. So, for example, if the couple's only property is a house bought on a mortgage during the marriage, the net value of the property at the relevant date will be the value of the house after deducting the outstanding loan.[1]

The relevant date is the date on which the parties cease to cohabit as husband and wife or the date of service of the summons in the action of divorce, if they continue living together.[2] Thus, if a couple cease to cohabit in June 1995, that will be the relevant date for this purpose even although the action for divorce is not brought until several years later.[3] Because a couple are deemed not to cohabit unless they are in fact living together as husband and wife,[4] the relevant date may occur before a couple finally separate if they were not in fact living together as husband and wife, albeit residing in the same house.[5] This is important as it will follow that the net value of their matrimonial property may be much less than the value of their property at the date they finally separated.

Matrimonial property is defined[6] as *all* the property belonging to the spouses or either of them at the relevant date which was acquired by the spouses(s):

a) before the marriage for use by them as a family home or as furniture or plenishings for such a home, ie the matrimonial home and its contents; or

1 Section 10(2)(a) and (b). 'Matrimonial property' is normally limited to property acquired during the marriage. Where a property transfer order is made, the payee may obtain an interest which is more valuable than the net value of the property at the relevant date, for example, because of the increase in value of the property between the relevant date and the date of divorce: *Little v Little* 1990 SLT 785; *Wallis v Wallis* 1993 SLT 1348. To avoid this injustice, the court should not make a property transfer order unless the increase in value corresponds to the transferee's share (or part of the share) of other matrimonial property or satisfies claims under other s 9 principles.
2 Section 10(3).
3 This is subject to s 10(7) which determines the relevant date after unsuccessful attempts at reconciliation. For discussion of s 10(7) see *Clive* p 475.
4 Section 27(2).
5 *Buczynska v Buczynski* 1989 SLT 558. For full discussion of the meaning of cohabitation see *supra* p 112 ff. The statutory definition of cohabitation for the purpose of divorce is identical to that in s 27(2).
6 Section 10(4).

b) during the marriage but before the relevant date.

However the following property is excluded:

a) property acquired before marriage, with the important exception of property acquired for use as a family home and its contents;

b) property acquired by a spouse *after* the relevant date; and

c) property acquired during the marriage from a third party by way of gift or succession.

We shall now consider the definition of matrimonial property in some detail.

The only property acquired before the marriage which can constitute matrimonial property is the family home and its furniture and plenishings. In *Mitchell v Mitchell*,[1] the Inner House of the Court of Session held that a house bought before the marriage would be treated as matrimonial property only if it was acquired by the purchaser with the intention that it was to be used as a family home for the purchaser and the other partner. Consider the following examples:

a) A buys a house as a bachelor pad. If A marries B, the house is not matrimonial property even if A and B live there: A did not acquire the house with the intention that it should be a family home for A and B.[2]

b) A buys a house when he is cohabiting with B with the intention that it should be a family home for A and B. *If* A and B marry, the house is matrimonial property as it was bought before the marriage with the intention that it should be a family home for A and B. It does not matter that at the time it was acquired, A did not intend to marry B: it is enough that it was intended as a family home for A and B.[3]

c) A buys a house when he is cohabiting with B with the intention that it should be a family home for A and B. A and B separate. A marries C. The house is not matrimonial property as it was not acquired by A as a family home for A and C.

d) H buys a house during his marriage to W_1. The house is matrimonial property. H and W_1 divorce. H remains in the house. H marries W_2. The house is not matrimonial property vis-a-vis the second marriage because it was not acquired with the intention of being a family home for H and W_2.[4]

e) H buys a house during his marriage to W. The house is matrimonial property. H and W divorce. H remains in the house. H and W remarry. The house is matrimonial property because although

1 1995 SLT 426.

2 The house *would* be a matrimonial home for the purpose of the Matrimonial Homes (Family Protection)(Scotland) Act 1981: see *supra* p 78.

3 *Mitchell v Mitchell* 1995 SLT 426 at 427 per Lord Justice Clerk (Ross).

4 *Ranaldi v Ranaldi* 1994 SLT (Sh Ct) 25.

acquired before the second marrige it was bought with the intention of being used as a family home for H and W, albeit when they were parties to the first marriage.[1]

f) H buys a house during his marriage to W. The house is matrimonial property. H and W divorce. H sells the house and buys a new property. H and W remarry. The house is not matrimonial property. It was bought before the second marriage when H did not intend it to be used as a family home for H and W.[2]

All property acquired by the spouses during the marriage but before the relevant date is prima facie matrimonial property. This includes the house, furniture, motor cars, jewellery, savings and investments. It is irrelevant whether as a matter of property law the property is owned individually or in common. Thus, for example, although money, vehicles and pets are not household goods[3] and therefore are not presumed to be owned in common, they nevertheless constitute matrimonial property if acquired during the marriage. Matrimonial property includes a business owned by a spouse.[4]

However, any property acquired by way of gift *from a third party* or inheritance is excluded. Several points should be noticed. First gifts from one spouse to the other constitute matrimonial property. If H gives W a necklace or W gives H a watch, the necklace and watch are matrimonial property: the exception only applies if H or W receive a gift from a third party, for example, their parents. Second, where a gift or inheritance increases in value during the marriage, the increase in value does *not* constitute matrimonial property and is excluded.[5] However, where a gift of money or an inheritance is used by a spouse to buy property during the marriage, the property acquired is matrimonial property. For example, W inherits £200,000 in shares. She sells £100,000 worth of shares to purchase a house. The house is matrimonial property but the unsold shares are not because they remain part of her inheritance. As Lord McLean observed,[6]

1 *Mitchell v Mitchell* 1995 SLT 426.
2 Unless H bought the house with the intention to allure W to remarry him.
3 Ie for the purposes of s 25: discussed *supra* p 64 ff.
4 *Crockett v Crockett* 1992 SCLR 591; *McConnell v McConnell* (OH) 1993. Acute difficulties can arise in the valuation of such a business: see Thomson 1995 SLG 113.
5 *Whittome v Whittome (No.1)* 1994 SLT 114 at 125 per Lord Osborne, disapproving dictum of Lord Marnoch in *Latter v Latter* 1990 SLT 805.
6 *Davidson v Davidson* 1994 SLT 506 at 508. These provisions must not be construed too technically. If, for example, W's parents wish to give H and W a house as a wedding present, the fact that they give W the money to pay for the house and the missives of sale are signed by W, would not prevent the house being regarded as a gift from W's parents and therefore *not* matrimonial property: see, for example, *Latter v Latter* 1990 SLT 805.

> ". . . any property acquired by the parties during the marriage
> but before separation is matrimonial proprty even if it is pur-
> chased with funds which one of the parties has acquired by way
> of gift or succession. The funds themselves before their appli-
> cation in acquiring the property, would not, according to s 10(4)
> be matrimonial property.'

Property acquired after the relevant date but before the divorce is not
matrimonial property for the purpose of s 9(1)(a) – although it would
be a part of the spouse's resources for the application of other provisions in the 1985 Act. Nevertheless, difficulties can arise. For example, a claim for damages awarded *after* the relevant date in respect of
a delict suffered by a spouse before the relevant date, is matrimonial
property.[1] A redundancy payment paid before the relevant date is
matrimonial property but *not* if paid after the relevant date.[2] A tax
refund paid after the relevant date in respect of income earned before
the relevant date is matrimonial property.[3]

Most importantly, matrimonial property includes the portion of
any rights or interests of either spouse (a) under a life policy or similar arrangement and (b) in any benefits under a pension scheme
which either party has or may have (including such benefits payable
in respect of the death of either party), which is referable to the period
of marriage before the relevant date.[4] In practice, difficulties have
been experienced in determining the appropriate valuation of the
spouse's interest in the pension.[5] However, by s 10(8)[6] the Secretary
of State has power to make regulations prescribing how the value of
the benefits under a pension is to be calculated and verified, and to
enable information to be obtained from the trustees or managers of

---

1 *Skarpaas v Skarpaas* 1993 SLT 343. Damages paid before the relevant date in
respect of a delict before the marriage would also be matrimonial property.
Damages paid after the relevant date in respect of a delict suffered before the marriage, would not be matrimonial property: *Petrie v Petrie* 1988 SCLR 190. See also
McGuire v McGuire's CB 1991 SLT (Sh Ct) 76 (criminal injuries compensation).
2 *Tyrrell v Tyrrell* 1990 SLT 406: the court refused to treat a redundancy payment as
analogous to an interest under a life policy or pension.
3 *Macritchie v Macritchie* 1994 SLT (Sh Ct) 72.
4 Section 10(5) as amended by s 167(2)(a) of the Pensions Act 1995. It is clear that
the widow's element of a husband's pension is now to be included: cf *Welsh v
Welsh* 1994 SLT 825; *Crosbie v Crosbie* 1995 SCLR 399; *Gribb v Gribb* 1995
SCLR 839; *Dible v Dible* 1995 SLT 1361.
5 See, for example, *Brooks v Brooks* 1993 SLT 184; *Bannon v Bannon* 1993 SLT 999.
The difficulty is whether the pension should be valued on a 'continuing service'
basis or a 'leaving service' basis: see Bissett-Johnson 1993 SLT (News) 321.
6 Added by s 167(2)(b) of the Pensions Act 1995. It is thought that the regulations
will recommend valuation on a 'leaving service' basis.

the pension scheme about the value. Where a lump sum is payable under the pension scheme on the death of one of the parties, the court on making a capital sum order under s 8(1) can direct the trustees or managers to pay the whole or part of the lump sum, when it becomes due, to the other party to the marriage: this is known as a pension lump sum order.[1]

In applying principle 9(1)(a) the first task is to identify the matrimonial property which should be shared fairly between the parties. In *Little v Little*,[2] the Inner House of the Court of Session held that there was no need for the court to calculate a single value of the total matrimonial property at the relevant date: moreover, the court could leave out certain items, for example, a couple's motor cars or personal possessions, if this would have no practical result on the claim for financial provision. In addition, it was accepted that the matrimonial home could be excluded if a property transfer order was desirable in the circumstances of the case.[3] It is submitted that the approach of the Inner House runs counter to the express language of s 10(4) which refers to *all* the couple's property at the relevant date and therefore a court should still proceed to calculate the total net value of their property at that date.[4] Consider the following example.

EXAMPLE

H bought a house for £5,000 shortly before he married W. H bought it intending that it should be used as their family home. H paid a down payment of £500 and raised the rest of the price by a mortgage. Title to the house was taken in H's name. When H left W after 16 years of marriage, the house was worth £70,000 with an outstanding mortgage of £1,000.

1 Section 12A as added by s 167(3) of the Pensions Act 1995.
2 1990 SLT 785. For full discussion, see Thomson 1990 SLT (News) 313.
3 The court maintained that the court's discretion to depart from equal sharing in special circumstances under s 10(1) and (6) was wide enough to exclude certain items from being treated as matrimonial property at all. However, it is thought that the discretion only operates *after* all the couple's matrimonial property at the relevant date has been valued: see *infra* p 134 ff. But cf *Jacques v Jacques* 1995 SLT 963.
4 Nevertheless the Inner House continues to allow judges at first instance considerable latitude: 'The sheriff decided to take a broad and practical approach, without finding it necessary to do what is required by a strict reading of s 10(4) of the Act, which is to take into account all the property belonging to the parties or either of them at the relevant date which is comprised within the definition of matrimonial property ... The question whether it was necessary to value every item of property comprised in the matrimonial property and to calculate a single lump sum representing the net value of the entirety of it was a matter for the discretion of the sheriff': *Jacques v Jacques* 1995 SLT 963 per Lord President (Hope) at 965. *Sed quaere.*

During the marriage, H bought furniture, a car, and golf clubs, worth £8,000, £5,000 and £500 respectively at the time that H left W. During the marriage, W bought furs and jewellery worth £2,000 and £3,000 respectively at the time tht H left W. She also inherited a diamond ring worth £5,000, at the time that H left W.

H had contributed to an occupational pension scheme which he joined four years before he married. The acturial value of H's interest in the scheme when H left W was £60,000. He has shares which he bought before the marriage which were worth £30,000 when H left W. W's savings made from her earnings during the marriage were worth £5,000. After H left W, she won £2,500 on the lottery.

The relevant date is the date when the parties ceased to cohabit, ie when H left W.

At that date, the net value of the matrimonial property consists of the following:

(i) the matrimonial home. While the property was acquired by H *before* marriage, it was acquired for use as a family home for H and W and therefore qualifies. Its net value at the relevant date was £70,000 – £1,000 (outstanding mortgage) = £69,000.

(ii) H's furniture, car and golf clubs, ie property acquired by him during the marriage and before the relevant date = £8,000 + £4,500 + £500 = £13,000.

(iii) W's furs and jewellery, ie property acquired by her during the marriage and before the relevant date, but excluding the diamond ring which was acquired by way of succession from a third party = £2,000 + £3,000 = £5,000.

(iv) W's savings made during the marriage and before the relevant date = £5,000. But H's shares are excluded as he acquired them *before* marriage. W's lottery winnings are excluded because she acquired them *after* the relevant date.

(v) the proportion of H's interest in the occupational pension scheme which is referable to the period of marriage before the relevant date. H has been in the scheme for 20 years, 16 of which were during the marriage and before the relevant date. At the relevant date value of interest is £60,000. Therefore portion referable to period of marriage is

$$\frac{£60,000 \times 16}{20} \quad = \quad £48,000$$

Thus the total value of the matrimonial property at the relevant date is £140,000.

By s 10(1) of the Act, fair sharing is prima facie equal sharing. Accordingly, in the example, H and W are prima facie entitled to £70,000. As W has already property valued at £10,000 *viz* £5,000 furs and jewellery and £5,000 savings, H must transfer to her £60,000. In deciding whether this should be done, the court must consider whether it is reasonable to do so, in the light of the couple's resources.[1] These will include the non-matrimonial property belonging to the spouses *viz* H's shares worth £30,000 and W's diamond ring and lottery win which are worth £5,000 and £2,500 respectively, ie £7,500. In these circumstances, it is thought that it would prima facie be reasonable to order H to make a payment to W of £60,000 – to be paid in instalments if his capital is not easily realisable.

It must always be remembered that the fund that is to be shared fairly is the net value of the matrimonial property at the relevant date. Consider the following situation: H and W own the matrimonial home in common. At the relevant date the house is worth £100,000, ie H and W have a one half *pro indiviso* share of £50,000. After separation, W remains in the matrimonial home. At the time of the divorce, the house is worth £120,000. W wishes to live in the house. In these circumstances, it might be thought sensible that H transfers his one half *pro indiviso* share to W, in return for a counter-balancing capital sum payment of £60,000, ie the value of H's *pro indiviso* share of the property *at the date of divorce*. However, in *Wallis v Wallis*[2] it was held that the maximum capital sum payment which could be awarded in this situation was half the value of the house *at the relevant date,* ie £50,000 in our example. Accordingly, if a property transfer order was made, W would receive an asset worth £60,000 in return for a capital sum payment of £50,000, ie W would obtain a windfall of £10,000! This result is clearly unfortunate. To avoid the apparent injustice, the court should *not* make a property transfer order in this situation unless there are other items of matrimonial property to be shared and W's 'windfall' represents her share or part of her share in that property. If W has claims for financial provision, based on other s 9 principles, the 'windfall' could be one of the ways in which her claims could be satisfied. Alternatively, the

1 Section 8(2)(b).
2 1992 SLT 672 (IH); 1993 SLT 1348 (HL). For discussion of the Inner House decision, which was approved by the House of Lords, see Clive 1992 SLT (News) 241; Thomson 1992 SLT (News) 245.

court could order the house to be sold[1] and the proceeds divided between the couple according to common law principles.

While fair sharing is prima facie equal sharing of the net value of all the matrimonial property, s 10(1) provides that the court can depart from the principle if other proportions are justified by special circumstances. Special circumstances include those listed in s 10(6) but the provision is general.[2] Considering the special circumstances in s 10(6):

a) the terms of any agreement between the parties on the ownership or division of any of the matrimonial property.[3] The most common example of such an agreement is a joint minute tendered to the court hearing the divorce but it could, of course, be an agreement made earlier in the marriage on how the matrimonial property should be divided on divorce.[4] While a gift made by one spouse to another is matrimonial property, the couple might agree expressly or impliedly that gifts inter se should be excluded from the division of matrimonial property;

b) the source of the funds or assets used to acquire any of the matrimonial property where these funds or assets were not derived from the income or efforts of the parties during the marriage. Where, for example, a spouse buys property during the marriage from funds which were not matrimonial property, for example the proceeds of the sale of a house prior to the marriage, the court can use this provision to give the spouse an increased share of the matrimonial property purchased from these funds.[5] While property acquired from a third party as a result of gift or inheritance is excluded from the definition of matrimonial property, where a spouse uses funds acquired in this way to purchase property during the marriage, for example, a painting or a motor car, this will prima facie be matrimonial property which is subject to fair sharing. However, in these circumstances, the court has been prepared to deviate from the principle that equality is

---

1 Section 14(2)(a): *Lewis v Lewis* 1993 SCLR 33; *Jacques v Jacques* 1995 SLT 963 (incidental orders for sale of property owned in common). The injustice could also be alleviated by an award of interest on the capital sum payment being backdated to the relevant date: see *supra* p 125.

2 See, for example, *Peacock v Peacock* 1994 SLT 40. The fact that the value of the matrimonial property has changed between the relevant date and the date of divorce is not *per se* a special circumstance for deviation under s 10(1): *Wallis v Wallis* 1993 SLT 1348; *Welsh v Welsh* 1994 SLT 828.

3 Where the agreement is concerned with heritable property, it does not have to be in writing: *Little v Little* 1990 SLT 785.

4 See, for example, *Jongejon v Jongejon* 1993 SLT 181.

5 See, for example, *Jesner v Jesner* 1992 SLT 999. *Cf Jacques v Jacques* 1995 SLT 963.

fairness, to compensate the spouse concerned as the matrimonial property was not bought from funds deriving from the income or efforts of the parties during the marriage.[1]

c) any destruction, dissipation or alienation of property by either party. This provision enables the court to deviate from the principle that fair sharing is equal sharing, when a spouse has destroyed, dissipated or alienated matrimonial property before or after the relevant date. This provision is additional to the general protection in s 18 against transactions likely to defeat claims for, inter alia, financial provision on divorce.[2]

d) the nature of the matrimonial property, the use made of it (including use for business purposes or as a matrimonial home) and the extent to which it is reasonable to expect it to be realised or divided or used as security. This is probably the most important of the special circumstances which may justify deviation from the principle that fair sharing is equal sharing. If, for example, H uses the family home for business purposes, it might be unreasonable to order H to sell the property in order to realise its value to make a capital payment to W. The court could, in those circumstances, allow H to retain the property and order him to pay whatever capital sum he could afford to W to compensate her for the loss of her prima facie entitlement to half the value of the house. This capital sum need not be equivalent to half the net value of the house, ie the court could decrease W's share, but it would normally still be substantial. H could be required to raise the capital by a second mortgage or the capital sum could be paid by instalments out of his income. Similarly, while a spouse's business assets acquired during the marriage consitute matrimonial property, the court may award less than half their net value to the other spouse as, clearly, they may not be easily realisable.[3]

Where there are children of the family who need a home, the court could order that the matrimonial home be transferred outright to the spouse who is looking after the children. This will usually be the wife. In these circumstances, W's share of the rest of the matrimonial property will be reduced proportionately, even if the reduction does not fully compensate H for the loss of half the value of all the matrimonial

---

1 See, for example, *Davidson v Davidson* 1994 SLT 506.
2 Section 18 is discussed *infra* pp 148–149.
3 *Morrison v Morrison* 1989 SCLR 574; *Crockett v Crockett* 1992 SCLR 591. Alternatively the capital sum could be ordered to be paid by instalments or payment delayed until a later date, with interest to run on the capital sum from the date of divorce (or earlier).

property.[1] In *Peacock v Peacock*,[2] for example, the couple had few assets except their house, title to which was in joint names. W looked after the children and H was unemployed and unable to contribute to the children's maintenance. W had paid the mortgage instalments after H left. The Inner House of the Court of Session ordered H to transfer his one half *pro indiviso* share of the house to W in return for W's assignation to him of her interest in a small life policy. The fact that there was little matrimonial property apart from the house, which was required as a home for the children, constituted special circumstances reducing H's share of the net value of the house to nil. On the other hand, if a couple have substantial resources, so that there would be little difficulty in the spouse who looks after the children acquiring suitable alternative accommodation for the family, the court might well simply order the home to be sold and the proceeds divided equally between the spouses, provided evidence was brought that it would not be contrary to the interests of the children to do so. If a spouse seeks the transfer of the matrimonial home, the court will more readily grant the order if the other spouse will thereby be relieved of liability for payment of mortgage instalments.[3]

Where the matrimonial property is a spouse's interest in a life policy or pension fund, the asset will often not be easily realisable. Unless the payer has other substantial capital,[4] it is not reasonable to expect that spouse to make a captial sum payment of half the net value of the interest to which the payee is prima facie entitled. In these circumstances, the courts have ordered capital sum payments of less than half the value of the interest;[5] the advantage to the payee of doing so, is that the capital sum payment, though less than the amount to which the payee is prima facie entitled, is paid at the date of the divorce. Alternatively, the court may delay the payment of the capital sum until the policy or the pension matures;[6] the disadvantage to the payee of doing so is that while the payee will obtain half the value of the interest, payment of the capital sum is deferred. To compensate the payee for the deferment, the court could increase the share beyond 50%[7] or order interest to be paid on the capital sum

---

1 *Cooper v Cooper* 1989 SCLR 347 (wife obtained a property transfer of the matrimonial home even although it was the couple's major capital asset: however, the husband did not require accommodation as he was seriously ill).
2 1994 SLT 40.
3 *Cooper v Cooper* 1989 SCLR 347.
4 *Brooks v Brooks* 1993 SLT 184.
5 *Muir v Muir* 1989 SCLR 445; *Carpenter v Carpenter* 1990 SCLR 206.
6 *Gulline v Gulline* 1992 SLT (Sh Ct) 71; *Bannon v Bannon* 1993 SLT 999; *Shand v Shand* 1994 SLT 387.
7 *Bannon v Bannon* 1993 SLT 999.

from the date of divorce (or earlier) – even though the capital sum does not have to be paid until a future date.[1]

If the matrimonial property is damages, there could be deviation on the grounds that they were intended to be used to support the spouse who was the victim of the injuries.[2]

e) actual or prospective liability for any expenses of valuation or transfer of property in connection with the divorce.

In applying the principle in s 9(1)(a), prima facie the conduct of either party to the marriage shall not be taken into account.[3] Thus if a marriage has irretrievably broken down as a result of a wife's adultery or a husband's behaviour, this is irrelevant and does not affect the principle that fair sharing of matrimonial property prima facie means equal sharing. However, where a spouse's conduct has adversely affected the financial resources of the couple, for example by dissipation of assets or unreasonably refusing to find employment, the conduct will be relevant.[4] Often, of course, such conduct may well have already been taken into account by virtue of s 10(6)(c), ie deviation from equality of sharing as a result of destruction, dissipation or alienation of property.[5] The reason why, as a general rule, matrimonial misconduct will not be relevant is that the principle in s 9(1)(a) is intended to recognise that a spouse deserves a fair share of the matrimonial property as a result of his or her contribution to the marriage and that responsibility for its breakdown should not undermine that entitlement unless the spouse's conduct has adversely affected the resources of the couple which are to be divided.

Principle 9(1)(b): Fair account should be taken of any economic advantage derived from either party from contributions by the other, and of any economic disadvantage suffered by either party in the interests of the other party or of the family

This principle is intended to compensate a spouse who has either (i) made a contribution to the economic advantage of the other, for example, by putting money into the other spouse's business or working in the business as an unpaid secretary, or (ii) has suffered an economic disadvantage in the interests of the other spouse or the family, for example, by a wife giving up a well paid job to bear and look after

1 *Gulline v Gulline* 1992 SLT (Sh Ct) 71: on interest, see *supra* p 125.
2 *Petrie v Petrie* 1988 SCLR 427.
3 Section 11(7).
4 Section 11(7)(a). In *Skarpaas v Skarpaas* 1991 SLT (Sh Ct) 15, H's alcoholism was regarded as such conduct.
5 Discussed *supra* p 135.

children.[1] Where a spouse has suffered an economic disadvantage, there need not be a corresponding economic advantage to the other spouse: it is sufficient if the economic disadvantage was suffered in the interests of the other spouse or the family.[2] Economic advantage includes gains in capital, income and earning capacity and economic disadvantage is to be construed accordingly.[3] Contributions include indirect and non-financial contributions, for example, gardening or decorating the matrimonial home. A contribution made by a spouse in keeping the home and caring for the family is specifically recognised.[4] It is important to note that principle 9(1)(b) applies to economic advantages made, economic disadvantages suffered and contributions made by a party *before* the marriage took place.[5] Thus, for example, if W had worked before a couple married in order to support H when he was undergoing training for a profession, that contribution would be taken into account under s 9(1)(b) even though it was made before the parties married.

Claims under this principle are particularly difficult to quantify. By s 11(2), the court must consider whether the economic advantages or disadvantages sustained by either spouse have been balanced by the economic advantages or disadvantages sustained by the other: it is only when there is an economic imbalance in the applicant's favour that an award can be made. The onus rests on the applicant to show such an imbalance.[6] Moreover, the court will also have to determine whether or not any resulting imbalance has been or will be corrected by a sharing of the value of the matrimonial property under principle 9(1)(a) or otherwise.[7] As any awards under principle 9(1)(b) must

1 Sums of money given by rich W to poor H during the marriage have been held to be economic advantages for the purpose of this principle: *Davidson v Davidson* 1994 SLT 506.
2 Where a wife had her jewellery forcibly removed from her this was held to constitute an economic disadvantage: *Tahir v Tahir (No 2)* 1995 SLT 451.
3 Section 9(2).
4 Section 9(2).
5 Contributions *after* the relevant date are also included.
6 *Petrie v Petrie* 1988 SCLR 190: *Welsh v Welsh* 1994 SLT 828. In *Louden v Louden* 1994 SLT 381, W's economic disadvantages were not set off by the life style she enjoyed during the marriage.
7 However, an award under s 9(1)(b) is intended to be *additional* to fair sharing of matrimonial property under s 9(1)(a): therefore it is thought that an imbalance will not have been corrected unless the payee had obtained more than half the net value of the matrimonial property under s 9(1)(a). This could arise, for example, if a wife had obtained the outright transfer of the matrimonial home under s 9(1)(a): see generally *Little v Little* 1990 SLT 230: In *Louden v Louden supra*, W's share of the matrimonial property was increased to 55%.

take the form of capital sum payments or property transfer orders, in practice principles 9(1)(a) and (b) are considered together. In *Ranaldi v Ranaldi*,[1] the couple's home was not matrimonial property and therefore W was not entitled to a share of its value under principle 9(1)(a). However, during the marriage, W had taken in boarders, paid off the mortgage and enhanced the value of the property. As a result of principle 9(1)(b), she was awarded a capital sum payment of half the increase in the value of the property during the marriage. However, where items of matrimonial property have simply increased in value between the relevant date and the date of divorce, the courts have consistently refused to allow s 9(1)(b) to be used to give the applicant a share in the increase in value of the asset: this is because the increase is not a result of any economic contribution of the applicant during that period.[2]

Thus, for example, having determined that a wife should receive compensation under principle 9(1)(b) for her contributions to the family during the marriage, the court may decide that the most appropriate form it should take is an outright transfer of the matrimonial home to her, even though she would thereby receive more than half the value of the matrimonial property to which she was prima facie entitled under principle 9(1)(a). As in principle 9(1)(a), in applying principle 9(1)(b) a spouse's matrimonial misconduct is irrelevant unless it has adversely affected the financial resources of the couple.[3]

Principle 9(1)(b) was intended to recognise the economic contributions made by women who had followed the traditional child rearing and housekeeping role in marriage. The economic contribution so made and the economic disadvantages sustained in doing so, were to be compensated by an award under s 9(1)(b). However, this has not occurred in practice. There are two main reasons. First, as we have seen,[4] an applicant must show that there is an economic imbalance in her favour: unless an attempt is made realistically to assess the economic value of housekeeping and child care services, there is likely to be equilibrium given that she will usually have been alimented by

---

1 1994 SLT (Sh Ct) 25.
2 See *Carroll v Carroll* 1988 SCLR 104; *Phillip v Phillip* 1988 SCLR 427; *Muir v Muir* 1989 SCLR 445 (inflationary increase in the value of heritage); *Tyrrell v Tyrrell* 1990 SLT 406 (increase in the value of husband's interest in a pension scheme between the relevant date and the date of divorce). Nor is the increase in value a special circumstance for deviation under s 10(1): see *supra* p 134, n 2.
3 Section 11(7)(a). In *Skarpaas v Skarpaas* 1991 SLT (Sh Ct) 15, H's alcoholism was held to amount to such conduct and increase W's claim.
4 *Supra* p 138.

her husband during the marriage.[1] Secondly, since only capital sum payments and/or transfer of property orders are available under s 9(1)(b), the courts are reluctant to make an award if the husband has no capital assets. However, it is submitted that a capital sum payment is nevertheless appropriate in these circumstances – to be paid by instalments out of the husband's income. As we shall see,[2] the courts are acutely aware of the economic difficulties facing middle aged women who have followed this traditional role. Their solution has been to award periodical allowances under principle 9(1)(e). In the present writer's view, this is often a distortion of the function of the s 9(1)(e) principle. Instead, recourse should be made to principle 9(1)(b) which has been designed to compensate women in this situation. The under-utilisation of s 9(1)(b) is perhaps the most disappointing feature of the way in which the 1985 Act has been applied in practice.

Principle 9(1)(c):   Any economic burden of caring, after divorce, for a child of the marriage under the age of sixteen years should be shared fairly between the parties

Where there are dependent children of a marriage[3] which ends in divorce, there cannot usually be a clean break as in most cases it will be in the children's best interests to retain contact with both parties.[4] As we have seen,[5] maintenance assessment and/or aliment for children of the family must be determined before the court will consider claims by the parties to the marriage for financial provision on divorce. But the parent who looks after the children may suffer economic disadvantages in doing so: for example, he or she may not be able to take up full time employment or may have to hire the services of a nanny. Principle 9(1)(c) was intended to ensure that the economic burden of child care is shared fairly between the parties. In practice this meant that the parent who looked after the children received additional financial provision in recognition of the economic burden of child care. However, where maintenance assessment is paid, an element of the maintenance is to provide support for the parent who cares for the child.[6] Accordingly, there should be a reduction of claims for financial provision based on 9(1)(c).

---

1 See, for example, *Welsh v Welsh* 1994 SLT 828. In *McCormack v McCormack* 1987 GWD 9–287, the wife received a capital sum which was the equivalent of £125 a year for these services!
2 *Infra* p 144 ff.
3 Children of a marriage include children who have been accepted by the parties as a child of the family: s 27.
4 See, generally, *infra* Ch 11.
5 *Supra* p 121.
6 On maintenance assessment, see *infra* p 180 ff.

In determining financial provision under principle 9(1)(c) the court must consider a) any decree or arrangement for the aliment of the child of the marriage, b) any expenditure or loss of earning capacity caused by the need to care for the child, c) the need to provide suitable accommodation for the child, d) the age and health of the child, e) the education, financial or other circumstances of the child, f) the availability and cost of suitable child care facilities or services, g) the needs and resources of the parties, and h) all the other circumstances of the case.[1] The court may also take into account the fact that the spouse from whom financial provision is sought is supporting a person who is maintained as a dependant in his or her household, whether or not he or she owes an obligation of aliment to that dependant; for example, where a husband leaves his wife and is living with and supporting his mistress and her children.[2] If the court does so, this will reduce the resources available for financial provision under principle 9(1)(c). Moreover, a spouse's matrimonial misconduct is again irrelevant unless it has adversely affected the financial resources of the couple. This is because principle 9(1)(c) recognises that by contributing to the family by caring for the children, the claimant deserves financial provision.

Unlike orders under principles 9(1)(a) and (b), the court has the power when applying principle 9(1)(c) to make an order for a periodical allowance, provided it is satisfied that a capital sum or property transfer is inappropriate or insufficient to satisfy the requirements of s 8(2).[3] Thus where a couple have little or no capital assets so that it is not reasonable in the light of their resources to make a capital sum payment or a property transfer order, a periodical allowance may well be justified under principle 9(1)(c). If a periodical allowance is made, it could – subject to recall or variation – last until the youngest child of the marriage reaches the age of 16.[4] If, however, the couple have extensive capital assets, financial provision under principle 9(1)(c) could take the form of the payment of a capital sum or property transfer order *in addition* to any financial provision under principles 9(1)(a) or (b). Alternatively, if the capital assets were not so

---

1 Section 11(3). See, for example, *Miller v Miller* 1990 SCLR 666 (adjusted aliment for children to satisfy claim); *Davidson v Davidson* 1994 SLT 506 (used to *reduce* H's claim against rich W).
2 Section 11(6).
3 Section 13(2).
4 A periodical allowance could be competent beyond the child's 16th birthday if the pursuer had incurred a substantial economic burden until the child reached 16 but the defender's means were not sufficient to pay the appropriate periodical allowance which would compensate the pursuer by the time the child reached 16: *Monkman v Monkman* 1988 SLT (Sh Ct) 37.

extensive, principle 9(1)(c) could be used to justify, for example, the transfer of the matrimonial home to the spouse who is looking after the children even although that spouse would thereby receive more than half the value of the matrimonial property to which he or she was prima facie entitled under principle 9(1)(a).

Principle 9(1)(d):   A party who has been dependent to a substantial degree on the financial support of the other party should be awarded such financial provision as is reasonable to enable him to adjust over a period of not more than three years from the date of the decree of divorce to the loss of that support on divorce

The purpose of this principle is to provide financial support for a spouse, in practice, a wife, who has been financially dependent on her husband, to enable her to readjust to life as a single person after the divorce.[1] The financial provision can take the form of a periodical allowance provided the court is satisfied that a capital sum or property transfer is inappropriate or insufficient to satisfy the requirements of s 8(2).[2] However, the payment of any periodical allowance is restricted to a maximum period of three years. It might be thought that a three year maximum period is too short to enable a spouse to readjust to life as a single person, but the view was taken that it was not the function of the law on financial provision on divorce to act as a panacea for the general problem of high unemployment. Moreover, it should also be noticed that any financial provision awarded under principle 9(1)(d) is *additional* to any capital sum or property transfer order awarded by virtue of principles 9(1)(a) or (b) and any financial provision awarded under principle 9(1)(c), which as we have seen,[3] can last until the youngest child reaches the age of sixteen.

Before the s 9(1)(d) principle applies, the applicant must have been to a substantial degree financially dependent on the other spouse. Accordingly, where a wife has been able to find a job during the period between separation and divorce, the principle may not be triggered at all or any support awarded will not be for the maximum period of three years.[4] However, provided she has continued to receive aliment from

1 *Morrison v Morrison* 1989 SCLR 574; *Mainland v Mainland* (9 December 1991, unreported) Sh Ct; *McConnell v McConnell* (1994, unreported) Inner House (W ordered to sell land transferred to her and invest proceeds to provide an income rather than have a periodical allowance under s 9(1)(d).
2 Section 13(2).
3 *Supra*.
4 *Dever v Dever* 1988 SCLR 352 (six months' support); *Muir v Muir* 1989 SCLR 445 (one year's support); *Miller v Miller* 1990 SCLR 666 (none at all).

her husband, a wife can expect some financial provision under this
principle, even if she has obtained part-time employment.[1]

In making any order the court must have regard to a) the age,
health and earning capacity of the applicant, b) the duration and
extent of the dependence prior to divorce: thus for example, a wife,
who has been a party to a short marriage and has given up her job
only shortly before the divorce, is unlikely to receive a periodical
allowance for the maximum three years as opposed to a wife who has
been dependent for many years before the divorce,[2] c) the applicant's
intention to undertake a course of education or training, d) the needs
and resources of the parties, and e) all the other circumstances of the
case.[3] The court may also take into account the fact that the spouse
from whom financial provision is sought is supporting a person who
is maintained as a dependant in his or her household whether or not
he or she owes an obligation of aliment to that dependant.[4] Unlike
s 9(1)(a), (b) and (c) principles, matrimonial misconduct will be
taken into account not only when it has affected the couple's financial
resources, but also if it would be manifestly inequitable to leave the
conduct out of account.[5] This is because principle 9(1)(d) is based on
equitable considerations and is not a recognition of what a spouse
has earned or will earn as a result of his or her contributions to the
marriage.

Given that financial provision under principle 9(1)(d) is *additional*
to any financial provision awarded under principles 9(1)(a), (b) or
(c), it is submitted that it will be useful in helping a spouse to readjust
to being unmarried. It will be particularly valuable when the applicant intends to embark on a course of further education or retraining.
But by restricting the payment of any periodical allowances under
this principle to a maximum of three years, any order will not be perceived by the payer as an indefinite financial burden.

**Principle 9(1)(e):   A party who at the time of divorce seems likely
to suffer serious financial hardship as a result of the divorce should
be awarded such financial provision as is reasonable to relieve him
of hardship over a reasonable period**

Principle 9(1)(e) is intended to be a 'long stop' measure where adequate financial provision for a spouse cannot be achieved by

1 *Tyrrell v Tyrrell* 1990 SLT 406.
2 *Sheret v Sheret* 1990 SCLR 799 (13 weeks only as very short marriage).
3 Section 11(4).
4 Section 11(6).
5 Section 11(7)(b); *Miller v Miller supra* (argued that W had bought too large a
  house).

applying the previous four principles. It deals with the situation where, *at the time of the divorce*, the applicant is old or is seriously ill[1] and, because he or she is unable to work, will suffer serious financial hardship. The principle does not apply if the spouse is overtaken by illness or other misfortune *after* the date of divorce: that is not the concern of a previous spouse.

Again financial provision can take the form of a periodical allowance provided the court is satisfied that a capital sum or property transfer is inappropriate or insufficient to satisfy the requirements of s 8(2).[2] In making any order, the court must have regard to a) the age, health and earning capacity of the applicant, b) the duration of the marriage, c) the standard of living of the parties during the marriage, d) the needs and resources of the parties, and e) all the other circumstances of the case.[3] The court may also take into account the fact that the spouse from whom financial provision is sought is supporting a person who is maintained as a dependant in his or her household, whether or not he or she owes an obligation of aliment to that dependant.[4] Moreover, matrimonial misconduct will be taken into account not only when it has affected the couple's financial resources but also when it would be manifestly inequitable to leave the conduct out of account.[5] This is because principle 9(1)(e) is clearly based on equitable considerations and accordingly an applicant's responsibility for the breakup of the marriage should be a relevant consideration. Nevertheless, it should be stressed that conduct will only be relevant when it would be *manifestly* inequitable to ignore it.

Recourse to the s 9(1)(e) principle should be rare. For example, if there has been a long marriage during which a wife has given up employment to look after her family, then, even if at the date of the divorce she is too old to enter the labour market, the s 9(1)(e) principle should not be applicable. For, in the circumstances of this type of marriage, the wife should have obtained substantial financial provision under principles 9(1)(a) and (b), particularly when it is remembered that matrimonial property includes the husband's interests under any life policies or occupational pension scheme.[6] Nevertheless, the courts have made awards of periodical allowance to

1 *Johnstone v Johnstone* 1990 SCLR 358.
2 Section 13(2).
3 Section 11(5).
4 Section 11(6).
5 Section 11(7).
6 Discussed *supra* p 130.

middle aged women who had already received generous capital settlements.[1] They had not, however, received an award under principle 9(1)(b) in recognition of their economic contributions in respect of caring for the children and running the household during a long marriage. The courts were concerned about their ability to survive comfortably without an income and therefore made an award of periodical allowance under s 9(1)(e). With respect, this is to distort the scope of s 9(1)(e) as the women were not in *serious* financial hardship since they had received substantial capital settlements. The proper course in these cases was to make an award under s 9(1)(b).

Moreover, since the serious financial hardship must arise *from the divorce* where a couple have very limited resources, principle 9(1)(e) should be inapplicable as any periodical allowance awarded thereunder simply reduces the amount of income support and other benefits to which the payee would otherwise be entitled as a divorced person.[2] On occasions, however, the courts have distorted the scope of s 9(1)(e) by awarding a periodical allowance in these circumstances. In *Stott v Stott*,[3] for example, the husband had a very low income and no capital assets. If there had been no divorce, any award of aliment for the wife would have been no greater than the income support and other benefits she would receive if she did divorce. Nevertheless the court awarded her a periodical allowance. In the present writer's view, s 9(1)(e) was inapplicable because her financial situation was the same whether or not she remained married and therefore no financial hardship arose from *the divorce*. The solution was to have recognised the wife's economic contribution in running the home and looking after the children by making an award of a capital sum under s 9(1)(b), payable by instalments over a long period.[4] The fact that matrimonial misconduct is generally irrelevant further restricts the scope of the principle.

1 *Bell v Bell* 1988 SCLR 457; *Humphrey v Humphrey* (25 May 1988, unreported). Cf approach of the Inner House in *McConnell v McConnell* (1994, unreported).
2 *Barclay v Barclay* 1991 SCLR 205: s 9(1)(e) not triggered where W was victim of multiple sclerosis and in hospital. Marriage was short and W was young. H living with cohabitee and child. Effect of stopping aliment to W would deprive her of only 5% of her total income. Therefore not *serious* hardship.
3 1987 GWD 17–645.
4 On the use of s 9(1)(b) in these circumstances, see discussion *supra* p 137 ff. In *Stott*, the sheriff awarded a periodical allowance under s 9(1)(d) to be followed after three years by a periodical allowance under s 9(1)(e). It is submitted that the order under s 9(1)(d) should not have been made; its purpose is to enable the payee to adjust to the loss of the payer's financial support: by awarding a periodical allowance under s 9(1)(e) to take effect three years later, the payer's financial support continues! In other words principles s 9(1)(d) and (e) are mutually exclusive. On principle s 9(1)(d), see *supra* p 142 ff.

Thus it should only be in very exceptional circumstances that principle 9(1)(e) will be relevant. For example, if there has been a short marriage and the couple have few capital assets but H has a reasonable income, the s 9(1)(e) principle might apply if W was seriously physically handicapped at the time of the divorce, provided her conduct was not responsible for the break-up of the marriage.[1] If a periodical allowance was ordered under this principle, while subject to recall or variation, it is not limited to any maximum period and can continue until the payee remarries or dies.[2] The fact that it gives rise to a potentially life long financial burden for the payer is another reason why principle 9(1)(e) should only be applicable in the most exceptional circumstances.

Conclusion

The s 9 principles provide sophisticated guidelines which judges must use when exercising their discretion in making orders for financial provision on divorce. Principles 9(1)(a) and (b) give recognition, through the payment of capital sums and property transfer orders, of the economic and other contributions made by the spouses to the marriage and provide compensation for any economic disadvantages suffered by a spouse in the interests of the family. As such, Clive has suggested[3] that they constitute a major step towards a system of deferred community of property and, in effect, perceive marriage as basically an equal partnership between the spouses. It is therefore to be regretted that more use has not been made of s 9(1)(b). At the same time, principle 9(1)(c) recognises the need to provide financial provision for a spouse who suffers an economic burden as a result of continued involvement in caring for any child of the marriage after the divorce[4] and principle 9(1)(d) is designed to help a spouse to readjust to life as a single person – though in this case a periodical allowance is restricted to a maximum period of three years. The final principle is a 'long stop' for very exceptional cases where at the time of the divorce serious economic hardship is likely to arise as a result of the divorce. Because of the under-utilisation of s 9(1)(b), it is submitted that too great a reliance has been made of s 9(1)(e), thus undermining the economic 'clean break' between the parties which was one of the

---

1 But even then it is doubtful if H has a low income: *Barclay v Barclay* 1991 SCLR 205. Loss of a wealthy wife has been held to be serious financial hardship for her destitute husband! See *Davidson v Davidson* 1994 SLT 506.
2 Section 13(7)(b); *Johnstone v Johnstone* 1990 SCLR 358.
3 *The financial consequences of divorce: reform from the Scottish perspective*, in *State, Law and The Family* (1984, ed Freeman) p 204.
4 But maintenance assessment has overtaken the issue by providing an element of financial support for the parent who cares for the child: see *infra* p 185.

major aims of the 1985 Act. Finally, matrimonial misconduct, unless it has adversely affected the couple's financial resources, is irrelevant, except in relation to principles 9(1)(d) and (e), where it should only be taken into account in so far as it would be manifestly inequitable *not* to do so.[1] This is, of course, consistent with a non-fault system of divorce.[2]

AGREEMENTS FOR FINANCIAL PROVISION

It was a cardinal principle of the pre-1985 law that a spouse could validly discharge his or her right to apply for financial provision on divorce.[3] Accordingly, spouses could agree for themselves the appropriate redistribution of their property and thus achieve an economic 'clean break' on divorce. The problem was, however, that because of the uncertainty on what financial provision a court was likely to order if the case was litigated, lawyers had difficulty in advising their clients on what in the circumstances of the marriage constituted a fair settlement. The introduction of the s 9 principles gives greater certainty as to the outcome of litigation and accordingly it is hoped that lawyers will now be in a better position to negotiate financial settlements on behalf of their clients.

Prior to the 1985 Act, an agreement on the financial provision to be made on divorce could not be set aside unless there was evidence of a vitiating factor such as error, fraud, undue influence or misrepresentation. Accordingly, it was and is important for the parties to be separately advised. Section 16 of the 1985 Act, however, gives the courts limited additional powers to set aside or vary agreements on financial provision to be made on divorce. First, any term in an agreement relating to the payment of a periodical allowance may be varied or set aside provided there is an express term in the agreement to this effect.[4] This can be done at any time after the divorce has been granted.[5] Second, any term relating to a periodical allowance can be

1 It is also significant that periodical allowances are most likely to be awarded under these principles.
2 On the operation of the Act in practice, see *The Impact of the Family Law (Scotland) Act 1985 on Solicitors' Divorce Practice* Scottish Office Central Research Unit Papers (November 1990).
3 *Dunbar v Dunbar* 1977 SLT 169; *Thomson v Thomson* 1982 SLT 521; *Elder v Elder* 1985 SLT 471.
4 Section 16(1)(a); *Mills v Mills* 1989 SCLR 213. It does not matter if the agreement refers – wrongly – to alimentary payments rather than periodical allowances: *Drummond v Drummond* 1995 SCLR 428.
5 Section 16(2)(a); *Mills v Mills* 1989 SCLR 213.

varied or set aside if the payer has become bankrupt or a child maintenance assessment has been made.[1] This can be done on, or at any
time after, granting decree of divorce. Third, on granting decree on
divorce,[2] the court may set aside or vary any agreement or any term
of such an agreement that was not 'fair and reasonable' at the time
when the agreement was made.[3] Thus, while the courts now have
power 'to police' such agreements to ensure that they were fair and
reasonable *at the time they were made*, because the power can only be
exercised when granting decree of divorce,[4] the aim of achieving an
economic 'clean break' between the parties after the divorce will not
be frustrated. It is thought that while this power was desirable for the
additional protection of parties to such agreements, its limited nature
will ensure that it does not operate to discourage spouses from self-
regulation of their financial arrangements on divorce.

PROCEDURAL MATTERS

By s 18 a spouse who has made a claim for an order for financial provision[5] may, not later than a year from the date of disposal of the
claim, apply to the court for an order setting aside or varying any
transfer of, or transaction involving, property which was effected by
the other party to the marriage not more than five years before the
date of making the claim.[6] The court will make such an order if satis-

---

1 Section 16(3) as amended by s 2(5) of the Child Support (Amendments to Primary
  Legislation) (Scotland) Order 1993, SI 1993/660.
2 Section 16(2)(b): the court may also exercise its power within such period as the
  court may specify on granting decree. While the court cannot set aside the agreement until in a position to grant decree of divorce, this does not prevent the court
  having a preliminary hearing to determine whether or not the agreement is fair:
  Gillan v Gillan (No 2) 1994 SLT 984.
3 Section 16(1)(b). The onus lies on the pursuer to prove that the agreement is not fair
  and reasonable. It is an objective test. The agreement is considered from the point
  of view of both parties. The quality of legal advice is important: *Gillon v Gillon (No
  1)* 1994 SLT 978. But the fact that the same solicitor advised both parties is not per
  se sufficient to render an agreement unfair: *Worth v Worth* 1994 SLT (Sh Ct) 54.
  The courts are reluctant to overturn agreements validly entered into by the parties.
  It is not enough that a spouse has been overgenerous and then changes his/her
  mind: *Anderson v Anderson* 1991 SLT (Sh Ct) 11. Nor does the fact that the assets
  are unevenly distributed per se give rise to an inference of unreasonableness or
  unfairness: *Gillon v Gillon (No 3)* 1995 SLT 678.
4 Or within a period specified by the court when granting decree.
5 The section also applies to an action for aliment, or variation or recall of a decree
  of aliment or order for financial provision.
6 The court has also the power to interdict the party from entering into such a transfer or transaction.

fied by the challenger that the transaction had, or was likely to have, the effect of defeating, in whole or in part, the applicant's claim for financial provision. This is an objective criterion: there is no need to establish whether the transfer was intended by the transferor to defeat the applicant's claim. Transactions will cover not only dispositions or settlements of property but also gifts of money and other moveables. An order under s 18 does not prejudice the rights of a third party in or to the property, where the third party has acquired the property or any rights therein in good faith and for value or has derived title to such property or rights from any person who has done so. Thus, for example, if three years before W's claim for financial provision H transferred £20,000 to his mistress, M, the court could set aside the transfer unless M was in good faith and had given value in respect of the money, eg sold H a painting worth £20,000.[1]

Finally, in an action for financial provision,[2] the court can order either party to provide details of his or her resources.[3] It should also be remembered that before the determination of a divorce action or an action of declarator of nullity, the court has the power to make an award of interim aliment to a party to the action.[4] Only periodical payments can be awarded which are payable until the date of the disposal of the action[5] when, of course, the court will make orders for financial provision.

---

1 Warrants for inhibition or arrestment on the dependence are also possible, on cause shown, in respect of any property which could be relevant in a claim for financial provision or aliment: s 19.
2 Or actions for aliment or interim aliment.
3 Section 20. *George v George* 1991 SLT (Sh Ct) 8; *Berry v Berry* 1991 SLT 42. Section 20 does not empower the court to order the defender to provide documents to vouch for the value of certain property nor written assurances that there are no further assets: *Nelson v Nelson* 1993 SCLR 149.
4 Section 6. Interim aliment can also be awarded in actions for aliment.
5 Section 6(3).

8   Parents and children

INTRODUCTION

In the law of Scotland, children have passive capacity in the sense that they enjoy a plethora of legal rights. But, as we shall see,[1] they lack active capacity in that they are unable to enforce these rights during their childhood. This must be done on their behalf by an adult, who will usually be a parent. In family law, children's most important rights are those which are exigible against their natural parents. The primary purpose of this chapter is to discuss how parentage is established. Before doing so, however, it is proposed by way of introduction to consider when a child first obtains legal rights.

Once a child is conceived, Scottish criminal law provides protection for the foetus by prohibiting the inducement of an abortion.[2] However, as a result of s 1(1) of the Abortion Act 1967,[3] a person will not be guilty of an offence if a pregnancy is terminated by a registered medical practitioner, provided two doctors in good faith are of the opinion –
(1) that the pregnancy has not exceeded its twenty-fourth week and that its continuance would involve risk, greater than if it were terminated, of injury to the physical or mental health of the pregnant woman or any existing children of her family; or
(2) that the termination is necessary to prevent grave permanent injury to her physical or mental health; or
(3) that the continuance of the pregnancy would involve risk to her life, greater than if the pregnancy were terminated; or
(4) that there is a substantial risk that if the child were born it would suffer from such physical or mental abnormalities as to be seriously handicapped.
Where an abortion is sought in the first trimester, ie during the first three months of the pregnancy, the termination will involve a risk to the mother's health which is considerably less than the risks involved

---

1 *Supra* Ch 9.
2 See generally Gordon *Criminal Law* (2nd edn, 1978) Ch 28; Norrie 1985 Crim LR 475.
3 As amended by s 34(1) of the Human Fertilisation and Embryology Act 1990.

in childbirth: accordingly, it is not too difficult to establish ground (1) for a lawful termination in these circumstances.

As in all cases of medical treatment, the patient, ie the woman, must consent. However, where the grounds for a lawful termination under s 1(1) are established, the consent of the father is not required nor can he obtain an interdict to prevent the pregnancy being terminated.[1]

While ground (1) cannot be used after the twenty-fourth week of the pregnancy, there is no time limit in relation to the other grounds. A later abortion may be necessary, for example, if there has been a delay in establishing that the foetus is abnormal for the purposes of ground (4). While not illegal per se, late termination, ie beyond 24 weeks, is not common in Scotland.[2]

While the Congenital Disabilities (Civil Liability) Act 1976 does not apply in Scotland, it is thought an action in delict will lie when a child is born physically or mentally handicapped as a result of injuries sustained in the womb.[3] No action in delict will lie unless the child is born alive; for it is only when the child is born that the child sustains damage and the delict is completed[4] – albeit that the injuries occurred while the child was a foetus. While there is no authority directly in point it is submitted that, in theory at least, an action would lie even where the injuries were caused as a result of the mother's negligence.[5] To this extent, the Scottish common law position is wider than the provisions of the 1976 Act.[6] A child's right to the physical integrity of its person therefore extends to injuries suffered before he or she was born. This conclusion is consistent with the *nasciturus* principle, *viz* that, in matters of private law, a child who is *in utero* should be deemed to be already born when this would operate for the child's benefit.[7] The principle has, for example, been used when a posthumous child has not received provision in his father's will: after birth, the will may be challenged on the child's behalf as a

1 *Paton v Trustees of BPAS* [1978] 2 All ER 1987, [1979] 2 QB 276; noted by Kennedy (1979) 42 MLR 324; *Paton v UK* [1980] 3 EHRR 408; *C v S* [1988] QB 135.
2 Before the amendments made by the Human Fertilisation and Embryology Act 1990 there was no time limit for termination in Scotland.
3 See *Liability for Antenatal Injury* (SLC No 30).
4 *Hamilton v Fife Health Board* 1993 SLT 624. For discussion see Thomson *Delictual Liability* (1994) p 196.
5 It has long been accepted that actions in delict are competent between parent and child for injuries sustained after the child's birth: *Young v Rankin* 1934 SC 499; *Wood v Wood* 1935 SLT 431.
6 Section 1(1) excludes the child's mother unless the injury to her foetus was the result of the mother's negligent driving: s 2.
7 See TB Smith *A Short Commentary on the Law of Scotland* (1962) p 246.

result of the presumption that the testator would not wish his will to be given effect in the altered circumstances – the *conditio si testator sine liberis decesserit*. A successful challenge revokes the will completely.[1]

In spite of these developments, in general a child only obtains the passive capacity to enjoy rights when he or she is born alive and has acquired an existence separate from his or her mother.[2]

ESTABLISHING PARENTAGE

In the context of family law, the rights which a child enjoys are those which are prima facie exigible against the child's natural parents. It is therefore important to have rules which establish parentage.

At one time there was little difficulty in determining who was a child's mother: she was the woman who gave birth to the child. Recent advances in reproductive techniques do, however, raise difficulties. If, for example, an ovum is donated, then fertilised and the resulting embryo transferred to the donee's womb, is she to be regarded as the child's mother, although genetically unrelated to the child? It was the present writer's view that a woman's act in carrying a foetus from implantation to full term should be the criterion of motherhood, rather than genetic relationship. This principle has now been enacted in s 27(1) of the Human Fertilisation and Embryology Act 1990 which provides that, 'The woman who is carrying or has carried a child as a result of the placing in her of an embryo or of sperm and eggs, and no other woman, is to be treated as the mother of the child'.

On the other hand, a child's father is determined solely by biological criteria: he is the man whose semen fertilised the ovum, leading to the birth of the child. In other words, he must be genetically related to the child. The difficulty, of course, is that more than one man may have had intercourse with the mother at the probable date of conception. The law therefore proceeds on the basis of a series of presumptions which can be rebutted by evidence to the contrary.

By s 5(1)(a) of the Law Reform (Parent and Child)(Scotland) Act 1986[3] a man is presumed to be the father of a child if he was married to the mother of the child at any time during the period beginning with the conception and ending with the birth of the child. Thus the presumption applies when –

---

1 See, for example, *Elder's Trustees v Elder* (1894) 21 R 704, (1895) 22 R 505.
2 For a stimulating discussion of antenatal issues, see *Wilkinson and Norrie* Ch 3.
3 In this chapter, references are to the Law Reform (Parent and Child)(Scotland) Act 1986 unless otherwise stated.

a) H and W were married both at the date of conception and birth;

b) H and W were married at the date of conception but not at the date of the birth: for example, if H had died before the child's birth – a posthumous child, or the couple had divorced before the child's birth;

c) H and W were not married at the date of conception but were married at the date of the birth;[1]

d) H and W were not married at the date of conception, were married during the pregnancy but were not married at the date of birth.[2]

The presumption does not apply where a child was conceived and born before H and W married.[3] The s 5(1)(a) presumption applies in the case of a void, voidable or irregular marriage in the same way as it applies in the case of a valid and regular marriage.[4]

However, even if s 5(1)(a) does not apply, a man will be presumed to be the father of a child, if *both* he and the mother of the child have acknowledged that he is the father and the child has been registered as such.[5] Thus, for example, a child of cohabitees will be presumed to be the child of the male cohabitee if he and the mother have acknowledged that he is the father and the child is registered as such.[6] The presumptions in s 5 may be rebutted by proof, on a balance of probabilities,[7] that the man was not the father of the child.

An interesting problem arises in relation to a child who is born as a result of artificial insemination from a donor (AID). If a married woman conceives as a result of AID, prima facie s 5(1)(a) will apply and her husband will be presumed to be the father of the

1 Cf the position at common law in *Gardner v Gardner* (1876) 3 R 695, (1877) 4 R (HL) 56.
2 For example, if H was a soldier who married W when she was pregnant but was killed before the baby was born.
3 This was also the position at common law: *Imre v Mitchell* 1958 SC 439; *James v McLennan* 1971 SLT 162.
4 Section 5(2). A difficulty arises if W marries H_1 and later goes through a ceremony of marriage with H_2. If W has a child, both H_1 and H_2 have the benefit of the s 5(1)(a) presumption as the presumption applies both to her valid marriage with H1 and her void 'marriage' with H_2. In these circumstances it is submitted that the statutory presumptions cancel each other and H_1 and H_2 must attempt to establish paternity by evidence. It is irrelevant that the parties to the void marriage were not in good faith: ie knew it was void. Cf s 3(2)(a) and (b) of the Children (Scotland) Act 1995, discussed *infra* p 197.
5 Section 5(1)(b) and para 8 of Sch 1 to the Act.
6 Cf the position at common law where no presumption applied from cohabitation: *A v G* 1984 SLT (Sh Ct) 65.
7 Section 5(4). At common law, the presumption *pater est quem nuptiae demonstrant*, ie the father is the man to whom the marriage points, applied when H was married to W at the date of conception. It was a presumption which could only be rebutted by evidence which established beyond reasonable doubt that H did not have access to W at the probable date of conception: see *S v S* 1977 SLT (Notes) 65.

child. However, as the husband is not the genetic father, the presumption could easily be rebutted. It is now provided, however, that unless the husband has not consented to the AID, he is to be treated in law as the father of the child and the donor is not to be treated as the child's father.[1] A marriage for this purpose includes a void marriage if either or both parties reasonably believed that the marriage was valid.[2]

Where the presumptions apply, the presumptive father – or the mother if she alleges her husband is not the father – can seek a declarator of non-parentage in the Court of Session or the sheriff court. Where the presumptions do not apply, a declarator of parentage may be sought in the Court of Session or the sheriff court.[3] Thus, if a woman has a child, she can seek declarator that a particular man is the father of her child.[4] Conversely, a man can seek declarator that he is the father of a woman's child. If declarator of non-parentage is granted, the presumptions in s 5 are displaced: if declarator of parentage is granted, it will give rise to a presumption to the same effect as the decree.[5]

The court shall not grant decree of declarator unless it is satisfied that the grounds of action have been established by sufficient evidence.[6] Thus, in an action of declarator of parentage, the pursuer – who will usually be the mother of the child – must establish, by evidence, that on the balance of probabilities the alleged man is the father of the child. Corroborated evidence is no longer required.[7]

---

1 Sections 28(2),(4) and 29 of the Human Fertilisation and Embryology Act 1990. A similar rule applies when AID is provided in the course of joint treatment of a couple and s 28(2) is inapplicable: s 28(3) and (4).

2 Section 28(7). There is a rebuttable presumption that one of the parties reasonably believed the marriage was valid: ibid.

3 The Court of Session has jurisdiction if the child was born in Scotland or the alleged or presumed parent or the child (a) is domiciled in Scotland on the date when the action is brought, or (b) was habitually resident in Scotland for not less than one year on the date when the action is brought, or (c) died before that date and either (i) was at the date of death domiciled in Scotland or (ii) had been habitually resident in Scotland for not less than one year immediately preceding the date of death; the sheriff court has jurisdiction if (a) the child was born in the sheriffdom or (b) an action could have been brought in the Court of Session and the alleged or presumed parent or the child was habitually resident in the sheriffdom on the date when the action was brought or on the date of death: ss 7(2) and (3).

4 The action of affiliation is probably no longer competent: *Canlon v O'Dowd* 1987 SCLR 771.

5 Section 5(3).

6 Section 8(1) of the Civil Evidence (Scotland) Act 1988.

7 Section 1(1) of the Civil Evidence (Scotland) Act 1988. The doctrine of corroboration by false denial has also been abolished: s 1(2).

Similarly, if a man seeks a declarator of parentage, he must establish, by evidence, that on the balance of probabilities, he is the father of the child.[1] Finally, in an action of declarator of non-parentage, it must be established, by evidence, that on the balance of probabilities the s 5 presumptions of paternity have been rebutted, by, for example, evidence of non-access by the husband to his wife at the probable date of conception. In this context it should be noted that courts have recognised the possibility of abnormal gestation periods.[2]

BLOOD TESTS AND DNA 'FINGERPRINTING'

In actions of declarator of parentage or non-parentage, blood test evidence can be of immense importance. These have become extremely sophisticated and highly accurate. By taking blood samples from a child, the mother and the alleged or presumptive father, it is possible to establish that because of his blood group the man could not be the father of the child: ie blood tests can lead to an exclusionary result. However, if a non-exclusionary result was obtained. the blood tests merely establish that any man within that blood group *could* be the child's father; blood tests cannot establish that a man genetically is the child's father. To some extent, the utility of blood test evidence has now been overtaken by developments in relation to DNA 'fingerprinting'. By taking samples of bodily fluid or tissue from the child, the mother and the alleged or presumptive father, it is possible by DNA profiling to establish positively whether or not the man is the child's father, ie an inclusionary result can be obtained.

The value of blood tests and DNA profiling evidence is obvious in determining issues of paternity. Nevertheless, at first the Scottish courts were sceptical of blood test evidence because of the possibility of inaccuracies. More recently, however, they have recognised the advances which have been made in serology and the increased

---

1 See, for example, *Docherty v McGlynn* 1985 SLT 237; *Campbell v Grossart* 1988 GWD 24–1004.
2 See, for example, *Currie v Currie* 1950 SC 10. (W gave birth 336 days after the couple last cohabited: held not to be an impossible period of pregnancy): cf *Preston-Jones v Preston-Jones* [1951] 1 All ER 124, [1951] AC 391, HL (alleged pregnancy of 360 days).

evidential importance of blood tests.[1] But the law on the subject was uncertain[2] and has now been put on a statutory basis.

The first problem is to consider who has the power to consent to samples of blood, bodily fluid or tissue being taken from a child. In civil proceedings relating to the determination of parentage, where such a sample is sought from a child below the age of 16 by a party to the proceedings or a *curator ad litem,*[3] any person having parental responsibilities may consent.[4] If a medical practitioner takes the view that a child under 16 understands the nature and purpose of the tests, the child has capacity to consent.[5] Where such a sample is sought from a person, for example, a baby, who is incapable of giving consent, the court has power to consent to the taking of a sample where (a) there is no person who is entitled to give such consent, for example, if the child is an orphan, or (b) there is such a person but it is not reasonably practicable to obtain his or her consent, for example, if the child's parents are abroad, or a parent is unwilling to accept the responsibility of giving or withholding consent.[6]

A particular difficulty arises if the person with parental responsibilities is the child's presumptive father. Consider the following example. H and W are married at the date of the child's conception and birth: s 5(1) will operate so that H will be presumed to be the child's father and consequently will have parental reponsibilities.[7] If H subsequently brings an action of declarator of non-parentage, can

1 Contrast the attitude of the court in *Imre v Mitchell* 1958 SC 439 and *Sproat v McGibney* 1968 SLT 33 with *S v S* [1970] 3 All ER 107, [1972] AC 24, HL; *Allardyce v Johnstone* 1979 SLT (Sh Ct) 54 and *Docherty v McGlynn* 1983 SLT 645, 1985 SLT 237.

2 See *Torrie v Turner* 1990 SLT 718 where the Inner House held that a court has no power to make a direction that a person should give a sample for the purposes of DNA screening though this could lead to a positive result of paternity. See generally, *Report on Evidence: Blood Group Tests DNA Tests and Related Matters (*SLC No 120). The Law Commission's recommendations in Part III of the Report were enacted by s 70 of the Law Reform (Miscellaneous Provisions) (Scotland) Act 1990, discussed *infra.*

3 A *curator ad litem* is a person appointed by the court to protect the interests of the child in the proceedings.

4 Section 6(1) and (2) as amended by s 70(3) of the Law Reform (Miscellaneous Provisions)(Scotland) Act 1990, para 42 of Sch 1 to the Age of Legal Capacity (Scotland) Act 1991, and para 38(3) of Sch 4 to the Children (Scotland) Act 1995. On parental responsibilities, see *infra* Ch 10.

5 Age of Legal Capacity (Scotland) Act 1991, s 2(4), discussed *infra* p 167 ff.

6 Section 6(3) as amended by s 70(3) of the Law Reform (Miscellaneous Provisions)(Scotland) Act 1990: it should be noted that s 6(3) applies to any person – not necessarily a child – who is incapable of consent, for example, a person suffering from mental illness.

7 Section 3(1)(b) of the Children (Scotland) Act 1995, discussed *infra* p 196.

he consent to samples being taken from the child when the purpose of so doing is to rebut the s 5 presumption by establishing on the balance of probabilities that he is not the father? While *Docherty v McGlynn*[1] is authority that a presumptive father may consent to samples being taken from a child, it is important to note that in this case he wished to do so to establish that he was in fact the child's genetic father. But could he rely on the presumption if his purpose was to deny that he was in fact the child's genetic father? In spite of dicta in *Docherty v McGlynn*[2] that he cannot do so, it is submitted that he can. Until the s 5 presumption is rebutted, H is the child's presumptive father and can act as the child's legal representative:[3] it is in that capacity that he has the power to consent to the blood or DNA test on the child. Even if his purpose is to establish that he is not the child's genetic father, this does not undermine the legality of his consent to samples being taken from the child, which was given in his capacity as the child's legal representative. As we shall see,[4] the court may refuse to admit the evidence so obtained if it would be against the child's interests to do so.

The second problem is that it is a cardinal principle of Scots law that in civil proceedings the courts will not make an order to compel a person to submit to a blood or DNA test against his or her will.[5] Similarly, the court will not make an order to compel a person with parental responsibilities to consent to samples of blood, bodily fluid or tissue being taken from the child.[6] Moreover, it would appear that at common law the court could not make a direction that a sample should be given and then draw adverse inferences if a sample was refused.[7]

Section 70(1) of the Law Reform (Miscellaneous Provisions) (Scotland) Act 1990 now provides that in civil proceedings the court[8] may request a party to the proceedings[9] to provide a sample of blood,

---

1 1983 SLT 645.
2 Ibid at 746 per Lord President (Emslie) approving *Whitehall v Whitehall* 1958 SC 252 and dicta in *Imre v Mitchell* 1958 SC 439.
3 Sections 3(1)(b) and 2(1)(d) of the Children (Scotland) Act 1995, discussed *infra* Ch 10.
4 *Infra*.
5 *Whitehall v Whitehall* 1958 SC 252; *Torrie v Turner* 1990 SLT 718.
6 *Docherty v Glynn* 1983 SLT 645; *Torrie v Turner supra*.
7 *Torrie v Turner* 1990 SLT 718; cf the approach of Lord Cameron in *Docherty v McGlynn* 1983 SLT 645 at 650.
8 Ie the Court of Session or the sheriff court: s 70(4). The court may make the request *ex proprio motu*: cf s 6(1).
9 A child's grandmother who defended an action of declarator of parentage in the capacity of executrix to her deceased son, the alleged father, has been held to be a party to the proceedings for this purpose: *MacKay v MacKay* 1995 SLT (Sh Ct) 30.

bodily fluid or tissue or consent to such a sample being taken from a child in relation to whom the party has power to give consent. This provision still does not give the court the power to *compel* a person to give such a sample or consent to such a sample being taken from a child. However, if the person refuses or fails to provide such a sample being taken from a child, the court may draw such adverse inference as seems appropriate.[1] In *Smith v Greenhill*,[2] it was held that the court has discretion (i) whether or not to draw an adverse inference at all, and (ii) if it decides to do so, the nature of the inference. In this case, the pursuer sought a declarator of parentage claiming to be the father of W's child. H had also had sexual intercourse with W at the probable date of conception. H refused to consent to samples being taken from the child. It was held that any adverse inference to be drawn from H's refusal was not per se enough to rebut the presumption that H was the father of the child.

Where a person has died, the Scottish courts are prepared to admit hospital records containing the blood group of the deceased, where the deceased's blood group is necessary to determine a child's paternity by the use of blood tests.[3]

Finally, in *Docherty v McGlynn*,[4] the Inner House of the Court of Session held that in the exercise of its inherent protective jurisdiction in relation to children, the court could intervene and refuse to admit such evidence if it was not in the child's interests to do so. Moreover, while it is expressly enacted that a court cannot exercise its powers under s 6(3) to consent to a blood sample being taken from a child unless satisfied that it would not be detrimental to the child's health to do so,[5] it is submitted that a court would not consent if the results of the blood tests would be contrary to the child's interests. In reaching its decision in *Docherty v McGlynn* the Inner House relied upon the English case of *S v S*[6] where Lord Reid concluded that 'the court ought to permit a blood test of a young child to be taken unless satisfied that it would be against the child's interest'.[7]

In what circumstances will the courts either refuse to make a request under s 70(1) of the Law Reform (Miscellaneous

1 Section 70(2) of the Law Reform (Miscellaneous Provisions)(Scotland) Act 1990.
2 1994 SLT (Sh Ct) 22.
3 *Docherty v McGlynn* 1985 SLT 237; s 7 of the Law Reform (Miscellaneous Provisions)(Scotland) Act 1966. Cf the position in English law in *The Ampthill Peerage* [1977] AC 547, HL at 583 per Lord Simon of Glaisdale.
4 1983 SLT 645.
5 Section 6(4).
6 [1970] 3 All ER 107, [1972] AC 24, HL.
7 Ibid at 45.

Provisions) (Scotland) Act 1990 that a party to the proceedings should consent to a sample of blood, bodily fluid or tissue being taken from a child or refuse to admit the results of blood or DNA tests which have been carried out on a child with the appropriate consents? In *Docherty v McGlynn*[1] the Inner House considered that there was a 'delicate balance' between the desire for truth in litigation and the advantages for a child in continuing to be regarded as legitimate; Lord Cameron, in particular, thought that 'the stigma of illegitimacy is one which in many cases and ranks of society is a cause of pain and distress'.[2] Thus, there is authority that the court should not exercise its power to make such a request or admit such evidence, if it was likely thereby to establish that a child who was presumptively legitimate was in fact illegitimate. But as we shall see,[3] the marital status of a child's parents is no longer of any major legal significance in relation to the child's rights[4] and consequently the force of the court's observations in *Docherty v McGlynn*[5] now carry little, if any, weight. It is therefore submitted that merely because the s 5 presumption of paternity is likely to be rebutted, is not per se sufficient for a court to conclude that it would be contrary to a child's interests to make a request under s 70(1) of the Law Reform (Miscellaneous Provisions) (Scotland) Act 1990 or admit the results of blood or DNA tests as evidence. Only in very exceptional circumstances[6] will it now be contrary to a child's interests that the truth of the child's paternity should be known. The present writer agrees with the observation that, 'The ascertainment of truth must always be in the interests of parties and will usually be in the interests of the child.'[7]

LEGITIMACY AND ILLEGITIMACY

Introduction

For centuries a child's rights in Scots law were dependent upon whether or not the child was legitimate. A child is legitimate if the

---

1 1983 SLT 645.
2 Ibid at 650.
3 *Infra.*
4 Section 1 as amended by para 38(2) of Sch 4 to the Children (Scotland) Act 1995.
5 1983 SLT 645.
6 For example, where the child is the product of an incestuous relationship.
7 *Petrie v Petrie* 1993 SCLR 391 at 393 per temporary Sheriff Principal (Coutts). (Direction for sample granted to H to remove his suspicions that W's child was *not* his child.)

parents were validly married at the date of the child's conception or birth or any time in between.[1] When the child is conceived during a valid marriage, the husband is presumed to be the child's father; *pater est quem nuptiae demonstrant*. Thus, for example, where a couple were validly married at the date of the child's conception the child is presumed to be the legitimate child of the husband, even if the husband died before the child's birth. If a child is conceived and born out of wedlock, the child is illegitimate.[2]

Where the parents' marriage is void, a child conceived or born during the void marriage can be regarded as legitimate as a result of the doctrine of putative marriage. Before this doctrine is applicable, at least one of the parties must have entered into the 'marriage' in the bona fide belief that the marriage was valid, ie in ignorance of any impediment to the marriage. However, the error has to be one of fact not of law: for example, if a man and a woman married without realising they were uncle and niece, the doctrine is applicable (error of fact) but it does not apply if they had married in the belief that uncle and niece had capacity to marry each other under the law of Scotland (error of law).[3] A child who is conceived or born during a voidable marriage retains the status of legitimacy even if a declarator of nullity of marriage is subsequently obtained.[4]

When a child was born illegitimate, at common law the child would be legitimated by the subsequent valid marriage of the parents; legitimation *per subsequens matrimonium*. While the effect of the doctrine was retrospectively to treat the child as legitimate from the date of birth, it did not apply if the child's parents lacked the capacity to marry each other at the date of the child's conception.[5] The law was, however, changed by the Legitimation (Scotland) Act 1968. This provides that a child will become legitimated as a result of the parents' subsequent marriage, provided that the child was living at the date of the marriage and the father was domiciled in Scotland at that date.[6] It is irrelevant that the parents lacked capacity to marry at

1 Bell's *Principles* 1624. If the child is conceived before marriage, and if the husband knew at the time of the ceremony that his wife was pregnant and he had intercourse with her at the probable date of conception, there is a strong presumption that the child is the legitimate child of the husband: *Gardner v Gardner* (1876) 3 R 695, (1877) 4 R (HL) 56.
2 *James v McLennan* 1971 SLT 162.
3 *Purves' Trustees v Purves* (1986) 22 R 513.
4 Section 4 of the Law Reform (Miscellaneous Provisions) Act 1949; since the only ground of a voidable marriage is incurable impotency, the number of children involved is very small: see *supra* Ch 2.
5 Erskine *Institute* I, 67, 52; Bell's *Principles* 1627; *Kerr v Martin* (1840) 2 D 752.
6 Section 1 of the Legitimation (Scotland) Act 1968.

the date of the child's conception,[1] but, unlike the common law position, the child is only treated as legitimate from the date of the marriage.[2] A marriage for the purposes of the Act includes a putative and
voidable marriage.[3]

The law took pains to preserve a child's status of legitimacy. Thus,
for example, the presumption *pater est* would only be rebuttable by
proof beyond reasonable doubt that the husband was not the father of
the child.[4] Moreover, because of the scope of the doctrine of putative
marriage and the possibility of legitimation by the subsequent marriage of a child's parents, the range of persons who are treated as
legitimate is wide. Nevertheless, the proportion of live illegitimate
births to live legitimate births continues to rise in the United
Kingdom. It became increasingly obvious how reprehensible it was
that the rights of children should continue to depend on the marital
status of their parents. Indeed, the legal discrimination against
illegitimate children appeared to be in breach of the United
Kingdom's international obligations under the European Convention
on Human Rights.[5] The matter was considered by the Scottish Law
Commission[6] and its recommendations were enacted in the Law
Reform (Parent and Child)(Scotland) Act 1986.

The current law

Section 1(1) of the Law Reform (Parent and Child) Scotland Act
1986 declares:

> 'The fact that a person's parents are not or have not been mar-
> ried to one another shall be left out of account in establishing
> the legal relationship between the person and any other person;
> and accordingly any such relationship shall have effect as if the
> parents were or had been married to one another'.

---

1 By s 4 of the Legitimation (Scotland) Act 1968 certain children who failed to be
  legitimated *per subsequens matrimonium* because their parents lacked capacity to
  marry at the date of their conception were to be treated as legitimate from the date
  of the commencement of the Act. Cf *Wright's Trs v Callander* 1992 SLT 498.
2 Section 1(1) of the Legitimation (Scotland) Act 1968.
3 Section 8(1) of the Legitimation (Scotland) Act 1968.
4 See, for example, *Ballantyne v Douglas* 1953 SLT (Notes) 10 at 11 per Lord
  Patrick. Proof of non-access by the husband to the wife at the probable date of conception would suffice: *Coles v Homer and Tulloh* (1895) 22 R 716. Now, of course,
  the s 5 presumption of paternity can be rebutted by proof on a balance of probabilities: s 5(4).
5 Arts 8 and 14: on these articles, see *Marckx v Belgium* (1979) 2 EHHR 330.
6 See *Illegitimacy* (SLC No 82).

The effect of this provision is that children have legal equality regardless of their parents' marital status at the time of their birth. In other words, the status of legitimacy and illegitimacy is no longer to have any legal significance.

To ensure its purpose, the Act provides that in any future deeds or statutes a reference to any relative shall, unless the contrary intention appears in the statute or deed, be construed in accordance with s 1(1).[1] The Act amends previous legislation[2] to remove legal inequalities between legitimate and illegitimate children[3] and, so far as possible, references to illegitimate children.[4]

There are, however, areas where the distinction between legitimate and illegitimate children remains important. First, s 1(1) does not apply to any deed executed *before* the commencement of the Act.[5] However, if the deed was executed after the commencement of the Law Reform (Miscellaneous Provisions)(Scotland) Act 1968, any reference in the deed to a relative includes, unless the contrary intention appears, an illegitimate as well as legitimate relationship.[6] Secondly, s 1(1) does not apply to any deed executed *after* the commencement of the Act, where the deed (however expressed) refers to a legitimate or illegitimate relationship.[7] Thus, for example, if a testator makes a bequest in his will to his daughter's legitimate children, her illegitimate children cannot benefit, even if the testamentary deed was executed after the commencement of the Act. Thirdly, the Act does not affect the right of legitim out of, or the right of succession to, the estate of any person who died before the commencement of the Act.[8] Fourthly, the Act does not apply to the succession or devolution of any title, coat of arms, honour or dignity transmissible on the death

---

1 Section 1(2).
2 Section 10(1) and Sch 1 to the Act.
3 For example, in relation to succession, para 7 of Sch 1 to the Act removes inequalities by the simple expedient of providing that any reference to relative in the Succession (Scotland) Act 1964 shall be construed in accordance with s 1(1) of the 1986 Act. On succession, see *supra* p 56 ff.
4 See, for example, para 15 of Sch 1, in relation to the Damages (Scotland) Act 1976, para 17 in relation to the Marriage (Scotland) Act 1977 (discussed *supra* Ch 2), and para 18 in relation to the Adoption (Scotland) Act 1978. But cf para 10 where the expression 'illegitimate person' is used in an amendment to the Law Reform (Miscellaneous Provisions)(Scotland) Act 1968.
5 Section 1(4)(b). See, for example, *Allan Petrs* 1991 SLT 203.
6 Section 5 of the Law Reform (Miscellaneous Provisions)(Scotland) Act 1968. See, for example *Russell v Woods* 1987 SCLR 207.
7 Section 1(4)(c).
8 Section 9(1)(d): on the rights of children on succession, see *supra* p 57 ff.

of the holder thereof.[1] Thus, it will still be necessary to resort to the law of legitimacy and legitimation for these, admittedly limited, purposes.

There remains a major difficulty in equating the legal position of a legitimate and illegitimate child. As we shall see,[2] parents have important parental responsibilities and rights in respect of their child. A mother automatically has parental responsibilities and rights.[3] However, the father of a child will automatically acquire parental responsibilities and rights only if he is or was married to the child's mother at the date of the child's conception or subsequently.[4] If he does not marry the child's mother, the father will not acquire parental responsibilities and rights unless by court order[5] or agreement with the mother.[6] It is expressly enacted that the principle of legal equality between legitimate and illegitimate children in s 1(1) of the 1986 Act does not affect the position of the father of an illegitimte child in respect of the acquisition of parental responsibilities and rights.[7] Thus, where the parents of a child never marry, prima facie it is only the child's mother who has parental responsibilities and rights. Consequently, the Act does not alter the rule that a child born out of wedlock takes the domicile of the mother as a domicile of origin or dependence,[8] nor the law of adoption under which the father of a child born out of wedlock plays little part in the proceedings unless he has obtained parental responsibilities and rights.[9]

In spite of the reforms in the 1986 Act, the status of illegitimacy still subsists in Scots law. The Scottish Law Commission has recommended that since there are now virtually no legal differences between legitimate and illegitimate children, a separate status of legitimacy and illegitimacy is unnecessary, and in the case of the latter, offensive. Consequently, the Commission suggests that s 1(1) of the Law Reform (Parent and Child)(Scotland) Act 1986 be

---

1 Section 9(1)(c).
2 *Infra* Ch 10.
3 Children (Scotland) Act 1995, s 3(1)(a).
4 Ibid, s 3(1)(b).
5 Ibid, s 11.
6 Ibid, s 4.
7 Section 1(3) as substituted by para 38(2) of Sch 4 to the Children (Scotland) Act 1995. For full discussion, see *infra* Ch 10.
8 Section 9(1)(a): a child who is born in wedlock prima facie takes the domicile of the father as the domicile of origin or dependence. The child has capacity to acquire an independent domicile on reaching the age of 16: s 7 of the Age of Legal Capacity (Scotland) Act 1991.
9 On adoption, see *infra* Ch 12.

amended so that it is expressly enacted that no person whose status is governed by Scots law shall be illegitimate.[1] However, where a person's parents have never married, this would remain significant in relation to the exceptions to the general principle of legal equality[2] and in the context of parental responsibilities and rights.

1 *Family Law: Pre-consolidation Reforms* SLC Discussion Paper No 85, paras 11.1–11.10. As a consequence, the Legitimation (Scotland) Act 1968 would be repealed as unnecessary and declarators of legitimacy, legitimation and illegitimacy would be incompetent.
2 *Supra* p 162.

9 Children's legal capacity and rights

INTRODUCTION

The purpose of this chapter is to examine some of the most important legal rights enjoyed by children and how these rights are enforced. However, as a child matures, there may be a conflict between the child's 'right' to self-determination and the parents' responsibilities and rights in relation to the child's upbringing. Full discussion of this important and controversial issue will be left to the following chapter, where parental responsibilities and rights will be discussed in some detail. At present, we are therefore concerned with a child's capacity to enter into juristic acts and to seek redress when the child's rights have been infringed; we shall also consider when children may incur liability in respect of their actions. In this context, Scots law makes an important distinction between a child below 16 and a young person over that age. At the age of 18, a young person becomes an adult.[1] At the outset, it must be emphasised that the treatment of the substantive law on many of these issues is not intended to be exhaustive.

LEGAL TRANSACTIONS

Children under 16

In Scots law, a child of any age has passive capacity ie the child enjoys the full complement of legal rights, for example, the right to own heritable and moveable property.[2] However, as a general rule, a child under 16 has no active capacity.[3] This means that the child cannot enter into juristic acts, for example, make a contract. Moreover, the child cannot pursue or defend actions when the child's rights have

---

1 Age of Majority (Scotland) Act 1969.
2 Age of Legal Capacity (Scotland) Act 1991, s 1(3)(e). In this section references are to the 1991 Act unless otherwise stated.
3 Section 1(1)(a).

been infringed. Instead, a person entitled to act as the child's legal representative must enter into juristic acts for the child's benefit and pursue or defend actions on the child's behalf. As we shall see,[1] the right to act as a child's legal representative is one of the parental responsibilities and rights[2] which prima facie parents have in respect of their children.[3] Accordingly, it is the parent who will usually enter into a transaction[4] on behalf of the child. If a child purports to enter into a transaction without the capacity to do so, the transaction is null.[5] Thus, for example, if a child of 10 purported to buy an Armani suit costing £500, the contract of sale is null.

Where a parent enters into a contract on behalf of a child, the contract is valid even if it is to the child's disadvantage. Any remedy[6] the child may have is against the parent, not the other party to the contract.[7] So, for example, if P enters into a contract with A on behalf of P's child, C, C has no remedy against A if the contract is disadvantageous to C, but may have a remedy against P for failing to act as a reasonable and prudent person.[8]

There are, however, important exceptions to the general rule of absence of legal capacity until the child reaches 16.

(i) A child under the age of 16 has legal capacity to enter into a transaction of a kind commonly entered into by persons of the child's age and circumstances provided the terms of the contract are not unreasonable.[9] If 'commonly' is interpreted as 'not unusually or surprisingly' as opposed to 'often', the scope of this section is potentially very wide. Not only would it cover such transactions as the purchase of sweets or bus and rail tickets, but also 'one off', but not unusual, contracts such as the purchase of a bicycle or computer. It should also be noted that before the child is bound by the transaction, its terms must not be unreasonable.

---

1 *Infra* Ch 10.
2 Children (Scotland) Act 1995, ss 1(1)(d) and 2(1)(d).
3 However, the father of an illegitimate child does not automatically acquire parental responsibilities and rights: see *supra* p 163. For full discussion, see *infra* Ch 10.
4 Transaction is defined as a transaction having legal effect: it includes unilateral transactions, the exercise of testamentary capacity, the exercise of a power of appointment, bringing or defending actions, acting as arbiter or trustee, acting as an instrumentary witness and giving consent having legal effect: s 9.
5 Section 2(5).
6 See *infra* p 195.
7 This is because the old remedy of reducing the contract as against the other party on the grounds of minority and lesion has been abolished: s 1(5). On reduction on the grounds of minority and lesion, see *Wilkinson and Norrie* pp 63–68.
8 Children (Scotland) Act 1995, s 10(1), discussed *infra* p 195.
9 Section 2(1)(a) and (b).

(ii) A child aged 12 or over has the legal capacity to make a will[1]; the child can test on both heritable and moveable property.[2]

(iii) An adoption order or an order freeing a child for adoption cannot be made in respect of a child aged 12 or over unless the child consents.[3]

(iv) A transaction includes giving any consent having legal effect.[4] Thus, giving consent to any surgical, medical or dental procedure on the child is a legal transaction. Where the child is under 16, the parent as the child's legal representative can give consent to such procedures on the child's behalf.[5] However, where a child is under 16, the child has capacity to consent if in the opinion of the qualified medical practitioner attending the child, the child is capable of understanding the nature and possible consequences of the procedure or treatment.[6]

Several points should be noticed. First, the child's capacity to consent is determined by the medical practitioner, ie it is the medical practitioner who decides whether or not the child is capable of understanding the nature and possible consequences of the procedure or treatment and, consequently, whether or not the child has legal capacity to consent.

Secondly, the language of s 2(4) is enabling. It empowers a child under 16 to consent. It is silent on whether a child, whom the medical practitioner has decided does understand the nature and possible consequences of the proposed procedure or treatment, has capacity to refuse consent. Since an invasion of bodily integrity is an assault in the absence of *positive* consent, it can be argued that inherent in the capacity to consent is the capacity to refuse consent, ie if a person does *not* positively consent, an invasion of bodily integrity cannot lawfully take place.[7] Further support for this view is to be found in s 90 of the Children (Scotland) Act 1995. This section provides that even if a court or children's hearing specifically directs that a child should undergo medical examination or treatment, this does not

1 Section 2(2).
2 On children's rights to legitim out of their parents' moveable estate, see *supra* p 57 ff.
3 Sections 2(3), 12(8) and 18(8) of the Adoption (Scotland) Act 1978, discussed *infra*.
4 Section 9.
5 For full discussion, see *infra* p 205 ff.
6 Section 2(4).
7 The patient does not have to say 'I refuse to consent': if the patient is silent, the proposed procedure or treatment cannot lawfully go ahead without the patient's positive consent. This is subject to the necessity principle where, for example, treatment can be carried out without consent if the patient is unconscious after an accident.

override the right of a child who has s 2(4) capacity to refuse consent.[1] However, where the proposed procedure or treatment is in the best interests of the child, the English courts have been prepared to override a young person's refusal to consent.[2] It remains to be seen whether the Scottish courts will find a way to reach a similar conclusion. In practice, if a child is refusing to consent to a proposed procedure or treatment, the medical practitioner is unlikely to take the view that the child is capable of understanding the consequences of the procedure or treatment and consequently the child will not have s 2(4) capacity. In these circumstances, the medical practitioner would then ask the parent as the child's legal representative to consent on behalf of the child.[3]

Finally, there is no express provision in s 2(4) that the procedure or treatment should be in the best interests of the child. So, for example, a child with s 2(4) capacity could consent to being a donor of non-regenerative tissue like a kidney!

(v) A child under 16 has legal capacity to instruct a solicitor in connection with any civil matter, provided the child has a general understanding of what it means to do so. A child aged 12 or more is presumed to be of sufficient age and maturity to have such understanding but a child below that age may instruct a solicitor if the child *in fact* has such understanding.[4]

(vi) If a girl under 16 has a baby, she will automatically have parental responsibilities and rights in respect of her child.[5] Although under 16, the mother may exercise her parental rights and responsibilities.[6] Where a child's father is under 16, he will not automatically have parental responsibilities and rights because he lacks capacity to marry the child's mother.[7] In the unlikely event of his obtaining

---

1 See generally, Chs 13 and 14.
2 *Re W (a minor)* [1992] 4 All ER 627.
3 For full discussion, see *infra* p 205 ff.
4 Section 2(4A) inserted by para 53(3) of Sch 4 to the Children (Scotland) Act 1995. If the child has s 2(4A) capacity he will also have capacity to sue or defend in civil proceedings: s 2(5A) inserted ibid.
5 Section 3(1)(a) of the Children (Scotland) Act 1995.
6 Section 1(3)(g) as amended by para 53(2)(b) of Sch 4 to the Children (Scotland) Act 1995.
7 See *supra* p 22. A father will only automatically acquire parental responsibilities and rights if he is or was married to the child's mother at the date of conception or subsequently: s 3(1)(b) of the Children (Scotland) Act 1995. He could, however, have responsibilities and rights if he and the mother had gone through a valid ceremony of marriage when domiciled abroad, or if the 'marriage' is voidable or void as a result of a bona fide error on the part of both parties: s 3(2) of the 1995 Act.

parental responsibilties and rights as a result of a court order,[1] or, more realistically, by agreement with the child's mother,[2] he could exercise these responsibilities and rights.[3]

YOUNG PERSONS OVER 16 BUT UNDER 18

A young person over 16 has active legal capacity to enter into transactions.[4] However, when a young person has entered into a transaction between the ages of 16 and 18, the court has power to set the transaction aside if it is a prejudicial transaction.[5] The court can set aside such a transaction until the young person reaches 21.[6] A prejudicial transaction is defined as a transaction which an adult, exercising reasonable prudence, would not have entered into in the circumstances of the young person at the time of entering into the transaction and has caused or is likely to cause substantial prejudice to the young person.[7]

Certain transactions cannot be set aside. These include consent to adoption orders, consent to medical or dental procedures or treatment, transactions in the course of the young person's trade, business or profession, transactions induced by the young person's fraudulent misrepresentation as to age or transactions ratified by the young person after the age of 18 when he or she knew that it could be set aside.[8] When a young person is between 16 and 18, all the parties to a proposed transaction may make an application to the court to have the transaction ratified.[9] The court cannot ratify the transaction if it is satisfied that an adult exercising reasonable prudence in the circumstances of the young person would not have entered into the transaction. If the transaction is ratified, it cannot be set aside as a prejudicial transaction.[10] Thus, for example, if A intends to purchase a house owned by B who is aged 17, A and B should apply to the court to have the proposed sale ratified. The court will ratify the proposed

1 Ie an order under s 11(2)(b) of the Children (Scotland) Act 1995: as a parent, he can obtain parental responsibilities and rights even though not 16. See *infra*.
2 See s 4, discussed *infra* p 197.
3 Section 1(3)(g) as amended by para 53(2)(b) of Sch 4 to the Children (Scotland) Act 1995.
4 Section 1(1)(b).
5 Section 3(1).
6 Ibid.
7 Section 3(2). A typical example of a prejudicial transaction would be if the young person undertook a cautionary obligation.
8 Section 3(3).
9 Section 4.
10 Section 3(3)(j).

sale if satisfied that an adult, exercising reasonable prudence, would have sold the house if in B's position. Once ratified, B cannot set the sale aside on the ground that it is a prejudicial transaction.

DELICTUAL LIABILITY

The Age of Legal Capacity (Scotland) Act 1991 does not affect delictual liability.[1] Where a child under 16 is injured by the wrongous or negligent act of another, the child's legal representative can sue for damages in delict on the child's behalf. Where the young person is over 16, he or she has capacity to bring the action. If a child is injured by his or her parent, an action for damages in delict is competent:[2] in these circumstances a *curator ad litem* will be appointed.

Conversely, children can be liable in delict for their wrongful acts if the requisite intention or negligence can be established. Since children are rarely wealthy or insured, there are few, if any, cases where they have been sued for damages in delict. This will, of course, not apply if a young person aged 17 causes injury through negligent driving. More importantly, it has been held that a child can be guilty of contributory negligence, leading to a reduction of the child's damages when he or she has been injured. Thus in *McKinnell v White*,[3] for example, Lord Fraser reduced the damages of a five year old child by 50% on the basis that the child had been contributorily negligent when he ran in front of a speeding motorist. Lord Fraser justified his decision on the basis that any child living in an urban area would be bound to be aware by the age of five of the danger of traffic.[4]

It should be noted that parents are not automatically vicariously liable for the delicts of their children[5] but a parent will incur personal liability if as a result of the parent's negligence, this caused or contributed to the child's delict, for example, failure to supervise a child properly.[6]

Where a child's parent has been killed as a result of a wrongous or negligent act of another, a child may claim damages in respect of the parent's death under the Damages (Scotland) Act 1976.[7] The fact that

1 Section 1(3)(c).
2 *Young v Rankin* 1934 SC 499; *Wood v Wood* 1935 SLT 431.
3 1971 SLT (Notes) 61.
4 Ibid at 62.
5 But, of course, the parents would be liable if they had authorised the child's action or the child was acting as an employee of the parents.
6 *Hastie v Magistrates of Edinburgh* 1907 SC 1102; *Hardie v Sneddon* 1917 SC 1.
7 A child has title to sue even though born after the parent has died: *Cohen v Shaw* 1992 SLT 1022.

the child's parents were never married to each other is irrelevant.[1] Damages are available for loss of support suffered or likely to be suffered as a result of the parent's death and also compensation for the loss of non-patrimonial benefits, for example, the parent's affection and guidance.[2]

MARRIAGE AND DOMICILE

As we have seen, a person has capacity to marry in Scots law when aged 16 or over.[3] A young person has the capacity to acquire a domicile of choice on reaching 16.[4]

CRIMINAL LIABILITY

The age of criminal responsibility is not changed by the Age of Legal Capacity (Scotland) Act 1991[5] and remains eight.[6] In most situations where a child under 16 has committed a criminal offence,[7] this will be a ground for the referral of the child's case by a Reporter to a children's hearing to determine whether or not the child is in need of compulsory measures of supervision.[8] However, a child will be prosecuted in the criminal courts on the instructions of the Lord Advocate if the child has committed a very serious crime, for example, murder or culpable homicide.[9]

SPECIFIC AGE LIMITS

The Age of Legal Capacity (Scotland) Act 1991 does not affect any age limits laid down for specific purposes by other statutes. In a work of this compass, it is not possible to explore these limits in major

1 Para 15 of Sch 1 to the Law Reform (Parent and Child) (Scotland) Act 1986.
2 For full discussion, see Thomson *Delictual Liability* (1994) Ch 13.
3 Section 1 of the Marriage (Scotland) Act 1977, discussed *supra* p 22.
4 Age of Legal Capacity (Scotland) Act 1977, s 7.
5 Section 1(3)(c).
6 Section 55 of the Children and Young Persons (Scotland) Act 1937; Criminal Procedure (Scotland) Act 1995, s 41.
7 But not when the child is below the age of eight: *Merrin v S* 1987 SLT 193, discussed *infra* p 284.
8 See generally, *infra* Ch 14.
9 For details, see *3 Stair Memorial Encyclopaedia* para 1218.

detail.[1] Sometimes a statute gives a child capacity before the child
reaches 16; for example, in Scotland a child aged 12 or more can
apply for a maintenance assessment under s 7 of the Child Support
Act 1991.[2] However, the statutory age limits usually prevent a young
person from engaging in a course of conduct until he or she reaches
an age beyond 16. Thus, for example, a young person has to be 17 or
over before he or she can hold a licence to drive a motor car,[3] or fly a
plane in order to obtain a pilot's licence.[4] Often Parliament makes it
a criminal offence to sell or supply particular goods or services to a
child or young person below a particular age, for example, to sell
tobacco to a child under 16[5] or alcohol to a young person below 18.[6]
It is also a criminal offence for a person under 18 to buy or attempt to
buy alcohol.[7] Similarly, there are offences relating to betting transactions[8] with young persons below 18.

In relation to sexual activities, it is a criminal offence to have sexual intercourse with a girl below 16.[9] The offence is committed even
although the girl consented. She does not commit any offence even if
she consented or seduced the man, because the offence was created to
protect vulnerable young women.[10] It is a defence if the man was
under 24, had not been previously charged with such an offence and
had reasonable cause to believe that the girl was aged 16 or over.[11] It
is a criminal offence for a boy below 18 to engage in homosexual acts
of any kind. However, the homosexual act is decriminalised if the
young man is 18 or over, his partner is 18 or over, the act takes place
in private and both parties consent.[12]

LITIGATION

Prima facie, the general rule of legal capacity applies. Thus, where
the child is below 16, any civil action must be pursued or defended on

1 For fuller discussion, see ibid para 1213 ff.
2 On the Child Support Act 1991, see *infra* p 180 ff.
3 Section 101 of the Road Traffic Act 1988.
4 Air Navigation Order 1989 S1 (1989/2004) reg 20(1)(b)(i).
5 Section 18(1) of the Children and Young Persons (Scotland) Act 1937.
6 Section 68(1) of the Licensing (Scotland) Act 1976.
7 Ibid, s 68(2).
8 See, generally, s 22 of the Betting, Gaming and Lotteries Act 1963.
9 Criminal Law (Consolidation) (Scotland) Act 1995, s 5. If the girl is below 12 the
   crime is rape as a girl below that age is presumed to be unable to consent. There
   are separate statutory offences when the girl is below 13 and between 13 to 16.
10 This could be a ground for compulsory measures of supervision, discussed *infra*
    Ch 14.
11 Criminal Law (Consolidation) (Scotland) Act 1995, s 5(5)(b).
12 Criminal Law (Consolidation) (Scotland) Act 1995, s 13(5).

behalf of the child by the child's legal representative. If the child has no legal representative or the legal representative refuses to act, the action can proceed in the child's name in spite of the fact the child is under 16.[1] In *any* civil proceedings, the court can appoint a *curator ad litem* to protect the child's interests.[2] If a child under 16 has legal capacity to consult a solicitor, the child also has capacity to pursue or defend in civil proceedings.[3] While a young person over 16 has legal capacity, the young person cannot assent to the variation of a trust until 18;[4] in these circumstances, a *curator ad litem* will be appointed for a young person between the ages of 16 and 18.[5]

It should be noted that prescriptive or limitation periods do not begin to run against a child until he or she reaches 16.[6]

CHILD WITNESSES

There is no minimum age for a child to be admissible as a witness in criminal or civil proceedings.[7] It is for the presiding judge to decide whether the child understands what he or she has seen or heard and knows the difference between truth and falsehood.[8] A child below the age of 12 is not put on oath, but admonished to tell the truth.[9]

In criminal cases, the judge can take steps to reduce the distress of

---

1 Section 1(3)(f)(i) of the Age of Legal Capacity (Scotland) Act 1991, as amended by para 53(2)(a) of Sch 4 to the Children (Scotland) Act 1995.
2 Section 1(3)(f)(ii) of the Age of Legal Capacity (Scotland) Act 1991. This would arise if, for example, there was a potential conflict of interest between the child and the parents and the child's parents were acting as the child's legal representatives.
3 Ibid, s 2(4A) and (4B) as inserted by para 53(3) of Sch 4 to the Children (Scotland) Act 1995: on s 2(4A), see *supra* p 168.
4 Section 1(2) of the Trusts (Scotland) Act 1961, as amended by s 1(3) of and Sch 1 to the Age of Majority (Scotland) Act 1969, and para 27 of Sch 1 to the Age of Legal Capacity (Scotland) Act 1991.
5 Section 1(3)(f)(iii) to the Age of Legal Capacity (Scotland) Act 1991.
6 Prescription and Limitation (Scotland) Act 1973, ss 17(3), 18(3), 18A(2), 22B(4), 22C(3) (limitation); s 6(4)(b) (five years' prescription); *McCabe v McLellan* 1994 SLT 346. There is no need for the young person's non-age (ie being below 16) to be causally related to the failure to pursue the action. In other words, there is a blanket protection due to non-age.
7 Or to give information at, or to be used in, a children's hearing: see *infra* Ch 14.
8 If the child is not asked if he or she knows the difference and is not told the truth, the child is not a competent witness: *F v Kennedy (No 1)* 1993 SLT 1277.
9 *Rees v Lowe* 1990 SLT 507. The oath is administered when the child is 14 or over: between the ages of 12 and 14, the judge has discretion whether or not to administer the oath: *Anderson v McFarlane* (1899) 1 F (J) 36.

a child witness, for example by removing wigs and gowns. On cause shown, provided an application has been made before the trial, the court has discretion to allow the child to give evidence in criminal proceedings through a live television link.[1] The judge will consider the effect on the child of giving evidence in court and whether or not the child would be better able to give evidence if the application is granted.[2] The judge can have regard to *any* factor considered relevant, for example the age and maturity of the child, the nature of the alleged offences, the child's relationship with the accused etc.[3] If the application is granted, the child need not identify the accused in court and evidence that the child identified the accused before the trial, for example at an identity parade, is admissible.[4]

The court also has power to appoint a commissioner to take the child's evidence before and, in exceptional circumstances, during the trial.[5] The proceedings are recorded on video and the video is admissible as evidence. The same criteria are relevant to such an application as in an application that a child should give evidence by a live television link.[6]

It should be noted that a child cannot witness a deed until 16.[7]

ALIMENT

A child has the right to be alimented by his or her parents. The law of aliment of children is to be found in the Family Law (Scotland) Act 1985.[8]

By s 1(1)(c) an obligation of aliment is owed by a father or mother to his or her child. *Both* parents are under an obligation to aliment their children. Thus liability must be divided between the father and the mother: aliment is not the primary responsibility of the father of a

---

1 Criminal Procedure (Scotland) Act 1995, s 271(5) and (7). Where there is more than one child involved in the case, there is no need for an application to be made on behalf of each child before the trial: *HM Advocate v Birkett* 1993 SLT 395.
2 Criminal Procedure (Scotland) Act 1995, s 271(7).
3 Ibid, s 271(8).
4 Ibid, s 271(11). The accused can challenge the child's evidence and can examine the child on identification using the television link.
5 Ibid, s 271(1).
6 Ibid, s 271(7). If the application is granted, the child need not identify the accused in court. It is also possible for the child to give evidence in court but screened from the accused: ibid, s 271(6).
7 Sections 1(1)(a) and 9 of the Age of Legal Capacity (Scotland) Act 1991.
8 In this section, references are to the 1985 Act unless otherwise stated.

child. The fact that the parents have never married each other is irrelevant.[1] However, s 1(1)(d) also places an obligation on a person to
aliment a child who has been accepted by that person as a child of the
family.[2] The absence of a blood tie is irrelevant. The obligation to aliment is therefore extended beyond parents and natural children to
include, for example, step-parents and step-children. But s 1(1)(d)
would equally apply where a grandparent brings up a grandchild or
an uncle or aunt brings up a niece.[3] It is not clear whether the acceptor must have a family before the child is accepted but it is expressly
provided by s 27 that family includes a one-parent family.[4]

But before the obligation arises under s 1(1)(d) the child must have
been 'accepted' as a child of the family. This could give rise to difficulties. Consider the following example.

EXAMPLE

H and W are married. W has a child. The presumption of paternity in s 5 of the Law Reform (Parent and Child)(Scotland) Act
1986 will apply. If, however, H later rebuts the presumption and
establishes that he is not the child's father, does he owe the
child an obligation of aliment? Section 1(1)(c) is inapplicable
as H is not the child's father. Section 1(1)(d) may not apply if
the court took the view that H did not accept the child as a child
of his family because he did not know that the child was not his
and had, therefore, not agreed with W to accept another man's
child as a child of the family.[5]

The difficulty could have been avoided if the criterion was whether a
person had 'treated', as opposed to 'accepted' the child as a child of
the family.[6]

---

1 Para 21 of Sch 1 to the Law Reform (Parent and Child)(Scotland) Act 1986.
2 Foster parents are not obliged to aliment children who have been boarded out by a
   local or other public authority or a voluntary organisation: s 1(1)(d).
3 See, for example, *Inglis v Inglis and Mathew* 1987 SCLR 608.
4 There is no obligation to aliment a child who had been accepted as a child of the
   family but was no longer accepted as such when the 1985 Act came into force:
   Forbes v Forbes 1991 SCLR 389. However, where a child has been accepted after
   the commencement of the 1985 Act, the obligation to aliment continues even if the
   acceptor no longer wishes a relationship with the child.
5 There is English authority that a non-parent does not accept a child as a child of the
   family unless there was full knowledge on the part of the non-parent of the child's
   paternity and he agreed to accept the child as a child of his family: *P(R) v P(P)*
   [1969] 3 All ER 777, sub nom *P v P* [1969] 1 WLR 898; cf *Kirkwood v Kirkwood*
   [1970] 2 All ER 161, [1970] 1 WLR 1042, DC; *Snow v Snow* [1972] Fam 74, CA.
6 'Treated' is now the criterion for the definition of a child of the family in other areas
   of Scots law, for example, ancillary orders for parental responsibilities and rights
   on divorce: s 12(4)(b) of the Children (Scotland) Act 1995.

A child for the purposes of aliment means a person under 18 or a person between 18 and 25 who is reasonably and appropriately undergoing instruction at an educational establishment, or training for employment or for a trade, profession or vocation.[1] Thus, for example, a parent's obligation to aliment a child continues while the child attends university.[2] The obligation to aliment a mentally handicapped child prima facie ceases when the child reaches 18[3] but will continue until 25 if the child attends any course of instruction designed to maximise the child's potential for life.

The obligation of aliment is to provide such support as is reasonable in the circumstances,[4] having regard to the factors which the courts use to determine the amount of aliment, *viz* the needs[5] and resources of the parties, their earning capacities and generally all the circumstances of the case.[6] Where two or more parties owe an obligation of aliment to a child, while there is no order of liability, the court, in deciding how much, if any, aliment to award against any of those persons, must have regard to the obligation of aliment owed to the child by the other person(s).[7] The following examples illustrate how this provision operates in practice.

1 Section 1(5)(a) and (b). See, for example, *Jowett v Jowett* 1990 SCLR 348.
2 Provided he or she is under 25.
3 *McBride v McBride* 1995 SCLR 1138.
4 Section 1(2). The test for what is reasonable is objective and does not turn on the view of the parent: *Winter v Thornton* 1993 SCLR 389 (whether aliment should be paid for the child's *private* education).
5 In *McGeachie v McGeachie* 1989 SCLR 99 the child was an infant and the mother was in receipt of child benefit; the court reduced an award of aliment on the ground that it was too generous in the light of the baby's existing needs! To be fair, this was an application for interim aliment.
6 Section 4(1). The court may take into account any support given by the defender to any person whom he maintains as a dependant in his household, whether or not the defender owes the dependant an obligation of aliment, for example, a mistress' children: s 4(3)(a). However, the mistress' income could be relevant: *Pryde v Pryde* 1991 SLT (Sh Ct) 26. Conduct is irrelevant unless it would be manifestly inequitable to leave it out of account: s 4(3)(b). In *Walker v Walker* 1991 SLT 649, the court took the father's conduct in lying about his income into account. The fact that a woman agreed to sexual intercourse without contraception – and, indeed, may have indicated to her lover that she was using contraceptives – will not be taken into account to reduce the amount of reasonable aliment to be paid by the father: *Bell v McCurdie* 1981 SC 64. Section 4(3) is discussed in detail in the context of aliment between husband and wife, *supra* p 49 ff.
7 Section 4(2). See, for example, *Inglis v Inglis and Mathew* 1987 SCLR 608 (action of aliment by uncle and aunt, who had accepted the child, against the child's parents: court took into account the fact that the aunt and uncle also owed an obligation to aliment the child).

EXAMPLE 1

H and W are married. They have a child, C. Both H and W therefore have an obligation to aliment C: s 1(1)(c). In quantifying the amount of aliment H should pay, the court must have regard to the fact that W also owes an obligation of aliment to C. Thus, if H was unemployed and W was in well-paid employment, the court could take the view that H should only be ordered to pay a fraction of the required aliment, or, indeed, no aliment at all, leaving C to pursue a claim against W.

EXAMPLE 2

A, mother, and B, father, have a child, C. Both A and B therefore have an obligation to aliment C: s 1(1)(c). A later marries H, who accepts C as a child of his family. H therefore has an obligation to aliment C: s 1(1)(d). In quantifying the amount of aliment H should pay, the court must have regard to the fact that both A and B owe an obligation of aliment to C. Thus, even if H was in employment, the court could take the view that H should only be ordered to pay a fraction of the required aliment, leaving C to pursue claims against A and the father, B.

Where a court makes an award of aliment in respect of a child under 16, it may include an amount for the reasonable expenses of the person having care of the child, where these are incurred in looking after the child.[1]

An action for aliment can be brought by the child.[2] Thus, for example, an 18 year old child who is attending university can bring a claim for aliment against his or her parents if they have refused to make an appropriate contribution towards the child's maintenance.[3] Where a child is below 18, an action can be brought on his or her behalf by the parent or guardian of the child, or any person, with whom the child lives or is seeking a residence order in respect of the child.[4] Thus, for example, if a grandmother is caring for her daughter's child, she can bring an action of aliment on the child's behalf against the child's mother and father. A woman, whether married or not, may bring an

1 Section 4(4) as inserted by para 5 of Sch 5 to the Child Support Act 1991.
2 Section 2(4)(a). If the child is between 16 and 18, the child has legal capacity to pursue the action: if below 16, the child will have legal capacity to pursue the action if the child has capacity to instruct a solicitor: see *supra* p 173.
3 See *Jowett v Jowett* 1990 SCLR 348.
4 Section 2(4)(c)(i) and (iii) as amended by para 40 of Sch 1 to the Age of Legal Capacity (Scotland) Act 1991 and para 36(b) of Sch 4 to the Children (Scotland) Act 1995. On residence orders, see *infra* Ch 11.

action for aliment on behalf of her unborn child as if the child had been born, but no such action will be heard or disposed of prior to the birth of the child;[1] however, on granting decree after the birth, the court has power to backdate the aliment to the date of the child's birth.[2]

An action for aliment of a child can be brought even if the child is living with the defender; so, for example, a child can seek aliment from his or her parents while still living at home with them.[3] In these circumstances, however, the parents will have a defence if they can show that they are fulfilling their obligation of aliment and are continuing to do so.[4] Where a couple have separated and the mother, for example, has taken a child under 16 with her, then if the mother brings an action for aliment on behalf of the child against the father, it is no defence to the action that the father has offered to receive the child into his household and thereby fulfil the obligation of aliment.[5] This is because the question of where a child should live is prima facie an issue in proceedings for a residence order where the child's welfare will be the paramount consideration.[6] However, where the child is over 16, the father will have a defence to a claim for aliment, if he had offered a home to the child which it was reasonable to expect the child to accept.[7] In determining whether it was reasonable for the child to accept such an offer, the defender's conduct will be taken into account.[8] Thus, for example, it might not be reasonable for a daughter to accept her father's offer of accommodation if the father's unreasonable behaviour towards her mother had led to the breakdown of the marriage and had been a cause of distress to both the mother and the child.[9]

While an action for aliment *simpliciter* is competent in both the Court of Session and the sheriff court,[10] in practice, a claim is more likely to be made in the course of other proceedings, such as declarator of parentage, actions in relation to parental responsibilities and rights, separation, divorce and financial provision.[11] For example,

1 Section 2(5). This provision is important, if, for example, the father was about to remove himself from the jurisdiction.
2 Section 3(1)(c).
3 Section 2(6).
4 Section 2(7).
5 Section 2(8).
6 The welfare principle is discussed *infra* Ch 11.
7 Section 2(8).
8 Section 2(9).
9 See, for example, *McKay v McKay* 1980 SLT (Sh Ct) 111. In *Bell v Bell* (unreported) the father's offer was held to be unreasonable as his daughter lived with her mother after the divorce and was currently engaged in higher education in a different town.
10 Section 2(1).
11 Section 2(2) as amended by para 36(a) of Sch 4 to the Children (Scotland) Act 1995.

when a woman has a child, if she seeks declarator of parentage,[1] she can bring a claim for aliment on behalf of her child against the alleged father in the same proceedings: if parentage is established, aliment can be ordered from the father of the child.

Similarly, in an action for divorce, the pursuer can bring claims for aliment on behalf of the children of the marriage: these will include not only the spouses' children but any children accepted by either of them as children of the family.[2] As we have seen,[3] any claims for aliment for the children must be satisfied before the court will order financial provision for the spouses. Where at any stage in the proceedings, an action for divorce or separation is dismissed, the court is not prevented from making inter alia an order for aliment for any children of the family.[4]

Aliment takes the form of periodical payments, whether for a definite or indefinite period or until the happening of a specified event.[5] The court cannot substitute a lump sum for a periodical payment.[6] But the court can order alimentary payments of an occasional or special nature to meet special needs which it would be unreasonable to expect the claimant to meet out of a periodical allowance.[7] This could, for example, be an order to pay school fees.[8] An award of aliment can be backdated to the date of the bringing of the action and, on special cause shown, to a date prior to the bringing of the action.[9] On a material change of circumstances since the date of the original decree, an award of aliment can be varied or recalled.[10] The variation can be backdated but not beyond the date of the decree which is being varied.[11] When a variation is backdated, any sums paid under the

1 Section 7 of the Law Reform (Parent and Child)(Scotland) Act 1986.
2 Section 1(1)(c) and (d). The court will not be able to make an order in relation to parental responsibilities and rights unless the child has also been treated as a child of the family (and vice versa): s 12 of the Children (Scotland) Act 1995. Cases where a child has been accepted but not treated as a child of the family will be rare – but a child *in utero* can be accepted as a child of the family though cannot be treated as such until born.
3 *Supra* Ch 7.
4 Section 21 of the Family Law (Scotland) Act 1985 as amended by Sch 5 to the Children (Scotland) Act 1995.
5 Section 3(1)(a): for example, aliment could be ordered until the child reaches 18.
6 Section 3(2).
7 Section 3(1)(b).
8 *McDonald v McDonald* 1995 SLT 72.
9 Section 3(1)(c).
10 Section 5(1). The making of a maintenance assessment in respect of the child for whom the decree of aliment was granted is a material change of circumstances: s 5(1A) as added by s 2(2) of the Child Support (Amendments to Primary Legislation) (Scotland) Order 1993, SI 1993/660.
11 Section 5(2) incorporating s 3(1)(c); *Walker v Walker* 1991 SLT 649; cf *Hannah v Hannah* 1988 SLT 82. This is because the material change of circumstances must have arisen after the original decree was awarded.

order before variation can be ordered to be repaid.[1] While an interim award of aliment can be varied or recalled, there is no power to back-date the variation.[2]

There is now no obligation on a child to aliment his or her parent, however wealthy the child or indigent the parent. Where a child is wealthy in his or her own right, a parent can use the child's income for his or her maintenance or education; resort will rarely be made to the child's capital for these purposes, unless the parent's circumstances are so reduced that he or she cannot aliment the child.[3]

Finally, the discretionary nature of awards of aliment must be emphasised. What a child will actually receive as an award of aliment depends not only on the child's needs but also the resources of his or her parents. For children of low income families, awards of aliment will be small. Increasingly, resort will have to be made to income support for basic maintenance of children whose parents are unemployed. However, where the parents have separated, in the vast majority of cases their child's right to aliment cannot be enforced in the courts. Instead, an application must be made to the Child Support Agency for maintenance assessment. It is to this statutory system of child support that we now turn.

THE CHILD SUPPORT ACT 1991

The Child Support Act 1991 represents a major change of approach to financial support for children. The White Paper, *Children Come First*,[4] which preceded the legislation suggested two main defects in the traditional system of aliment described above, *viz* (i) that judicial discretion as to the amount to be awarded meant that awards were difficult to predict and inconsistent, and (ii) that the aliment awarded was often not paid or badly in arrears. The White Paper also emphasised the growing numbers of lone parents, the low proportion of lone parents in employment, and the high proportion of lone parents who were dependent on means-tested benefits – many of whom were receiving no aliment from the other parent of the child(ren). The

1 Section 5(4).
2 *McColl v McColl* 1993 SLT 617.
3 The parent on ceasing to act as the child's legal representative is liable to account for intromissions with the child's property, but there is no liability if the child's money was used in the proper discharge by the parent of the parent's responsibility to safeguard and promote the child's welfare: s 10 of the Children (Scotland) Act 1995, discussed *infra* p 195.
4 (1990) Cm 1264.

White Paper echoed the widespread dissatisfaction with the private law system of aliment which had become apparent some years before its publication. However, it has been suggested that the government's dominant motive in reform was to reduce public expenditure rather than to improve the situation of lone parents.[1]

The main elements of the system introduced by the Child Support Act 1991 ('the 1991 Act') and associated secondary legislation are (a) the assessment of the amount of maintenance for a child by a mathematical formula rather than the exercise of judicial discretion, and (b) the transfer in most cases of the jurisdiction to assess maintenance from the courts to a new government organisation, the Child Support Agency, which operates under the aegis of the Department of Social Security. Once introduced the system proved highly controversial. Some adjustments were made to the formula for calculating maintenance assessments in February 1994. More far-reaching changes were proposed in a second White Paper, *Improving Child Support*,[2] some of which were implemented by changes to the regulations, others of which required fresh primary legislation – the Child Support Act 1995.

The reformed system of financial support for children is not fully in effect. The original intention was to phase it in over the period 1993/97, but there has since been some adjustment of the timetable. The following paragraphs describe the system as if it were fully in effect. They are followed by a brief summary of the transitional provisions. The primary and secondary legislation together form a large and complex body of law. What follows should be considered merely an outline of its main features.[3]

Who is covered by the 1991 Act?

The central legal concept of the 1991 Act is that of the 'qualifying child'.[4] This concept is described in more detail below, but, in general, a child is only a qualifying child when one or both of the child's parents are not living with the child. Each parent of a qualifying child is responsible for maintaining the child, but shall be taken to have met that responsibility by making periodical payments of child

---

1 See, for example, Garnham and Knights *Putting the Treasury First: The Truth About Child Support* (Child Poverty Action Group, 1994).
2 (1994) Cm 2745.
3 For more detailed accounts, see Bird *Child Maintenance: The Child Support Act 1991* (2nd edn, 1993); Mostyn, *Child's Pay* (1993); Knights, Garnham, and McDowell *Child Support Handbook* (3rd edn, 1995/96).
4 The Child Support Act 1991, s 3. References in this section are to the 1991 Act unless otherwise stated.

maintenance in accordance with the Act.[1] Where a maintenance assessment requiring payments is made under the 1991 Act, it is the duty of the absent parent to whom the assessment is addressed to make those payments.[2] The person with day-to-day care of the child in effect meets his or her responsibility to maintain by looking after the child, and need make no payments to, or for the benefit of, the child. In most cases covered by the Act, the child is being cared for by one of his or her natural parents ('the person with care'), who is separated from the other ('the absent parent'). However, the person with care need not be a parent, and it is, therefore, possible for two persons to be absent parents for the purposes of the Act.

A child is a qualifying child if one or both of the child's parents are 'absent parents'.[3] A parent is an absent parent if he or she is not living in the same household with the child, and the child has his or her home with another person who is 'a person with care'.[4] A person with care is the person with whom the child has his or her home, and who usually provides day-to-day care for the child provided that person does not fall within a prescribed category. The person need not be an individual, but may be, for example, a children's home. The prescribed categories for those who may not be persons with care are local authorities and those looking after children who have been boarded out with them by local authorities.[5]

A person only counts as a 'child'[6] for the purposes of the 1991 Act if (a) under 16; (b) under 19 and receiving full-time, non-advanced eduction; or (c) under 18, and registered for work or youth training while a parent is still claiming child benefit in respect of the child. Category (b) covers those attending school or a further education college, but not students at universities or similar institutions. In addition, a person who is or has been married is not a child, and this includes cases where the person has celebrated a marriage which is void, or a decree of nullity has been granted. Where a person does not fall within the definition of 'child', that person is not a qualifying child for the purposes of the 1991 Act and, therefore, no maintenance assessment relating to him or her may be made.[7]

The definition of 'parent' is also important as a person cannot be either a parent with care or an absent parent unless he or she falls

---

1 Section 1.
2 Ibid.
3 Section 3.
4 Ibid.
5 SI 1992/1813, reg 51.
6 Section 55.
7 However, since the person is not a qualifying child, he or she may be able to pursue an action for aliment in the courts: see *infra* p 186 ff.

within the definition of parent. The Act defines 'parent' as 'any person who is in law the mother or father of the child'.[1] This means that the expression covers both natural and adoptive parents but not step-parents. A person is not, therefore, liable to maintain a step-child under the Act.[2] The Act makes special provision for determining disputes about parentage for its purposes.[3]

The Act is therefore concerned with defining and enforcing the obligations of parents to maintain their natural and adopted children, in those cases where at least one of the parents is neither living with nor looking after the child, and the child is living with and being looked after by the other parent, or a third party. In most cases to which the Act applies, the courts have no power to award aliment.

Maintenance assessments

Under s 4 of the 1991 Act, either the person with care or the absent parent of a qualifying child may apply to the Secretary of State for a maintenance assessment to be made. The assessment is made by a child support officer appointed by the Secretary of State. The person applying for the assessment may also authorise the collection and enforcement of the maintenance payable. The authority to make an assessment, and to collect and enforce maintenance may be withdrawn by the applicant. However, an application under s 4 may not be made when there is in force a maintenance assessment under s 6.

Whereas the making of a child maintenance assessment under s 4 occurs at the option of the person applying for it, s 6 provides for a compulsory assessment in certain cases. Section 6 stipulates that a parent with care (but not any other person with care) of a qualifying child *must* authorise the Secretary of State to take action to recover child support maintenance from the absent parent if he or she is being paid one of the following means-tested benefits: income support, family credit and disability working allowance. However, a parent with care may not be required to give such authorisation if the Secretary of State considers there are reasonable grounds for believing that there would be a risk of the parent or any child living with him or her suffering harm or undue distress as a result of being required to give, or actually giving, the authorisation. Unless this exception applies, the parent with care must provide information required to trace the absent parent, make an assessment, and recover

---

1 Section 54. On the legal concept of parent see *supra* Ch 8.
2 This means that the child can pursue an action for aliment in the courts against a step-parent who has accepted the child as a child of the family: discussed *supra* p 175.
3 Sections 26–28.

the maintenance assessed from him or her. If the parent with care refuses to give such authority, or fails to give the necessary information, the child support officer has a discretion to issue a reduced benefit direction which has the effect of reducing the amount of benefit received for 78 weeks.[1]

By virtue of s 7 a qualifying child who is habitually resident in Scotland and is 12 or over may apply for a maintenance assessment in his or her own right, provided no application has already been made by either a person with care or an absent parent under s 4, and provided also that the Secretary of State has not been authorised to take action in a benefit case under s 6.

Once a maintenance assessment has been made under any of ss 4, 6, or 7, the absent parent comes under a duty to make payments of the amounts specified in the assessment. The Secretary of State has power to arrange for the collection and enforcement of maintenance in the case of all compulsory assessments made under s 6, and those voluntary assessments under ss 4 or 7 where the applicant has authorised the Secretary of State to collect and enforce the amounts due.

Where payments are required under a maintenance assessment they may be made in a variety of ways, but the Secretary of State has two important powers. The first is to make a deduction from earnings order,[2] which is in effect an instruction to an employer to deduct maintenance from earnings at source and remit them to the Secretary of State. Such orders may be used both to collect arrears and to collect current maintenance even where there are no arrears. The second is to apply for a liability order,[3] but this may be done only where there are arrears, and either a deduction from earnings order would be inappropriate, or has been tried already and proved ineffective as a means of securing payment. A liability order may be enforced by the usual forms of diligence (other than an earnings arrestment).[4]

This is an appropriate point at which to mention the obligation imposed on the Secretary of State and child support officers by s 2; *viz* when considering the exercise of any discretionary power conferred by the 1991 Act they are to 'have regard to the welfare of any child likely to be affected by [their] decision'. This may be contrasted with the obligation of the court in s 11(7) of the Children (Scotland) Act 1995 to regard the welfare of the child as the paramount consideration in any proceedings relating to parental responsibilities and rights.

1 Section 46.
2 Sections 31, 32.
3 Section 33.
4 Section 38.

The formula

The amount of maintenance payable is worked out according to a complicated formula detailed in Sch 1 to the 1991 Act and associated secondary legislation.[1] The formula takes into account the needs and resources of both the absent parent and the person with care, but only the absent parent may be required to make any payment. The formula has four elements:
a) the maintenance requirement;
b) assessable income;
c) the rate of deduction;
d) the protected income level.

The method of calculation produces weekly amounts for elements a), b) and c).

a) *The maintenance requirement* is the basic amount required to meet the needs of the child or children for whom maintenance is being assessed. It is based on the amounts provided for the support of children under the income support system, and includes an amount for supporting the person with care. It is not necessarily the amount of maintenance which is required to be paid. The absent parent only pays the full amount of the maintenance requirement if he or she can afford to do so; a well-off absent parent may have to pay more.

b) *Assessable income* is that part of a parent's (or carer's) income which is available for child maintenance. It is calculated by subtracting the person's exempt income from their net income. Exempt income originally consisted of amounts based on income support rates, and an allowance for housing costs. Since April 1995, additional amounts have been allowed in order to take into account high travel to work costs, and the effect of capital or property settlements entered into before 5 April 1993. The assessable income of both parents is calculated but, as explained above,[2] it is only the absent parent who is liable to make payments. No allowance is made for the support of any new partner or step-children of the absent parent at this stage.

c) *The rate of deduction* is the rate at which an absent parent pays child maintenance from assessable income. The effect of the formula is that an absent parent will normally pay half his or her assessable income up to the point where the maintenance requirement is fully satisfied. If the absent parent has more than enough assessable income to meet the maintenance requirement child maintenance will then consist of a basic element, plus an additional element. In such

1 See s 11 and Sch 1, and SI 1992/1815.
2 Page 182.

cases, the basic element amounts to half of the absent parent's assessable income up to the point where the maintenance requirement is met in full. In addition, the absent parent pays 15–25% of his or her remaining assessable income, depending on the number of children to be supported by the assessment. However, the basic and additional elements combined may not exceed a prescribed maximum figure. Once the maximum has been reached the absent parent pays no more maintenance on any surplus income.

The first three stages of the calculation produce only a provisional figure which may be restricted in order to guarantee a minimum income level to the absent parent and any 'second family' he or she may have.

d) *The protected income level* is the level below which the income of the absent parent and any second family is not permitted to fall. If the effect of paying the amount calculated from the first three steps of the formula would be to take the absent parent's income below the protected level then the amount of child maintenance payable is reduced by an appropriate figure. There are two aspects to protected income. The first aspect, introduced in April 1995, is the requirement that an absent parent pays no more than 30% of net income in child maintenance. The second aspect, which has been part of the scheme since its inception, and is now applied after the 30% calculation has been made, is a more complicated calculation, the effect of which is to leave the absent parent and any second family better off than they would be if claiming income support. The amount of maintenance payable is reduced to the point necessary to ensure that the absent parent and any second family do have the protected income level fixed by this fourth element of the formula.

Thus, although the interests of any new partner and step-children of the absent parent are ignored at stage b) (assessable income) they are taken into account when calculating protected income. The effect of this will in most cases be to reduce the maintenance payable. However, even where the protected income calculation would indicate otherwise, there is a prescribed minimum weekly amount that must be paid (£2.35 in 1995/96) although some categories of persons are exempt from paying it.

An example of a child maintenance assessment is given in Appendix 1 in order to indicate the method of calculation.[1]

---

1 In future, however, there will be some circumstances in which the amount of child maintenance assessed is different from that fixed by the formula. Sections 1–9 and Schs 1, 2 of the Child Support Act 1995 provide for a system of 'departure directions' under which there is discretion to depart from the formula in specified circumstances. These provisions are not yet in force but may become so before the end of 1996.

Respective roles of the courts and the Child Support Agency

The jurisdiction of the courts to award aliment for qualifying children has been largely, but not entirely, replaced by the powers of child support officers employed by the Child Support Agency to make maintenance assessments.[1] Section 8 of the 1991 Act provides that no court shall exercise any power which it would otherwise have to make, vary, or revive an award of aliment in any case where a child support officer would have jurisdiction to make a maintenance assessment. In other words, it is not competent for the court to make any order which has the effect of awarding aliment in cases where a child support assessment may be made under ss 4 or 7,[2] or where a person with care may be required to authorise the Secretary of State to take action under s 6. This has the effect of excluding the court's jurisdiction to award aliment under the Family Law (Scotland) Act 1985 in cases where at least one of the parents of the relevant child or children is an absent parent for the purposes of the Act. However, s 8 does not prevent an order for aliment being made against a person with care of the child. A child might, therefore, sue the person caring for him or her for aliment, even where a maintenance assessment could be made against the absent parent.

There are four exceptions to the general principle that no award of aliment may be made where a maintenance assessment could be made. First, under s 8(6), an order for aliment may be made where the absent parent has more than enough assessable income to meet fully the maximum child maintenance allowable under the formula, and the court is satisfied that the circumstances of the case make it appropriate for an award to be made. This is colloquially referred to as a 'top-up' award. However, the great majority of absent parents will not be sufficiently well-off to reach the threshold for top-up awards. Secondly, under s 8(7), an award for aliment may be made solely for the purpose of meeting some or all of the expenses incurred by a child in receiving instruction at an educational establishment or undergoing teaching for a trade, profession or vocation. Thirdly, under s 8(8), an award of aliment may still be made where the child is disabled and the order is made solely for the purpose of meeting some or all of the expenses due to the disability. This exception applies where a disability living allowance is being paid in respect of the child, or the child is blind, deaf or dumb or substantially and permanently

---

1 Sections 11 and 13.
2 It should be emphasised that the court's jurisdiction is excluded if maintenance assessment *could* be made: there is no need for assessment to have taken place before the court's jurisdiction is excluded.

handicapped. These exceptions apply where a person is a qualifying child for the purposes of the Act, and their effect is to allow the court to make an award of aliment even though a child maintenance assessment has been or could be made. However, since the court's jurisdiction is only excluded in the first place where a child support officer would have jurisdiction to make a maintenance assessment, it follows that the general law of aliment is still relevant in all cases where a child *who is not a qualifying child* is owed an obligation of aliment. Thus, a university student may sue a parent for aliment, and a step-child may sue a step-parent.

The fourth exception is potentially of broader application. Power has been conferred on the courts under s 8(5)[1] to make an order which is, in all material respects, in the same terms as a written maintenance agreement providing for periodical payment by the absent parent to or for the benefit of the child. For so long as the transitional provisions are operative, this has the effect of allowing parents to 'contract out' of the 1991 Act by agreement.[2]

More generally, in terms of s 9, there is nothing to prevent persons entering into a maintenance agreement even though a child maintenance assessment has been or might be made. However, the existence of such an agreement does not prevent any party to it from applying for a maintenance assessment with respect to any child covered by the agreement, and any provision of the agreement to the contrary effect is void. In any case where the jurisdiction of the court to make an award of aliment would be excluded by s 8, the court has no power to *vary* any maintenance agreement by inserting a provision requiring an absent parent to pay aliment, or by increasing the amount payable under such an existing provision.

Phasing in child support assessments

The 1991 Act did not take immediate effect with respect to all claims for child maintenance. Arrangements were made for phasing-in to stagger the workload of the Child Support Agency. The original phasing-in arrangements have been adjusted by the Child Support Act 1995, and are now summarised.

With effect from 5 April 1993, child support officers were given jurisdiction in: (a) all new cases, ie cases in which there was no pre-existing court order for aliment or written maintenance agreement; (b) all cases in which the parent with care of the qualifying child claims or is paid income support, family credit, or disability working

1 See SI 1993/620. The order appears to apply to Scotland as well as England.
2 See SI 1992/2644 (as amended) and s 18 of the Child Support Act 1995.

allowance (benefit cases). Such parents with care may not apply for a 'voluntary' assessment under s 4 of the Act. In all such cases it ceased to be competent to apply to the courts for aliment for qualifying children from that date. However, not all cases falling under (b) were actually assessed immediately because of the workload of the CSA.

For other cases, ie those where there was in force a court order for aliment or written maintenance agreement made before 5 April 1993, there was a transitional period, during which the courts were to continue to have jurisdiction. During this period the right to apply for an assessment was to be postponed. Applications under s 4 were to be phased in according to a timetable which would have brought these cases on stream in four phases during 1996/97. The transitional period has now been extended indefinitely. Accordingly, written agreements and court orders in non-benefit cases will prevent applications for maintenance assessments for some time to come, ie until the government comes up with a new timetable. Indeed it is possible that the phasing in of such cases will be postponed indefinitely. This applies mainly to pre-April 1993 orders and agreements, but, as described above,[1] couples can in effect still contract out of the 1991 Act by making a written agreement and asking the court to make an order *in the same terms as the agreement* as allowed by s 8(5) of the Act. Such post-5 April 1993 orders will postpone the right to apply for assessment.

There is special provision for cases which are 'pending' during the transitional period, ie where proceedings seeking aliment or the variation of a written maintenance agreement had begun before 5 April 1993, but no order of the court had been made by that date. In such cases the courts retain jurisdiction to make an order even after 5 April 1993. The court has no power to make an order in cases not begun before 5 April 1993, although the view has been expressed that in Scotland the court's power to make an order also applies to cases *begun during the transitional period.*[2]

Reviews and appeals

Assessments can be queried, challenged and updated through processes of review and appeal. Reviews are conducted by child support officers. On a review, a maintenance assessment may be varied or cancelled. There are four kinds of review: (1) periodical reviews which take place automatically every two years and which ensure that changes in child support rates allowance is made for;[3]

1 *Supra* p 188.
2 *Pope v Pope* 1995 SCLR (Sh Ct) (Notes) 963.
3 Section 16.

(2) reviews on change of circumstances at the instigation of an absent parent, parent with care, or child applicant;[1] (3) reviews at the instigation of child support officers which may take place where a child support officer is satisfied that an assessment, or any of a range of other decisions relating to assessment, is defective because made in ignorance of a material fact, based on a mistake as to a material fact, or wrong in law;[2] (4) reviews of decisions of child support officers.[3] Whilst changes in circumstances will be taken into account in periodical reviews, the second and third types of review allow changes in circumstances to be considered during the intervals between periodical reviews. The fourth category of review ('a s 18 review') is the major avenue of challenge to decisions regarding assessments. The person aggrieved may apply for a review of (i) a refusal to make an assessment; (ii) a refusal to make a review; (iii) an existing assessment; (iv) the cancellation of or refusal to cancel an assessment. The review is by a child support officer who had no part in the decision which is the subject of the review. A child support officer's decision is reviewable where it was made in ignorance of a material fact or based on a mistake as to a material fact or wrong in law. An aggrieved person should seek such a review within 28 days of being notified of the decision he or she wishes reviewed. The time limit may be waived in cases of unavoidable delay.

The appellate structure is analogous to that for most social security benefits. The 1991 Act provides for child support appeal tribunals[4] and child support commissioners[5] to hear appeals. However, in most cases there is no right of appeal direct to a child support appeal tribunal from a decision relating to child maintenance. Instead the Act provides for an appeal to a tribunal only from a section 18 review or refusal of an application for a s 18 review.[6] The effect is that in general an appeal must be preceded by an internal review. The only exception is an appeal against a reduced benefit direction which may be made directly to a tribunal.[7] An appeal must be brought within 28 days of the decision appealed against being given or sent to the appellant. Where an appeal is allowed, the tribunal remits the case to the Secretary of State where it will be dealt with by a child support officer. The tribunal in remitting a case may give such directions as it considers appropriate.

1 Section 17.
2 Section 19 as substituted by s 15 of the Child Support Act 1995.
3 Section 18.
4 Section 21 and Sch 3.
5 Section 22 and Sch 4.
6 Section 20.
7 Section 46(7).

Where the ground for appeal against a s 18 review raises a dispute about parentage it must be made to the ordinary courts rather than to a tribunal.[1] Appeal may be made to a court in Scotland if (a) the child was born in Scotland, or (b) the child, absent parent, or parent with care is domiciled or habitually resident in Scotland on the date when the appeal is made. Appeal may be made to a particular sheriff court in the sheriffdom where (a) the child was born, or where (b) the child, absent parent, or parent with care is domiciled or habitually resident on the date when the appeal is made.

There is a further appeal from a tribunal decision 'on a question of law' to a child support commissioner.[2] Leave to appeal is required (from the chairman of the tribunal within three months or, if he or she refuses, from a commissioner within 42 days of the refusal). The appeal must be made within 42 days of leave being granted. There is a final appeal on a question of law to 'the appropriate court'.[3] This means either the Court of Appeal or, if the child support commissioner so directs, the Court of Session. An appeal to the courts may be made only with leave of the commissioner or, if he or she refuses, leave of the appropriate court. Although there is no express provision in the 1991 Act, there is a final appeal to the House of Lords.

1　SI 1993/961.
2　Section 24.
3　Section 25.

10 Parental responsibilities and rights

INTRODUCTION

It is a hallmark of a democratic society that while parents have the primary responsibility to look after their children, they are free to bring them up in the manner which they deem best for the children's welfare. In order to fulfil their responsibilities, parents enjoy important rights in respect of the upbringing of their children. However, parental autonomy is not absolute. The criminal law protects children from serious physical, emotional or sexual abuse by their parents. Moreover, if a parent neglects or physically ill-treats a child, the child can be made subject to compulsory measures of supervision under the Children (Scotland) Act 1995 and can, if necessary, be removed from the parents.[1] But within these parameters, Scots law gives parents the rights, for example, to choose a child's religion, to decide how a child should be educated, to discipline the child, to consent to medical treatment on the child's behalf and to determine, generally, the place and manner in which the child's time is spent. As maturity is gained, increasingly children will wish to make important decisions in relation to such matters as medical treatment for themselves. Accordingly, it is submitted that the nature of a parental right alters as the child matures: beginning with the right to take decisions on the child's behalf, it becomes, in time, a right merely to give guidance to the child.

The purpose of this chapter is to examine the nature and extent of parental responsibilities and parental rights. We shall consider a) what, in general, these responsibilities and rights are; b) who has parental responsibilities and rights, and c) some specific parental responsibilities and rights.

---

1 On the Children (Scotland) Act 1995, see *infra* Chs 13 and 14.

WHAT ARE PARENTAL RESPONSIBILITIES AND RIGHTS?

A parent[1] has the following responsibilities to a child:[2]

a) to safeguard and promote the child's health, development and welfare;

b) to provide direction and guidance to the child in a manner appropriate to the stage of the child's development;

c) if the child is not living with the parent, to maintain personal relations and direct contact with the child on a regular basis; and

d) to act as the child's legal representative.[3]

These responsibilities supersede any analogous duties imposed on a parent at common law;[4] but they do not replace specific statutory duties, for example, to aliment the child[5] or to ensure the child's education.[6] The parental responsibilities have to be carried out to the extent that it is practicable and in the interests of the child to do so.[7]

In order to fulfil these responsibilities, a parent has the following rights:

a) to have the child living with the parent or otherwise to regulate the child's residence;

b) to control, direct or guide the child's upbringing in a manner appropriate to the child's stage of development;

c) if the child does not live with the parent, to maintain personal relations and direct contact with the child on a regular basis;

d) to act as the child's legal representative.[8]

These parental rights supersede any analogous right enjoyed by a parent at common law;[9] but they do not replace specific statutory rights.[10] Because these rights are given in order that parents can fulfil their parental responsibilities, they can only be exercised in so far as it is practicable and in the interests of the child to do so.[11]

1 A parent is the child's genetic mother or father: s 15(1) of the Children (Scotland) Act 1995. The father of an illegitimate child prima facie is not a parent for these purposes: ibid, s 3(1)(b). A person is a parent if parentage is established by ss 27–30 of the Human Fertilisation and Embryology Act 1990, in spite of the absence of a genetic relationship: s 15(1) of the 1995 Act. On the 1990 Act see *supra* p 152 ff. An adoptive parent is a parent: ibid. In this chapter references are to the 1995 Act unless otherwise stated.

2 A child is a person below 18: s 15(1).

3 Section 1(1)(a), (b), (c) and (d).

4 Section 1(3).

5 Section 1(1)(c) and (d) of the Family Law (Scotland) Act 1985, discussed *supra* p 174 ff.

6 Under the Education (Scotland) Acts.

7 Section 1(1).

8 Section 2(1)(a),(b),(c) and (d).

9 Section 2(5).

10 For example, under the Education (Scotland) Acts.

11 Section 1(1).

Parental rights end when the child reaches 16.[1] Parental responsibilities end at that age, except the responsibility to give a child guidance, which lasts until a young person reaches 18.[2] When reaching
any major decision in fulfilling parental responsibilities or exercising
parental rights, the parent must have regard so far as practicable to
the views of the child, if the child wishes to express them.[3] Account
should be taken of the child's age and maturity. It is presumed that a
child of 12 or over is of sufficient age and maturity to form a view;
but the views of younger children are relevant if they have *in fact* sufficient maturity. This obligation to consult the child may be difficult
to enforce,[4] but it is indicative of the child centred decision-making
process which the 1995 Act is intended to promote. It should be
noted, however, that the obligation arises only in respect of *major*
decisions. It is thought that the importance of a decision will be determined objectively rather than from the child's or parent's perspective.

If two or more persons have parental rights, each can exercise a
right without the consent of the other.[5] However, a child cannot be
removed from the United Kingdom without the consent of a person
who has the parental rights relating to the child's residence or contact
with the child.[6]

The parental responsibility in s 1(1)(a) is sufficiently amorphous to
cover a wide range of matters: the child's education, health, religion,
discipline etc. Similarly, the s 1(1)(b) responsibility is of wide
import, *viz* the provision of counsel for the child in every aspect of
the child's life. The s 1(1)(c) responsibility is of the utmost significance. The 1995 Act proceeds on the basis that it is in a child's best
interests to have the benefit of two parents: thus the responsibility –
and corresponding right in s 2(1)(c) – of a parent to maintain personal
relations and direct contact with the child, when that parent no longer
lives with the child. The parental rights in s 2(1)(a) and (b) are to help
a parent fulfil the parental responsibilities in s 1(1)(a) and (b). We
shall consider these responsibilities and rights in greater detail later
in this chapter.

1 Section 2(7).
2 Section 1(2)(a) and (b).
3 Section 6(1). The views of other persons having parental responsibilities and rights
  should also be considered.
4 What would Leopold Mozart have thought if told he had to consult the five year old
  Wolfgang as to the wisdom of going on a concert tour – albeit that Wolfgang
  Amadeus Mozart was an infant prodigy?
5 Section 2(2).
6 Section 2(3) and (6). If the child's parents have such rights the consent of both is
  required.

The parental responsibility[1] and right[2] to act as a child's legal representative enables a parent to enter into transactions on behalf of a child, when the child lacks active legal capacity.[3] The parent should consult the child before entering any major transaction[4] on the child's behalf; but if the other party to the transaction entered into it in good faith, the transaction cannot be challenged on the ground of the legal representative's failure to consult the child.[5] Where a parent, acting as the child's legal representative, administers the child's property,[6] the parent must act as a reasonable and prudent person would act on his or her own behalf.[7] While enabled to do anything in relation to the property which the child could do if of full age and capacity,[8] the parent is liable to account to the child for the intromissions with the child's property.[9] This will usually occur when the child reaches 16. No liability is incurred by the parent in respect of funds which have been used in proper discharge of the parent's responsibility under s 1(1)(a), ie to safeguard and promote the child's health, development and welfare.[10] As we have seen,[11] if a parent enters into a transaction on behalf of a child below 16, the transaction cannot be set aside on the ground that it is prejudicial to the interests of the child. If the transaction involved the use of the child's own funds, redress may be sought by the child against the parent under s 10.[12]

Transaction is widely defined.[13] Accordingly, the parent acting as the child's legal representative can enter into a wide range of juristic acts on behalf of the child, as well as administer the child's own property.[14] Moreover, as legal representative, a parent can give consent on

1 Section 1(1)(d).
2 Section 2(1)(d).
3 On the legal capacity of children, see *supra* Ch 9.
4 On the duty to consult, see *supra* p 194.
5 Section 6(2).
6 Where the child is the beneficiary under a trust or executory, the property may be administered by a judicial factor or the Accountant of Court: s 9. Where a child is awarded damages, the court can order that the fund is to be administered by persons other than the parents, for example, the Accountant of Court: s 13. On the previous position, see *Riddoch v Occidental Petroleum (Caledonian) Ltd* 1991 SLT 721; *Scott v Occidental Petroleum (Caledonian) Ltd* 1990 SLT 882.
7 Section 10(1)(a).
8 Section 10(1)(b); for example *sell* the child's property, including heritage.
9 Section 10(1).
10 Section 10(2).
11 *Supra* p 166.
12 A parent is no longer a trustee for the purposes of the Trusts (Scotland) Act 1921: para 6 of Sch 4 to the Children (Scotland) Act 1995.
13 It has the same meaning as in s 9 of the Age of Legal Capacity (Scotland) Act 1991, discussed *supra* p 166: s 15(1).
14 Section 15(5)(a).

behalf of the child.[1] Thus, for example, while the responsibility to obtain medical care for a child falls within s 1(1)(a), the duty and right to consent to medical treatment on the child's behalf derives from the parent being the child's legal representative.[2]

Parents cannot abdicate parental responsibilities and rights but can arrange for them to be carried out by other people, for example, the headmaster of a boarding school;[3] liability for failure to fulfil the responsibilities remains with the parents.[4]

WHO HAS PARENTAL RESPONSIBILITIES AND RIGHTS?

A child's mother automatically has parental responsibilities and rights in relation to her child.[5] It does not matter that she has never been married to the child's father: her age is also irrelevant.[6] A child's father automatically obtains parental responsibilities and rights only if he is or was married to the child's mother at the date of the child's conception or at any time thereafter.[7]

EXAMPLES

a) H and W are married at the date of conception and birth; H is presumed to be the father of the child[8] and will automatically have parental responsibilities and rights;

b) H and W are married after the date of conception but before the birth; H is presumed to be the father of the child and will automatically have parental responsibilities and rights;

c) H and W marry after the date of conception and birth; H will *not* be presumed to be the father of the child,[9] but if H's paternity is established, H will automatically acquire parental responsibilities and rights when H marries W.

Marriage to his child's mother is therefore crucial if the father is automatically to obtain parental responsibilities and rights. For this pur-

1 Section 15(5)(b).
2 Sections 1(1)(d) and 2(1)(d).
3 Section 3(5).
4 Section 3(6).
5 Section 3(1)(a).
6 Section 1(3)(g) of the Age of Legal Capacity (Scotland) Act 1991 as amended by para 53(2)(b) of Sch 4 to the Children (Scotland) Act 1995.
7 Section 3(1)(b).
8 Section 5(1)(a) of the Law Reform (Parent and Child)(Scotland) Act 1986, discussed *supra* p 152 ff.
9 Unless both H and W have acknowledged that H is the father of the child and the child has been registered as such: ibid, s 5(1)(b), discussed *supra* p 153.

pose, marriage includes a voidable marriage; and a 'marriage' which is void, provided *both* parties believed in good faith that the marriage was valid (whether or not the error was one of fact or law).[1]

Where a father never marries the child's mother prima facie he has no parental responsibilities and rights. There are, however, two ways that he can obtain parental responsibilities and rights. First, if the mother has not previously been deprived of some or all of her parental responsibilities and rights,[2] she may enter an agreement with the father under which he is to obtain the responsibilities and rights which he would have got if he had married the mother.[3] Thus a father can obtain *all*[4] the parental responsibilities and rights by agreement with the mother. The agreement will stipulate the appropriate date upon which the father is to acquire the responsibilities and rights. It is expressly enacted that the mother and father have capacity to make such an agreement 'whatever age they may be'.[5] This means that if the parent(s) are below 16, the age of legal capacity,[6] they can still enter into such an agreement and both will be able to exercise their parental responsibilities and rights in respect of their child.[7] Such an agreement does not have effect unless it is in the prescribed form and registered in the Books of Council and Session at a time when the mother still has the parental responsibilities and rights that she had when she made the agreement.[8] It is important to note that the father acquires his responsibilities and rights solely by the mother's agreement: no court is involved. Once registered, the agreement is irrevocable,[9] except by court order.[10]

1 Section 3(2)(a) and (b). Accordingly, if W is in bad faith, H does not obtain parental responsibilities and rights under this provision: W will of course have parental responsibilities and rights by virtue of being the child's mother. Cf s 5(1) and (2) of the Law Reform (Parent and Child) (Scotland) Act 1986 discussed *supra* p 152 ff.
2 For example, as a result of the child having been adopted: a s 11(1)(a) order or a parental responsibilities order. On adoption see *infra* Ch 12; on s 11 orders see *infra* p 217 ff; and parental responsibilities orders, see *infra* p 267 ff. If the mother has been deprived of *any* responsibilities and rights, she cannot make such an agreement.
3 Section 4(1).
4 Unless there is a s 11 order in force affecting some of those responsibilities and rights, for example, if there was a residence order in favour of a third party. Such an order does not normally *deprive* the parent of his or her responsibilities and rights: s 11(11), discussed *infra* p 220. Accordingly the mother could still enter into a s 4 agreement with the father, even if a residence order had been made in favour of the child's grandparents.
5 Section 4(1).
6 Discussed *supra* Ch 9.
7 Section 1(3)(g) of the Age of Legal Capacity (Scotland) Act 1991, as amended by para 53(2)(b) of Sch 4 to the 1995 Act: for discussion see *supra* p 168 ff.
8 Section 4(2)(a) and (b). The date of registration is the appropriate date, ie the date when the father obtains parental responsibilities and rights.
9 Section 4(4).
10 Section 11(11).

Secondly, the father could apply to the sheriff court or Court of Session under s 11 of the Children (Scotland) Act 1995, for an order giving him parental responsibilities and rights.[1] He has title to sue as a person who 'not having, and never having had, parental responsibilities and rights in relation to the child, *claims an interest*'.[2] His genetic and/or emotional ties towards the child are per se sufficient to constitute an interest.[3] The welfare of the child is the paramount consideration,[4] and the court will give the father parental responsibilities and rights if it is in the child's interests to do so.

Similarly, any person, for example the child's grandparents or a step-parent, could apply under s 11(3)(a)(i) to obtain parental responsibilities and rights; again their genetic and/or emotional ties would constitute sufficient interest. Moreover, it is open to any person with an interest in the welfare of a child to apply under s 11(3)(a)(ii) for a specific parental responsibility or right; for example, a doctor seeking the right to consent to medical treatment on behalf of a child whose parents are refusing to consent. Section 11 orders are discussed in detail in the next chapter.

Where a person aged 16 or over has de facto care or control of a child below that age then, if the carer does not have parental responsibilities or rights in relation to the child, the carer has a statutory responsibility to do what is reasonable in all the circumstances to safeguard the child's health.[5] Even although the carer does not have the right to act as the child's legal representative,[6] in fulfilling the responsibility to safeguard the child's health the carer can consent to any surgical, medical or dental treatment or procedure on behalf of the child. However, this right to consent only applies if (i) the child does not have legal capacity to consent on his or her own behalf[7] *and* (ii) the carer has no reason to believe that the child's parent would refuse to consent.[8] Thus, for example, a person who has care of a child and knows that the child's parents are Jehovah's Witnesses cannot consent to a blood transfusion on behalf of the child. If in fulfill-

---

1 Section 11(1), (2)(b)(i) and (ii). The court can do so, even if he is under 16: ibid.
2 Section 11(3)(a)(i). Italics added.
3 *D v Grampian Regional Council* 1994 SLT 1038 (Inner House); upheld 1995 SLT 519 (House of Lords).
4 Section 11(7)(a).
5 Section 5(1).
6 Section 2(1)(d).
7 On the capacity of a child below 16 to consent to medical treatment etc, see s 2(4) of the Age of Legal Capacity (Scotland) Act 1991, discussed *supra* p 167 ff.
8 Section 5(1).

ing this responsibility the carer must make a major decision, the child has to be consulted.[1] The responsibility does *not* arise when a person has care or control of a child at school.[2]

A child's parent can appoint a person to be the child's guardian in the event of the parent's death.[3] To be effective the appointment must be in writing and signed by the parent.[4] In addition, the parent must have been entitled to act as the child's legal representative at the date of the parent's *death*.[5] When a parent appoints a guardian, this is regarded as a major decision and there is a duty to consult the child.[6] An appointment as guardian does not take effect unless the person named in the deed accepts the appointment, either expressly or by acts which are not consistent with any other intention.[7]

Once the appointment is accepted, the guardian automatically acquires the full complement of parental responsibilities and rights.[8] Where the child has a surviving parent, the parent's responsibilities and rights continue and are fulfilled and exercised along with the parental responsibilities and rights of the guardian.[9] Guardianship ends when the child reaches 18, or the child or guardian dies, or is terminated by an order under s 11 of the Children (Scotland) Act 1995.[10]

---

1 Section 6(1)(a). On the duty to consult the child, see *supra* p 194.
2 Section 5(2).
3 Section 7(1). A guardian of a child may appoint a person to be the child's guardian in the event of the guardian's death: s 7(2). The same rules apply as in the appointment of a guardian by the child's parent.
4 Section 7(1)(a)(i). The appointment will usually be in the parent's will or a codicil to the will. If the will or codicil is revoked, the appointment is also revoked: s 8(4). Where the appointment is made in a deed other than a will or codicil, it is revoked if the deed is destroyed by the granter or the granter has another person destroy the deed in the granter's presence: s 8(3). If A appoints B to be the guardian, then B's appointment is revoked if A later appoints C to be the guardian, unless it is clear that the appointment of C is an additional appointment: s 8(1). However, the appointment of B is not revoked unless the appointment of C is in writing and signed by A: s 8(2). It does not matter if the appointment of B is in an unrevoked will or codicil.
5 Section 7(1)(a)(ii).
6 Section 7(6).
7 Section 7(3). If two or more persons are appointed, any one can accept the appointment even if the other(s) refuse to do so, unless the appointment otherwise provides.
8 Section 7(5). This is subject to any s 11 orders and any parental responsibilities order in force at the time the appointment was accepted.
9 Section 7(1)(b). Each can exercise a parental right without the consent of the other: s 2(3), discussed *supra* p 194.
10 Section 11(2)(h).

SPECIFIC PARENTAL RESPONSIBILITIES AND RIGHTS

In this section, we shall consider some of the most important parental responsibilities and rights.[1] The statutory responsibilities and rights are expressed in very general terms and it is valuable to consider specific aspects. The responsibility to safeguard and promote the child's health, development and welfare and to give the child direction and guidance, will be considered along with the right to have the child living with the parent and the parent's right to control, direct or guide the child. The responsibility and right to act as the child's legal representative have already been discussed.[2] It must always be remembered that a parent is expected to fulfil the statutory responsibilities only in so far as it is practicable for the parent to do so.[3] However, in exercising parental rights there is a duty to consult the child when making a major decision and the parent must always act in the child's interests.[4] Accordingly, parental rights can be regarded as prima facie rights, in the sense that any purported exercise of the right must further the child's welfare or, at least, must not be against the interests of the child: this is known as the welfare principle. If a purported exercise of a parental right is against the child's interests, there is no obligation on the child or a third party to act in accordance with the parent's decision. The ultimate arbiter of whether or not a purported exercise of parental rights is *in fact* contrary to a child's welfare is the Court of Session or the sheriff court which have the power to make any order in relation to parental responsibilities and rights.[5] Thus, for example, a child or a third party can petition the court for a declarator that a purported exercise of a parental right by a parent is not in the interests of the child or that a parent's acts or omissions are in breach of the parent's statutory responsibilities.

Residence

Parents have the right to have their child live with them or otherwise to regulate their child's residence,[6] for example to allow the child to holiday with friends. It is generally accepted that children thrive in a

---

1 For full discussion see *Wilkinson and Norrie* Chs 5–8.
2 *Supra* p 195 ff. It will arise incidentally in the present discussion.
3 Section 1(1). There would, for example, be no failure to comply with s 1(1)(a) if a parent had to refuse a child's request to be educated at boarding school, or holiday in Florida, if the parent could not afford to do so.
4 Sections 1(1), 2(1) and 6. On the duty to consult, see *supra* p 194.
5 Section 11(1) and (2). The orders listed in s 11(2) are 'without prejudice to the generality' of s 11(1).
6 Section 2(1)(a).

stable home environment, and consequently this right can be seen as enabling parents to fulfil their responsibility to promote the child's development.[1] However, it is only a prima facie right and must be exercised in the child's interests. Thus, parents may lose the right to have their child live at home if it would be against the child's interests to remain with or be returned to the parent.

This is illustrated by the leading case of *J v C*,[2] a decision of the House of Lords in an English appeal, but accepted as authoritative in Scotland.[3] When a couple had a child, they were advised that because of the child's health, he should remain with foster parents in England and not return with his parents to Spain where the family lived. The parents left their child in England, but retained contact with him through visits etc. When, several years later, the child's health had improved, the parents decided that the child should come to Spain and live there with the rest of the family. The child was made a ward of court. The court had then to determine whether or not the parents should be permitted to take their child to Spain. The proceedings were protracted and the case was eventually heard by the House of Lords. The House decided that in spite of the fact that the parents' conduct was unimpeachable, the child should nevertheless remain with his foster parents in England. After eight and a half years, the boy had become integrated into his foster parents' family and to remove him to Spain would be likely to cause him distress and possible long term psychological harm: and so the parents could not exercise their prima facie right to have their child live with them because it would be contrary to the child's interests to do so.

J v C is therefore authority for the proposition that the parental right of residence is governed by the welfare principle.[4] Accordingly, a parent cannot validly exercise the right if it is not in the best interests of the child to do so. A striking example is provided by *M v Dumfries and Galloway Regional Council*.[5] A child was being looked after by a local authority. The mother, who had not been deprived of her parental rights,[6] asked the local authority to return her child. The local authority refused. The sheriff held that since there was

---

1 Section 1(1)(a).
2 [1969] 1 All ER 788, [1970] AC 668, HL
3 See *Cheetham v Glasgow Corporation* 1972 SLT (Notes) 50.
4 See, in particular, the speech of Lord McDermott, [1970] AC 608 at 701. This is now enacted in s 1(1) of the Children (Scotland) Act 1995.
5 1991 SCLR 481.
6 For example, as a result of a parental responsibilities order, see *infra* p 267 ff. The child was not subject to compulsory measures of supervision: discussed *infra* Ch 14.

suspected abuse, the return of the child was not in the child's interests and consequently the authority was not under any obligation to accede to the mother's request.[1]

Discipline

A parent has the right to control a child.[2] This can include physical chastisement.[3] In theory, the exercise of this right must be in accordance with the welfare principle: in practice, physical chastisement must be reasonable. Excessive physical ill-treatment of a child will lead to criminal proceedings for cruelty[4] and will constitute grounds for compulsory measures of supervision under the Children (Scotland) Act 1995.[5] Thus, where the parent's intention is to punish the child, no crime is committed and no ground for compulsory measures of supervision exists, provided the force used is moderate: it is irrelevant that the parent lost his or her temper at the time of the chastisement.[6] On the other hand, loss of control or temper will not prevent a conviction, if the intention to injure, as opposed to discipline the child, can be inferred from the severity of the parent's conduct.[7] Attempts to abolish or moderate the parental right of physical chastisement have failed.[8] The right lasts until the child reaches 16.[9] While the exercise of this right is limited by the welfare principle, it is thought that there are more practical limitations:

1 The case of the child should, of course, have been referred to a Reporter to consider whether the child was in need of compulsory measures of supervision.
2 Section 2(1)(b).
3 The recognition of this right is inherent in the decision of the European Court of Human Rights in *Campbell v Cosans* (1982) 4 EHHR 293. In that case, the court indicated that at least the threat of a strapping using the tawse did not amount to torture or inhuman or degrading treatment.
4 Section 12(1) of the Children and Young Persons (Scotland) Act 1937: s 12(7) provides that a parent's and teacher's right to discipline is not affected.
5 On compulsory measures of supervision, see *infra* Ch 14.
6 *B v Harris* 1990 SLT 208 (mother lost her temper and strapped daughter who had called her 'a fucking bastard'!).
7 *Peebles v MacPhail* 1990 SLT 245 (slap on face knocked over child); *Boyd v Wither* 1991 SLT 206 (child seriously beaten); *Kennedy v A* 1993 SLT 1134 (father spanked a distressed baby). See also *Cowie v Tudhope* 1987 GWD 12–395 where a father who had hit his 15 year old son with the leg of a table was convicted of assault.
8 For discussion see *Report on Family Law* (SLC No 135) para 2.67 ff.
9 Section 2(7).

a mother, for example, may find difficulty in disciplining her son for refusing to dry the dishes if he is a 15 year old, twelve stone prop forward.[1]

Education

Parents are under a duty to ensure that their children receive a suitable education until they reach 16.[2] In particular, they must ensure that the child attends school.[3] In order to fulfil these specific obligations and fulfil the general statutory responsibility to promote the child's development,[4] a parent has the right to choose a child's education.[5] This right must be exercised in accordance with the welfare principle.[6] In practice, unless the parent has sufficient means to afford private education, the exercise of this right will be limited. However, parents' rights to choose a local authority school which is suitable for the needs of their children have been strengthened as a result of legislation.[7]

It should be noted that the rights and obligations in respect of a child's education vest not only in the parent but also the child's guardian, any person obliged to aliment the child and any person having day-to-day care of the child.[8]

1 At common law, school teachers have an independent right physically to chastise school children: *McShane v Paton* 1922 JC 26. However, corporal punishment has been abolished in local authority schools and in relation to pupils in state assisted places at independent schools: s 48A of the Education (Scotland) Act 1980 as amended by s 294 of the Education Act 1993. Even where the right exists ie in respect of non-state assisted pupils at independent schools, the punishment must not amount to inhuman or degrading treatment: s 48A(1A).
2 Sections 30–31 of the Education (Scotland) Act 1980.
3 Section 35 of the Education (Scotland) Act 1980; the parent is relieved of this obligation if the parent provides the child with effective education by other means. A parent's failure, without reasonable cause, to ensure that a child attends school is an offence: see, for example, *Wyatt v Wilson* 1994 SLT 1135.
4 Section 1(1)(a).
5 Where both parents have parental rights any dispute over choice of school etc can be resolved a specific issue order under s 11(2)(e) of the 1995 Act.
6 *J v C* [1969] 1 All ER 788, [1970] AC 668, HL at 702 per Lord McDermott.
7 Sections 28 and 28A–H of the Education (Scotland) Act 1980 (as amended): see Seager 1982 SLT (News) 291. The right is not absolute: *Keeney v Strathclyde Regional Council* 1986 SLT 490. Note also the parental involvement in school boards: see School Boards (Scotland) Act 1988 as amended by para 46 of Sch 4 to the Children (Scotland) Act 1995.
8 Section 135(1) of the Education (Scotland) Act 1980 as amended by para 28(5) of Sch 4 to the Children (Scotland) Act 1995.

Religion

In an increasingly pluralistic society, religious toleration is of the first importance. Scots law recognises that in fulfilment of their responsibility for the child's development, parents have a prima facie right to choose a child's religion. This right must be exercised in accordance with the child's welfare. Where, for example, a parent's or, indeed, a child's, religious convictions will result in physical harm to the child, the parents' and the child's wishes will be overridden. Thus, for example, while parents are free to decide that a child should be brought up as a Jehovah's witness, if the child should require a blood transfusion, the law will not countenance the parent's refusal to consent to such treatment.[1]

Scottish courts have accepted that where parents are of different religions,[2] it matters little to the child whether he or she is brought up in one faith rather than another: the matter will be decided in the light of all the circumstances of the case in accordance with the welfare principle. Thus, for example, in *McNaught v McNaught*,[3] a mother who was a Protestant had the children of the marriage living with her. In spite of the fact that she had agreed to bring up the children in her husband's Roman Catholic faith, the husband failed to obtain an order that at least his youngest child, a son, should continue to be brought up as a Roman Catholic. As it was otherwise in the child's best interests to be with his mother, she was free to bring up the child as a Protestant since either faith was for the benefit of the child.

Hitherto, the courts have been adamant that it is in a child's welfare to be brought up in a religious faith. In *M'Clements v M'Clements*,[4] the Lord Justice Clerk (Thomson) said that in his opinion a child 'ought not to be denied the opportunity of being brought up in the generally accepted religious beliefs of the society in which he lives'.[5] Nevertheless, it is thought that today parents would not be in breach of any parental responsibility if they choose to bring up their child as

---

1 In practice an application would be made for a child protection order and the sheriff can give a direction in the order that the child should have medical treatment: s 58(5). On child protection orders, see *infra* p 272 ff. Alternatively, a person could apply for the parental right to consent to medical treatment by bringing proceedings for a specific issue order under s 11(2)(e) of the Children (Scotland) Act 1995: see *infra* p 48.
2 The cases are concerned with parents of different Christian denominations, but it is thought that the same principles would apply if, for example, one parent was Christian and the other Moslem.
3 1955 SLT (Sh Ct) 9.
4 1958 SC 286.
5 Ibid at 289.

an atheist or agnostic.[1] It is, however, interesting to note in this context that religious instruction is a 'compulsory' element in the curricula of public, ie education authority, schools.[2]

On reaching 16, a young person can choose his or her own religion.[3] While parents retain the responsibility to guide their child on such matters,[4] they have no power to veto the child's choice. A child below 16 may wish to choose a religion different from the child's parents. Given their duty to consult the child, parents may fulfil their statutory responsibilities by agreeing with the child's choice. The parents would only be in breach of their parental responsibilities if it would be against the child's interests to change religion. This could arise, for example, if the child proposed to join an extreme sect, for example, scientologists.

Medical procedures

In fulfilment of their responsibility to safeguard and promote their children's health,[5] parents have the prima facie right to consent to medical treatment on the child's behalf.[6] However, the exercise of this right is subject to the welfare principle. There is little Scottish authority on the point, but English decisions are instructive. In *Re D (a minor)*,[7] for example, a mother consented to the sterilisation of her mentally handicapped daughter who had reached the age of puberty. Before the operation took place the child was made a ward of court. The court overrode the mother's decision on the ground that the operation was not in accordance with the welfare of the child. Heilbron J based her decision on the grounds that while mentally handicapped, the child probably had sufficient capacity to enter into marriage, there was no evidence that she was promiscuous and any unwanted pregnancy could be terminated. In those circumstances, the proposed operation was not in the child's interests. On the other hand, in *Re B (a minor)*,[8] the House of Lords held that a sterilisation operation could be carried out on a mentally handicapped girl of 17 who had a

1 Cf *MacKay v MacKay* 1957 SLT (Notes) 17 per the Lord President (Clyde).
2 Sections 8–10 of the Education (Scotland) Act 1980. Religious observance can only be discontinued after a poll of local government electors: s 8(2). Parents can, however, elect that their child should not take part in religious observance or education.
3 The parental responsibility and right ceases when the child is 16: ss 1(2)(a) and 2(7).
4 The parental responsibility to give guidance lasts until the child is 18: s 1(2)(b).
5 Section 1(1)(a).
6 This is by virtue of their responsibility and right to act as the child's legal representative: ss 1(1)(d) and 2(1)(d).
7 [1976] 1 All ER 326, [1976] Fam 185.
8 [1988] AC 199, [1987] 2 WLR 1213.

mental age of 5. Pregnancy and childbirth would have been physically and mentally disastrous for the young woman and therefore it was in her best interests that the operation go ahead.[1]

The right to consent implies the right to refuse consent to medical treatment. This right must again be exercised in accordance with the welfare principle. Thus, in *Re B (a minor)*[2] the Court of Appeal overrode the parents' refusal to consent to an operation to remove an intestinal blockage from their new born infant who was suffering from Down's syndrome. The parents had taken the view that since the child was mentally handicapped, it was better for the child to die as a result of the blockage rather than live. The Court of Appeal held that this purported exercise by the parents of their prima facie right to withhold consent was not in accordance with the child's welfare. The child had the prospect of a reasonably happy life, albeit suffering from the syndrome. In the circumstances, the court overrode the parents' decision and consented to the operation on behalf of the child. On the other hand, *Re B (a minor)* was distinguished in *Re C (a minor)*[3] where a new born baby, suffering from congenital hydrocephalus, was dying. It was in the infant's best interests to receive care which merely relieved her suffering and there was no need to give treatment which might achieve a short prolongation of life.

Where the proposed treatment is generally accepted as therapeutic, it is thought that a parent's consent to such treatment on a child will be upheld as a valid exercise of the parent's prima facie right, since it would be in the child's best interests to consent. Conversely, where a parent refuses to consent to therapeutic medical treatment on a child, the purported exercise of the prima facie right will be overridden as it

---

1 The court indicated that before such an operation was to be performed, the consent of the court should always be obtained: ibid at 1218, per Lord Templeman. In Scots law this could be done by an application under s 11(1) of the Children (Scotland) Act 1995. Given that consent can only be given where it is in the child's best interests to do so, it could be argued that the consent of the court is otiose: however, it is thought that it would nevertheless be prudent to obtain the court's approval in such a sensitive area. In England, the court has approved such an operation on a mentally handicapped adult: in *Re F* [1989] 2 WLR 1025. In Scotland, this result could be obtained by the appointment of a tutor dative who could consent on behalf of the incapax adult. Indeed, this would have been the case if *Re B* had arisen in Scotland; the young woman was over 16 and therefore her mother's right, as her legal representative, to consent on her behalf would have terminated: s 2(7). On the sterilisation of a mentally handicapped adult, see now the decision of Lord MacLean in *L, Petrs* 22 February 1996, OH.
2 [1981] 1 WLR 1421, CA.
3 [1990] Fam 26. See also *Finlayson (Applicant)* 1989 SCLR 601 where a ground for compulsory measures of supervision was established when parents refused medical treatment for their haemophiliac son even though they were genuinely concerned that the child might be infected with AIDS as a result of the treatment: the child's physical condition had deteriorated as a result of non-treatment.

would be against the child's interests not to have the benefit of the treatment. But difficulties arise where the proposed medical procedures are not unarguably in the child's best interests. If an analogy be taken from the law on blood tests,[1] *S v S*[2] and *Docherty v McGlynn*[3] suggest that a medical procedure can be carried out on a child provided it is not positively *against* the child's interests to do so. Thus, it is submitted that in Scots law parents can lawfully consent to medical procedures on their children, which, while not in the child's best interests, are not positively against the child's interests. These would include, for example, non-therapeutic circumcision of male infants,[4] the taking of blood samples from healthy children for the purpose of medical research and the donation of regenerative tissue, for example, bone marrow.[5]

When a child reaches 16, the child can consent on his or her own behalf.[6] Given the importance of patient autonomy, this must include the right to refuse medical treatment. But, as we have seen,[7] a child below 16 may have capacity to consent by virtue of s 2(4) of the Age of Legal Capacity (Scotland) Act 1991. However, the 1991 Act does not expressly stipulate that parents lose their right to consent on behalf of a child who has s 2(4) capacity. Where the proposed medical treatment is unarguably therapeutic, there is no difficulty if the parents and the child both consent. Moreover, if the child has s 2(4) capacity, the child's consent is sufficient – even if the parents would not consent. The difficulty arises if the child has s 2(4) capacity and refuses to consent. Can the parents override their child's refusal and consent on the child's behalf? Conversely, if a child with s 2(4) capacity consents to medical treatment which is not unarguably therapeutic, can the parents veto the child's decision: for example, if the child consents to a termination of pregnancy or to donate non-regenerative tissue?

There are two possible views. The first is that when the child has s 2(4) capacity, then the parents lose their right to consent as the right

1 Discussed *supra* p 155 ff.
2 [1970] 3 All ER 107, [1972] AC 24, HL at 45 per Lord Reid.
3 1983 SLT 645.
4 Non-therapeutic female circumcision cannot lawfully be carried out in the United Kingdom: Prohibition of Female Circumcision Act 1985.
5 The donation of non-regenerative tissue, for example, a kidney would be *against* the child's ie the donor's interests: consequently a parent cannot consent to this procedure on behalf of a child. However, if the child had capacity under s 2(4) of the Age of Legal Capacity (Scotland) Act 1991, it would appear that the *child* could consent. For full discussion, see *supra* p 167 ff.
6 Section 1(1)(b) of the Age of Legal Capcity (Scotland) Act 1991.
7 For discussion, see *supra* p 167 ff.

is no longer needed. The second is that as the parents retain the responsibility to give direction to the child until the child is 16[1] – and guidance until the child is 18[2] – the parents cannot simply be ignored. The difficulty is that if the parents are to give direction or guidance, they must be told of the proposed medical treatment.

In the case of *Gillick v West Norfolk and Wisbech Area Health Authority*,[3] the House of Lords in an English appeal held that, in exceptional circumstances, a parent need not be informed when a girl under 16 seeks contraceptives or contraceptive advice from a doctor. There are two threads of reasoning in the speeches of the majority. Lord Scarman took the view that parental rights exist only in so far as a child lacks the capacity to take decisions for him or herself: thus, when a girl has sufficient understanding, intelligence and maturity to make decisions in relation to inter alia sexual matters, the parent's rights cease.[4] But whether or not the child has gained this degree of maturity is a question of fact and it is difficult to see how this will be determined, particularly in relation to sexual matters. Parents will argue that a child has not reached that degree of maturity when the child's proposed course of conduct appears to be contrary to the parent's concept of what is in the best interests of the child. Lord Fraser, on the other hand, did not deny that the parents had a prima facie right to be informed. But he maintained that there could be exceptional circumstances where this was not necessary *viz* when the child (i) understood the nature and effect of contraceptives, (ii) had been persuaded to consult her parents but had refused, (iii) was likely to have or continue to have sexual intercourse without contraceptives, (iv) her physical or mental health would suffer without contraceptive advice, and (v) that it was in the child's best interests to be prescribed contraceptives without the parents' knowledge or consent. Whether an exceptional case had arisen could in his Lordship's opinion safely be left to the clinical judgment of the doctor concerned.[5] It should be noticed that before Lord Fraser's exception applies, the proposed course of treatment must be in the child's best interests. This could provide a solution to the problem where a child with s 2(4) capacity refuses to have medical treatment which would be in the child's best interests, for example, a blood transfusion. Since the child is acting *against* his or her interests, Lord Fraser's exception would *not* apply

1 Section 1(1)(b)(i) and (2)(a).
2 Section 1(1)(b)(ii) and (2)(b).
3 [1985] 3 All ER 402, HL.
4 Ibid at 422. This supports the first view outlined above.
5 Ibid at 413.

and the parental consent would be valid. In other words, if Lord Fraser is correct, a child with s 2(4) capacity can in exceptional circumstances consent without the parent's knowledge to medical procedures which are in the child's interests but cannot refuse to consent to such procedures if this would be clearly against the child's interests.[1]

Gillick was, of course, an English decision and is not binding on Scottish courts where the matter is ultimately one of construction of s 2(4) of the 1991 Act. However, to the extent that the House of Lords rejected the contention that parents have a right to veto such treatment, it is important. On the other hand, it is precisely where medical treatment is not unarguably in the child's best interests that parents should have the right to be informed and be able to advise their children before they embark on a course of action which they might later regret. In the context of the prescription of contraceptives to girls under 16, her parents have a statutory obligation to proffer advice, to discuss, for example, whether or not it is in her long term interests to enter sexual relationships at such an early age. If they persuade her that this is not in her interests, then no further difficulties arise; but if they do not, they cannot prevent her obtaining contraceptives if she has s 2(4) capacity. In the case of a sexually active girl who is determined to continue to have sexual intercourse, it is the present writer's view that the Scottish courts would accept that it was not against her interests to be prescribed contraceptives without her parents' consent. But this would be a decision that the parents had purported to exercise their right improperly, ie in a way which was contrary to the welfare principle – not that the right to be informed does not exist.[2]

It is thought that a similar approach would be taken in respect of other medical procedures. If, for example, a 14 year old girl sought termination of a pregnancy, then even if she had s 2(4) capacity, her parents have the right to be informed in order to discuss with her the alternatives to termination and the possible long term effect on her of having an abortion. If the child was still determined to have the termination, it is submitted that any purported veto by her parents would be ineffective as it is surely against a child's interests to compel her to continue with an unwanted pregnancy.[3] On the other hand, if, for example, parents purported to veto a 14 year old boy's decision to

1 Lord Fraser's approach was followed by the Court of Appeal in *Re W* [1992] 4 All ER 627. (If a child refuses to consent to life-saving treatment, the parents can give a valid consent.)
2 Cf the approach of Lord Scarman, ibid at 402 and the first view of the effect of s 2(4) capacity discussed *supra* p 207.
3 See, for example, *Re P (a minor)* (1982) 80 LGR 301.

donate a kidney for a school friend, the parent's decision would probably be upheld even if the boy had s 2(4) capacity since it is prima
facie contrary to his interests to donate non-generative tissue.[1]
However, this remains an uncertain area of the law until s 2(4) has
been the subject of authoritative judicial scrutiny.

Looking after children

Ensuring that a child receives medical care is only one aspect of a
parent's responsibility to safeguard and promote the child's health,
development and welfare.[2] Apart from alimenting the child,[3] parents
should give their children love and affection, and provide them with
opportunities to play and socialise with other families.[4] Parents must
ensure the safety of their children and that their children are looked
after in the parents' absence. In the event of abandonment or neglect,
not only could the child be in need of compulsory measures of supervision,[5] but the parents could be liable to criminal sanctions under
s 12(1) of the Children and Young Persons (Scotland) Act 1937.
Wilful abandonment is a question of fact and degree, depending on
the period during which the children have been left and the steps, if
any, which were taken for their care.[6] Merely to leave a child unattended is not wilful neglect: it will depend on all the circumstances of
the case including the age of the child, the age of any babysitter, the
time the child was left alone and the reason why the child was left
unattended. But it is neglect if a very young child is left alone for a
substantial period, and through the absence of care is likely to experience unnecessary suffering.[7]

Parents must also be prepared to give their children direction and
guidance whenever it is in the child's interest to do so.[8] This clearly
covers a wide range of issues, for example, recreational pursuits, educational opportunities, career opportunities etc. In practice this will
merge with the parent's obligation to consult the child on any major

1 But the parents would not be able to do so if the first view of the effect of s 2(4) was
   correct: *supra* p 207.
2 Section 1(1)(a).
3 On aliment, see *supra* Ch 9.
4 For full discussion, see *Wilkinson and Norrie* p 192 ff.
5 Discussed *infra* Ch 14.
6 *M v Orr* 1995 SLT 26.
7 *H v Lees; D v Orr* 1994 SLT 908 (not neglect when mother was intoxicated and unable
   to look after baby for several hours when no evidence that child required food or
   changing during that period; not neglect when father left 13 year old son alone for
   several hours); *M v Normand* 1995 SLT 128 (not neglect merely to leave a child of
   20 months sleeping unattended in a car for 45 minutes: there must be circumstances
   which suggest that the child would be likely to experience unnecessary suffering).
8 Section 1(1)(b).

decision which will affect the child, for example, moving house, changing school etc.[1]

Names

Parents will usually determine the name of the child. It is customary for a legitimate child to take the surname of the father. Difficulties arise, however, when parents divorce and the children live with their mother. If she remarries, can she unilaterally change the children's surname to that of their step-father? Where, as a result of the retention of their surname, the children experience difficulties at school or settling into their new family, it could be argued that it would be in their best interests to alter their surnames. On the other hand, the retention of their original surname is a valuable link in maintaining the children's relationship with their father: this would be particularly important if the children knew their father before the divorce and he had been having successful contact with them. In those circumstances, unless there was evidence of genuine distress to the children in being known by their original surname, as opposed to inconvenience for the mother and step-father, it is submitted that it would be contrary to the children's interests to alter the surname. On the other hand, if the children had had little contact with their father, there would be a strong case that a change of surname to that of their step-father would be in the children's interests as this would strengthen their relationship with their step-father who is, in the circumstances, the only father figure that they have known.[2] It is thought that the change of name is a matter relating to parental responsibility under s 1(1)(a) as it concerns the welfare of the child and that the court has jurisdiction to consider a dispute over the matter by virtue of s 11(1) of the 1995 Act.[3]

Contact

We have been considering specific examples of the nature of parental responsibilities and rights where the child is living with the parents. However, a parent who is not living with a child has the responsibility to maintain personal relations and direct contact with the child on a regular basis;[4] and the parent enjoys the corresponding right to

---

1 On the duty to consult, see *supra* p 194.
2 *W v A* [1981] 1 All ER 100, [1981] Fam 14, CA; cf *Cosh v Cosh* 1979 SLT (Notes) 72.
3 Cf the position taken by the sheriff under the pre-1995 Act legislation: *GSF v GAF* 1995 SCLR 189. It is submitted that this decision is wrong.
4 Section 1(1)(c).

maintain the relationship and have direct contact with the child.[1] As with the other parental rights, the right to contact is a prima facie right in the sense that it must be exercised in accordance with the welfare principle. Before the enactment of the 1995 Act, Scottish courts insisted that a father was not entitled to have contact with his child unless he could show that it was positively in the child's best interests to do so.[2] The onus lay on the father to provide such evidence: there was no presumption that contact would be in the interests of the child.[3] The position can be summarised as follows:

> 'The father's application for access [contact] was made by him on his own admission, because he is the father. He gave no other reason for his application. A father does not have an absolute right to access to his child. He is only entitled to access if the court is satisfied that it is in the best interests of the child.'[4]

Accordingly, before an application for contact was successful, the parent had to prove that contact was positively in the child's best interests: the fact that contact was not against the child's interests was not enough. In these circumstances, the right to contact was a right without substance.[5]

However, the Children (Scotland) Act 1995 not only gives parents the right to have contact with their children but imposes an obligation upon them to do so. The rationale for such an obligation is that prima facie it is in the interests of children to have a continuing relationship with the parent who does not live with the child. The opportunity is open for the courts to assert that there is now a presumption that contact is in a child's best interests and that a parent should only be denied contact if it is established that contact would be contrary to the interests of the child. The views of the children will be of the utmost importance in determining whether or not contact would be in their interests.[6] In this way, the right to contact – albeit, defeasible if contrary to the welfare principle – would have the significance it clearly deserves.

---

1   Section 2(1)(c).
2   *Crowley v Armstrong* 1990 SCLR 361; *Sanderson v McManus* 1995 SCLR 902.
3   *O v O* 1995 SLT 238. But see the dissenting judgment of Lord McCluskey in *Sanderson supra.*
4   *Porchetta v Porchetta* 1986 SLT 105 per Lord Dunpark.
5   For full discussion see Thomson 1989 SLT (News) 109. The position in England was the same: *Re KD (a minor)* [1988] AC 806.
6   The case will be brought under s 11(2)(d): for further discussion, see *infra* p 228 ff.

11 Actions in relation to parental responsibilities and rights

INTRODUCTION

As we have seen, a mother automatically has parental responsibilities and rights in relation to her child.[1] The child's father will also automatically have the full complement of parental responsibilities and rights, if he was married to the child's mother at the date of conception or subsequently.[2] But it is possible for other persons to acquire parental responsibilities and rights as a result of an application to the court under s 11 of the 1995 Act. For example, unless he has obtained parental responsibilities and rights under an agreement with the child's mother,[3] the father of an illegitimate child can only obtain parental responsibilities and rights by virtue of a s 11 order. Moreover, on divorce, the court has power to regulate the parental responsibilities and rights of the parties in relation to any children of the marriage. The purpose of this chapter is to discuss the procedures which are applicable and the principles which are applied in litigation relating to parental responsibilities and rights.

TITLE TO SUE

(i) Independent applications in relation to parental responsibilities and rights

The Court of Session and the sheriff court have the power to make any order in relation to parental responsibilities and rights as it thinks fit.[4] An application can be brought by the following persons:

1 Section 3(1)(a) of the Children (Scotland) Act 1995, discussed *supra* p 196. References in this chapter are to the 1995 Act unless otherwise stated.
2 Section 3(1)(b), discussed *supra* p 196.
3 Section 4, discussed *supra* p 197.
4 Section 11(1)(a), (b) and (2). The court can also make any order relating to the guardianship of the child and the administration of the child's property: s 11(1)(c) and (d). See *supra*. Jurisdiction in an application in relation to parental responsibilities and rights is based on the child's habitual residence in Scotland (or sheriffdom): s 9 of the Family Law Act 1986. The presence of the child in Scotland (or

213

a) A person who does not have and never has had parental responsibilities and rights in relation to the child, but claims an interest.[1] In other words, *any* person claiming an interest can bring an application. An interest can be a genetic or emotional tie between the applicant and the child; thus, for example, the father of an illegitimate child, a step-parent or the child's grandparents could use this provision to obtain parental responsibilities and rights in relation to a child.[2] In addition, a person with an interest in the outcome of the specific application as it relates to the welfare of the child, also has title to sue.[3] Thus, for example, a doctor could apply under this provision for the right to consent to medical treatment on behalf of a child whose parents were refusing to consent. It is expressly enacted that a child has title to sue in respect of the fulfilment of parental responsibilities and rights vis-a-vis him or herself.[4] Accordingly, if a child wished to live elsewhere than at home, or the child was unhappy with parental decisions relating to the child's education etc, or was concerned about how his or her property was being administered, the *child* could apply under s 11(1) for a ruling by the court. However, a local authority has no title to sue under s 11 for an order in relation to parental responsibilities and rights.[5] If the local authority wishes to assume parental responsibilities and/or rights, it must apply for a parental responsibilities order under s 86.[6] If a social worker considered the child to be in need of compulsory measures of supervision, the case should be referred to a Reporter.[7]

---

sheriffdom) will suffice if the child is not habitually resident in any part of the United Kingdom and, in the case of an application in the sheriff court, the pursuer or defender is habitually resident in the sheriffdom: s 10 of the Family Law Act 1986. In an emergency, jurisdiction can be taken on the presence of any child in Scotland (or sheriffdom) if it is necessary to make such an order immediately: s 12 of the Family Law Act 1986. Habitual residence of the child in Scotland (or sheriffdom) is a basis for jurisdiction in an application in relation to guardianship: s 16 of the Family Law Act 1986 as amended by para 46 of Sch 2 to the Age of Legal Capacity (Scotland) Act 1991. Where the application is concerned with the administration of a child's property, the Court of Session has jurisdiction if the child is habitually resident in, or the property is situated in, Scotland: s 14(1) of the Children (Scotland) Act 1995: the sheriff has jurisdiction in such applications if the child is habitually resident in, or the property is situated in, the sheriffdom: ibid, s 14(2).

1 Section 11(3)(a)(i).
2 *D v Grampian Regional Council* 1994 SLT 1038 (IH); approved 1995 SLT 519, HL. For discussion of the position of the father of an illegitimate child, see *supra* p 198.
3 Ibid.
4 Section 11(5): we are assuming the child has legal capacity to sue, see *supra* Ch 9.
5 Section 11(5).
6 On parental responsibilities orders, see *infra* p 267 ff.
7 On compulsory measures of supervision, see *infra* Ch 14.

b) Any person who has parental responsibilities or rights in relation to a child.[1] Thus, for example, if both parents have parental rights and responsibilities but cannot agree on the child's religion or education etc, either could apply under s 11 for a ruling by the court on the matter.

c) Any person who has had parental responsibilities or rights in relation to the child.[2] For example, if a mother has been deprived of her parental responsibilities and rights by a s 11(1)(a) order because she was a drug addict, she could apply for parental responsibilities and rights when she was successfully cured of her addiction and wished to resume her responsibilities towards her children. However, persons deprived of parental responsibilities and rights by the following orders, have no title to sue:[3]

   (i) when the parental responsibilities and rights have been extinguished as a result of an adoption order. Thus, for example, if a child has been adopted the natural mother cannot seek parental responsibilities and rights under s 11.[4]

   (ii) when the parental responsibilities and rights have been transferred to an adoption agency as the result of an order freeing the child for adoption. While no application can be made under s 11, the relevant parent whose responsibilities and rights have been transferred by the freeing order, can seek to hve the freeing order revoked.[5]

   (iii) when the parental responsibilities have been extinguished by virtue of s 30(1) of the Human Fertilisation and Embryology Act 1990 (fast track adoption procedure for child born as a result of surrogacy).[6]

   (iv) where the parental responsibilities and rights have been transferred to a local authority by a parental responsibilities order. In this situation, the parent can apply to have the parental responsibilities order varied or discharged.[7]

In these four situations, decisions have been made for the long term future of the child and the parents' interests will have been taken into account on making the relevant order. It would defeat the certainty inherent in adoption and parental responsibilities orders if the whole procedure could be undermined by applica-

---

1 Section 11(3)(a)(ii).
2 Section 11(3)(a)(iii).
3 Section 11(4)(a)–(d).
4 She could, theoretically, apply to adopt the child. On adoption generally, see *infra* Ch 12.
5 On freeing orders, see *infra* p 244 ff.
6 Discussed *infra* p 254.
7 Section 86(5), discussed *infra* p 269.

tions under s 11 for parental responsibilities and rights by parents who had recently been denuded of these rights and responsibilities as a consequence of such orders.[1]

(ii) Ancillary actions in relation to parental responsibilities and rights

We have been considering the question of title to sue when a person brings an application relating to parental responsibilities and rights independently of other proceedings. However, courts have the power to make s 11 orders in any action of divorce, judicial separation or declarator of nullity of marriage.[2] Even if no application has been made, the court must consider whether or not to make a s 11 order in the light of such information as is before the court, relating to the arrangements or proposed arrangements for the upbringing of any child of the family.[3] A child of the family is *either* a child of both parties to the action *or* any other child (other than a child placed with them as foster parents by a local authority) who has been treated by both of them as a child of the family.[4] A child is a person below the age of 16.[5] The court can postpone granting decree in the principal action if it feels unable to make a s 11 order without further consideration and there are exceptional circumstances which make it desirable in the interests of the child to delay granting decree until the court is able to exercise its s 11 powers.[6] In these circumstances, the court can call on a local authority to provide a report as to the arrangements for the upbringing of the child.[7] The report will often contain recommendations with regard to the residence of the child and while the decision is that of the court alone,[8] in practice the recommendations will often be followed.[9] The use of this power is not

---

1 This was also the position before the enactment of s 11(4): *D v Grampian Regional Council* 1995 SLT 519.
2 Section 12(1). The court is the Court of Session, or the sheriff court in an action of divorce or separation. Jurisdiction is determined by the rules in respect of the principal action. See also s 13 of the Family Law Act 1986 as amended by para 41(3) of Sch 4 to the Children (Scotland) Act 1995.
3 Ibid.
4 Section 12(4)(a) and (b). But the court cannot order aliment for such a child unless the child was also accepted as a child of the family: ss 1(1)(d) and 2(2)(a) of the Family Law (Scotland) Act 1985; see *supra* p 175.
5 Section 12(3).
6 Section 12(2).
7 Section 11 of the Matrimonial Proceedings (Children) Act 1958 as amended by para 43 of Sch 8 to the Social Work (Scotland) Act 1968 and para 9 of Sch 4 to the Children (Scotland) Act 1995.
8 *MacIntyre v MacIntyre* 1962 SLT (Notes) 70.
9 Eekelaar and Clive *Custody after Divorce* (1977) p 53.

extensive and even if social background reports were made mandatory in all divorce actions, it is considered that in the vast majority of cases, they would merely confirm the arrangements agreed by the parties. Moreover, with the gradual acceptance of the value of conciliation, parties are increasingly making voluntary agreements as to the upbringing of their children after divorce.[1] Conciliation is not compulsory but the court has power to recommend conciliation in relation to disputes over parental responsibilities and rights.[2]

Where the court considers that a s 11 order should be made, it can make the order even if there was no application for such an order: moreover, the court can make a s 11 order even if it declines to make an order in respect of the principal action.[3] Thus, for example, if H brings an action of divorce against W, the court could order that their children should reside with W, even although the court refuses H's action for divorce.

THE NATURE OF S 11 ORDERS

Whether a s 11 order is sought in an independent action or as an ancillary action, the court has the power to make any order in relation to parental responsibilities and rights as it thinks fit.[4] Without prejudice to the generality of this power, the 1995 Act specifies the following orders:[5]

(a) An order depriving a person of some or all of that person's parental responsibilities and rights. For example, if H is convicted of sexual abuse of his children, W could apply under s 11(2)(a) for an order depriving H of his parental responsibilities and rights.

(b) An order (i) imposing upon a person parental responsibilities and (ii) giving a person parental rights. The person must be 16 or over unless that person is a parent of the child.[6] This is the provision under which a person who does not have parental responsibilities and rights can obtain them: for example, the father of an illegitimate child, a step-parent or the child's grandparent.

(c) An order regulating the arrangements as to (i) with whom a child

1 Solicitors are enjoined to encourage clients to use conciliation in appropriate cases: Practice Notes of 11 March, 1977.
2 Rules 170B(15) and 250D(10) (Court of Session); Rule 132F (sheriff court). For information on conciliation consult Family Conciliation Scotland, 127 Rose Street, South Lane, Edinburgh. See *Clive* p 576 ff.
3 Section 11(3)(b).
4 Section 11(1) and (2).
5 Section 11(2).
6 Parent is the genetic mother or father, subject to the Adoption (Scotland) Act 1978 and ss 27–30 of the Human Fertilisation and Embryology Act 1990. On applications by parents below 16, see *supra* pp 168 ff, 198. A mother under 16 would only have to apply if she had been deprived of her parental responsibilities and rights as a result of a s 11(2)(a) order.

under 16 is to live or (ii) if with different persons alternately or periodically, with whom during what periods, a child under 16 is to live. This is known as a residence order. This order can be used where, for example, H and W divorce and the court wishes to regulate the residence of their children, for example, that they are to live with W for six days a week and with H for the other day. Because the court can make any order 'it thinks fit', residence need not be awarded to H or W but to a third party, for example, the child's grandparent. It should be noted that a child can apply for a residence order.[1]

(d) An order regulating the maintenance of personal relations and direct contact between a child under 16 and a person with whom the child is not living. This is known as a contact order. This order can be used where, for example, H and W divorce and W obtains a residence order: H can apply for a contact order in order to maintain his personal relationship with his children who are living with W. It is also the way in which, for example, the father of an illegitimate child or a grandparent, who has successfully applied for the parental right of contact, can exercise that right. A child can also apply for a contact order.[2]

(e) An order regulating any specific question which has arisen in respect of parental responsibilities and rights, guardianship or the administration of a child's property. This is known as a specific issue order. The scope of such orders is potentially very wide. Consider the following examples:

   (i) H and W cannot agree on the education or religion of their child. An application could be made for a specific issue order to resolve the impasse.

   (ii) A child is unhappy with his/her parents' decision to send the child to boarding school or to move house or not to holiday in Florida. The child could apply for a specific issue order to resolve the matter.

   (iii) The mother of a mentally handicapped girl wishes to have her daughter sterilised: the doctors are concerned. The mother or the doctors can apply for a specific issue order to determine whether the operation is in the girl's interests and, as a consequence, whether or not the sterilisation can go ahead.

   (iv) The parents of a child refuse to consent to medical treatment on the child. A doctor could apply for a specific issue order to give the doctor the right of legal representation to consent on behalf of the child.

1 Section 11(5).
2 Ibid.

(f) An interdict to stop any conduct which purports to be done in fulfilment of parental responsibilities or to be an exercise of parental
rights relating to a child or the administration of the child's property. Again the scope of this provision is potentially very wide.
Consider the following examples:

  (i) The parents of a 12 year old girl with s 2(4) capacity[1] consent
on her behalf to the termination of their daughter's pregnancy, even though the girl refuses to consent. The girl or a
nurse or a doctor could apply for an interdict prohibiting the
operation going ahead until the court has made a specific
issue order as to the legality of the operation.

  (ii) The parents enter into the sale of a house owned by their 12
year old child. The child could apply for an interdict preventing the sale going ahead until the court had determined
whether or not the sale was in the child's interests.

(g) An order appointing a judicial factor to manage a child's property
or remitting the matter to the Accountant of Court.

(h) An order appointing or removing a person as guardian of the
child.[2]

In practice, the most common orders are likely to be residence orders,
contact orders and orders giving or depriving persons of parental
responsibilities and rights.

A s 11 order includes an interim order, the variation of an order or
the discharge of an order.[3] A child, for the purpose of s 11, is a person
below 18, except in the case of a residence order and a contact order
when the child must be below 16.[4] If, in the course of s 11 proceedings,[5] the court considers that a ground of referral exists,[6] it may refer
the case to a Reporter who can arrange a children's hearing to consider whether or not the child requires compulsory measures of
supervision.[7]

It will be clear that often more than one person will have parental
responsibilities and rights in respect of a child.[8] Where this is the

---

1 Ie capacity to consent to medical treatment by virtue of s 2(4) of the Age of Legal
Capacity (Scotland) Act 1991, discussed *supra* p 167 ff.
2 On guardianship, see *supra* p 199.
3 Section 11(13).
4 Sections 15(1), 11(2)(c) and (d).
5 Section 54(1)(b). This power also exists in an action of divorce, judicial separation,
declarator of marriage, nullity of marriage, parentage or non parentage: s 54(1)(a).
The child must normally be below 16.
6 On grounds of referral, see *infra* p 281 ff. The provision does not apply where the
ground of referral is that the child has committed an offence: s 54(1).
7 Section 54(3). The ground of referral is deemed to have been established in accordance with s 68. For full discussion, see *infra* Ch 14.
8 For full discussion, see *supra* p 196 ff.

case, each can exercise a parental right without the consent of the other(s).[1] What then is the effect of a s 11 order on a person's parental responsibilities and rights? Consider the following example:

> H and W are married. Both have parental responsibilities and rights in respect of C. H and W divorce. W obtains a residence order in respect of C. H is awarded a contact order in respect of C. How do these orders affect H and W's parental responsibilities and rights?

By s 11(11), an order has the effect of depriving a person of parental responsibilities and rights[2] only in so far as the order expressly so provides and only to the extent that it is necessary to do so to give effect to the order. Thus, in the example, the residence order will not deprive H of *any* of his parental responsibilities and rights unless this is expressly stipulated in the order. However, while not being deprived of his responsibilities and rights, H cannot act in any way which would be incompatible with the residence order.[3] So, even though he has still the prima facie right to have his child living with him, H cannot insist that the child live with him rather than W during the periods stipulated in the residence order that W was to have C living with her. Similarly, W retains the full complement of parental responsibilities and rights but cannot prevent H from seeing C at the times stipulated in the contact order. However, if the court took the view that H and W would not act sensibly, it could in the residence order *expressly* deprive H of his s 2(1)(a) right to have C living with him and in the contact order *expressly* deprive W of her right to have contact with C during the period C is to have contact with H. However, the court is enjoined not to do so, unless satisfied that it would be better for the child to make such orders than that no order to that effect be made at all.[4]

The importance of s 11(11) cannot be over-emphasised. The 1995 Act takes the view that a child should have the benefit of the support and guidance of both parents: therefore a s 11 order should have the minimal effect on the parents' existing parental responsibilities and rights. Indeed, if, for example, a child's parents agree on the steps to be taken in respect of the child's upbringing after they divorce,[5] there should be no need for a s 11 order as the court *cannot* make a s 11 order unless satisfied that it is better for the child to make the order

1 Section 2(2): see *supra* p 194.
2 But the court can revoke a s 4 agreement if necessary to do so: s 11(11). On s 4 agreements, see *supra*.
3 Section 3(4). (Or in any way that is incompatible with a supervision requirement: on supervision requirements, see *infra* Ch 14.)
4 Section 11(7)(a).
5 Discussed *supra* p 217.

than that none should be made at all. Moreover, even if a s 11 order is made and a person is expressly deprived of a parental responsibility or right, this must be the *minimum* necessary to give effect to the order. If, in the example, H was deprived of his right to have C live with him,[1] H still retains the right to determine, for example, C's education[2] or act as C's legal representative:[3] these rights are exercised *along with* W, who, of course, also retains parental responsibilities and rights.

Where a residence order is made which requires a child to live with a person who does not have pre-existing parental resonsibilities and rights in relation to the child, the effect of the order is to give that person the parental responsibilities in section 1(1)(a),(b) and (d)[4] and the parental rights in section 2(1)(b) and (d),[5] for as long as the order is in force.[6] So, in the example, if residence was awarded to C's grandmother, she would have the relevant responsibilities and rights as a result of the residence order.[7] Unless H or W was expressly deprived of parental responsibilities and rights in the residence order, they would continue to fulfil their responsibilities and exercise their rights *along with* C's grandmother, provided they did not act in any way which was incompatible with the order.[8]

The 1995 Act therefore adopts a minimalist approach to orders relating to parental responsibilities and rights. No s 11 order can be made unless the court is satisfied that it is better for the child to make an order than that none should be made at all.[9] This is particularly pertinent where a residence order or a contact order is sought when a marriage breaks down. In these circumstances, the parties are to be encouraged to reach agreement, if necessary through conciliation services, on how their children are to be brought up after divorce. If this can be done, each parent will retain the full complement of parental responsibilities and rights after divorce. There will be no need for a residence or contact order: indeed, the court *cannot* make the orders.[10] However, if this policy is to be achieved, it will necessitate radical changes in the practice of solicitors and advocates, who

1 Section 2(1)(a).
2 Section 2(1)(b).
3 Section 2(1)(d).
4 Discussed *supra* p 193 ff.
5 Ibid.
6 Section 11(12). These are known as relevant responsibilities and rights.
7 Subject to any provision in the order that she was *not* to have any relevant responsibility or right.
8 Section 3(4) discussed *supra* p 220.
9 Section 11(7)(a).
10 Ibid.

regarded ancillary orders for residence[1] or contact[2] as part and parcel of a divorce 'package'; in the legal culture of judges, who must now regard making such orders as the exception rather than the rule; and in the attitude of parents, who must put the interests of their children first and recognise the importance of the children's need to retain personal relationships with both parents after the breakdown of the marriage.

THE WELFARE PRINCIPLE

In considering whether or not to make a s 11(1) order and, if so, the nature of the order, the court has to exercise discretion. In so doing the court 'shall regard the welfare of the child concerned as its paramount consideration and shall not make any such order unless it considers that it would be better for the child that the order be made than that none should be made at all'.[3] We have discussed the non-interventionist aspect of this provision in the preceding section; in this section we shall explore the welfare principle in some detail.

It is a fundamental tenet of the 1995 Act that decisions relating to parental responsibilities and rights should be child centred. Accordingly, not only is the child's welfare the paramount consideration in s 11 proceedings, but the court is enjoined so far as practicable, taking account of the child's age and maturity, to do the following:[4]

(i) give the child an opportunity to indicate whether the child wishes tc express any views;

(ii) if the child so wishes, give the child an opportunity to express his or her views; and

(iii) have regard to such views as the child may express.

We shall call this the duty to consult the child. A child aged 12 or over is presumed to be of sufficient age and maturity to form a view, but the views of a child below that age can be taken into account if the child *in fact* is of sufficient age and maturity.[5] In giving his or her views, the child does not have to be legally represented if he or she does not wish to be.[6] Thus, the views of the child at the centre of the

---

1 Pre-1995 Act known as custody.
2 Pre-1995 Act known as access.
3 Section 11(7)(a).
4 Section 11(7)(b)(i), (ii) and (iii).
5 Section 11(10).
6 Section 11(9): the presumption in s 11(10) applies to a child's decision under s 11(9).

proceedings must be fed into the court's decision-making process. However, it is the *court's* view of what is in the child's best interests which will ultimately prevail, not the views of the child.

The welfare principle is the paramount consideration in any application under s 11. It would apply in deciding, in what would be exceptional circumstances, that a parent should be deprived of parental responsibilities. Conversely, it will be the paramount consideration in determining whether or not to give parental responsibilities and rights to the father of an illegitimate child, a step-parent or relative of the child. Difficult problems can be envisaged in specific issue orders but again the welfare principle is paramount. An exception is made to this in proceedings relating to a child's property, to the extent that the court must endeavour not to affect adversely a person who has 'in good faith and for value, acquired any property of the child concerned, or any right or interest in such property'.[1] This could arise, for example, if the child's parents had leased heritable property owned by the child to a bona fide tenant, when it was not in the child's best interests to do so.

Where the welfare principle was most commonly applied before the enactment of the 1995 legislation was in actions for custody and access. These cases are illustrative of how it may be used in applications for residence and contact orders. However, the decisions must be used with caution given that under the 1995 Act (i) the court should not make any order unless it is better for the child to do so than that no order should be made at all[2] and (ii) the court *always* has a duty to consult the child.[3]

The relevant factors in applying the welfare principle in residence orders

While the welfare of the child is the paramount consideration, all the factors of the case are considered to the extent that they point to the course of action which is best for the child. As Lord MacDermott explained in *J v C*,[4] the welfare principle connotes

'a process whereby, when all the relevant facts, relationships, claims and wishes of parents, risks, choices and other

---

1 Section 11(8).
2 Discussed *supra* p 220 ff. For an example of this approach being adopted before the 1995 Act, see *Potter v Potter* 1993 SLT (Sh Ct) 51 (sheriff refused to grant mother custody, leaving the child in her care and father having generous access but both retaining their parental rights).
3 *Supra* p 222.
4 [1969] 1 All ER 788, [1970] AC 668, HL at 710–711.

circumstances are taken into account and weighed, the course
to be followed will be that which is most in the interests of the
child's welfare . . .'.[1]

Thus, specific factors remain relevant in so far as they pertain to the
child's welfare. However, in determining what is best for the child's
welfare, a judge will be influenced not only by medical and psychological knowledge of the development of children but, inevitably, by
his or her own conception of how a child should be brought up. This
is recognised in the rule that in such cases[2] an appellate court will not
interfere with the decision of the judge at first instance unless the
court is satisfied either that the judge exercised his or her discretion
upon a wrong principle, or that the decision is so plainly unreasonable that the judge must have exercised his or her discretion wrongly.[3]

Early this century, it was the practice of the Court of Session in
divorce actions to apply a presumption that the 'innocent' spouse
whose conduct was not responsible for the breakup of the marriage
should be granted custody; this presumption was rebuttable on evidence that it would be against the child's welfare to award custody to
the innocent spouse.[4] However, such a presumption has no place in
modern Scots law where the welfare of the child is the paramount
consideration in s 11 proceedings and the law of divorce is, theoretically at least, based on the non-fault concept of irretrievable breakdown of marriage.[5] Instead, a person's 'conduct' should only be
relevant in so far as it suggests that it would not be in the child's best
interests to live with that person. So, for example, if all other factors
suggest that it would be in a girl's interests that she should live with
her mother, the fact that the mother was an adulterous wife is irrelevant. Similarly, it should also be irrelevant that a woman is a prosti-
tute provided she is a competent mother and has satisfactory
accommodation for the child. But if the accommodation was such
that the child was in danger of physical or sexual assault by the
woman's clients then the prostitution would be relevant because of its
probable effects on the welfare of the child.

It is submitted that a similar approach should be taken when the
person seeking residence or contact is homosexual. However, it is
clear that a parent's sexual orientation has been considered to be an

---

1 In *Campins v Campins* 1979 SLT (Notes) 41 at 42, Lord Cameron emphasised that
   nothing can override or be superior to the child's welfare.
2 It is thought that this is true for all applications under s 11(1) of the 1995 Act, not
   merely residence and contact orders.
3 *Britton v Central Regional Council* 1986 SLT 207; *Early v Early* 1990 SLT 221.
4 *Hume v Hume* 1926 SC 1008.
5 See *supra* Ch 6.

important factor. In *Early v Early*[1] a mother lost custody of her child who had lived happily with her for several years: the court held, inter alia, that the boy who was approaching adolescence required a suitable male role model and could better adjust to his mother's sexuality if he lived with his father and siblings.[2]

In weighing up the factors which determine what is best for the child, the Scottish courts have, in the past, given considerable importance to ensuring that a child obtains a religious upbringing. The 'solace and guidance' of a religious faith was regarded as so important for the welfare of a child that on divorce it was difficult for an atheist spouse to obtain custody if the other spouse was prepared to provide a religious environment. Thus, for example, in *M'Clements v M'Clements*,[3] an adulterous mother was awarded custody rather than an atheist father because she would give the children a religious upbringing.[4] Where both parties were prepared to offer the child a religious upbringing, there was no bias in favour of any particular Christian denomination and custody was determined by weighing up other factors in accordance with the welfare principle.[5] These cases were decided 40 years ago. It is submitted that given our increasingly secular society, religious upbringing should no longer be such an important factor in applying the welfare principle.

The Scottish courts have rejected any presumption that a young child should prima facie live with his or her mother. In *Hannah v Hannah*,[6] the Lord Ordinary had proceeded on the basis that it was 'more in accordance with nature' that a child should be removed from the custody of her father and his mistress where he had been living for several years after the marriage had broken down, and be returned to the mother. In reversing the judge's decision, in the Inner House of the Court of Session, Lord Walker observed[7]

'What exactly the Lord Ordinary meant by nature, or what precisely nature has to do with it, I must confess I find difficulty in appreciating as a proper test in matters of this kind. It is not nature but the welfare of the child which is the material matter.'

1 1989 SLT 114, approved 1990 SLT 221.
2 However, in *Hill v Hill* 1990 SCLR 238, a child was returned to his homosexual father in Canada on the ground that the father was not a danger to the child with whom he had had a good relationship.
3 1958 SC 286.
4 Cf *MacKay v MacKay* 1957 SLT (Notes) 17 when the atheist father was awarded custody on condition that the child's grandmother gave the child religious instruction.
5 *McNaught v McNaught* 1955 SLT (Sh Ct) 9.
6 1971 SLT (Notes) 42.
7 Ibid at 43.

The evidence established that the child, who had lived with her father for six years, was happy and well adjusted; in these circumstances, the court held that it was in her best interests that custody be awarded to her father.

In *Brixey v Lynas*[1] the sheriff awarded custody to the father of an illegitimate child. The decision was upheld by the Sheriff Principal. Since her birth and throughout the proceedings, the child had been in the care of her mother and was well looked after. In reversing the decisions of the sheriff and Sheriff Principal, the Inner House of the Court of Session held that the child should remain with her mother. In the course of his judgment, Lord Morison took the view that the sheriff had given insufficient weight to 'the practice of the courts in Scotland to recognise as an important factor which has to be fully taken into account in a dispute concerning custody between the mother and father of a very young child, that during his or her infancy the child's need for the mother is stronger than the need for a father'.[2] However, Lord Morison also recognised that 'This principle should not be regarded as creating any presumption in favour of the mother, nor, certainly, as a rule of law'.[3] It is thought that while Lord Morison overstates the importance of a *mother's* – as opposed to a *parent's* – role in the upbringing of a child, the result in this case is justified on the basis that the child was thriving in the de facto care of her mother.[4]

It is submitted that *Hannah v Hannah* and *Brixey v Lynas* illustrate the most important factor which the court will take into account in determining where a child should live *viz* the preservation of the status quo. Provided a child is secure in the environment where he or she has lived since the breakdown of the marriage or relationship, prima facie it is in the child's best interests to remain in the care of that parent. Thus, for example, in *Whitecross v Whitecross*[5] a mother failed to obtain the custody of a young child who had lived with his father since the breakup of the marriage. The court took the view that it was in the child's best interests not to disturb the continuity of the child's relationship with his father with whom he had been living:

> 'To disturb the situation which admittedly is satisfactory in all respects and would involve removing the child from the custody of a parent with whom he has lived in family since his

1 1994 SLT 847.
2 Ibid at 849.
3 Ibid. Nevertheless 'motherly love' is still regarded as an important factor: see, for example, *Clark v Clark* 1987 GWD 35–1240; *Beaney v Beaney* 1987 GWD 36–1268; *McCluskey v Gardiner* 1988 GWD 16–680.
4 For an excellent critique of *Brixey*, see E Sutherland 1994 SLT (News) 375.
5 1977 SLT 225.

birth inevitably involves a certain degree of disturbance of his life, the effects of which it is impossible to assess or estimate with any accuracy.'[1]

Consequently, other things being equal, it is considered to be in a child's best interests to preserve the status quo and allow the child to live with the parent who has looked after the child since the breakup of the marriage or the relationship.[2]

It must be stressed that this is only a prima facie presumption. If it is established that it is in the best interests of the child to be moved, the courts should not hesitate to do so. Thus, in *Hastie v Hastie*,[3] a child aged nine had been in the care of his father's mother, ie the child's grandmother, for four years. The grandmother, who was 63, attempted to indoctrinate the child against his mother. In these circumstances, Lord Davidson ordered that the child should live with his mother because this would restore a 'normal' parent-child relationship which was in the child's best interests.[4] Similar concern for a 'normal' family relationship has resulted in a child being removed from the care of his homosexual mother to that of his father.[5] Other factors, for example, if a child would be removed from a school where he/she was settled, may result in the child residing with a parent who has not hitherto had care and control of the child.[6]

Because it is generally accepted that the preservation of the status quo operates for the benefit of the child, an important consequence follows. When a marriage or relationship breaks down, the children will generally remain in the care of their mother. In practice, there are few disputed cases.[7] Instead, the couple agree that the child should continue to reside with the parent who has cared for the child since the breakup: in the vast majority of the cases, this will be the mother.

1 Ibid at 228 per Lord Cameron.
2 The preservation of the status quo is consonant with the 'least detrimental' criteria for custody disputes advocated by Goldstein, Freud and Solnit in their influential book, *Beyond the Best Interests of the Child* (1973, New York). In *Breingan v Jamieson* 1993 SLT 186, a child who had been living with her mother was allowed to remain with her mother's family, after the mother's death. In refusing the father's application for custody Lord McLean observed at 190: 'Her [the child's] life has been disturbed enough so far. To remove her now to a totally different environment would be disruptive of her settled, happy life and detrimental to her best interests . . .'.
3 1985 SLT 146.
4 See also *Clark v Clark* 1987 GWD 35–1240 (child removed from grandparents to mother).
5 *Early v Early* 1989 SLT 114, approved 1990 SLT 221.
6 *Clark v Clark* 1987 GWD 13–441. See also *Jesner v Jesner* 1992 SLT 999.
7 Eekelaar and Clive *Custody after Divorce* (1977) p 52. In the Scottish sample, custody was disputed at the time of the divorce proof in only 1% of the cases.

An award of custody simply reflected this arrangement.[1] Even in the few contested cases, the courts were reluctant to disturb the status quo.[2] *A fortiori*, given the principle of non-intervention in s 11(7)(a), even fewer residence orders should be awarded, since it will not be in the child's interests to make an order which simply reflects what the parties have already agreed.[3]

Relevant factors in applying the welfare principle in contact orders

As we have seen,[4] in actions for access before the 1995 Act, the Scottish courts insisted that the onus lay on the pursuer to prove that access was positively in the child's best interests.[5] As a result of the 1995 Act,[6] where a person already has parental responsibilities and rights, prima facie that person has both the duty and the right to maintain a personal relationship with a child who is no longer living with him or her. This responsibility and right to contact remains even if the child is subject to a residence order, unless the person has been expressly deprived of the responsibility and right.[7] In other words, the whole thrust of the 1995 legislation is that it is prima facie in a child's best interests to have contact with an absent parent, as this reinforces the child's sense of identity.[8] Accordingly, it is submitted that if a person who already has parental responsibilities and rights applies for a contact order, the court should approach the case in the following way:

a) consider whether it is better for the child to make the order than that none should be made at all. Since *ex hypothesi* the applicant has the right to see the child, an order should normally not be necessary as the parties should have made suitable arrangements. An order will be required if the applicant has had difficulties in seeing the child;

b) if an order would be better for the child, the court should assume that prima facie contact is in the child's best interests and the onus

---

1 Thus Eekelaar and Clive found that the wife was awarded custody in 76% and the husband awarded custody in 9% of the cases: ibid p 56 and Table 34.
2 It was irrelevant whether or not the preservation of the status quo favoured the child's father or mother. For full discussion, see Maidment *Child Custody and Divorce* (1984) pp 61–66.
3 Discussed *supra* p 220 ff.
4 *Supra* p 212.
5 *Porchetta v Porchetta* 1986 SLT 105; *Crowley v Armstrong* 1990 SCLR 361; *O v O* 1995 SLT 238; *Sanderson v McManus* 1995 SCLR 902.
6 Sections 1(1)(c) and 2(1)(c).
7 Section 11(11); see *supra* p 220.
8 *Cooper v Cooper* 1987 GWD 17–628; *McCabe v Goodall* 1989 GWD 30–114.

should shift to the person denying contact on a voluntary basis to
establish that contact would be against the child's interests. Here
the duty to consult the child is important but where the child does
not wish to see the applicant, the courts should follow their previous practice and take pains to ensure that the refusal is genuine.[1]
Only if satisfied that contact is against the child's interests, should
a contact order be refused: this would be most unlikely unless the
child had never had a personal relationship with the applicant,[2] or
the applicant had seriously ill-treated the child or voluntary contact was causing the child great distress.[3]

On the other hand, if a contact order was sought by a person who did
not have any parental responsibilities and rights, for example the
father of an illegitimate child, it is submitted that the applicant should
have to adduce evidence that on the balance of probabilities[4] contact
would positively be in the child's best interests.[5]

It remains to be seen whether or not the courts will take the
approach outlined above in applications for contact orders.[6]

Difficulties sometimes arise where the persons with whom the
child is living wish to emigrate abroad with the result that a parent's
right to contact is frustrated. The courts have taken the view that provided that the emigration of the family is in the child's interests, the
fact that a person may have difficulty in exercising contact should not
prevent the child leaving the country.[7]

CONCLUSION

We have seen how, in theory, any proceedings in relation to parental
responsibilities and rights are determined by the welfare principle.

1 *Cosh v Cosh* 1979 SLT (Notes) 72; *Clement v Clement* 1987 GWD 18–660; *Brooks v Brooks* 1990 GWD 2–62.
2 This could arise, for example, if H₁ and W were married but separated before C was born. C lives with W who divorces H₁ and marries H₂. If H₁ has failed to implement his parental responsibility since C was born, contact with H₁ would not be in C's interests if the only parental figures C knew were W and H₂: cf *Porchetta v Porchetta* 1986 SLT 105; *Naismith v Naismith* 1987 GWD 17–628.
3 *Russell v Russell* 1991 SCLR 429 (child distressed: fact mother stopped agreed contact did not prevent her showing that a contact order would be against the child's interests).
4 *Sloss v Taylor* 1989 SCLR 407; *Crowley v Armstrong* 1990 SCLR 361; cf *McEachan v Young* 1988 SCLR 98.
5 *Montgomery v Lockwood* 1987 SCLR 525; *Crowley supra*; *Johnston v Carson* 1990 SCLR 460.
6 The approach suggested in the text is similar to that advocated by Lord McCluskey in his dissenting judgment in *Sanderson v McManus* 1995 SCLR 902.
7 *Johnson v Francis* 1982 SLT 285; *Borland v Borland* 1990 GWD 33–1883.

But in relation to the residence of children whose parents' marriage ends in divorce, Maidment[1] has concluded that British socio-legal studies have produced three findings:

> 'Firstly, about 94 per cent of divorcing parents agree between themselves the arrangements for the care of their children after the divorce. Secondly, about 90 per cent of these arrangements provide for the mother being the main caretaker in that the children live with her. Thirdly, the court, which need not but usually is asked to confirm the private consensual arrangements, rarely disturbs parents' agreements and almost invariably preserves the residential status quo of the child . . .'.

Whatever the theoretical powers of the court, even if a residence order was thought necessary, the judge will invariably 'rubber stamp' the arrangements which have been negotiated by the parties. In so far as these arrangements will normally confirm that the child should live with the mother where she has had the care of the child since the breakup of the marriage, this preserves the status quo. This is thought to be conducive to the child's welfare as it does not disturb the continuity of the child's relationship with the de facto caring parent. Moreover, unless he has been expressly deprived of his parental responsibilities and rights, a residence order does not deprive the father of exercising his rights and fulfilling his responsibilities in relation to the upbringing of the child. It will often have been agreed that the non-residential parent should have contact with the child. Before the 1995 Act, such contact often became irregular, particularly if the parents subsequently entered into new family relationships. It is hoped that since parents now have a statutory responsibility under the 1995 Act to maintain personal relations with children who are not living with them, this will reinforce the importance of continuing to see the child.[2] However, the normal arrangements under which a child lives with the mother operates to reinforce the traditional view that women should bear the major burden of the child-rearing function.

There is growing evidence that children will make a better recovery from the traumatic effects of the breakdown of their parents' marriage when they can sustain an emotional tie with both parents. As a consequence of the principle that no s 11 order should be made unless it is better for the child to make the order than that none should be made at all, and that such orders, even when made, should have the

---

1 Maidment *Child Custody and Divorce* (1984) p 68.
2 Section 1(1)(c).

minimum effect on a parent's existing responsibilities and rights, the 1995 Act has given Scots law the framework to achieve this end. It remains to be seen whether, by jettisoning their previous practices, the courts, legal practitioners and parents will take the opportunity provided by the Act to make this aspiration everyday actuality.

INTERNATIONAL ASPECTS

In recent years there has been growing concern over the problem of international child abduction. When, for example, a court has awarded custody to a parent in state A and the non-custodial parent kidnaps the child to state B, it would appear desirable that there should be a quick and easy procedure by which the child should be returned to the custodial parent in state A, always provided that it is not against the child's interests to do so. This matter has been the subject of international conventions which have been enacted into Scots law.[1] These and related issues will be discussed in this section.

Common law

At common law, the Scottish courts will recognise decrees relating to parental responsibilities and rights granted by the court of the country where the child was habitually resident.[2] However, that decree will only be enforced if it is in the child's best interests to do so. Accordingly, a Scottish court can refuse to enforce the foreign decree and instead make its own s 11 order in relation to the residence of the child, when, of course, the child's welfare is the paramount consideration.[3] In *Sinclair v Sinclair*,[4] for example, Lord Prosser refused to order the return to Germany of children who had been abducted by their father to Scotland in breach of an interim custody order in favour of their mother, on the ground that he was not satisfied that the German court had made sufficient inquiries: the welfare of the children was the paramount consideration and it was in their best interests that the children should remain in Scotland.

1 The Child Abduction and Custody Act 1985 implementing (i) the European Convention on Recognition and Enforcement of Decisions concerning Custody of Children (the European Convention) and (ii) the Convention on the Civil Aspects of International Child Abduction (the Hague Convention).
2 Section 26 of the Family Law Act 1986 as amended by para 41(6) of Sch 4 to the Children (Scotland) Act 1995. Previously the courts recognised decrees of the court where the child was domiciled.
3 Section 11(7)(a); *Campins v Campins* 1979 SLT (Notes) 41.
4 1988 SLT 87.

United Kingdom decrees

The common law position has now been overtaken where the 'foreign' decree emanates from a court in another part of the United Kingdom. In these circumstances, the order[1] relating to parental responsibilities and rights is to be automatically recognised by the Scottish courts as having the same effect as an order of the Court of Session.[2] When the custody order has been registered in the Court of Session,[3] proceedings can be brought for its enforcement.[4] The Court of Session has the same powers to enforce the order as if it was its own order.[5]

The European Convention

The European Convention provides for the mutual recognition and enforcement of custody decisions[6] between contracting states. Where a person has obtained a custody decision in a contracting state, he can seek to have it recognised and enforced in Scotland. He can approach 'the central authority' for help in tracing the child and securing the recognition and enforcement of the decision. In Scotland, the central authority is the Secretary of State.[7] The custody decision is to be recognised as if it was made by a Scottish court unless there are grounds upon which the Court of Session can refuse recognition.[8] Once registered in the Court of Session, the decision can be enforced as if it was an order of that court.[9]

There are several grounds upon which the Court of Session can refuse to recognise or enforce a decision. For the present purpose, the

---

1 Technically the term 'Part I order' should be used: this defines the relevant orders for parental rights including residence, custody, care or control and contact. See s 1 of the Family Law Act 1986 as amended by para 62 of Sch 13 to the Children Act 1989 and para 41(2) of Sch 4 to the Children (Scotland) Act 1995.
2 Section 25(1) of the Family Law Act 1986; the Court of Session is the 'appropriate court' in Scotland: s 32(1).
3 An application for registration is made to the court which made the order and then passed on to the Court of Session: s 27.
4 Section 29 of the Family Law Act 1986. In *Woodcock v Woodcock* 1990 SLT 848, the Lord President (Hope) held that the new statutory regime did not elide the limited protective jurisdiction of the Court of Session to refuse to give effect to a custody order if satisfied that the enforcement of the order would result in physical or moral injury to the child: ibid at 853.
5 Ibid.
6 Ie orders relating to parental responsibilities and rights. Access, ie contact decisions, are also included: art 11.
7 Section 14(1) of the Child Abduction and Custody Act 1985.
8 Ibid, s 15.
9 Ibid, s 18. The Court of Session is 'the appropriate court' : ibid, s 27(2).

most important are to be found in art 10.[1] First, a decision will not be recognised if its effects are manifestly incompatible with fundamental principles of the law of Scotland.[2] For example, a decision reached on the basis that the custody of a child should automatically be awarded to the father would not be recognised as it was made without reference to the welfare of the child and therefore manifestly incompatible with s 11(7)(a) of the Children (Scotland) Act 1995. Secondly, a decision will not be recognised if by reason of a change of circumstances, including the passage of time but *not* a mere change in residence, the effects of the decision are manifestly no longer in accordance with the child's welfare.[3] In other words, it must be established that the enforcement of the decision by, for example, returning the child to the custodial parent, would be manifestly against the child's interests; the fact that the Court of Session, applying the welfare test, would have reached a different decision from the foreign court is not enough to refuse to recognise or enforce the decision on this ground.

The Hague Convention

The Hague Convention is concerned with the wrongful removal of a child from one contracting state to another. Where a child has been wrongfully removed to or wrongfully retained in Scotland, a parent can seek the help of the Secretary of State, as the central authority in Scotland,[4] to obtain the return of the child. Proceedings for recovery of the child take place in the Court of Session.[5] The removal or retention of the child is wrongful if it is in breach of a parent's rights of custody. These rights can arise *ex lege* or as a result of a custody order.[6] Thus, the Convention applies where a person automatically enjoys parental rights under the law of a contracting state;[7] there is no need to have obtained parental rights as the result of a custody order.[8] Before the removal or retention is unlawful, it must be in breach of

1 For full discussion see *10 Stair Memorial Encyclopaedia* para 1328 ff.
2 Article 10(1)(a).
3 Article 10(1)(b). See generally *Campins Coll* 1989 SLT 33.
4 Section 3(1) of the Child Abduction and Custody Act 1985.
5 The Court of Session is 'the appropriate court': ibid, s 4.
6 Article 3 of the Convention.
7 As, for example, the mother and married father enjoy under Scots law; see *supra* Ch 10. Of course, the applicant must have parental rights: *C v S* [1990] 2 All ER 449. Whether or not a parent has parental rights is determined by the law of the child's habitual residence; whether these amount to rights of custody within the meaning of the Convention is a matter for Scots law: *Bordera v Bordera* 1995 SLT 1176. A right of access per se is not sufficient: ibid.
8 This point appears to have been overlooked in *Hill v Hill* 1990 SCLR 238.

the applicant's custody rights under the law of the state in which the child was *habitually resident* immediately before the removal or retention.[1] Habitual residence is primarily a question of fact. Where both parents have custodial rights, habitual residence cannot be changed unilaterally.[2] If one parent removes the child from country A without the other's consent, the child remains habitually resident in country A. If both agree that the child can leave country A, then the child will not be habitually resident in A, even although the child has not become habitually resident in country B.[3] If both agree that the child can leave country A for a temporary period, the child remains habitually resident in A and if not returned after the period has expired, the retention is unlawful and the Convention applies.[4]

Moreover, before the Convention applies, the applicant must have been exercising parental rights or would have done so but for the removal or retention.[5] It is not enough that the applicant could have applied to a court for such rights.[6] Where the applicant has a custody order in his favour, his refusal to allow the child to leave the country is an exercise of parental rights.[7]

Wrongful retention and removal are mutually exclusive.[8] A parent who has a custody order in his favour does not wrongfully remove a child unless the order prohibits the child's removal from the country.[9] Retention is a 'one-off' act of omission or commission,[10] for example, a parent's failure to return with a child after a holiday abroad agreed with the applicant.

When satisfied that the removal or retention is unlawful, the court *must* order the return of the child if a period of less than one year has elapsed since the date of the wrongful removal or retention.[11] If more than a year has elapsed, the court should still order the child to be returned unless it is demonstrated that the child is now settled in Scotland.[12] The court can refuse to return the child if satisfied (i) that

1 Article 3.
2 *Dickson v Dickson* 1990 SCLR 692 at 703 per Lord President (Hope).
3 Ibid.
4 *Findlay v Findlay* 1994 SLT 709; *Findlay v Findlay (No 2)* 1995 SLT 492.
5 Article 3.
6 *Seroka v Bellha* 1995 SLT 204. Nor is it enough that the parent had a right of access which necessarily involved responsibilities when the child was actually in his care: ibid.
7 *McKiver v McKiver* 1995 SLT 790.
8 *Findlay v Findlay* 1994 SLT 709.
9 *Taylor v Ford* 1993 SLT 654; *Re H (A Minor)* [1990] 2 FLR 439.
10 *Findlay v Findlay (No 2)* 1995 SLT 492.
11 Article 12.
12 Ibid. It must be established that, as a result of the connections the child has made in Scotland, it would be against the child's interests to be uprooted from Scotland: *Perrin v Perrin* 1995 SLT 81; *Soucie v Soucie* 1995 SLT 414.

the applicant did not have custody rights at the time of the removal or retention or had consented to the child's removal or retention[1] or (ii) that there is a grave risk that the child's return would expose the child to physical or psychological harm or otherwise place the child in an intolerable situation.[2] In establishing that there is such a risk, the onus rests on the person objecting to the child's return. The risk has to be greater than that normally to be expected when a child passes from the care of one parent to another; moreover there must be a risk of substantial harm which amounts to the child being placed in an intolerable situation. The court can consider what is likely to happen to the child if the child was returned.[3] However, it will only be in exceptional circumstances that such a risk would occur.[4] The fact that the Court of Session, applying the welfare principle, does not think that it is in the child's best interests to be returned is insufficient.[5]

The court has also discretion to refuse to return the child if the child objects.[6] In *Urness v Minto*,[7] it was held that a child had sufficient maturity for his views to be considered; these included his reasons for staying in Scotland as well as those for not liking the US. The court exercised its discretion and allowed him to remain in Scotland. As a result, the court also refused to return his younger sibling to the US; although the younger child had not sufficient maturity for his views to be considered, he would be placed in an intolerable situation if he was returned to his father in the US without his elder brother and his mother.[8]

---

1 *Zenel v Haddow* 1993 SLT 975 (consent does not have to be to a particular removal).
2 Article 13.
3 *Macmillan v Macmillan* 1989 SLT 350.
4 See, for example, *Re E (a minor)* [1989] 1 FLR 135; *C v C* [1989] 1 FLR 11.
5 *Viola v Viola* 1988 SLT 7, in particular at 10, per Lord McCluskey: *McCarthy v McCarthy* 1994 SLT 743.
6 Article 13.
7 1994 SLT 988.
8 For the criminal aspects of the law on child abduction, see *10 Stair Memorial Encyclopaedia* paras 1342–1343.

12 Adoption

INTRODUCTION

Adoption is the legal process by which the relationship of parent and child is created by the order of a court. The law has been consolidated in the Adoption (Scotland) Act 1978.[1] The effect of an adoption order is to vest parental responsibilities and rights in relation to the child in the adoptive parents.[2] An adopted child is treated in law as the legitimate child of the adopter, as if he or she had never been the child of any person other than the adoptive parents.[3] Thus, the parental responsibilities and rights of the natural parents towards their child are extinguished when the child is adopted and the child's rights are enforceable against the adopters and not the natural parents.

There are exceptions to the general principle that on adoption the child is no longer regarded as the child of his or her natural parents. In determining prohibited degrees of relationship for the purpose of the law of marriage and incest, the child remains the child of his or her natural parents;[4] in addition, an adopted child cannot marry an adoptive parent.[5] A child who is a citizen of the United Kingdom and Colonies retains that status even if adopted by aliens.[6] A child who is

---

1 As amended by Pt II of Sch 10 to the Children Act 1989, para 4 of Sch 4 to the Human Fertilisation and Embryology Act 1990 and Pt III of and Sch 2 to the Children (Scotland) Act 1995. References in this chapter are to the 1978 Act unless otherwise stated. On the law generally, see PGB McNeill *Adoption of Children in Scotland* (3rd edn, 1996). For an account of the law before the amendments made by the Children (Scotland) Act 1995, see *Wilkinson and Norrie* Chs 19 and 20.
2 Section 12(1).
3 Section 39(1)(a) and (c). Where the person adopting a child is married to the child's natural parent in whom are vested parental responsibilities and rights, the effect of the adoption order is to treat the child as the legitimate child of the marriage and not the child of any other person except the adopter and the natural parent: ss 15(1)(aa) and 39(1)(b). The adoption order does not affect the parental responsibilities and rights vested in the natural parent: s 12(3A). If an illegitimate child is adopted by one of his or her natural parents as sole adopter, the child will be treated as the legitimate child of both parents if they subsequently marry: s 39(2). The adoption order can then be revoked: s 46.
4 Section 41(1).
5 Adoptive siblings can marry: s 39(2). For full discussion, see *supra* p 26.
6 Section 41(2).

not, will, however, acquire that status if adopted by a citizen of the United Kingdom and Colonies.[1]

An adopted child remains entitled to certain social security benefits in respect of his or her natural family, for example, death grant.[2] Similarly, adoption does not affect a child's entitlement to a pension which was in payment at the time of the adoption.[3] Finally, while, as a general rule, an adopted child is treated for the purposes of the law of succession as the child of the adopters and no other person,[4] the child retains rights in relation to a natural parent's estate if the adoptive parent died before the commencement of the Succession (Scotland) Act 1964 and the natural parent dies after the commencement of the Law Reform (Miscellaneous Provisions) (Scotland) Act 1966.[5]

In spite of these exceptions it must be emphasised that the effect of an adoption order on the child's relationship with his or her natural parents is drastic. Put simply, the natural parents lose all parental responsibilities and rights when their child is adopted. Because of this, the law of adoption must have regard to the rights of the child's natural parents as well as the interests of the child. While traditionally considered as a way of providing a home for a newborn infant, usually with a childless couple, adoption is increasingly perceived as a long term solution for children in need.[6] In these circumstances, adoption orders should not be made without the agreement of the natural parents unless they have clearly forfeited their prima facie rights and responsibilities to bring up their child.

ADOPTION AGENCIES

It is the duty of every local authority to establish and maintain a comprehensive adoption service to meet the needs of all those who are involved in adoption – the children, their parents and the adoptive parents.[7] The facilities to be provided include arrangements for assessing children and prospective adopters, placing children for

---

1 Section 40: in the case of a joint adoption, the adoptive father must be a citizen of the United Kingdom and Colonies.
2 Section 41(3), (4) and (5).
3 Section 42.
4 Section 23(1) of the Succession (Scotland) Act 1964.
5 Section 5 of the Law Reform (Miscellaneous Provisions) (Scotland) Act 1966.
6 See *infra* Chs 13 and 14.
7 Section 1(1).

adoption and providing assistance, counsel and advice.[1] The adoption service is to be provided in conjunction with the local authority's other social services, so that help can be given in a co-ordinated manner.[2] Where a local authority does not have an adoption service it may use the services of an adoption society which has been approved by the Secretary of State.[3] For the purpose of the 1978 Act, the local authority adoption service and an approved adoption society is known as an adoption agency.[4]

It is a fundamental tenet of the 1978 Act that all the preliminary arrangements for an adoption should be made by an adoption agency. Accordingly, it is a criminal offence for a person other than an adoption agency to make arrangements for the adoption of a child or place a child for adoption.[5] The person who makes the placement and the person who receives the child, knowing the placement is with a view to adoption, can be prosecuted.[6]

There are two exceptions where arrangements made by persons other than an adoption agency are lawful. First, a private person can place a child for adoption where the proposed *adopter* is a relative of the child.[7] Thus, for example, a mother can place her child for adoption by her sister, ie the child's aunt. Secondly, a children's hearing is entitled to make a condition in a supervision requirement that a child who is in need of compulsory measures of supervision should live with persons who are suitable prospective adoptive parents.[8] This recognises the increasing importance of adoption as a way of providing a long term solution for at least some children in need.

WELFARE OF CHILDREN

Section 6(1) of the Act provides:

> '. . . in reaching any decision relating to the adoption of a child, a court or adoption agency shall have regard to all the circumstances but –

1 Section 1(2).
2 Section 1(2) and (3).
3 Section 1(1): on approval, see ss 3–5.
4 Section 1(4). The services maintained by local authorities are to be known collectively as 'the Scottish Adoption Service'.
5 Section 11(1) and (3).
6 Section 11(3).
7 Section 11(1).
8 Section 70(3) of the Children (Scotland) Act 1995. If the court makes an adoption order in respect of a child who is subject to a supervision requirement, it may determine the requirement if it considers compulsory measures of supervision are no longer necessary: s 12(9) of the 1978 Act. On children in need of compulsory measures of supervision, see *infra* Ch 14.

(a) shall regard the need to safeguard and promote the welfare of the child concerned throughout his life as the paramount consideration; and

(b) shall have regard so far as practicable –

   (i) to his views (if he wishes to express them) taking account of his age and maturity; and

   (ii) to his religious persuasion, racial origin and cultural and linguistic background.'[1]

A child of 12 or more is presumed to be of sufficient age and maturity to form a view;[2] but the views of a child below 12 should be taken into account, if the child has *in fact* sufficient age and capacity to form a view.

Thus, at *every* stage of the adoption procedure when a court or adoption agency makes a decision which involves a degree of discretion – as opposed to a finding of fact – the welfare of the child is the paramount consideration[3] and the views of the child must be fed into that decision-making process.

Before placing a child for adoption, an adoption agency *must* consider whether or not adoption is the best way to meet the needs of the child, or whether there is some better, practicable alternative.[4] For example, if H₁ and W divorce and W marries H₂, it may be better for the children of H₁ that he retains his parental rights and responsibilities than that his children are adopted by H. H could, of course, obtain parental responsibilities and rights in respect of the children;[5] these would be exercised jointly with H₁. Similarly, if the prospective adopters are relatives of the child, for example the child's grandparents or siblings, it may be better for the child that they apply for parental responsibilities and rights rather than distort the natural relationships through the adoption process.

In placing a child for adoption, an adoption agency must have regard (so far as practicable) to any wishes of the child's parents and

1 This is without prejudice to the need for the consent of a child aged 12 or over to the adoption order or order freeing the child for adoption: ss 6(1), 12(8) and 18(8), discussed *infra*.
2 Section 6(2).
3 For example, in *H v M* 1995 SCLR 401 when the child's mother died, the father who had never married the child's mother obtained parental rights including residence. The sheriff refused the father's application to adopt his daughter on the basis that adoption was no better for the child's welfare than the existing situation which allowed the child to have contact with her maternal grandmother. The child was too young to express an informed opinion.
4 Section 6A.
5 H₂ would apply under s 11 of the Children (Scotland) Act 1995; for discussion, see *supra* Ch 11.

guardians in relation to the religious upbringing of the child.[1] Nevertheless, the child's welfare is the paramount consideration[2] and the adoption agency should give effect to parental wishes in relation to religion only when it is consistent with the child's welfare to do so. Only children who are under 18[3] and are and have not been married[4] can be adopted in Scots law. An adopted child can be adopted again.[5] Where the child is aged 12 or over, an adoption order cannot be made without the child's consent.[6] However, in reaching any decision, the views of a child of any age must be given due consideration by a court or adoption agency.[7]

PROSPECTIVE ADOPTERS

An unmarried person aged 21 or over may apply to adopt a child alone.[8] Applications can be made to adopt a child jointly only if (i) the applicants are a married couple both of whom are 21 or over or (ii) one of the spouses is the child's parent and is 18 or over and the other spouse is 21 or over.[9] A married person can adopt the child alone if the court is satisfied that (i) the other spouse cannot be found or (ii) the spouses have separated and are living apart and the separation is likely to be permanent or (iii) the other spouse is incapable of making a joint application because of physical or mental ill health.[10] Where a person is married to the natural parent of the child and the natural parent has parental responsibilities and rights, that person can adopt the child alone.[11] Thus, if A is married to M, the child's mother, A can adopt the child alone: after the adoption A will share parental

1 Section 7.
2 Section 6(1)(a). The *child's* religious persuasion is a factor to be fed into the welfare principle: s 6(1)(b)(ii).
3 Section 65(1). An adoption order can be made in respect of a person aged 18 or over, if the application was made before the child was 18: s 12(1).
4 Section 12(5).
5 Section 12(7).
6 Section 12(8). The court may dispense with the child's consent if satisfied that the child is incapable of giving consent. This also applies to orders freeing the child for adoption: s 18(8).
7 Section 6(1). In *C, Petrs* 1993 SLT (Sh Ct) 8, it was held to be impracticable to ascertain the views of a 6 year old child, when the prospective adopters refused to allow her to be interviewed, since they did not wish her to know that she was adopted: the prospective adopters were the child's natural mother and step-father. The adoptive order was nevertheless made.
8 Section 15(1)(a).
9 Section 14(1), (1A) and (1B).
10 Section 15(1)(b).
11 Sections 15(1)(aa) and 39(1)(b).

responsibilities and rights with M. There is, accordingly, no need for M to adopt her own child.[1]

While a parent can adopt his or her own child,[2] an adoption order shall not be made

> 'on the application of the mother or father of the child alone unless the court is satisfied that
>
> (a) the other natural parent is dead or cannot be found or by virtue of section 28 of the Human Fertilisation and Embryology Act 1990, there is no other parent, or
> (b) there is some other reason justifying the exclusion of the other natural parent.'[3]

PROCEDURE

Where the child was placed with the applicants by an adoption agency or where the applicant is a parent, step-parent or relative of the child, the child must be at least 19 weeks old before an adoption order can be made and have lived with the applicant at all times during the preceding 13 weeks.[4] If, however, a child was not placed with the applicants by an adoption agency and they are not related to the child, the child must be at least 12 months old before an adoption order can be made and have lived with the applicants at all times during the preceding 12 months;[5] this would apply where, for example, foster parents want to adopt a child who has been looked after by them.

Where a child has not been placed with the applicants by an adoption agency, the applicant must give notice to the local authority within whose area the child has his or her home of their intention to adopt the child. The notice must be given at least three months before

---

1 If the child's natural father has parental responsibilities and rights this is a situation where adoption by A may not be in the best interests of the child as it would destroy the father's responsibility to retain contact with the child. A could obtain parental responsibilities and rights under s 11 of the Children (Scotland) Act 1995 which A could exercise jointly with M and the child's father. See s 6A of the 1978 Act, discussed *supra*. On s 11 of the 1995 Act, see *supra* Ch 11.
2 This might be done if, for example, it was important for succession purposes that the child be treated as legitimate and there was no other way in which the child could be legitimated. Such situations would be rare.
3 Section 15(3). Where such an order is made the reason justifying the exclusion of the other natural parent must be recorded by the court. As to s 28 of the 1990 Act, see *supra* p 154.
4 Section 13(1).
5 Section 13(2).

the date of the order. During that period the local authority investigates the suitability of the adoptive parents etc and makes a report to the court.[1] Where a child has been placed by an adoption agency, the adoption agency submits a report to the court on the suitability of the adoptive parents etc.[2] An adoption order will not be made unless the court is satisfied that the applicants have afforded the adoption agency or the local authority sufficient opportunities to see the child in the home environment.[3]

Where an application for an adoption order is made by a person with whom the child has had his or her home for the preceding five years, no person can remove the child from the applicant's home while the application is pending, except with the leave of court or under authority conferred by any enactment.[4] This protection extends to foster parents who decide to adopt a child who is being looked after by a local authority but who has lived with the applicants for the preceding five years.[5]

An application for an adoption order can be made to the Court of Session or the sheriff court of the sheriffdom where the child lives.[6] The proceedings are heard in private.[7] A *curator ad litem* must be appointed with the duty of safeguarding the child's interests; in particular, it is the curator's duty to provide the court with a comprehensive report dealing with all the circumstances of the adoption application.[8] Thus, the court will have an independent assessment of whether the adoption will be in the interests of the child.

Difficulties can be experienced when an application is made for an adoption order in respect of a child who at the same time is also the subject of an action for parental responsibilities and rights in another court. These conflicts of jurisdiction should be avoided in the best interests of the child.[9]

---

1 Section 22. Where the child is subject to a supervision requirement, the adoption agency refers the case to a Reporter who arranges a children's hearing to review the supervision requirement in the light of the proposed adoption: s 22A. On supervision requirements, see *infra* Ch 14.
2 Section 23.
3 Section 13(3).
4 Section 28(1). Similar protection exists for the period during which a prospective adopter has given notice of intention to adopt a child to a local authority but before the application is made; the child must have lived with the prospective adopters for the preceding five years: s 28(2).
5 Section 28(3).
6 Section 56.
7 Section 57.
8 Section 58(1)(a). A reporting officer must also be appointed for witnessing agreements etc: s 58(1)(b). The same person can be both *curator ad litem* and reporting officer.
9 See, for example, *F v F* 1991 SLT 357.

PARENTAL AGREEMENT

It is a fundamental principle of the law of adoption that an adoption order cannot be made unless the court is satisfied that each parent or guardian of the child 'freely, and with full understanding of what is involved, agrees unconditionally to the making of an adoption order'.[1] For this purpose, parent means the mother and father of the child where both have parental responsibilities and rights or where either of them has parental responsibilities and rights.[2] Consider the following examples:

(i)   M and F are married at the child's conception or subsequently: both have parental responsibilities and rights and are parents;[3]
(ii) M is an unmarried mother: she has parental responsibilities and rights and is a parent;[4]
(iii) F has not married M: he has no parental responsibilities and rights and is not a parent;[5]
(iv) F has not married M but has obtained a contact order under s 11(2)(d) of the Children (Scotland) Act 1995: he has the parental responsibility and right to contact and is a parent;[6]
(v)   M and F are married at the child's conception but both have been deprived of parental responsibilities and rights under s 11(2)(a) of the Children (Scotland) Act 1995: neither has parental responsibilities and rights and therefore neither is a parent.[7]

A guardian is a person appointed to be the child's guardian by deed or will or court order.[8] The agreement of a person, other than the child's mother or father, who has parental responsibilities and rights is *not* required unless that person has been appointed to be the child's guardian. A mother's agreement is ineffective if given less than six weeks after the child's birth.[9]

---

1 Section 16(1)(b); agreement is necessary whether or not the parent or guardian knows the identity of the applicants.
2 Section 65(1). For full discussion of parental responsibilities and rights, see *supra* Ch 10.
3 Section 3(1)(a) and (b) of the Children (Scotland) Act 1995.
4 Ibid, s 3(1)(a).
5 Ibid, s 3(1)(b).
6 On s 11(2)(d), see *supra* p 218. F would also be a parent if he obtained the responsibilities and rights by agreement with M: s 4 of the 1995 Act, discussed *supra* p 197.
7 On s 11(2)(a), see *supra* p 217. A parent's right to agree to an adoption is *not* transferred to a local authority by a parental responsibilities order, see *infra* p 269.
8 Section 65(1). On guardianship, see *supra* p 199.
9 Section 16(4).

Freeing a child for adoption

When a parent or guardian agrees to an adoption, while the application is pending they cannot remove the child from the care and possession of the prospective adoptive parents except with leave of the adoption agency who placed the child or of the court.[1] But if the parent or guardian withdraws agreement before the order is made, the adoption cannot go ahead unless the court is prepared to dispense with the parent's or guardian's agreement.[2] To alleviate the difficulties which can arise if agreement is withdrawn, the Act provides a procedure whereby an order can be obtained which 'frees' the child for adoption.

An application for an order freeing the child is made by an adoption agency, which is a local authority, with the consent of the child's parent[3] or guardian.[4] If, however, the child is already being looked after by the adoption agency, an application can be made without such consent provided the agency is applying to the court to dispense with the agreement of the parent or guardian.[5] Thus, this procedure facilitates the adoption of children being looked after by a local authority or who have been subject to a supervision requirement because they are in need of compulsory measures of supervision.[6] While an application is pending in these circumstances, the parents or guardian cannot without leave of the adoption agency or the court remove the child from the person with whom the child is living while being looked after by the adoption agency.[7]

If the requisite consents have been obtained or dispensed with, the court will make an order if this is in accordance with the welfare principle in s 6(1).[8] Where the child is aged 12 or over, the child's consent is also required.[9] If the child's father has never married the child's mother and has no parental responsibilities and rights, before making the order the court must satisfy itself that any person claiming to be the child's father has no intention (i) of applying for parental responsibilities and rights under s 11 of the Children (Scotland) Act 1995 or

1 Section 27(1).
2 On dispensation, see *infra* p 245 ff.
3 A mother's consent is ineffective if given less than six weeks after the child's birth: s 18(4).
4 Section 18(2)(a): the consent of one parent or guardian will suffice.
5 Section 18(2)(b). No dispensation will be made unless the child is already placed for adoption or the court is satisfied that it is likely the child will be placed for adoption: s 18(3). Dispensation of agreement is discussed *infra* p 245 ff.
6 On compulsory measures of supervision, see *infra* Ch 14.
7 Section 27(1).
8 Section 18(1).
9 Section 18(8).

that if he did apply, his application would be refused; and (ii) of entering into an agreement with the child's mother under s 4(1) of that Act, or that no agreement is likely to be made.[1]

The effect of a freeing order is to transfer to the adoption agency all the parental responsibilities and rights in relation to the child.[2] Accordingly, once the child has been freed for adoption, the agreement of the parents or guardian to the adoption order is no longer required. But unless the parents or guardian have made a declaration before the order is made that they prefer not to be involved in future questions concerning the adoption of the child,[3] they are entitled after a year to progress reports from the adoption agency informing them whether the child has been adopted or placed for adoption.[4] If the child has not been adopted or placed for adoption, the parent or guardian may apply to a court to revoke the freeing order and so attempt to recover their parental responsibilities and rights.[5] A freeing order will only be revoked if this would be in accordance with the welfare principle in s 6(1). As a general rule, an application for revocation of an order freeing a child for adoption can only be made once.[6] If it revokes the freeing order, the court makes an order under s 11 of the Children (Scotland) Act 1995, determining who should obtain parental responsibilities and rights in respect of the child.[7]

Dispensation with agreement

If a child has been freed for adoption, there is no need to obtain the parent's or guardian's agreement to the adoption order.[8] But where the child has not been freed for adoption, the agreement of the child's parent or guardian is necessary before an adoption order can be made. However, the court has power to dispense with its agreement in certain circumstances;[9] these will be discussed in this section. It should be noted that this power also exists to dispense with the

1 Section 18(7).
2 Section 18(5).
3 Section 18(6).
4 Section 19.
5 Section 20(1). The adoptive agency can apply for an order revoking a freeing order at any time: s 20(1A).
6 Section 10(4) and (5). If unsuccessful the adoption agency is no longer obliged to make progress reports.
7 Section 20(3). Accordingly, the parental responsibilities and rights may not necessarily be given to the parent or guardian who successfully obtained the revocation order.
8 Section 16(1)(a).
9 Section 16(1)(b) and (2).

agreement of a child's parent or guardian in relation to an order free-ing the child for adoption.[1]

Section 16(1) provides that:

> 'An adoption order shall not be made unless
> (a) the child is free for adoption . . .; or
> (b) in the case of each parent or guardian of the child the court is satisfied that –
>> (i) he freely, and with full understanding of what is involved, agreed unconditionally to the making of an adoption order . . .; or
>> (ii) his agreement to the making of the adoption order *should* be dispensed with on a ground specified in sub-section (2).'[2]

The grounds specified in s 16(2) are that the parent or guardian –

a) is not known, cannot be found or is incapable of giving agreement;
b) is withholding agreement unreasonably;
c) has persistently failed, without reasonable cause, to fulfil one or other of the following parental responsibilities in relation to the child –
  (i) the responsibility to safeguard and promote the child's health, development and welfare; or
  (ii) if the child is not living with him or her, the responsibility to maintain personal relations and direct contact with the child on a regular basis;
d) has seriously ill-treated the child, whose reintegration into the same household as the parent or guardian is, because of the serious ill-treatment or for other reasons, unlikely.

It has been emphasised that dispensation with agreement involves the court in a two-stage process.[3] First, the court must be satisfied that a s 16(2) ground exists. This is primarily a question of fact.[4] If a ground is established, the court must then consider whether the agreement of the parent or guardian *should* be dispensed with on that ground. In reaching this decision, the court must apply the welfare principle in s 6(1), ie the welfare of the child is the paramount consideration. But it must be emphasised that s 6(1) is only relevant at this second stage, ie *after* a s 16(2) ground has been established. In considering the

---

1 Section 18(1)(b). See, for example, *P v Lothian Regional Council* 1989 SLT 739; *L v Central Regional Council* 1990 SLT 818.
2 Italics added.
3 *L v Central Regional Council* 1990 SLT 818 (IH).
4 *Re P (infant)* [1977] 1 All ER 182 , [1977] Fam 25, CA.

s 16(2) grounds, it is proposed to leave discussion of s 16(2)(b) until the end, as this is the ground which has caused considerable controversy.

(i) *Is not known, cannot be found or is incapable of giving agreement*

Whether a parent or guardian is not known or cannot be found is usually decided on the information contained in the report of the *curator ad litem* and the productions. The court must be told what steps were taken to discover the identity of, or to find, the parent or guardian, and in particular it is important to 'follow up' evidence that relatives or friends may still be in contact with the missing person.[1] Evidence of incapacity to give agreement will usually be a medical report on the parent's or guardian's physical or mental condition.

Once the ground is established, the court must apply s 6(1) to determine whether agreement *should* be dispensed with. Consider the following examples:

EXAMPLE 1

A mother is unconscious in hospital after a road accident. Clearly the s 16(2)(a) ground is established as she is incapable of giving agreement. The medical prognosis is that she is likely to regain consciousness within a month. This evidence is relevant to the second stage, ie whether the court *should* dispense with her agreement on the ground that she is incapable of giving it. The issue is determined by s 6(1). Since it is prima facie in a child's best interests to be brought up by his or her mother, giving paramount consideration to the welfare of the child, it is thought that the court should not dispense with the mother's agreement and the adoption order should therefore not be made.

EXAMPLE 2

A mother is unconscious in hospital after a road accident. Clearly the s 16(2)(a) ground is established as she is incapable of giving agreement. The medical prognosis is that she is severely brain damaged and unlikely to regain consciousness. This evidence is relevant to the second stage, ie whether the court *should* dispense with her agreement on the ground that she is incapable of giving it. The issue is determined by s 6(1). Giving paramount consideration to the welfare of the child, it is

1 *Re F (R) (infant)* [1969] 3 All ER 1101, [1970] 1 QB 385, CA.

thought that the court should dispense with the mother's agreement on this ground and make the adoption order.

(ii) *Persistent failure without reasonable cause to safeguard and
promote the child's welfare*

What is required for this ground is a pattern of behaviour which amounts
to neglect of the child. The court must consider the past history of the
case, not the child's future prospects.[1] An important factor in such
behaviour will be failure to pay aliment, but all the circumstances of
the case should be considered. A temporary withdrawal from the household when a marriage was breaking down has been held to lack the element of permanancy inherent in the concept of persistent failure.[2]
Provided the parent aliments the children, this aspect of the ground is
unlikely to be established.[3] It might be thought that the phrase 'without reasonable cause' suggests that an element of culpability is required;
however, it has been held[4] that the standard is objective, ie whether by
the standard of a reasonable parent there was a reasonable cause for the
failure. By that standard, ill health would probably amount to reasonable cause, while imprisonment would not. It has been held that a father
who had failed to aliment his child because he was unemployed had
reasonable cause for his failure to do so.[5] The ground will also be established by persistent failure to provide a child with care and attention.

Neglect is a negative concept. But it is thought that the ground
could also be established by a pattern of positive, ill-treatment of the
child by the parent or guardian. The accumulative effects of persistent positive acts of physical or mental abuse of the child – even
though a single act might appear trivial – should be enough to establish the ground.[6]

Even if the ground is established, the court must apply s 6(1) to
determine whether the agreement *should* be dispensed with. Thus, for
example, if the ground was established but the reason for the failure

---

1 *L v Central Regional Council* 1990 SLT 818. The child's future prospects are, of
   course, relevant under s 6(1) in determining whether agreement *should* be dispensed with if the ground is established.
2 *Re D (minors)* [1973] 3 All ER 1001, [1973] Fam 209, DC; cf *H and H v
   Petitioners* 1976 SLT 80 where the father had 'washed his hands' of the child.
3 *A and B v C* 1977 SLT (Sh Ct) 55.
4 *Central Regional Council v B* 1985 SLT 413, construing the phrase in the context
   of s 16(2)(e) of the Social Work (Scotland) Act 1968 (repealed); *D v Kelly* 1995
   SLT 1220.
5 *A v B* 1967 SLT (Sh Ct) 121.
6 It is thought that the conduct need not be wilful; cf *Central Regional Council v B*
   1985 SLT 413.

was the parent's imprisonment, if the parent has been released from prison and is anxious to regain a relationship with the child the court could hold that, even giving paramount consideration to the welfare of the child, it should not dispense with the parent's agreement.[1]

(iii) *Persistent failure without reasonable cause* to have contact with a child

This ground is established where there is a pattern of behaviour whereby the parent or guardian has failed, without reasonable cause, to maintain personal relations and direct contact with the child on a regular basis. Reasonable cause is tested objectively. So, for example, if a father chooses to work abroad for five years and makes no effort to have contact with his child, the ground is established. Similarly, if the father was in jail. Even if the ground is established, the court must consider whether the agreement of the parent *should* be dispensed with in accordance with the welfare principle in s 6(1); for example, if the father had returned from abroad or was out of jail and wished to resume relations with the child.

(iv) *Seriously ill-treating the child*

It has been argued that ground (ii) can be established by evidence of positive ill-treatment of the child: but there must be a pattern of behaviour. Unlike (ii), this ground can be established by evidence of one incident which caused the child serious harm. However, it must also be shown that the reintegration of the child into the same household as the parent or guardian is unlikely because of the serious ill-treatment, or for other reasons. Thus, if, for example, a child was seriously assaulted by his father when he was under the influence of LSD, the ground would not be established unless it could be shown that the father is an addict and consequently the child's reintegration into the father's household is unlikely.

Where reintegration is likely, it would, of course, be in accordance with the welfare principle in s 6(1) to refuse to dispense with parental agreement. The point to be made, however, is that serious ill-treatment is not a ground at all if reintegration of the child in the household of the parent or guardian is likely.[2] If, however, the ground

---

1 If, for example, the neglect or ill-treatment was due to alcohol or drug abuse, the court might not dispense with the agreement, if the parent had successfully undergone treatment and was capable of, and anxious to, look after the child.
2 If the serious ill-treatment was the result of a persistent course of conduct, then ground (ii) might be satisfied; the court would then have to apply s 6(1) to determine whether it should dispense with parental agreement given that the reintegration of the child is likely.

is established, it will almost always be in the child's interests for the court to dispense with the parent's agreement.

(v)   *Withholding agreement unreasonably*

It has been argued that the question of dispensation of agreement falls into two stages viz (1) does a s 16(2) ground exist and (2) should agreement be dispensed with on that ground.[1] The s 6(1) welfare principle is only relevant after the ground is established. Thus, a parent or guardian is not withholding agreement unreasonably merely because, giving paramount consideration to the welfare of the child, ie applying s 6(1), adoption would be better than living with the natural parent or guardian. If that were the law, whenever a court considered that an adoption order was in the best interests of a child, it could dispense with agreement under s 16(2)(b) and the right of a parent or guardian to refuse to agree to the adoption of a child would be rendered nugatory. As Lord Hodson emphasised in the leading case of *Re W (infant)*,[2] 'it has been repeatedly held that the withholding of consent could not be held unreasonable merely because the [adoption] order, if made, would conduce to the welfare of the child'.

The difficulty is that, even more than the other grounds, s 16(2)(b) is a question of fact and degree. It involves the court in an exercise of judgment to determine whether or not the agreement is being withheld unreasonably. In *P v Lothian Regional Council*[3] the Second Division of the Court of Session held that s 6(1) was relevant at the first as well as the second stage, ie s 6(1) was to be used to determine whether or not the agreement was being unreasonably withheld. The Lord Justice-Clerk (Ross) explained:[4]

> 'In my opinion "any decision relating to the adoption of a child" clearly includes the decision as to whether or not to make an adoption order. It also, in my opinion, includes the decision whether or not to dispense with parental consent on the ground that it is being withheld unreasonably . . . . The result of all this is that in determining whether a parent has unreasonably withheld consent a number of factors must be laid in the balance. The test is an objective one. The question is – would a reasonable parent have withheld consent? Regard must be had to the

1 *L v Central Regional Council* 1990 SLT 818; *Lothian Regional Council v A* 1992 SLT 858.
2 [1971] 2 All ER 49, [1971] AC 682, HL at 718.
3 1989 SLT 739.
4 Ibid at 741. The case was, of course, concerned with the construction of the 1978 Act before the 1995 amendments; in the unamended s 6 the child's welfare was the 'first' not the 'paramount' consideration.

interests of the child, of the natural parents, and of the prospective adopter. The welfare of the child is the first consideration, and in the particular case may be the paramount consideration.'[1]

However, in *Lothian Regional Council v A*[2] the First Division of the Court of Session approved the two-stage process, recognising that 'strictly speaking, s 6 is directly relevant only at the second stage'.[3] Although the distinction between stage one and stage two is less obvious where the ground concerned is s 16(2)(b), the Lord President (Hope) accepted[4] that at the first stage, 'the issue is not what decision the court itself should take as to whether or not the parent's consent should be dispensed with – that matter must be reserved for the second stage – but whether a reasonable parent would have withheld consent. This question must be looked at objectively, and the test will be satisfied if no reasonable parent, in all the circumstances, would withhold agreement to the making of the adoption order'. It is thought that Lord Hope's approach is to be preferred to that of Lord Ross.[5]

A parent or guardian is therefore withholding agreement unreasonably when in the particular circumstances of the case a reasonable parent would not have withheld agreement. In *A v B and C*[6] Lord Guest took the view that 'other things being equal, it is in the best interests of a child to be with its natural parents . . .'. Accordingly, it is reasonable for a parent or guardian to refuse to agree to the adoption. But a reasonable parent will regard the child's welfare to be an important factor to be taken into account in determining whether or not to agree to the adoption of the child. While it is an important consideration, the weight to be given to the child's welfare is not the parent's paramount consideration, but will depend on the circumstances. If, for example, the child had been with the adoptive parents for only a short period, a reasonable parent could take the view that natural ties of love and affection outweighed any possible disadvantage to the child in being removed from the adoptive parents' home;[7] on the other hand, if the child had been with the adoptive parents for a long period, a reasonable parent would give great weight to the disruptive

---

1 See also ibid at 744 per Lord Wylie and at 745 per Lord Cowie.
2 1992 SLT 858.
3 Ibid at 862 per the Lord President (Hope).
4 Ibid at 862.
5 Lord Hope observed (ibid at 863) that his own analysis was 'not precisely' that described by Lord Ross, but that 'the practical result is the same'. Technically it could be argued that the First Division was bound as a matter of precedent by the decision of the Second Division.
6 1971 SC (HL) 129 at 143.
7 *A v B* 1987 SLT (Sh Ct) 121.

effects on the child of removing him or her from that environment
and would regard the child's welfare as outweighing natural ties of
love and affection.[1]

All the circumstances of the case must be considered including the
personal characteristics of the parents. Thus, in *A v B and C* itself,
while at the date of the appeal the child's parents were married and
had a home available for the child, because there was evidence that
they were emotionally unstable and since the child had been with the
adoptive parents for several years, the House of Lords held that a reasonable parent would not, in those circumstances, have withheld
agreement. There is, of course, a degree of artificiality involved. In *R
v Lothian Regional Council*[2] the court was faced with the question
whether a mother who was an alcoholic was withholding her agreement unreasonably. In the course of his judgment, the Sheriff
Principal (O'Brien) said:[3]

> 'I readily accept that the question is what a reasonable woman
> in the place of the appellant [the mother] would do in all the cir-
> cumstances, but do not find myself much nearer the answer in a
> case where a reasonable woman has to put herself in the shoes
> of an alcoholic mother claiming to have given up drinking.'

In *Re D (infant)*[4] the House of Lords upheld a decision that a father
who was homosexual was withholding his agreement unreasonably
when his former wife and her husband applied to adopt his son. The
trial judge had taken the view that the father who had had a series of
homosexual relationships with males under the age of 21, had nothing to offer his child. In these circumstances, a reasonable parent –
whether homosexual or heterosexual – who had nothing to offer his
child, would not have withheld agreement, much as he loved his
child.

It will be clear that it is not necessary for there to be any degree of
culpability on the part of the parent or guardian: on the other hand,
because the child's welfare is not the paramount consideration, the
ground is not established merely because adoption is in the child's
best interests. As Lord Hailsham said in *Re W (infant)*:[5]

---

1 *O v Central Regional Council* 1987 GWD 22–813; *Lothian Regional Council v R*
  1988 GWD 28–1172.
2 1987 SCLR 362.
3 Ibid at 363.
4 [1977] 1 All ER 145, [1977] AC 602, HL.
5 [1971] 2 All ER 49, [1971] AC 682, HL at 700.

'Two reasonable parents can perfectly reasonably come to opposite conclusions on the same set of facts without forfeiting their rights to be regarded as reasonable. The question in any given case is whether a parental veto comes within the band of possible reasonable decisions and not whether it is right or mistaken. Not every reasonable judgment is right, and not every mistaken exercise of judgment is unreasonable. There is a band of decisions within which no court should seek to replace the individual's judgment with his own.'

Accordingly, it is only when the refusal is outwith the band of reasonable responses that the s 16(2)(b) ground is established.[1]

When a parent or guardian is withholding agreement unreasonably, it will almost inevitably follow that the court should dispense with their agreement in the light of the welfare principle in s 6(1).

THE ADOPTION ORDER

If the child is freed for adoption or the relevant agreements have been obtained or dispensed with, the court can then proceed to make the adoption order.[2] It will do so having regard to s 6(1), ie giving paramount consideration to the welfare of the child. A court has refused to make an order, for example, when the purpose of the adoption was to avoid immigration requirements and not to integrate the child into the proposed adopters' family.[3] But the most common situation where an adoption order would not be made would be if the court was not satisfied with the verification of the statements in the petition. If an order is refused, the child is returned to the adoption agency.[4]

1 Cf *AB v CB* 1985 SLT 514: father refused to agree to the adoption of his children by his former wife and her husband. Although the court was doubtful, it dispensed with his agreement inter alia on the basis that informal access should be agreed by the mother to the younger child and that adoption was in the child's long term welfare. It is submitted that the father's refusal was not outwith the band of reasonable responses and therefore the s 16(2)(b) ground was not established. It should also be remembered that in the light of s 6A the adoption agency must now consider whether adoption is best for the child or whether there is a better, practicable alternative. See *supra* p 239.
2 Interim orders are possible: s 25(1).
3 *In Re W (a minor)* [1985] WLR 945, CA; cf *Re H (a minor)* [1982] 3 All ER 84, [1982] Fam 121.
4 Section 30. If the court takes the view that grounds of referral are established, the case can be referred to a Reporter to consider whether the child is in need of compulsory measures of supervision. Section 54(1), (2)(c) of the Children (Scotland) Act 1995.

By s 12(6) the court has power to attach any terms or conditions to the order as it thinks fit. This discretion is, of course, governed by the welfare principle in s 6(1). In England, this power has often been used to allow the child to have contact with his or her natural family after the adoption.[1] Scottish courts appear reluctant to impose such conditions but, nevertheless, it should be remembered that the power exists.

Adoption orders are registered in the Adopted Children Register. On reaching 16, an adopted person is entitled to obtain information in respect of his birth, and counselling services are available for adopted persons who have received such information.[2]

Surrogacy

Where a married couple have commissioned a surrogate mother, and either H or W (or both) is the genetic parent,[3] after the child is born, they can apply within six months of the birth for a parental order.[4] Both H and W must be 18 or over. The agreement is required of the surrogate mother, ie the woman who gave birth to the child.[5] The agreement of the mother is ineffective if given within six weeks of the birth.[6] The effect of the order is that the commissioning couple, in effect, adopt the child, ie the child becomes the child of the married couple for all legal purposes.[7]

---

1 Re *C (a Minor)* [1989] AC 1. Cf *AB v CB* 1985 SLT 514.
2 See generally s 45 and Sch 1 to the Act.
3 H by supplying sperm or W by supplying the ovum.
4 Section 30 of the Human Fertilisation and Embryology Act 1990.
5 Ibid, ss 27(1) and 30(5). The agreement of the child's father is also required. He could be the man presumed to be father under the provisions of the 1990 Act itself; for example, the surrogate mother's husband. For discussion, see *supra* p 154.
6 Ibid, s 30(6).
7 See *Wilkinson and Norrie* p 143 ff; Willock 1995 SLT (News) 41.

13 Children in need – duties and powers of local authorities

INTRODUCTION

While family autonomy may be regarded as a hallmark of a democratic society, it is accepted that there is a duty on a modern state to make provision through its social work agencies for the assistance, support and protection of children who are vulnerable when the family of which they are part becomes dysfunctional. At one extreme, this provision may simply take the form of advice and guidance to the family; at the other, it might involve the compulsory removal of a child from the family. In the latter situation, two points must be stressed. First, not only are parental responsibilities and rights being overridden but the child is being deprived of liberty. It is therefore important that the law should provide procedural safeguards to ensure that these interests are adequately represented before a decision is made which would deprive parents of their child and the child of his or her family – even if, ultimately, this step must be taken to secure the welfare of the child. Secondly, while a large degree of discretion must be given to social work agencies, their decisions in relation to a child may have serious consequences for the child and the child's family; it is therefore crucial that the parameters in which this discretion can lawfully be exercised are clearly laid down. In the following account of the duties and powers of the state in relation to the support and protection of vulnerable children, the extent to which contemporary Scots law achieves these two important policies will be considered. The law in this area has been the subject of extensive review and has been radically reformed by the Children (Scotland) Act 1995.[1]

---

1 References in this chapter are to the Children (Scotland) Act 1995 unless otherwise stated. For an exhaustive commentary on the Act, see Norrie *Children (Scotland) Act 1995* (Greens Annotated Statutes).

THE DUTIES OF LOCAL AUTHORITIES

By s 12 of the Social Work (Scotland) Act 1968[1] it is the duty of a local authority to make available general advice, guidance and assistance to persons living in its area. Assistance can be given to a relevant person in kind or, in exceptional circumstances constituting an emergency, in cash. A relevant person is any person aged 18 or over.[2] Assistance can only be given in kind or cash if to do so would avoid the local authority incurring greater expense in giving assistance to that person in some other way either then or in the future;[3] for example, giving a mother cash to avoid having to look after her child in local authority accommodation. In this way, by helping adult members of their family, the local authority indirectly helps children in need.

However, by s 22(1) of the Children (Scotland) Act 1995, a local authority is under an obligation (a) to safeguard and promote the welfare of children[4] in their area who are in need and (b) so far as is consistent with that duty, to promote the upbringing of such children by their families so that the children can be helped within their home environment. In providing child care services, the local authority should, so far as is practicable, have regard to the child's religion, racial origin and linguistic background.[5] It is envisaged that services may be provided for a particular child and members of the child's family, if it will safeguard or promote the child's welfare to do so.[6] The services may include giving assistance in kind or, in exceptional circumstances, cash.[7]

Consonant with the policy that children in need should be supported within their families, the Children (Scotland) Act 1995 requires local authorities to prepare and publish plans for the provision of relevant services within their areas.[8] These plans are to be reviewed from time to time.[9] Information about the services available for children is to be publicised.[10] There is emphasis on co-operation between the local authority, the health boards, national health trusts and other local authorities in the provision of appropriate services.[11]

---

1 As amended by para 15(11) of Sch 4 to the 1995 Act.
2 Section 12(2) of the Social Work (Scotland) Act 1968.
3 Ibid, s 12(1). Giving assistance in kind or cash is also subject to the provisions in s 12(3),(4) and (5) of the 1968 Act.
4 A child is a person under 18: s 93(2)(a).
5 Section 22(2).
6 Section 22(3)(a).
7 Section 22(3)(b).
8 For details, see s 19.
9 Section 19(3).
10 Section 20.
11 Section 21.

Among its services, a local authority should provide help for physically and mentally disabled children[1] and day care for pre-school age children.[2]

A local authority *may* provide accommodation for any child within its area if it considers that it would safeguard or promote the child's welfare to do so.[3] However, a local authority *must* provide accommodation for any child, residing or found in its area, if it appears to the local authority that the child requires accommodation because –

a) no one has parental responsibility[4] for the child;

b) the child is lost or abandoned;

c) the person who has been caring for the child is prevented, whether or not permanently and for whatever reason, from providing the child with suitable accommodation or care.[5]

A child for these purposes is a child who has not attained 18.[6]

Before providing a child with accommodation, the local authority, so far as practicable, must have regard to the child's views (if the child wishes to express them), taking account of the child's age and maturity; a child aged 12 or over is presumed to be of sufficient age and maturity to form a view, though the views of younger children should be considered if they *in fact* have sufficient maturity.[7]

As we have seen, it is the policy of the Act to enable children in need to be supported at home rather than in local authority accommodation. Accordingly, a local authority cannot provide accommodation for a child if any person with parental responsibilities and s 2(1)(a) and (b) parental rights[8] objects *and* is willing and able to provide or arrange accommodation for the child.[9] Moreover, any such person can remove the child from local authority accommodation at any time.[10] However, the child cannot be removed from local authority accommodation if the child is 16 or over and agrees to remain in the local authority accommodation.[11] Where the child is subject to a

---

1 Section 23.

2 Section 27.

3 Section 25(2).

4 On parental responsibilities, see *supra* Ch 10.

5 Section 25(1).

6 Section 93(2)(a). A local authority *may* provide accommodation for a young person in their area aged between 18 and 21, if it would safeguard or promote that young person's welfare to do so; s 25(3).

7 Section 25(5).

8 On s 2(1)(a) and (b) parental rights, see *supra* p 193 ff.

9 Section 25(6)(a).

10 Section 25(6)(b).

11 Section 25(7)(a)

residence order[1] the child cannot be removed by a person with parental responsibilities and s 2(1)(a) and (b) parental rights, if the person in whose favour the residence order was made agrees that the child should be looked after in accommodation provided by the local authority.[2] Where a child has been provided with accommodation by a local authority for a continuous period of six months or more, any persons with the relevant parental rights and responsibilities cannot remove the child without having given the local authority at least 14 days' notice in writing of their intention to do so.[3]

The accommodation provided by the local authority can be with foster parents or the child's relatives or any other suitable person; but the child cannot be accommodated with any persons who have parental responsibilities or with whom the child has been living.[4] The child can also be maintained in a residential establishment or other appropriate place.[5]

When a local authority is looking after a child for whom it is providing accommodation, the authority must act to promote and safeguard the child's welfare: this is the paramount consideration.[6] Use can be made of the services available for children who are being cared for by their parents.[7] The authority must take steps to promote personal relationships and direct contact between the child and any person with parental responsibilities, provided it is practicable and appropriate to do so.[8] In reaching any decision in relation to the child, the local authority, so far as is reasonably practicable, must ascertain the views of the child, the child's parents, any person with parental rights who is not a parent of the child and any other person whose views the authority considers relevant.[9] The child's views, if any, those of the other persons described above and the child's religion, race and cultural and linguistic background must all be regarded by the local authority in making its decision,[10] ie all these factors must be fed into the welfare principle which is the paramount consideration.[11] The authority can only depart from the welfare

1 On residence orders, see *supra* p 218 ff.
2 Section 25(7)(b).
3 Section 25(7).
4 Section 26(1)(a).
5 Section 26(1)(b) and (c).
6 Section 17(1)(a). This includes the duty to provide the child with advice and assistance to prepare the child for when he or she is no longer cared for by the local authority: s 17(2). See *infra*.
7 Section 17(1)(b).
8 Section 17(1)(c).
9 Section 17(3).
10 Section 17(4).
11 Section 17(1)(a).

principle if it is necessary for the protection of the public from serious harm.[1] When a child is being looked after by a local authority, the child's case must be reviewed periodically.[2]

It is important to emphasise that this duty to look after the child arises not only when the child has been provided with accommodation under s 25 but also when the child is in local authority accommodation as a result of a supervision requirement[3] or any order, warrant or authorisation made under the 1995 Act, as a result of which the local authority has responsibilities in respect of the child.[4]

When a child, after ceasing to be of school age, continues to be looked after by a local authority,[5] the local authority is under a duty to provide the young person with advice, guidance and assistance when the young person leaves local authority accommodation.[6] This obligation lasts until the young person reaches 19. However, between the ages of 19 and 21, the young person can apply to the local authority for such advice, guidance and assistance; and the local authority may grant the application unless satisfied that the young person's welfare does not require it.[7] The assistance may include assistance in kind or cash.[8] The local authority can also make grants to help such a young person meet expenses in relation to education and training,[9] and can contribute towards the costs of the young person's maintenance and accommodation in any place where the young person is, or is seeking, employment or receiving education or training.[10] A grant or contribution in respect of training or education can continue after the young person reaches 21 until the relevant course is completed.[11] These 'after care' provisions are important as they help the young person make the difficult transition from the local authority environment to independence in the general community.

---

1 Section 17(5).
2 Section 31(1). Where a child is being looked after by a local authority, any natural person who has parental responsibilities must inform the local authority of any change of address: s 18(1).
3 See *infra* Ch 14.
4 Ibid.
5 Or is initially provided with local authority accommodation after ceasing to be that age.
6 Section 29(1).
7 Section 29(2).
8 Section 29(3).
9 Section 30(1)(a).
10 Section 30(1)(b).
11 Section 30(3).

The Act also provides for short term refuges for children at risk of harm.[1] When a *child* requests refuge and it appears to the local authority (or the manager of a registered residential establishment) that the child is at risk of harm, the local authority may provide the child with accommodation for a period of up to 7 days or, in exceptional circumstances, 14 days. During that period the local authority can determine what further steps should be taken to safeguard and promote the welfare of the child.[2]

THE POWERS OF LOCAL AUTHORITIES

We have seen that when children are in need a major objective of the Children (Scotland) Act 1995 is that local authorities should provide services to support children in their family environment.[3] The 1995 Act also gives a local authority the right to apply to the sheriff for a range of court orders to help the local authority fulfil its obligations in respect of children. These orders are discussed in this section.

The court's duty to consult the child

At the outset, it is important to appreciate that in determining any matter relating to the child, the welfare of the child throughout his or her childhood is the paramount consideration of the court.[4] Where a local authority applies to a sheriff for an assessment order,[5] exclusion order,[6] or a parental responsibilities order,[7] the sheriff must, so far as is practicable and taking account of the age and maturity of the child concerned, give the child an opportunity to indicate whether or not he or she wishes to express a view; if so, give the child an opportunity to express that view; and have regard to the view expressed.[8] A child of

---

1 Section 38.
2 A local authority is also under an obligation to safeguard and promote the welfare of a child if the authority receives notice from the managers of a hospital in its area that the parents of a child in the hospital have not been in contact with their child for a continuous period of three months or more (or it is likely that there will be no contact with the child for three months or more taking into account any preceding period of absence of parental contact). On receipt of such notice the local authority must consider what further steps, if any, it should institute under the 1995 Act to safeguard and promote the child's welfare: see s 36.
3 Section 22(1)(a) and (b).
4 Section 16(1).
5 See *infra* p 261.
6 See *infra* p 263.
7 See *infra* p 267.
8 Section 16(2) and (4)(b)(i).

12 or more is presumed to be of sufficient age and maturity to form a view, but younger children's views must also be heard if they *in fact* have sufficient age and maturity.[1] Moreover, consonant with the underlying philosophy of the 1995 Act that help for a child in need should take place within the child's own family environment, the sheriff should not make any order unless satisfied that it would be better for the child that the order be made than that none should be made at all.[2] We shall call this the duty to consult.

The importance of the obligation to consult the views of the child cannot be over emphasised. It is a central policy of the Act that the child at the centre of the judicial proceedings should have the opportunity to state his or her views and that these are fed into the sheriff's decision-making process which is ultimately governed by the welfare principle, the paramount consideration. A sheriff can only depart from the welfare principle if this is necessary for the protection of the public from serious harm.[3]

Child assessment orders

In order to safeguard and promote the welfare of children, local authority social workers may require access to the child in order to make an assessment of the child's needs. After the assessment is made, the local authority can determine what steps should be taken to help the child, by way of provision of services or taking further proceedings under the 1995 Act.

If the local authority social workers experience difficulties in seeing the child, for example, if the child's family denies access, the local authority can apply to a sheriff for a child assessment order.[4] The purpose of this order is to assess the state of the child's health or development or the way in which the child has been treated. For the purpose of a child assessment order a child is a person below 16.[5] Before an order can be made the sheriff must be satisfied that (a) the local authority has reasonable cause to suspect that the child is suffering or is likely to suffer *significant* harm as a result of the way the child is being treated or neglected; (b) assessment is required in order to establish whether or not there is reasonable cause to believe that the child is being badly treated or neglected; *and* (c) the local

1 Ibid.
2 Section 16(3).
3 Section 16(5).
4 Section 55(1).
5 Section 93(2)(b). Also included is a child between 16 and 18 who is subject to a supervision requirement: on supervision requirements, see *infra* Ch 14.

authority is unlikely to be able to make such an assessment unless the order is made.[1] The duty to consult the child applies in proceedings for an assessment order[2] and the sheriff must also be satisfied that it is better to make the order than that none should be made at all.[3]

The sheriff must specify the date on which the assessment is to begin and the period during which the child is to be assessed.[4] This period must not exceed seven days beginning with the date specified in the order.[5] An assessment order cannot be renewed. The person who has the child must produce the child, allow the assessment to be carried out and comply with any conditions in the order.[6] The assessment is carried out by an authorised person, ie the local authority or any person authorised by the local authority, for example, a doctor or social worker.[7] The sheriff has the power to order the child to be taken to any place for the purpose of making the assessment (for example, a hospital) and can authorise the child to be kept there for a specified period. During that time, the court can make directions for the child to have contact with any person (for example, the child's parents).

The assessment will usually involve the medical examination of the child. If the child is under 16 but has capacity to consent under s 2(4) of the Age of Legal Capacity (Scotland) Act 1991,[8] the child's rights are preserved by s 90 of the 1995 Act. Thus, the child could refuse to consent to the medical examination.

As we have seen, the order lasts for a maximum period of seven days. It may be for this reason that the Act does not expressly provide an appeals procedure for such orders. This may appear odd given that the child can be removed from home for the purposes of the assessment. However, it is thought that the normal appeals procedure from an order of a sheriff is available, but given the constraints of time an appeal would only be possible where the assessment was not to take place until several weeks after the proceedings in court.

By s 55(2), where an application is made for an assessment order, if the sheriff considers that the conditions exist for making a child protection order under s 57(1), the sheriff must proceed as if the application was made under s 57(1) and grant a child protection

---

1 Section 55(1).
2 Section 16(2) and (4)(b)(i).
3 Section 16(3).
4 Section 55(3)(a) and (b).
5 Ibid.
6 Section 55(3)(c).
7 Section 55(3)(d) and (6).
8 Discussed *supra* p 167 ff.

order.[1] However, if this was done as a matter of course it would frustrate the purpose of an assessment order. Moreover, although the language of s 55(2) is mandatory, ie a child protection order *shall* be made, it is thought that the effect of the provision is that the application is to be treated as an application for a child protection order under s 57, where the sheriff clearly has discretion whether or not to make such an order.[2]

After the assessment has taken place, the local authority will be in a position to determine what steps should be taken to help the child. These could include further orders under the 1995 Act, referral of the case to a Reporter to arrange a children's hearing[3] or, if practicable, support for the child at home through the provision of services.[4]

Exclusion orders

The philosophy underlying an exclusion order is simple; *viz* that where a child is being abused it is better for the alleged abuser to leave the home environment than that the child be removed from home. This is, of course, consonant with the aim of the 1995 Act that, so far as it is consistent with the local authority's duty to safeguard and promote the child's welfare, a child should be brought up by his or her own family.

A local authority can apply to a sheriff for an order excluding any person named in the order (a named person) from the child's family home.[5] A child for the purpose of an exclusion order is a person below 16.[6] Family home means any house, caravan, houseboat or other structure used as a family residence in which the child ordinarily resides with a person who has parental responsibilities[7] in relation to the child or who ordinarily has charge of, or control over, the child; it includes any garden or other ground or building attached to, or usually occupied with, the home.[8]

The sheriff *may* grant an exclusion order if the following conditions are satisfied:

a) that the child has suffered, is suffering, or is likely to suffer, *significant* harm as a result of any conduct, or any threatened or reasonably apprehended conduct, of the named person;

1 On child protection orders, see *infra* p 272 ff.
2 Ibid.
3 On children's hearings, see *infra* Ch 14.
4 Section 22(1)(a) and (b).
5 Section 76(1).
6 Section 93(2)(b). Also included is a child between 16 and 18 who is subject to a supervision requirement: on supervision requirements, see *infra* Ch 14.
7 On parental responsibilities, see *supra* Ch 11.
8 Section 76(12).

b) that the making of an exclusion order against the named person –
   (i) is *necessary* for the protection of the child, irrespective of whether the child is for the time being residing in the family home; and
   (ii) would better safeguard the child's welfare than the removal of the child from the family home; and
c) that, if an order is made, there will be a person specified in the application who is capable of taking responsibility for the provision of appropriate care for the child and any member of the family who requires care and who is, or will be, residing in the family home (an appropriate person).[1]

While condition b) prescribes that the test is 'necessity', unlike the position under s 4 of the Matrimonial Homes (Family Protection) (Scotland) Act 1981,[2] in an application for an exclusion order under the 1995 Act, the welfare of the child *is* the paramount consideration.[3] Moreover, in determining whether an exclusion order should be made, the sheriff has a duty to consult the child.[4] In addition, the sheriff cannot make an order unless satisfied that making the order is better than that none should be made at all.[5] The present writer envisages that difficulties will arise in giving the appropriate weight to the statutory conditions for an exclusion order within the context of the paramount consideration being the welfare of the child. For if the welfare of the child is indeed paramount, some, at least, of the statutory conditions would be redundant. Only time – and the courts – will resolve this conundrum. What is clear is that an exclusion order can be made even where the child is not residing in the family home at the time of the application, thus avoiding the problems initially experienced in relation to exclusion orders under s 4 of the Matrimonial Homes (Family Protection)(Scotland) Act 1981.[6]

An exclusion order cannot be finally determined unless the named person has been afforded an opportunity of being heard, or represented before, the sheriff, and the sheriff has considered the views of any person on whom notice of the application has been served.[7] However, if the sheriff is satisfied that the conditions in s 76(2) are met but the conditions in s 76(3) are not fulfilled, ie the named person etc has not been

1 Section 76(2).
2 Discussed *supra* p 81 ff.
3 Section 16(1).
4 Section 16(2) and (4)(b)(i).
5 Section 16(3). This provision appears to make little sense in the context of exclusion orders: *sed quaere*.
6 For discussion, see *supra* p 81 ff.
7 Section 76(3).

heard, the sheriff may grant an interim order which will have the effect of an exclusion order pending a hearing before the sheriff within a period to be specified in rules.[1] At that hearing, the sheriff can confirm or vary the interim order until the case is finally determined.[2] An interim order can be made, even if the conditions in s 76(3) are met, at any time before the final determination of the case. As an exclusion order is defined as including an interim exclusion order,[3] the obligation to consult the child applies in proceedings for such an order.

As a consequence of provisions similar to those in s 4 of the Matrimonial Homes (Family Protection) (Scotland) Act 1981,[4] the sheriff is enjoined *not* to make an exclusion order if it appears to the sheriff that it would be unjustifiable or unreasonable to do so having regard to all the circumstances of the case[5] including (a) the conduct of the members of the child's family (whether in relation to each other or otherwise); (b) the respective needs and financial resources of the members of the family; and (c) the extent, if any, to which the family home and any relevant item in that home is used in connection with a trade, business or profession by any member of the family.[6] Other relevant factors in this context are whether the named person must reside in the family home because it is or is part of an agricultural holding, or is let to the named person by an employer as an incident of employment. As in s 4 of the 1981 Act, it is difficult to envisage situations where it would be unjustifiable or unreasonable not to grant an exclusion order when *ex hypothesi* the sheriff is satisfied that the condition in s 76(2)(b)(i) is met, ie the order is *necessary* for the protection of the child.[7] *A fortiori* this would appear to be the case, when we remember that the welfare of the child is the paramount consideration in determining whether or not to make an exclusion order under the 1995 Act.[8]

If in an application for an exclusion order, the sheriff considers that the conditions for a child protection order under s 57 are satisfied, the sheriff *may* make a child protection order rather than an exclusion order if it is in the child's best interests to do so.[9]

1 Section 76(4).
2 Section 76(5).
3 Section 76(12).
4 Discussed *supra* p 81 ff.
5 Section 76(9).
6 Section 76(10).
7 A possible scenario is when other orders are available under the 1995 Act which would equally protect the child.
8 Cf the Matrimonial Homes (Family Protection)(Scotland) Act 1981.
9 Section 76(7). On child protection orders, see *infra* p 272 ff. Unlike the position in relation to a child assessment order, it is not mandatory on the sheriff to make a child protection order: see discussion *supra* pp 262, 263.

The effect of an exclusion order is to suspend the named person's rights of occupancy[1] (if any) in the family home and to prevent the named person from entering the home except with the express permission of the *local authority* which applied for the order. A wide range of ancillary orders is available.[2] These include a warrant for the summary ejection of the named person from the home, an interdict prohibiting the named person from entering the home without the express permission of the local authority, an interdict preventing the named person removing any item from the home (ie an item reasonably necessary to enable the home to be used as a family residence), an interdict prohibiting the named person from entering or remaining in a specified area in the vicinity of the home, an interdict prohibiting the named person from taking any step specified in the interdict in respect of the child, for example, meeting the child at school or telephoning the child, and an order regulating contact between the child and the named person.[3] With the exception of an interdict prohibiting the named person from entering the home, the sheriff cannot make any of these ancilliary orders if the named person satisfies the sheriff that it is unnecessary to do so.[4] A contact order can be made by the sheriff *ex proprio motu* if it is in the best interests of the child to do so.[5] But it must be remembered that unless the named person is interdicted from seeing the child, if the named person has parental responsibilities and rights he or she will retain the responsibility and right to have contact with the child on a regular basis, and a contact order is not necessary.[6]

The local authority may at any time an exclusion order is in force apply to the sheriff to have a power of arrest attached to any interdict granted by the sheriff. This power applies to an interim exclusion order as well as a final order. The detailed provisions in respect of powers of arrest are to be found in s 78.

A final exclusion order ceases to have effect six months after being made[7] unless the sheriff directed that it should end earlier or any permission given by a third party to the spouse or partner of the named person to occupy the home is withdrawn.[8] Partners are persons who live together as if they were husband and wife.[9] On the application of

1 On occupancy rights, see *supra* p 77 ff.
2 Section 77(3).
3 Section 77(3). On contact orders, see *supra* p 228 ff.
4 Section 77(4).
5 Section 77(6).
6 See generally *supra* Ch 10.
7 Section 79(1).
8 Section 79(2)(a) and (c).
9 Section 79(4).

the local authority or the named person or an appropriate person (ie a person who has responsibility for the care of the child) or the spouse or partner of the named person (if not excluded from the home or is not an appropriate person), the sheriff may vary or recall an exclusion order or any ancillary order:[1] the welfare of the child is, of course, the paramount consideration. If the exclusion order is recalled, it ceases to have effect.[2]

An exclusion order cannot be renewed. Accordingly, it only allows a breathing space of six months to enable appropriate steps to be taken by the local authority for the long term support of the child. In this context, the crucial role given to local authorities in relation to exclusion orders can be seen as an aspect of their general obligations under the Act to safeguard and promote the welfare of children in need.

Parental responsibilities orders

Although a local authority must endeavour to support a child who is in need within the child's own family environment,[3] situations arise when it is neither practicable nor conducive to the child's welfare to do so. The child's case may be passed to a Reporter to refer the matter to a children's hearing to determine whether the child is in need of compulsory measures of supervision.[4] However, the local authority could apply to the sheriff for a parental responsibilities order, transferring the parental responsibilities and rights from the child's parents to the local authority. The effect of such an order is that the child will often be removed from home and the local authority will have the right to make the major decisions in relation to the upbringing of the child. In doing so, the local authority must act in accordance with the principles already discussed in the context of the provision of accommodation for children being looked after by the authority.[5]

By s 86(1) a local authority may apply to a sheriff for an order transferring the appropriate parental rights and responsibilities in respect of a child from a relevant person to the local authority. A child for these purposes is a person under 18.[6] A relevant person is the child's parent or any persons having parental rights in respect of the child.[7] A parental responsibilities order shall not be made unless the sheriff is satisfied that each relevant person either:

1 Section 79(3).
2 Section 79(2)(b).
3 Section 22(1)(a) and (b).
4 On compulsory measures of supervision, see *infra* Ch 14.
5 Section 17(6): the principles are discussed *supra* p 258.
6 Section 93(2)(a).
7 Section 86(4): on parental rights, see *supra* Ch 10.

a) freely, and with full understanding of what is involved, agrees unconditionally that the order be made; or
b) is a person who
  (i) is not known, cannot be found or is incapable of giving agreement;
  (ii) is withholding such agreement unreasonably;
  (iii) has persistently failed, without reasonable cause, to fulfil one or other of the following parental responsibilities in relation to the child, that is to say the responsibility to safeguard and promote the child's health, development and welfare or, if the child is not living with him, the responsibility to maintain personal relations and direct contact with the child on a regular basis; or
  (iv) has seriously ill-treated the child, whose reintegration into the same household of that person is, because of the serious ill-treatment or for other reasons, unlikely.[1]

It will be noticed that these conditions are exactly the same as those in s 16 of the Adoption (Scotland) Act 1978 in respect of making an adoption order.[2]

In proceedings for a parental responsibilities order the sheriff is under an obligation to consult the child.[3] The welfare of the child is the paramount consideration[4] and no order is to be made unless the sheriff considers that it would be better for the child that the order be made than that none should be made at all.[5] It is *not* a precondition for an order that the child is already being looked after by the local authority at the time of the application.[6] Thus, an application can be made in respect of any child, for example, where the child is living with his or her parents, or is living in local authority accommodation as a result of s 25 of the 1995 Act,[7] or is subject to a supervision requirement.[8] A *curator ad litem* may be appointed to safeguard the interests of the child.[9]

---

1 Section 86(2).
2 For discussion of the grounds, see *supra* p 246 ff.
3 Section 16(2) and (4)(b)(i). But the agreement of a child aged 12 or over is not required unlike the position in adoption: see *supra* p 240.
4 Section 16(1).
5 Section 16(3).
6 Cf the former position in respect of resolutions assuming parental rights under s 16 of the Social Work (Scotland) Act 1968 (repealed); see Thomson *Family Law in Scotland* (2nd edn, 1991) p 232 ff.
7 Discussed *supra* p 257.
8 On supervision requirements, see *supra* Ch 14.
9 Section 87(4).

If an order is made, the parental responsibilities and rights of a relevant person are transferred to the local authority (subject to any conditions the sheriff may make).[1] Prima facie, therefore, a relevant person is denuded of *all* his or her parental rights and responsibilities.[2] However, the right to agree to the child being freed for adoption or adopted is not transferred;[3] but if the conditions for a parental responsibilities order are satisfied, the relevant person's agreement can readily be dispensed with under the Adoption (Scotland) Act 1978.[4] While the order is in force it is the duty of the local authority to fulfil the transferred parental responsibilities.[5] If it is for the benefit of the child, the local authority may allow the child to reside with a parent, guardian, relative or friend;[6] this is, of course, consonant with the general aim of the 1995 Act that children in need should be supported in their home environment, whenever possible.

When a parental responsibilities order is being made, or is in force, the child has the right to reasonable contact with a relevant person and any person who had a residence order in respect of the child immediately before the order was made.[7] Accordingly, the child, the local authority or any person with an interest may apply to the sheriff for a contact order.[8] But even if no application is made, the sheriff may make a contact order *ex proprio motu*.[9] This provision is interesting as it is one of the few in the Act which gives a positive right to the child.[10] At any time the sheriff may vary or discharge a parental responsibilities order on the application of the child, a relevant person immediately before the order was made, any person claiming an interest or the local authority.[11] The order is terminated if the child is adopted or freed for adoption or reaches 18.[12]

As we have seen, a relevant person will usually be the child's parent and the effect of the order is to denude the parent of parental responsibilities and rights in relation to the child. This means that

1 Section 86(5).
2 Section 86(3).
3 Ibid.
4 Discussed *supra* p 245 ff.
5 Section 87(1).
6 Section 87(2).
7 Section 88(2).
8 Section 88(3).
9 Section 88(4).
10 Section 88(2).
11 Section 86(5).
12 Section 86(6)(a) and (b).

while the local authority has a duty to ascertain the parent's views[1] before making any decision with respect to the child, the parent has no title to challenge the merits of the local authority's decision.[2] Only if the decision is so unreasonable that it is not a legitimate exercise of the local authority's discretion does the possibility lie for a judicial review of the case. However, the parent can apply to the sheriff under s 88(3)[3] to have contact with the child and, of course, can apply to have the order discharged under s 86(5). But while the parental responsibilities order is in force, it is expressly enacted that a parent has no title to sue for an order relating to parental responsibilities under s 11.[4] Conversely, a local authority has no title to sue for an order under s 11;[5] if parental responsibilities are sought by a local authority, it must apply for a parental responsibilities order and satisfy the stringent conditions in s 86(2).

1 Section 17(3) and (6). For discussion, see *supra* p 258.
2 *Beagley v Beagley* 1984 SLT 202; for example, if the authority decided that the child should be innoculated against measles or whooping cough.
3 On the assumption that a parent has title to sue as a person 'with an interest' for the purposes of s 88(3).
4 Section 11(4)(d). On s 11 orders, see *supra* Ch 11.
5 Section 11(5).

14 Children in need – emergency procedures and compulsory measures of supervision

INTRODUCTION

We have been discussing the obligations and powers of a local authority to provide support for children in need. As we have seen, the local authority should endeavour to safeguard and promote the child's welfare by providing support within the child's home environment. As such, the child and the child's family voluntarily accept the local authority's help through its social work department.[1] However, circumstances can arise where it is not possible to provide support for a child on a voluntary basis and the only way to safeguard and promote the child's welfare is through *compulsory* measures of supervision for the child. In Scots law, compulsory measures of supervision are made by a children's hearing.[2] A child's case is referred to a children's hearing by a Reporter[3] to the children's panel, who acts independently of any local authority.[4] In this chapter we shall examine the operation of this system.[5] At the outset, it is important to emphasise that in deciding any matter in relation to a child, the welfare of the child throughout his or her childhood is the paramount consideration of the children's hearing.[6] A children's hearing can only depart from the welfare principle for the purpose of protecting the public from serious harm.[7] Moreover, as a general rule when reaching its decision, the children's hearing is under the same obligation to

---

1 An exception is, of course, a parental responsibilities order.
2 On the constitution of children's hearings, see *infra* p 280.
3 The Act refers to 'the Principal Reporter'. But this includes other officers of the Scottish Children's Reporter Administration to whom the Principal Reporter's functions are delegated ie Reporters: s 93(1) of the Children (Scotland) Act 1995. In this chapter references are to the 1995 Act unless otherwise stated.
4 A Reporter cannot be an employee of a local authority without the consent of the Scottish Children's Reporter Administration.
5 On the role of the Reporter in the system, see *infra*.
6 Section 16(1).
7 Section 16(5). This would appear to undermine the ethos of the children's hearing system which hitherto has *always* acted in the child's best interests.

271

consult the child as a sheriff when making a court order.[1] The children's hearing is also enjoined not to make a supervision requirement unless the hearing considers that it would be better for the child to make the requirement than that none should be made at all.[2]

EMERGENCY PROCEDURES – CHILD PROTECTION ORDERS

Situations can arise where it is necessary to act quickly to protect a child from serious ill-treatment by removing the child to a place of safety. A Reporter can then consider whether the child is in need of compulsory measures of supervision and, if so, arrange a children's hearing. A child for these purposes is a person below 16.[3]

On an application by any person (for example a police constable, or a local authority) a sheriff *may* make a child protection order if satisfied that (a): (i) there are reasonable grounds to believe that the child is suffering *significant harm* as the result of the way the child is being treated or neglected; or (ii) the child will suffer such harm if not removed to and kept in a place of safety (or does not remain in the place where the child is currently being accommodated), whether or not actually resident there, *and* (b) a child protection order is *necessary* to protect the child from significant harm.[4] When the applicant is a local authority, a sheriff *may* make a child protection order if satisfied (a) that the local authority has reasonable grounds to suspect that the child is suffering or will suffer significant harm as the result of the way the child is being treated or neglected, (b) the local authority is making inquiries to allow it to decide whether it should act to safeguard the welfare of the child and (c) those inquiries are being frustrated by access to the child being unreasonably denied (the local authority having reasonable cause to believe that such access is required as a matter of urgency).[5] It should be noted that, theoretically at least, the sheriff has a discretion whether or not to make the order. Yet, if the application is for an assessment order and the sheriff considers that the conditions for a child protection order are satisfied, it would appear that there is a mandatory obligation upon the court to

1 Section 16(2) and (4)(a). On the obligation to consult, see *supra* p 260 ff.
2 Section 16(3) and (4).
3 Section 93(2)(b). Also included is a child between 16 and 18 who is already subject to a supervision requirement.
4 Section 57(1).
5 Section 57(2).

make a child protection order.[1] The application must identify the applicant and, where it is practicable, the child concerned; state the grounds for the application and be accompanied by supporting evidence.[2] Notice of the application must be given to the Reporter and the relevant local authority, if the local authority is not the applicant.[3]

The effect of the order is to require any person in a position to do so to produce the child and to authorise the removal of the child to a place of safety[4] (or prevent the child being removed from the place the child is currently being accommodated).[5] The order can provide that the location of the place of safety should not be disclosed to any person specified in the order.[6] An applicant's actions in respect of the child are restricted to those acts the applicant believes are necessary to safeguard or promote the welfare of the child.[7]

The sheriff has power to make directions in respect of contact between the child and the child's parent,[8] any person with parental responsibilities, and any specified person or class of persons; the direction can only be made if the sheriff considers that it is *necessary* to do so.[9] The sheriff can order contact or prohibit contact or direct that contact take place under conditions.[10] The applicant may apply for a direction in relation to the exercise or fulfilment of parental responsibilities and rights, if the applicant considers such a direction *necessary* to safeguard and promote the welfare of the child.[11] Such a direction can authorise a medical examination of, and related treatment for, the child, as well as any other assessment of the child.[12] If the child has capacity under s 2(4) of the Age of Legal Capacity (Scotland) Act 1991,[13] no examination or treatment can take place if the child refuses to consent.[14] Unless the Reporter discharges the

---

1 Section 55(2). On child assessment orders, see *supra* p 263. There it is argued that instead of being compelled to make a child protection order, the sheriff simply treats the application as one for a child protection order rather than an assessment order.
2 Section 57(3).
3 Section 57(5).
4 A place of safety is a residential or other establishment provided by a local authority, a community home, a police station, or a hospital or surgery: s 93(1).
5 Section 57(4).
6 Ibid.
7 Section 57(6).
8 Ie genetic mother and father; the wider definition of parent in s 15(1) does *not* apply as it is restricted to Pt I of the Act. See *supra*.
9 Section 58(1). On contact orders, see *supra*.
10 Section 58(1) and (2).
11 Section 55(4). On parental responsibilities and rights, see *supra*.
12 Section 58(5).
13 Discussed *supra* p 167 ff.
14 Section 90.

child from the place of safety under s 60(3) or has received notice of an application to set aside or vary the protection order under s 60(7) and (9), the Reporter must arrange a children's hearing to determine whether or not the protection order should continue.[1] This initial children's hearing must take place on the second working day after the order has been implemented.[2] If satisfied the conditions for making a child protection order are established, the children's hearing can continue the order and any directions (with or without variations) until a second children's hearing can be arranged to consider whether or not the child is in need of compulsory measures of supervision.[3] This second hearing must take place on the eighth working day after the order was implemented. The duty to consult the child does *not* arise in proceedings before the sheriff under s 58 or before the initial children's hearing under s 59(2).

An application can also be made by any person to a justice of the peace for authorisation to remove a child to, or prevent the child's removal from, a place of safety.[4] The justice of the peace must be satisfied that the conditions in s 57(1) would be satisfied, that it is probable the sheriff would give authorisation to remove the child to, or prevent the child's removal from, a place of safety, and that it is not practicable in the circumstances for an application for a child protection order to be made to a sheriff.[5] If an application is made by a local authority, authorisation can be granted if the justice of the peace is satisfied that the conditions in s 57(2) would be satisfied, that it is probable that the sheriff would authorise the removal of the child to or prevent the child's removal from, a place of safety and that it is not practicable in the circumstances for an application for a child protection order to be made to a sheriff.[6] This is an emergency procedure. The duty to consult the child does not arise. The authorisation ceases after 12 hours, if arrangements have not been made to remove the child to, or prevent the child's removal from, a place of safety.[7] Where these steps have been taken, the authorisation ceases after 24 hours or when an application to a sheriff for a child protection order has been disposed of, if earlier.[8] In other words, it is essential to apply to a sheriff for a child protection order as soon as possible within the

1 Section 59(2). This is known as an initial hearing.
2 Section 59(3).
3 Section 59(4).
4 Section 61.
5 Section 61(1).
6 Section 61(2).
7 Section 61(4)(a).
8 Section 61(4)(b).

24 hours that the authorisation lasts and that steps are taken to protect the child within 12 hours of the authorisation being granted.

There is no appeal from the sheriff's decision to grant a child protection order or the decision of the initial children's hearing to continue the order.[1] However, an application can be made to a sheriff (presumably a different sheriff) to set aside (or vary) the protection order and directions (if any): this must be done *before* the initial children's hearing has commenced to consider whether or not the order should be continued.[2] An application can also be made to a sheriff to set aside (or vary) a decision of the initial children's hearing that the order and directions (if any) should continue: this must be done within two working days of the hearing's decision.[3] The application can be brought by the child, a person with parental rights, a relevant person, ie persons including parents with parental responsibilities or rights, or who is in charge of, or has control over, the child,[4] any person to whom notice of the original application was given, and the applicant for the original order.[5] Notice of the application must be given to the Reporter,[6] who can arrange a children's hearing to provide advice for the sheriff hearing the application.[7] After hearing the parties and the Reporter, if the Reporter wishes to make representations, the sheriff must determine whether the s 57 conditions for making a child protection order are satisfied or, where the application relates only to a direction, whether the direction should be varied or cancelled.[8] In these proceedings, the sheriff is under an obligation to consult the child.[9] If the sheriff finds that the conditions are satisfied, he can (a) confirm or vary the order or any condition on which it was granted; (b) confirm or vary any direction; (c) give a new direction; or (d) continue in force the order and directions (if any) until the commencement of a second children's hearing arranged to consider whether the child is in need of compulsory measures of supervision.[10] If the sheriff decides that the conditions for making a child protection order are not satisfied, the order is recalled and any directions cancelled.[11] In effect, a s 60(7) application is a rehearing of the case.

1 Section 51(15).
2 Section 60(7) and (8)(a).
3 Section 60(7) and (8)(b).
4 Section 93(2).
5 Section 60(7).
6 Section 60(9).
7 Section 60(10). In this situation, the children's hearing *is* under an obligation to consult the child: s 16(2) and (4)(a)(iii).
8 Section 60(11).
9 Section 16(2) and (4)(b)(ii).
10 Section 60(12).
11 Section 60(13).

However, the application must be determined within three working days of being made; if the case is not decided within this period, the original child protection order ceases to have effect.[1]

A child protection order ceases to have effect in the following circumstances *viz*:

(i)   if no attempt has been made to implement the order by the end of 24 hours of a child protection order being made;[2]

(ii) where the initial children's hearing does not continue the order;[3]

(iii) where an application under s 60(7) to have the order set aside is not determined timeously, ie within three days of the application;[4]

(iv) where a sheriff recalls the order;[5]

(v)   where the Reporter considers that the conditions for a child protection order are no longer satisfied and the person who implemented the order has received notice of the Reporter's decision;[6]

(vi) where the Reporter decides not to arrange a second children's hearing under s 65(2) to consider whether the child is in need of compulsory measures of supervision and the person who implemented the order has received notice of the Reporter's decision;[7]

(vii) where a child protection order has been continued, on the commencement of a second children's hearing under s 65(2) to consider whether the child is in need of compulsory measures of supervision.[8]

The second children's hearing, arranged under s 65(2) to consider the case of a child who is subject to a child protection order, has exactly the same powers as a hearing arranged in respect of a child who has not been subject to such an order.[9] These include the power to issue a warrant under s 66 which will, in practice, be particularly relevant to a child who has been subject to a child protection order. Section 66 provides inter alia that if the hearing is unable to dispose of the case, for example if the child or a relevant person does not accept the

1 Section 60(2) and (8).
2 Section 60(1).
3 Section 60(6)(a).
4 Section 60(2).
5 Section 60(6)(b).
6 Section 60(6)(d).
7 Section 60(6)(c).
8 Section 60(6)(e).
9 On children's hearings, see *infra* p 280 ff.

ground(s) of referral,[1] they can issue a warrant keeping the child in a place of safety provided they are satisfied that the child should be kept in a place of safety in order to safeguard or promote the child's welfare.[2] The warrant may contain such conditions as appear to the children's hearing to be necessary or expedient, including regulation of contact between the child and any person, for example, a parent, and a requirement that the child submit to any medical or other examination or treatment.[3] Where the child has capacity under s 2(4) of the Age of Legal Capacity (Scotland) Act 1991,[4] the medical examination or treatment cannot be carried out if the child refuses to consent.[5] The hearing can order that the location of the place of safety should not be disclosed to a person or class of persons.[6] The children's hearing has a duty to consult the child in these proceedings[7] and cannot grant the warrant unless satisfied that it would be better for the child to grant the warrant than that no warrant should be granted at all.[8]

The warrant lapses 22 days after it has been granted[9] but during that period the children's hearing can continue the warrant, on cause shown by the Reporter, for a further period(s) not exceeding 22 days.[10] A child cannot be kept in a place of safety under a warrant (which has been continued) for a period exceeding 66 days from the day the child was first taken to a place of safety under the warrant.[11] However, at any time prior to the expiry of the warrant, the Reporter can apply to a sheriff for a warrant to keep the child in a place of safety after the warrant granted by the children's hearing has expired.[12] The sheriff can only grant the warrant on cause shown.[13] The warrant must specify the date on which it expires and may contain any conditions which a children's hearing could include in a warrant granted under s 66.[14] An application can be made to the sheriff for a further warrant(s) at any time before the warrant granted by the sheriff has expired.[15] Unlike s 66 warrants, there is no maximum

---

1 See *infra* p 281 ff.
2 Section 66(1), (2)(b) and (3)(a).
3 Section 66(4).
4 Discussed *supra* p 167 ff.
5 Section 90.
6 Section 66(7).
7 Section 16(2)and (4)(a)(ii).
8 Section 16(3).
9 Section 66(3)(a).
10 Section 66(5).
11 Section 66(8).
12 Section 67(1).
13 Section 67(2).
14 Section 67(2)(a) and (b).
15 Section 67(1).

period beyond which the child cannot be kept in a place of safety as a result of a warrant(s) granted under s 67! The children's hearing and the sheriff are obliged to consult the child in these proceedings[1] and cannot grant the application unless satisfied that it is better for the child to do so than refuse to grant (or continue) a warrant.[2] However, unlike the position relating to the continuation of a child protection order, an appeal lies to a sheriff from a children's hearing's decision to grant a warrant to keep a child in a place of safety.[3] The appeal can be brought by the child or a relevant person and must be lodged within three weeks beginning with the date of the decision.[4] The appeal must be disposed of within three days of lodging the appeal: failure to do so results in the warrant ceasing to have effect.[5] If the sheriff is satisfied that the decision of the children's hearing is not justified in all the circumstances of the case, the sheriff must recall the warrant.[6] There is a duty to consult the child in the appeal proceedings.[7] There is no express appeal procedure in relation to the sheriff's decision to grant a warrant under s 67: it is thought that this will be subject to the normal appeals procedure in respect of sheriff court orders.

Child protection orders have been discussed in considerable detail. The reason for doing so is that these orders deprive the child of his or her family and parents of their child. They are paradigmatic of the tension inherent in any system of child protection law between the autonomy of the family and the obligation of the state to intervene in order to protect a child. In the 1995 Act, Parliament has enacted a complex system of strict time limits, rehearings and appeals in order to balance these two potentially competing interests. It is to be hoped that this system will prevent children in danger from slipping through the child protection safety net while, at the same time, ensuring that children are not removed from their families as a result of inappropriate, if well intentioned, applications by social work and other agencies for emergency orders.

---

1 Section 16(2),(4)(a)(ii) and (4)(b)(iii).
2 Section 16(3), (4)(a)(ii) and (4)(b)(iii).
3 Section 51(1)(a).
4 Ibid.
5 Section 51(8).
6 Section 51(5)(a).
7 Section 16(2) and (4)(c).

COMPULSORY MEASURES OF SUPERVISION

Information that a child may be in need of compulsory measures of supervision

We have been considering the situation where a child enters the children's hearing system as a result of a child protection order. This is an emergency procedure which should only be used in exceptional circumstances. The more usual route is that the Reporter receives information that a child may be in need of compulsory measures of supervision. Any person who has reasonable cause to believe that a child requires such measures may inform a Reporter;[1] a police constable is obliged to inform the Reporter.[2] If a local authority acquires information, for example from social workers, that a child may be in need of compulsory measures of supervision, the local authority must cause inquiries to be made in relation to the child, unless satisfied that inquiries are unnecessary.[3] After the inquiries have been completed, if the local authority takes the view that compulsory measures of supervision are required, it must pass the information to the Reporter. A court has also the power to refer a case to the Principal Reporter, if during relevant proceedings[4] it is satisfied that one (or more) of the grounds of referral for compulsory measures of supervision[5] – other than the commission by the child of an offence – exists.[6] Where criminal proceedings are not to be proceeded with against a child who has been detained in a place of safety, the Reporter must arrange a children's hearing to consider the child's case, unless the Reporter is satisfied that the child does not require compulsory measures of supervision.[7]

1 Section 53(2)(b).
2 Section 53(2)(a).
3 Section 53(1)(a). This could involve the application for a child assessment order: for discussion, see *supra* p 261 ff.
4 *Viz* actions for divorce, judicial separation, declarators of marriage, nullity of marriage, parentage or non parentage, proceedings in relation to parental responsibilities and rights, actions for adoption orders or orders freeing a child for adoption and proceedings in relation to offences under the Education (Scotland) Act 1980: s 54(2).
5 On these grounds, see *infra* p 281 ff.
6 Section 54(1). In this situation, the ground of referral is deemed to be established so that the children's hearing can immediately consider the appropriate disposal of the case.
7 Section 63 as amended by the Criminal Procedure (Consequential Provisions) (Scotland) Act 1995, Sch 4, para 97(5). The children's hearing may grant a warrant to keep the child in a place of safety if the conditions in s 66(2) of the Act are satisfied: see *supra* p 276 ff.

The role of the Reporter

When a child has entered the system by the routes described above, the decision whether or not to refer the case to a children's hearing is that of the Reporter. The Reporter (an officer of the Scottish Children's Reporter Administration) acts independently of a local authority.[1] The Reporter may have a legal background but this is not essential. After making an initial investigation, the Reporter may take the view that no further action is necessary.[2] Alternatively, the Reporter may consider that the family may be able to benefit from social work support; in these circumstances, the Reporter refers the case to the local authority concerned.[3] However, if the Reporter feels that the child is in need of compulsory measures of supervision, it is the Reporter's duty to arrange a children's hearing to consider the case[4] and to call upon the local authority for a report on the child and the child's social background. As we shall see, the Reporter has important powers and duties in relation to the conduct of the children's hearing and subsequent proceedings. The Reporter is, in effect, the lynch pin of the whole system and the importance of the Reporter's role cannot be over-emphasised.

The children's hearing

Whether or not a child is in need of compulsory measures of supervision and, if so, what steps should be taken to promote the child's welfare, are prima facie issues for a children's hearing. For every local authority area there is a children's panel consisting of persons with a knowledge of, or interest in, children, who are appointed by the Secretary of State to serve on the panel for the purposes of the 1995 Act.[5] A children's hearing consists of three members of the panel, one of whom acts as a chairman:[6] the hearing shall not consist solely of male or female members.[7]

It must be emphasised that a children's hearing is not a court. Its proceedings are relatively informal[8] and conducted in private with

---

1 The Reporter normally cannot be a local authority employee: s 40(2).
2 Section 56(4). The Reporter must inform the child, any relevant person and the person who brought the case to the Reporter's notice of the decision.
3 Section 56(4)(b).
4 Section 56(6).
5 The Children's Panel Advisory Committee advises the Secretary of State of suitable panel members and the general administration of the panels; see generally Sch 1.
6 Section 39(5).
7 Ibid.
8 See Rose 1994 SLT (News) 137.

the Reporter, the child and any relevant person usually present.[1] The parties are not normally legally represented but have the right to representation.[2] The basic rules of evidence apply.[3] However, it has been held that in exceptional circumstances the rules of natural justice can be suspended in the interests of the child.[4] The Secretary of State has power to make rules governing procedure at a children's hearing.

The conditions for compulsory measures of supervision – grounds of referral

Before a child will be considered to be in need of compulsory measures of supervision, one or more of the following conditions must be satisfied. A child for these purposes is a person under 16.[5] A relevant person in relation to a child is (a) any parent who enjoys parental responsibilities and rights;[6] (b) any person in whom parental responsibilities are vested as a result of the 1995 Act, for example a person who has a residence order in respect of a child;[7] and (c) any person who appears to be a person who ordinarily (and other than by reason only of employment) has charge of, or control over, the child.[8] The grounds of referral are listed in s 52(2)[9] *viz*:

a) the child is beyond the control of any relevant person; or
b) the child is falling into bad associations or is exposed to moral danger. A child will probably be regarded as falling into bad associations or exposed to moral danger if his or her parents or friends are prostitutes, drug addicts, alcoholics or homosexuals;[10] or
c) lack of parental care is likely to cause the child unnecessary suffering or seriously to impair the child's health or development. Earlier incidents of parental neglect can be used to show the likelihood of the child's suffering or impairment of health or development.[11] In *McGregor v L*[12] the Inner House of the Court of

---

1 On relevant persons, see *infra*.
2 Section 42(2)(i). The representative can be a lawyer but legal aid is not available.
3 *Kennedy v B* 1973 SLT 38; *F v Kennedy (No 2)* 1993 SLT 1284.
4 *Kennedy v A* 1986 SLT 358 at 362 per Lord Justice Clerk (Ross).
5 Section 93(2)(b). Also included is a person between 16 and 18 who is already subject to a supervision requirement. In relation to failure to attend school, a child includes a person over 16 who is not over school age.
6 On parental responsibilities and rights, see *supra* Ch 10.
7 On residence orders, see *supra* p 2.
8 Section 93(2)(b).
9 As amended by the Criminal Procedure (Consequential Provisions) (Scotland) Act 1995, Sch 4, para 97(3).
10 See, for example, *B v Kennedy* 1987 SLT 765.
11 *Kennedy v S* 1986 SLT 679. The fact that the child was put out of the house at night by the father's cohabitee did not prevent the court establishing the ground against the father.
12 1981 SLT 194.

Session held that this ground was established in relation to a new-born infant who had never left hospital but whose parents had a history of neglecting their children. It was not necessary for the child actually to have suffered parental neglect before the ground was made out:

> 'If it is proved that the habits and mode of life of these parents are such as to yield the reasonable inference that they are unlikely to care for this child in a manner likely to prevent unnecessary suffering or serious impairment of her health or development, the ground of referral would be established.'[1]

The test whether lack of parental care is likely to cause a child unnecessary suffering or seriously to impair a child's health or development is objective, ie whether a reasonable person could draw that inference from the nature and extent of the parental lack of care;[2] or

d) the child is a victim of a Sch 1 offence.[3] The ground is established if on the balance of probabilities an offence was committed against the child.[4] It is not necessary to be able to identify the perpetrator of the offence. Even if the alleged perpetrator is identified, the balance of probabilities is still the correct standard of proof: it is irrelevant that the alleged perpetrator is ultimately acquitted of the offence in criminal proceedings;[5] or

1 Ibid at 196.
2 *M v McGregor* 1982 SLT 41; *D v Kelly* 1995 SLT 1220. Thus the ground was established in *Finlayson (Applicant)* 1989 SCLR 601, although the parents' refusal to allow conventional medical treatment on their haemophiliac child was the result of concern that the child might thereby be infected by AIDS.
3 Ie an offence listed in Sch 1 to the Criminal Procedure (Scotland) Act 1995: the offences include physical and sexual abuse of a child. They are not restricted to crimes against children; for example, incest with an adult is included. The ground can be established if, for example, physical chastisement of a child is not reasonable: see *B v Harris* 1990 SLT 208, discussed *supra* p 202. A serious lacuna in the original list of Sch 1 offences in the Criminal Procedure (Scotland) Act 1975 was uncovered in *F v Kennedy* 1988 SLT 404 where no Sch 1 offence was committed if a child under 12 had been the victim of lewd, indecent or libidinous practices but had not suffered physical injury. Similarly, if a child had been the victim of a homosexual offence, no Sch 1 offence was committed unless the child had suffered physical injury. This was because Sch 1 had not been appropriately amended when s 7 of the Sexual Offences (Scotland) Act 1976 had been repealed and replaced by s 80(7) of the Criminal Justice (Scotland) Act 1980. This serious situation was remedied by para 51 of Sch 15 to the Criminal Justice Act 1988 which made the relevant amendments to Sch 1. These amendments were held to be retrospective: *Harris v E* 1989 SLT (Sh Ct) 42. The current relevant offences are in Sch 1 of the 1995 Act.
4 *S v Kennedy* 1987 SLT 667.
5 *Harris v F* 1991 SLT 242. Evidence can be led to establish the ground even if criminal proceedings are imminent: *P v Kennedy* 1995 SLT 476.

e) the child is, or is likely to become, a member of the same household as a child who has been a victim of a Sch 1 offence. The extent of the concept of household is illustrated by *McGregor v H*.[1] Child A's brother, B, had been a victim of a Sch 1 offence. At the date of the hearing, B was being looked after by foster parents, ie was no longer physically in the same house as A. However, the Inner House of the Court of Session was prepared to give 'household' an extended meaning. In the court's view, 'household' connoted a family unit, *viz* a group of persons held together by a particular tie, usually a blood relationship: while a family unit normally lived together, it did not cease if individual members were temporarily separated. Although at the time of the hearing B was physically separated from A, they were still part of the same family unit and therefore the same household. Accordingly, the ground of referral was applicable vis-a-vis A, as A was a member of the same household as B, who had been the victim of a Sch 1 offence. In *A v Kennedy*,[2] the ground was established in respect of a child whose sibling had died of a Sch 1 offence almost ten years before! Although there had been changes in the membership of the family, it was still the same household as at the time the child had died. Where the perpetrator of a Sch 1 offence has physically left the family this is *not* decisive of the question whether or not a child is a member of the perpetrator's household. Since the criterion for the existence of a household turns on relationship rather than locality, the household could continue if the person who looked after the child still felt affection for the perpetrator and there was regular contact between them.[3] In particular, the court will be reluctant to accept that a household has changed if the separation only took place as a consequence of intervention by a local authority when investigating whether or not a child was in need of compulsory measures of supervision.[4] The definition of household also applies in relation to grounds f) and g); or

f) the child is, or is likely to become, a member of the same household as a person who has committed a Sch 1 offence. There is no need for the Sch 1 offence to have been committed against a child; for example, a conviction for non-consensual homosexual acts against an adult would satisfy the ground; or

---

1 1983 SLT 626.
2 1993 SLT 118.
3 *Kennedy v R's Curator ad Litem* 1993 SLT 295.
4 Ibid. See Norrie 1993 SLT (News) 192.

g) the child is, or is likely to become, a member of the same household as a person who has been the victim of incest or intercourse
with a step-parent or person in a position of trust, committed by a
member of that household;[1] or

h) the child has failed to attend school regularly without reasonable
excuse. In the absence of an allegation of misconduct on the
child's part, it has been held that an order excluding the child
from school is a reasonable excuse for non-attendance;[2] or

i) the child has committed an offence. The Children (Scotland) Act
1995 proceeds on the basis that when a child commits a criminal
offence this is merely symptomatic of the child's failure to
develop social skills. This failure will often be the result of dysfunctionalism in the child's family. The child who commits an
offence is therefore in need of help not punishment.[3] In exceptional cases, for example very serious crimes such as murder or
where the child has committed an offence with an adult, the child
may be prosecuted in the High Court or sheriff court. But as a
general rule, where a child has committed an offence, the case
will be referred by the Reporter to a children's hearing to determine whether the child is in need of compulsory measures of
supervision. In *Merrin v S*[4] the Inner House of the Court of
Session held that before this ground can be used the child must
have reached the age of criminal responsibility, ie be aged eight or
over. The case proceeds in exactly the same way as the case
where a referral is made on any other of the s 52(2) grounds; or

j) the child has misused alcohol or any drug, whether or not a con-
trolled drug within the meaning of the Misuse of Drugs Act 1971;
or

k) the child has misused a volatile substance by deliberately inhaling
its vapour, other than for medicinal purposes, ie glue sniffing; or

l) the child is being provided with accommodation by a local
authority under s 25[5] or is the subject of a parental responsibilities

---

1 The offences are to be found in the Criminal Law (Consolidation) (Scotland) Act
1995, ss 1, 2 and 3.
2 *D v Kennedy* 1988 SCLR 31.
3 See generally, *Report on Children and Young Persons* (the Kilbrandon Report)
Cmnd 2306 upon which the Social Work (Scotland) Act 1968 was based and, in this
respect, has been followed in the 1995 Act.
4 1987 SLT 93. In the present writer's view there is force in the dissenting judgment
of Lord Dunpark who emphasised that the child need only have committed an
offence: cf been *guilty* of an offence.
5 On the provision of accommodation, see *supra* p 257 ff.

order under s 85[1] and, in either case, the child's behaviour is such that special measures are necessary for the adequate supervision of the child, in the child's own interests or the interests of others.

Procedure in referrals

Where a case is referred by the Reporter to a children's hearing, the child has the right to attend all stages of the hearing and is obliged to do so.[2] However, the child can be released from the obligation to attend if the children's hearing is satisfied (a) in a case concerned with a Sch 1 offence that the child's presence is not necessary for a just hearing or (b) in any case, that it would be detrimental to the interests of the child to be present.[3] However, because the child has a statutory *right* to be present, the child can insist on attending.[4] It is the Reporter's responsibility to secure the child's attendance.[5] Where a children's hearing is considering a child's case, a relevant person has the right to attend all stages of the hearing and is obliged to do so.[6] The children's hearing can exclude a relevant person (and his or her representative) from any part(s) of the case for so long as it is necessary in the interests of the child, where the hearing is satisfied that it must do so in order to obtain the child's views or because the presence of the relevant person is causing, or is likely to cause, significant distress to the child.[7] After the relevant person (or representative) has returned the chairman of the hearing must explain to the relevant person the substance of what has occurred during the excluded person's absence.[8]

1 On parental responsibilities orders, see *supra* p 267 ff.
2 Section 45(1)(a) and (b).
3 Section 45(2)(a) and (b) as amended by the Criminal Procedure (Consequential Provisions) (Scotland) 1995, Sch 4, para 97(2).
4 The position before the 1995 Act was controversial: *Sloan v B* 1991 SLT 30; *Wilkinson and Norrie* p 464 ff. This is one of the few situations where the 1995 Act gives a child a positive right.
5 Section 45(3). If a child fails to attend, or on cause shown it is necessary to do so, the children's hearing can grant a warrant for the detention of the child in a place of safety for up to 7 days: s 45(4) and (5). There is no need to consult the child.
6 Section 45(8): unlike the child's right to attend, the relevant person's right is expressly subject to the children's hearing's power to exclude a relevant person under s 46. A relevant person's attendance is not necessary if the hearing thinks it is unreasonable to require that person's attendance or that the attendance is unnecessary for the proper consideration of the case.
7 Section 46(1).
8 Section 46(2). This may satisfy any potential breach of art 8 of the European Convention on Human Rights: *McMichael v UK* 51/1993/446/525. Regulations must ensure that a relevant person has access to the documents before the children's hearing; but this may lead to a child being reluctant to disclose information which the child knows will be given to a relevant person.

When the child and the relevant persons appear, it is the chairman's duty to explain to them the ground(s) of referral.[1] If the relevant persons and the child accept that the ground(s) of referral exist, the hearing will then consider how best to dispose of the case.[2] But if either a relevant person or a child does not accept the ground(s) of referral, unless they are prepared to discharge the referral, the hearing must direct the Reporter to make an application to the sheriff for a finding whether or not the ground(s) of referral are established.[3] A direction for an application by the Reporter to the sheriff is also necessary[4] if the child is not capable of understanding or has not understood the explanation of the ground(s) of referral.[5] The chairman must explain to the child and the relevant person(s) the purpose of the application to the sheriff and inform the child that he or she must attend the hearing before the sheriff.[6] Where the hearing is unable to dispose of the case because the grounds of referral have not been accepted, they may grant a warrant to keep the child in a place of safety if (a) there is reason to believe the child may not attend a subsequent hearing or (b) that it is necessary that the child should be kept in a place of safety in order to safeguard or promote the child's welfare.[7]

The application by the Reporter must be heard by the sheriff within 28 days of being lodged.[8] The child has both the right to attend and the duty to do so.[9] The sheriff can release the child from the obligation to attend if satisfied (a) in an application concerned with a s 52(2)(d), (e), (f) or (g) ground of referral[10] that the child's attendance is not necessary for the just hearing of the application *and* (b) in any application that it would be detrimental to the interests of the child to be present.[11] But once again, as the child has a statutory right

1 Section 65(4).
2 Section 65(5). The hearing can dispose of the case even if the relevant person(s) and the child only accept the ground(s) in part: s 65(5).
3 Section 65(7); *JF v McGregor* 1981 SLT 334.
4 Unless the hearing discharges the case.
5 Section 65(9).
6 Section 65(8).
7 Section 66 (1) and (2). For full discussion on the hearing's powers in relation to such warrants, see *supra* p 276 ff.
8 Section 68(2).
9 Section 68(4)(a) and (b).
10 On these grounds, see *supra* p 282 ff.
11 Section 68(5)(a) and (b). Unlike the parallel provision in respect of children's hearings, s 45(2) discussed *supra* p 285, s 68(5) places 'and' as opposed to 'or' between the two grounds. It is not thought that there is significance in this difference in drafting. In the present writer's view 'and' should not be construed as cumulative in s 68(5); in other words, a child can be released from the obligation to attend by virtue of s 68(5)(a) even although it would not be detrimental to the interests of the child to be present.

to be present, the child can insist on attending.[1] The child and the relevant persons have the right to be represented.[2] The onus lies on the reporter to establish by evidence that the ground(s) of referral exist. The sheriff can dispense with hearing evidence if (a) the child and the relevant persons accept the ground(s) in the course of the hearing; or (b) if the application has been brought because of the child's incapacity to understand the explanation of the grounds and the relevant persons accept the grounds, provided it appears to the sheriff reasonable to do so.[3] In these circumstances the grounds of referral are deemed to have been established. The standard of proof normally required is that on the balance of probabilities the ground(s) exist.[4] There is no need for corroboration.[5] There is an important exception. When the ground of referral is that the *child* has committed an offence, the standard of proof is the criminal standard, ie it must be proved to the sheriff beyond reasonable doubt that the child committed the offence and corroboration is required.[6]

If the sheriff decides that none of the grounds of referral is established, the sheriff dismisses the application and discharges the referral.[7] If a ground of referral is established (or deemed to be established), the sheriff remits the case to the Reporter to arrange a children's hearing to consider and determine the case.[8] The sheriff can issue an order that the child be kept in a place of safety for up to three days, if this is necessary in the child's best interests or there is reason to believe the child will run away before the children's hearing sits to consider the case.[9]

Disposal of the case

If the child and the relevant persons accept the ground(s) of referral or if the ground(s) of referral have been established in s 68 proceedings before the sheriff, the children's hearing will then consider how

---

1 If the child fails to attend, the sheriff can make an order to bring the child before the court and keep the child in a place of safety for 14 days: s 68(6) and (7).
2 Section 68(4). If the representative is a lawyer legal aid is available.
3 Section 68(8). For example, if the child is a baby and the relevant persons accept the ground that they neglected the infant.
4 *S v Kennedy* 1987 SLT 667; *Harris v F* 1991 SLT 242.
5 Section 1(1) of the Civil Evidence (Scotland) Act 1988.
6 Section 68(3).
7 Section 68(9). The sheriff recalls, discharges or cancels any order, warrant or direction which has been made.
8 Section 68(10)(a).
9 Section 68(10)(b) and (12).

it should dispose of the case.[1] The hearing will have the social background report and any other relevant information.[2] If the hearing considers that further investigation is necessary into the child's circumstances, the case can be continued to a subsequent hearing.[3] The child can be required by the hearing to attend or reside in a hospital or clinic for the purpose of such investigations for a period not exceeding 22 days.[4] If the child fails to fulfil this requirement, the hearing may grant a warrant removing the child to a place of safety so that the examination can go ahead.[5] This warrant can only last for 22 days.[6] Moreover, if it is necessary to safeguard or promote the child's welfare or there is reason to believe that the child will not attend a subsequent hearing, the children's hearing may grant a warrant removing the child to a place of safety for a maximum period of 22 days.[7] These warrants may contain conditions regulating contact with the child and requiring the child to submit to any medical or other examination or treatment.[8] But if the child has capacity under s 2(4) of the Age of Legal Capacity (Scotland) Act 1991,[9] the child can refuse to consent.[10] In granting a warrant, the children's hearing has a duty to consult the child: moreover, a warrant cannot be granted unless it would be better for the child to grant it than if no warrant was granted at all.[11] There is no provision for the continuation of these warrants beyond 22 days. This is in striking contrast to the position when a warrant is granted under s 66, ie when the children's

---

1 Section 69(1). This is also the situation where the case has been referred to the Reporter by a court which is satisfied in relevant proceedings that a ground of referral exists: s 54(1), discussed *supra* p 279.
2 This can include allegations against a relevant person which were not used in respect of the ground of referral which was accepted or established: *O v Rae* 1993 SLT 570. See Norrie 1995 SLT (News) 353. But the hearing cannot rely on allegations specifically rejected by the sheriff: *M v Kennedy* 1993 SLT 431.
3 Section 69(2).
4 Section 69(3). If the children's hearing has reason to believe before the ground(s) of referral have been accepted or established that a child would not attend the hospital etc if it exercised its powers under s 69(3), the hearing can grant a warrant to remove the child to a place of safety: s 66(1) and (2)(a)(ii). The children's hearing's powers under s 66 are discussed *supra* p 276 ff.
5 Section 69(4) and (5).
6 Section 69(6).
7 Section 69(7) and (8).
8 Section 69(9)(a) and (b).
9 Discussed *supra*.
10 Section 90.
11 Section 16(2),(3), and (4)(a)(ii).

hearing is unable to dispose of the case because the grounds of referral have not been accepted or established.[1]

Children in need of supervision

The children's hearing must proceed on the course which, in its view,
is in the best interests of the child.[2] If it feels that no further action is
required, it can discharge the referral.[3] If, however, the children's
hearing decides that the child is in need of compulsory measures of
supervision, it can make a 'supervision requirement'.[4] In doing so,
the hearing is under a duty to consult the child and must be satisfied
that it is better for the child to make a supervision requirement than
that none be made at all.[5] The hearing can impose any condition
which will safeguard and promote the child's welfare. It must consider whether to impose a condition regulating contact between the
child and any specified person or class of persons, for example the
child's parents.[6] The supervision requirement may order the child to
reside at any place specified in the requirement, for example local
authority accommodation.[7] A condition may require the child to submit to any medical or other examination or treatment;[8] but if the child
has capacity under s 2(4) of the Age of Legal Capacity (Scotland) Act
1991,[9] the child can refuse to consent.[10] As a general rule, the child
must comply with any condition contained in the requirement.[11]

A supervision requirement ceases to have effect after the child
reaches 18.[12] However, the supervision requirement should not continue any longer than is necessary in the interests of the child.[13] If a
local authority takes the view that the requirement should cease to
have effect, it can refer the case to the Reporter for review by a children's hearing who can terminate the requirement if it thinks this

---

1 Discussed *supra* p 276 ff. On a literal construction of s 66(1) it could be argued
 that a children's hearing could grant warrants under that section *in addition* to its
 powers to grant warrants under s 69. It is thought, however, that if this were so,
 the provisions of s 69 would be otiose; *sed quaere.*
2 Section 16(1).
3 Section 69(1)(b) and (12).
4 Sections 69(1)(c) and 70(1).
5 Section 16(2), (3) and (4)(a)(i).
6 Section 70(2) and (5)(b). The hearing is not, however, obliged to impose such a
 condition: *Kennedy v M* 1995 SLT 717.
7 Section 70(3)(a).
8 Section 70(5)(a).
9 Discussed *supra* p 167 ff.
10 Section 90.
11 Section 70(3)(b).
12 Section 73(3).
13 Section 73(1).

would be the proper course.[1] Moreover, a supervision requirement cannot remain in force after a year unless it has been continued as a result of a review by a children's hearing.[2] The child and any relevant person have the right to a review of the requirement.[3] On review, the children's hearing may continue the requirement, vary the requirement, or terminate it.

The child or relevant person may appeal to the sheriff against any decision of the children's hearing.[4] An appeal is competent not only in relation to the making of the supervision requirement itself but also as to any of the conditions laid down, for example as to contact.[5] The sheriff has a duty to consult the child.[6] If the sheriff is satisfied that the decision of the children's hearing is not justified in all the circumstances the sheriff may (a) remit the case to the children's hearing, with reasons for his or her decision, for reconsideration by the hearing of its decision; (b) discharge the child from any further hearing or other proceedings in relation to the ground(s) of referral of the case; or (c) substitute for the disposal by the children's hearing any requirement which it could have imposed under s 70.[7] When the supervision requirement contains a condition, the sheriff can direct that the condition shall cease to have effect.[8] Because the sheriff can substitute his or her decision for that of the children's hearing, this provision appears to be a serious inroad into the autonomy of the children's hearing.[9]

If the appeal is unsuccessful, the sheriff will confirm the decision of the children's hearing.[10] Where the appeal is from a review by the children's hearing of the case and the sheriff is satisfied that the

---

1   Section 73(4)(a) and (8)(i). If the child has been looked after by a local authority, after care services can be provided: see *supra* p 259.
2   Section 73(2) and (9)(e); *Stirling v D* 1995 SLT 1089.
3   Section 73(6). They can do so after three months from the making or continuation or variation of the requirement: ibid. A review can take place at any time if a local authority refers the case to a Reporter: s 73(4)(a) and (8)(i); and a Reporter is entitled to arrange a review, if a supervision requirement is due to expire within three months: s 73(8)(v). This is the only circumstance where a Reporter can initiate a review on his/her own volition.
4   Section 51(1): the appeal must be made within three weeks of the decision of the children's hearing.
5   *Kennedy v A* 1986 SLT 358.
6   Section 16(2) and (4)(c).
7   Section 51(5)(c).
8   Section 51(5)(b).
9   Before the 1995 Act the sheriff could not give the hearing directions on the steps it should take when reconsidering the case after a successful appeal: *Kennedy v A* 1986 SLT 358.
10 Section 51(4).

appeal is frivolous, the sheriff can order that there should be no subsequent appeal for 12 months from a decision of the hearing to continue the supervision requirement.[1]

Safeguarding the child's interests

In any proceedings before a children's hearing or in an application before the sheriff court for a finding that the ground(s) of referral exist, a child assessment order, an exclusion order or an appeal to the sheriff against a decision of a children's hearing, in addition to any existing power to appoint a *curator ad litem*, the chairman or sheriff may appoint an independent person to safeguard the child's interests.[2] The safeguarder's report can be used by the sheriff as a check on the view that the sheriff had formed of the evidence.[3] A safeguarder cannot be appointed in relation to proceedings for a child protection order.[4]

Further appeals and review

There is an appeal to the Sheriff Principal and/or the Inner House of the Court of Session by way of stated case, on a point of law or in respect of any irregularity in the conduct of a case, from any decision of the sheriff on an appeal to the sheriff against a decision of a children's hearing or an application to the sheriff to establish the ground(s) of referral.[5] On deciding the appeal, the Sheriff Principal or the Inner House of the Court of Session shall remit the case to the sheriff for disposal in accordance with such directions as the court may give.[6]

Before the enactment of the 1995 Act difficulties were experienced when, after the sheriff had found the ground(s) of referral established, new evidence became available which suggested that the ground(s) of referral did not in fact exist. Resort could be made to the *nobile officium* of the Inner House of the Court of Session but the court would only intervene in very exceptional circumstances.[7] The 1995

---

1 Section 51(7). It is competent to appoint one safeguarder where there are a number of children concerned, even though the interests of the children may be different: *DH and JH v Reporter for Strathclyde Region* (IH) (20 Dec 1991, unreported).
2 Section 41(1). The safeguarder's appointment should not extend beyond the initial disposal of the proceedings in which he or she was appointed: *Catto v Pearson* 1990 SLT (Sh Ct) 75.
3 *Kennedy v M* 1989 SLT 687.
4 Section 41(2): on child protection orders, see *supra* p 272 ff.
5 Section 51(11). There is no appeal from the Inner House of the Court of Session to the House of Lords.
6 Section 51(14): see, for example, *Kennedy v A* 1986 SLT 358.
7 *R, Petr* 1993 SLT 910; *L, Petr (No 1)* 1991 SLT 1310; *L, Petr (No 2)* 1993 SLT 1342.

Act introduces a procedure under which a sheriff's finding that ground(s) of referral are established[1] (the original application) can be reviewed in the light of new evidence.[2] An application for review of the original application is made to a sheriff by the child or a relevant person.[3] The applicant must claim (a) to have evidence which was not considered by the sheriff in the original application, the existence or significance of which might materially have affected the determination of the original application; (b) that the evidence is likely to be credible and reliable, and would have been admissible in relation to the ground(s) of referral in the original application; and (c) that there is a reasonable explanation for the failure to lead such evidence in the original application.[4] If these claims are satisfied, the sheriff can consider the new evidence.[5] If in the light of the new evidence the sheriff finds that none of the grounds in the original application is established, the sheriff can discharge the referral of the case to the children's hearing on those ground(s) and order any supervision requirement to be terminated either immediately or at a specified date.[6] The sheriff may order a variation of the supervision requirement to take effect before the specified date of termination.[7] If the sheriff finds any ground in the original application established or there is sufficient evidence to establish a ground of referral which was not stated in the original application, the sheriff must remit the case to the Reporter to arrange a children's hearing under s 68(10).[8] There is an appeal from the sheriff's decision in the review proceedings to the Sheriff Principal and Court of Session.[9]

It should be noted that the grounds of the review are restricted to the introduction of new evidence, as opposed to the quality of the evidence in the original application. The s 85 procedure could not be used if, for example, a child retracted allegations of abuse against a relevant person made in the original application; in this situation, the

---

1 Section 68(10), discussed *supra* p 286 ff.
2 Section 85(1).
3 Section 85(4).
4 Section 85(3).
5 Section 85(6). If the claims are not established, the application must be dismissed: s 85(5).
6 Section 85(6)(a) and (7).
7 Section 85(8). The sheriff could, for example, order contact between children who have been looked after by a local authority and their parents, to enable the family to readjust to the children returning to their home when the supervision requirement is ultimately terminated.
8 Discussed *supra* p 287.
9 Section 51(11)(a)(iii) and (b).

relevant person could seek a review by the children's hearing to consider the case in the light of the child's retraction.[1]

The effect of a supervision requirement

A child who is subject to a supervision requirement may be required to live in local authority accommodation. If this is the case, the child is regarded as being looked after by the local authority.[2] Consequently, the principles in s 17 which determine how a local authority is to look after the child apply.[3] However, the local authority must operate within any conditions imposed by the children's hearing, for example in relation to access, unless or until the conditions are varied or terminated by the hearing when reviewing the requirement.[4] Where a children's hearing has specified in a supervision requirement that the child shall be liable to be placed and kept in secure accommodation in a named residential establishment, the child can be placed in such accommodation for such period as the person in charge of the establishment, with the agreement of the chief social worker of the local authority, considers necessary.[5]

Parents do not lose their parental responsibilities and rights in respect of a child who is subject to a supervision requirement.[6] Thus, for example, not only does a court have jurisdiction to regulate residence or contact in relation to such children, but the parent retains title to sue.[7] However, this is of little value, for even if the parent is awarded residence or contact, the parent cannot *exercise* the parental

---

1 Cf *R, Petr* 1993 SLT 910; *K v Kennedy* 1993 SLT 1281.
2 Section 17(6)(b). If the supervision requirement provides that the child should reside with his or her family, the local authority must investigate from time to time to see whether or not any conditions in the supervision are being carried out: s 71(2) and (3).
3 On the s 17 principles, see *supra* p 258.
4 Section 71(1). The local authority can refer the case to a reporter to arrange a children's hearing to decide whether or not a requirement should be varied or terminated: s 73(4)(a).
5 Section 70(9) and (10). This is only possible where (a) the child having previously absconded is likely to abscond and, if he or she absconds, it is likely that his or her physical, mental or moral welfare will be at risk, or (b) the child is likely to injure him or herself or some other persons, unless the child is kept in secure accommodation. On the provisions relating to residence in secure accommodation see s 75(1). A children's hearing can authorise a child to be liable to be placed and kept in secure accommodation in warrants granted under s 66 and s 69; a sheriff can do so in warrants granted under s 67 and an order under s 68(10) and (11).
6 On parental responsibilities and rights, see *supra* Ch 10.
7 *W v Glasgow Corpn* 1974 SLT (Notes) 5; *Aitken v Aitken* 1978 SLT 183; *D v Strathclyde Regional Council* 1985 SLT 114; *Borders Regional Council v M* 1986 SLT 222. On residence and contact orders, see *supra* Ch 11.

responsibilities and rights if it would be incompatible with the supervision requirement and any conditions it contains,[1] for example, in
relation to the parent's contact with the child. As a relevant person,
however, the parent could seek a review and ask the children's hearing to vary the condition in relation to contact.[2]

The reason why parental responsibilities and rights do not automatically cease when a supervision requirement is made is because in
many cases it is desirable that the child should continue to live or, at
least, to retain links with his or her family. If, however, the local
authority social workers take the view that in order to safeguard and
promote the welfare of the child it is necessary that the child should
no longer be part of his or her family, several steps are open. The
local authority could apply for a parental responsibilities order[3] or
place the child for adoption or apply for an order freeing the child for
adoption.[4] Before doing so, the local authority must refer the case to
the Reporter who must arrange a children's hearing to review the
case.[5] If the children's hearing agrees that it is in the best interests of
the child to do so, it can vary the supervision requirement to allow the
local authority to proceed.

CONCLUSION

The Children (Scotland) Act 1995 gives extensive power to state
agencies to act to assist children who are in need. The system of children's hearings is not only a bold attempt to introduce a welfare
based approach to the problem of juvenile crime but also provides
personnel with expertise and experience to make decisions which are
in the best interests of children who, because of the dysfunctionalism
of their family or otherwise, are in need.[6] However, the danger of
such paternalistic legislation is that insufficient weight is given to the
rights of children and their families. By insisting that a hearing cannot proceed unless the child and relevant persons accept the grounds
of referral or where they do not, that the grounds are established to

---

1 Section 3(4).
2 Section 73(6), discussed *supra* p 290.
3 Section 86, discussed *supra* p 267 ff.
4 On adoption generally, see Ch 12.
5 Section 73(4)(c), (8)(a)(i).
6 For a comprehensive account of the children's hearing system before the enactment
  of the 1995 Act, see 3 *Stair Memorial Encyclopaedia* para 1275 ff; *Wilkinson and
  Norrie* Ch 17. For detailed discussion of the post 1995 system, see Norrie *Children
  (Scotland) Act 1995*.

the satisfaction of a judge, the present system recognises the importance of family autonomy. By imposing a duty to consult the child at all the important procedural stages, the 1995 Act also places emphasis on children's rights. But however sophisticated the system – and there is no doubt that the 1995 Act strives for a genuine balance between the interests of the state and the family – it will only be successful if those who administer the Act do so with professional competence and integrity. As a first step, sheriffs, Reporters, lawyers and social workers must gain a thorough knowledge of the statute's complex provisions. More importantly, perhaps, they must implement those provisions in accordance with the spirit of the legislation. At a time when, as a result of unemployment, alcohol and drug abuse, mental illness and marital breakdown, families are increasingly unable to cope and children are becoming more and more vulnerable, the utility of the provisions of the Children (Scotland) Act 1995 to assist children in need, should not be underestimated.

Appendix

METHOD FOR CALCULATING MAINTENANCE ASSESSMENT
UNDER CHILD SUPPORT ACT 1991

This is merely an example to illustrate how the formula for computing child maintenance works in a relatively straightforward case. It sets out a simplified version of the method for computing maintenance, and should not be relied on as an authoritative exposition of the formula.

The maintenance assessment is done in four steps:
1. calculation of maintenance requirement
2. calculation of each parent's assessable income
3. calculation of deduction from income
4. protected income calculation

The first three steps produce an amount which may be called 'proposed maintenance'. However, this amount is only paid if that does not cause the absent parent to fall below the protected income level.

The method may be illustrated by the following example:

EXAMPLE

Sally and Peter are divorced. They have two children, Jemima and William aged 8 and 12 who live with Sally. Sally works part-time and earns £80 net per week. She now lives in the former matrimonial home. Their house which had been jointly owned was transferred to Sally as part of the divorce settlement in 1992. The house was then worth £48,000 but was subject to a mortgage of £39,000.

Peter now lives with Sharon. They have one child aged two living with them of whom Peter is the father. Sharon does not work, but Peter earns £250 net per week. They have an endowment repayment mortgage on their home. Interest payments are £75 per week and the endowment premium works out at £15 per week giving total housing costs of £90 per week.

Peter has a ten mile round trip to work every day.

Step 1 – calculation of maintenance requirement

Add:
personal allowance for each child
personal allowance for the caring parent
family premium
lone parent premium where the caring parent has no partner

Subtract from the total:
child benefit for each child (but not one parent benefit)

This can be applied to Sally and Peter:

	£ per week
child 1	5.95
child 2	23.40
caring parent	46.50
family premium	10.25
lone parent premium	5.20
subtotal	101.30
less child benefit	18.85 (10.40 + 8.45)
total maintenance requirement	82.45

The amount for the caring parent is reduced by one quarter when the youngest child reaches the age of 11, and by another quarter when the youngest child reaches the age of 14. The amount would, therefore, be £34.88 if Jemima were 11, and £23.25 if Jemima were 14.

Step 2 – calculate each parent's assessable income

Assessable income is based on net income minus exempt income. To establish *net income*, the income of a person from all sources (subject to exceptions) is taken into account. However, child benefit at the basic rate is not counted. In relation to *earnings from employment*, net income means gross income after deduction of income tax, national insurance contributions and 50% of contributions to an occupational or personal pension scheme.

Assessable income is obtained by subtracting exempt income from actual net income. To get exempt income:

Add:
adult personal allowance
housing costs
high travel to work costs, if applicable
allowance for pre-April 1993 property and/or capital settlements of at
    least £5,000

plus any of the following which are applicable:
personal allowance for each natural or adoptive child living with the
   parent
disabled child premium for each natural or adoptive child living with
   the parent
family premium
lone parent premium or disability premium (not both)
severe disability premium
carer premium
fees for residential accommodation

This can be applied to Peter.

Step 2 – Peter

	£ per week
net income	250.00
exempt income:	
adult allowance	46.50
child allowance	15.95
family premium	10.25
housing costs	90.00
travel to work costs	0.00
pre-April 1993 capital settlement	0.00
total exempt income	162.70
assessable income (net – exempt)	87.30

Peter has £87.30 of assessable weekly income available to meet the
maintenance requirement.

High travel to work costs. An addition to exempt income for travel
to work costs is allowed only where the parent is employed and the
total weekly distance exceeds 150 miles. Peter only travels 100 miles
per week (10 miles × 5 days) and, therefore, cannot claim any addition to exempt income.

Pre-April 1993 property/capital settlements. Again these are taken into
account by adding an allowance to the transferor's exempt income.
This is done by translating the value of the property or capital transferred into a notional weekly amount as shown in the table below.

Relevant Value	Weekly Allowance
less than £5,000	nil
£5,000–£9,999	£20
£10,000–£24,999	£40
£25,000 or more	£60

The value of the property transferred to Sally is £4,500 (£48,000 – £39,000 ÷ 2) so the weekly amount is nil and does not increase Peter's exempt income.

Step 2 – Sally

We need not display this calculation. Because of her child care responsibilities and housing costs, Sally's exempt income exceeds her net income. Her assessable income is, therefore, nil.

Step 3 – calculate deduction from income

Add together the assessable income of both the caring parent and the absent parent and divide the total by two.

Where half of the total is equal to or less than the maintenance requirement, the absent parent pays half his assessable income. In other words, the absent parent pays 50% of his assessable income in child maintenance up to the point where the maintenance requirement is met in full.

Where half of the total is more than the maintenance requirement, the absent parent's liability consists of a basic element and an additional element. If the caring parent has substantial income, that will affect the calculation of the additional element.

The calculation for deduction from income can be applied to Peter and Sally.

	£ per week
maintenance requirement	82.45
combined assessable income	87.30 (87.30 + 0.00)
half combined assessable income	43.65

Since half the combined assessable income is less than the maintenance requirement, Peter pays 50% of his assessable income.

half of Peter's income	43.65

The proposed maintenance for Peter to pay is £43.65 per week.

Step 4 – do protected income calculation

The purpose of the protected income level is to ensure that the absent parent (and his family, if any) are no worse off than if he was on income support. There are two separate protected income calculations – the 30% cap and protected family income.

(a) *The 30% cap*

To establish this aspect of protected income simply assess whether payment of proposed maintenance would leave the absent parent with less than 30% of his/her net income. However, in a case where arrears are also being recovered the cap is 33%.

Step 4a

	£ per week
net income	250.00
30% of net income	75.00
proposed maintenance	43.65

Therefore, there is no reduction of maintenance on this account.

(b) *Protected family income*

The calculation is based on the total family income of the absent parent together with any new partner and children. All children who are members of the household are counted and not just natural children of the absent parent. If, after making the maintenance payments indicated by the formula, the absent parent's (and family where relevant) income would fall below the protected income level, then maintenance payments are reduced by the appropriate amount. However, the minimum allowable payment is £2.35 even if a protected income calculation suggests a lesser figure. The income of an absent parent (and partner, if any) from all sources is taken into account. For this purpose, child benefit *is* counted as income. Allowable housing costs include only interest payments where there is a mortgage.

To establish the protected income level:

Add:

adult personal allowance for single person or couple
housing costs
plus any of the following which are applicable:
personal allowance for each child
disabled child premium for each child
family premium
lone parent premium or disability premium (not both)
severe disability premium
carer premium

pensioner premium
enhanced pensioner premium
higher pensioner premium
council tax (net figure after deducting any council tax benefit)
fees for residential accommodation
high travel to work costs
and
£30.00 (the standard margin)
Adding these gives a preliminary figure, to which:
add:
15% of the difference between the preliminary figure and disposable income (the additional margin)

This can be applied to Peter and his 'second family' – Sharon and Sharon's children.

Step 4b – do protected income calculation (see below)

	£ per week
disposable income	260.40
(earnings + £10.40 child benefit)	
protected income:	
adult couple allowance	73.00
child allowance	15.95
family premium	10.25
housing costs	75.00
council tax	15.40
£30.00	30.00
subtotal	219.60
15% × (£260.40 − 219.60)	6.12
total protected income	225.72

disposable income (£260.40) – maintenance payments (£43.65) = £216.75

This is less than the protected income level, therefore maintenance is reduced to £34.68.

CHILD SUPPORT RATES

The various personal and child allowances and premiums are based on income support rates. The amounts used in this example are the 1995/96 rates. New rates take effect at the beginning of each financial year. The rates most frequently used in maintenance assessments which are all weekly amounts are given below.

Adult personal allowance	£46.50
(person aged 25 or over)	
Adult couple personal allowance	£73.00
Childrens' personal allowances:	
aged under 11	£15.95
aged 11 to 15	£23.40
aged 16 to 17	£28.00
aged 18	£36.80
Premiums:	
family	£10.25
lone parent	£5.20

Index